Religion and Morality

A Collection of Essays

EDITED BY
GENE OUTKA and JOHN P. REEDER, JR.

1973
Anchor Books
Anchor Press/Doubleday
Garden City, New York

The Anchor Books edition is the first publication of RELIGION AND MORALITY.

Anchor Books edition: 1973

ISBN: 0-385-03992-1
Library of Congress Catalog Card Number 72–84966
Copyright © 1973 by Gene Outka and John P. Reeder, Jr.
All Rights Reserved
Printed in the United States of America
First Edition

CONTRIBUTORS

Robert Merrihew Adams, Associate Professor of Philosophy, University of California, Los Angeles

K. O. L. Burridge, Professor of Anthropology, University of British Columbia

Eric D'Arcy, Senior Lecturer in Philosophy, University of Melbourne

Donald Evans, Professor of Philosophy, University of Toronto

William K. Frankena, Professor of Philosophy, University of Michigan

James M. Gustafson, University Professor of Theological Ethics, Divinity School, University of Chicago

R. M. Hare, White's Professor of Moral Philosophy in the University of Oxford and Fellow of Corpus Christi College, Oxford

Louis Jacobs, Lecturer in Talmud, Leo Baeck College; Rabbi of New London Synagogue; Formerly Tutor at Jews' College, London

Godfrey Lienhardt, Reader in Social Anthropology in the University of Oxford and Fellow of Wolfson College, Oxford

David Little, Associate Professor of Religious Studies, University of Virginia

Gene Outka, Associate Professor of Religion, Princeton University

John P. Reeder, Jr., Assistant Professor of Religious Studies, Brown University

Sumner B. Twiss, Jr., Instructor in Religious Studies, Brown University

CONTENTS

INTRODUCTION

Gene Outka and John P. Reeder, Jr.

The question of how religion and morality are related arises in a variety of contexts—both ancient and modern, theoretical and practical. Socrates asks in Plato's *Euthyphro*: "Is what is holy holy because the gods approve it, or do they approve it because it is holy?" Aquinas maintains that certain kinds of action are divinely prohibited because they are wrong, rather than the reverse. William of Ockham, on the other hand, has been interpreted to say that rightness simply means, or is equivalent to, commanded by God. Many English moralists have opposed the theory that ordinary moral words like right and wrong can be simply equated with what a sovereign wills or forbids, even if that sovereign is God. Perhaps especially during the last two centuries, thinkers have struggled with the implications for morality of a loss of religious belief. Some have seen chaos and nihilism, as expressed in the dictum of Dostoyevsky's Ivan Karamazov: "Without God, everything is lawful." Others, like Sartre and Camus, have striven to erect a viable "existentialist" morality for those who view the universe as alien and uncaring. One also encounters the question in areas of contemporary politics and public policy. Can democratic values and institutions be sustained without the presupposition of a "Supreme Being"? Should moral education in schools involve recourse to religious beliefs, or does such recourse in effect indoctrinate? What beliefs should society allow as a basis for conscientious objection?

These instances show that the question has had a long and varied life. But the attention given it recently is scarce. Those who would appear to be especially well equipped to shed some light—for example, moral philosophers, theologians, and anthropologists—have been often preoccupied elsewhere. Moreover, when a representative of one of these groups addresses the question, he seems all too frequently to talk past those who belong to the others. Religious persons find their moral life anchored in their beliefs; philosophers point out that one can certainly be moral without being religious, and that even if one is religious, the precise relation of religion to morality is not at all clear. Is the relation logical, epistemological, psychological, or some other kind?[1] Anthropologists sometimes offer widely inclusive definitions of both religion and morality. Their notions of religion may seem too unspecified to suit thinkers steeped in the major Western religious traditions; and their concepts of morality too imprecise to satisfy moral philosophers who discuss their subject according to the rigorous standards of clarity found in Anglo-American analytic philosophy.

We hope this book will serve as a modest remedy of recent neglect. All of the essays appear here for the first time and most of them were written expressly for this volume. The contributions include philosophical assessments of certain recurrent claims, interpretations of influential strands in Judaism and Christianity, and anthropological studies of particular societies. A major question addressed throughout the volume is whether morality is logically or epistemologically dependent on religion. In addition, some contributors discuss definitions of religion and morality, beliefs about the influence of God on the moral agent, and convictions which give a "point" to moral endeavor. Unfortunately the scope of the volume does not permit essays which treat in detail the meaning of religious and moral norms,[2] although certain ones are mentioned particularly in Section I.

---

[1] Jews and Christians, of course, believe in a creator God, upon whom the world is dependent both for its origin and continued existence. In a sense, then, it could be said that morality, like all that is human, is *metaphysically* dependent on God. In addition, a *historical-causal* dependence of morality on religion has often been maintained. Within the matrix of definite religious communities, certain commandments have been formulated, such as, "you shall love your neighbor as yourself." Yet to give an account of their origin is not necessarily to offer a justification. And many (especially those who follow Kant) have wanted to hold that a moral principle is logically independent of the historical-social context in which it may have first received expression.

[2] See, for example, Gene Outka, *Agape: An Ethical Analysis* (New Haven: Yale Univ. Press, 1972).

We propose now to help to set the stage by offering some brief exposition and commentary on the individual essays and the relations between them. We wish also to place the essays in a wider historical frame of reference and to identify pivotal issues and possible ambiguities. Naturally some of our interpretations may be disputed and our queries reflect misunderstanding. Our general aim will be realized, however, if the reader is alerted to several critical questions which the essays address.

I

The first section is entitled "Definitions of Religion and Morality." We begin with essays which attempt to provide broad conceptual and methodological bearings. David Little and Sumner B. Twiss, Jr., directly address the task of constructing definitions of religion and morality. Kenelm Burridge works out a definition of religion and relates it to the Tangu, a people of New Guinea. Godfrey Lienhardt makes no attempt to formulate general definitions of either religion or morality but employs implicit concepts of both in order to discuss the life of the Dinka of the Southern Sudan. Since his aim is to relate the culture of the Dinka to notions of "morality and happiness" with which philosophers work, his essay is appropriate in this section.

One can note significant similarities and differences in the definitions proposed or assumed in these three essays. One common theme concerns the nature of a basic moral norm, principle, or "action-guide."

Little and Twiss present a notion of the necessary and sufficient characteristics of a "moral action-guide," e.g., a rule, principle, or prescription which is used to "guide behavior and attitudes." They consider various kinds of characteristics which have been proposed in recent discussions, for instance, prescriptivity, universalizability, supremacy, and reference to the interests of others.[3] They see the problem or function of morality as the regulation of possible or actual conflicts of interests for the sake of some form of social "co-operation." By "co-operation" they do not mean to suggest a

[3] See A. D. M. Walker and G. Wallace, eds., *The Definition of Morality* (New York: Barnes & Noble; London: Methuen, 1970), esp. W. K. Frankena, "The Concept of Morality," pp. 146–73.

normative principle, but a method by which the interests of various individuals or groups may be adjusted. They propose that a moral action-guide must be, among other things, "other-regarding." It not only has to do with actions which in fact impinge on the welfare of others, it involves on the part of the agent *"some* consideration of the effects of the actions of one person on the welfare of others." Even an "enlightened" ethical egoism, which recognizes that the welfare of the individual depends on the welfare of others, would meet the criterion, just as norms of fairness or disinterested concern for others would.

The meaning given to "other-regarding" by Little and Twiss appears not to be the usual one. In ordinary usage, policies of other-regard and ethical egoism, however "enlightened," are normally distinguished. The agent pursues an other-regarding policy when he acts predominantly for "the other person's own sake," even when his own interests are not always enhanced. He may, though he need not, espouse pure altruism in the sense that he has a moral obligation to pursue the interests of others, but not his own. He is usually thought at least to employ the criterion of fairness *for all* affected; if you like, to count himself as one and no more than one and never accord himself a privileged position. At a minimum, he applies this criterion to members of the community of which he is a part. The ethical egoist, on the other hand, aims predominantly in all of his actions at the realization of his own interests. He is formally at liberty to concede that the actions which are in his interests by no means reduce to the actions which *only* benefit him. Still, attention to the interests of others must be justified solely by self-benefiting considerations.[4]

Little and Twiss, then, are claiming that the "enlightened" form of egoism, which does pay attention to the interests of others on self-benefiting grounds, not only *can* meet their criterion but that it is the only type of egoism which *does.* They may assume as a cross-cultural fact—which they find reflected in the beliefs of Ladd's Navahos—that the welfare of the agent depends on the welfare of others. Thus the egoist is constrained to be enlightened. He will argue, in a way reminiscent of Hobbes, that while he surrenders

[4] For a representative depiction of ethical egoism and its distinction from e.g., utilitarianism, see John Hospers, *Human Conduct* (New York: Harcourt, 1961), esp. pp. 157–74.

something in belonging to a social group with definite rules of behavior, he gains considerably more. Social co-operation pays invariably in private benefits. Many ethical egoists would, however, be prepared to go no further than a prudent recognition that the agent's interests happen to coincide much of the time with the interests of those around him. (Or at any rate they coincide much of the time with one or more distinctive groups within a particular society, which is a further complication.) These egoists would nonetheless deny factual coincidence in a relevantly large number of cases and maintain, of course, that whenever conflicts occur, self-interest should always override. Is their position excluded by the very definition of what Little and Twiss take the problem of morality to be, i.e., "co-operation"? Does the exclusion derive from a factual mistake on the egoists' part? Such egoists could reply that whether they are mistaken is far from obvious. Empirical and conceptual questions are, then, intimately linked at this point and the assumptions in the Little-Twiss account of a moral action-guide need to be pondered.

Burridge identifies the "moral order" as a set of rules which determine which actions are right and wrong (compare Little and Twiss on the "prescriptive component"). He furnishes support of a kind for the claim of Little and Twiss that morality functions at the very least to regulate "human conduct so that co-operative living is possible." Without some limitation on the unrestrained pursuit of individual self-interest, human beings could not have, he contends, "community life." Moral rules are based on the criterion of "reciprocity" or "like for like." Every individual has to pay this "price" if he is to live in community. Burridge's account seems intended to apply cross-culturally; reciprocity appears universally as the criterion in accordance with which community life is governed. He does not say, however, whether reciprocity or fairness is acknowledged by men across the world for its own sake, or is adopted for the sake of self-interest. It is also uncertain whether, in reference to the distinction drawn by Little and Twiss, reciprocity is construed as a substantive moral principle or is tantamount to a formal characteristic of morality as such.

While Burridge emphasizes reciprocity, Lienhardt identifies happiness as the pivotal concept of Dinka morality. Little and Twiss treat happiness as a kind of satisfaction which involves certain attitudes and depends on the particular experiences of the individual, over and beyond his "welfare." For the Dinka, as Lienhardt presents them, welfare in the Little-Twiss sense is part of "happiness." Moreover, social unity, concord, or unanimity, over against "self-gratification" (compare Burridge's unilateral or non-reciprocal action), is itself the *chief* ingredient of happiness. To take into account the welfare of others is not only a duty—this alone would meet the Little-Twiss criterion for a "moral" action-guide—but a good or value in itself; it is not only a means to happiness but is constitutive of it.

A number of comparisons may thus be made between the detailed accounts of morality in given cultures provided by Burridge and Lienhardt and the theoretical characterization of a moral action-guide offered by Little and Twiss. All three essays, moreover, in their discussion of religion, touch issues which are of central interest in the rest of the volume.

Little and Twiss argue, for instance, that part of the "superiority" (or supremacy) of a moral action-guide is its "autonomy," its "sufficiency," and "ultimacy." These features depend on the "logical requirement" that moral conclusions cannot be deduced from premises which are entirely nonmoral. As W. K. Frankena points out in his essay, this requirement is unexceptional as far as it goes. The issue, however, on which the question of deduction hinges, is whether a moral term or concept can be *defined* in a nonmoral, e.g., exclusively religious, way, as Frankena thinks some theologians try to do.

Little and Twiss do allow that in systems of religious ethics one finds combinations of moral and purely religious action-guides. A religious action-guide consists in a guide to behavior and attitudes which is an "appropriate response" to a "religious object." The relation of the religious object to men answers certain fundamental problems of "interpretability," in regard to the natural world, death and suffering, and "puzzles inherent in human conduct." A combined action-guide is accordingly a response both to the problem of interpretability and to the problem of co-operation. A moral/religious action-guide is explicitly viewed as religious, but also meets the criteria of a moral one. In contrast, a religious/moral action-guide is one which is explicitly taken as moral but which upon examination is found to include religious elements.

As part of their "descriptive" theory, Little and Twiss allow to both sorts of action-guides a "weak" or *prima facie* type of priority. A purely religious action-guide can override a moral one, e.g., as in Kierkegaard's *Fear and Trembling* (which is discussed by Gene Outka and also by Louis Jacobs in this volume). In contrast, a god who demands human sacrifice is deposed in favor of one who asks only for goats and cows. Any view which gives a religious or a moral action-guide *absolute* priority involves, in their view, "normative argumentation." Whenever a clash occurs, one must look to see which action-guide happens to override; evidently one must also ask whether it is given absolute status on normative grounds.

Little and Twiss treat certain motifs which link the religious object to action-guides—charismatic authority, an "evaluative standard" related to the religious object, and a role relation between man and the religious object—as purely religious. Thus where one finds action-guides that are both commanded by God and based on natural law, one has a moral/religious action-guide, one which has a purely religious component—commanded by God—and a moral action-guide which can be taken autonomously—natural law. In some traditions in Judaism and Christianity, however, the notion of divine commands is not so purely religious or the notion of natural law so purely moral as these authors suggest. In fact, the notion of an "appropriate" religious response is often given content in moral terms, as the essays by Jacobs, Gustafson, and Evans testify. Doubtless Little and Twiss do not mean to exclude the concepts Gustafson identifies where religious and moral elements are intertwined. They would hold that even if particular concepts are composed of both moral and religious elements, the moral element is still autonomous, in the sense that it is not derived or deduced from the religious. Frankena makes a similar point based on his view that the attempt to provide a nonmoral definition of a basic moral term or concept inevitably fails. What is somewhat misleading about the conclusion of the Little-Twiss essay is that the religious input to a combined religious and moral action-guide seems to have to do wholly with the problem of interpretability and the moral to do only with co-operation. What several authors, not only Gustafson but also Frankena, recognize is the way in which religious beliefs sometimes provide crucial subsidiary premises for the derivation of particular *moral* norms. Moreover, moral action-guides are not always presented solely in the context of human social experience, but also as a determinative part of men's relation to the divine.

Burridge presents what seems to be a rather different definition of religion but it has affinities to the one offered by Little and Twiss. Religion has to do with the relation between the moral "level" of experience and man's beliefs about the "truth of things." Part of these beliefs are about the sorts of "powers" which affect human experience, powers seen as beneficial or harmful. Religion is concerned to order these powers, to gain some sort of "control" over what in another sense is beyond man's power. Moreover, the "redemptive process" by which men seek to deal in some way with their obligations ("discharge, or evade or defy") is "dependent on a continuing search for the truth of things, one of whose sources [is] the 'spiritual' experience." Burridge believes that especially when man seems confronted by forces or powers which are non-reciprocal or which his "system of order" cannot accommodate, he turns to the "level" of the spiritual, beyond the moral. Myths of origin picture man as a "free-mover" not subject to morality but "at one with Creator and All-being." It is the business of religion not only to "maintain" morality but to enable man to transcend it "as ultimate conclusion to the redemptive process," to overcome the "limitations of time and space," to reverse the movement from animal to cultural and moral being. To "transcend" the moral is not necessarily to come into conflict with it, but, "in full awareness of [its] dictates," to go beyond its sphere of validity.

Thus Burridge's theory, like that of Little and Twiss, involves the effort to gain an interpretation of the ultimate context of man's experience. Man seeks to respond in an "appropriate" way or "in accord with the truth of things." Little and Twiss seek a characterization of the "religious object," in relation to which the problems of interpretability are resolved, which is nonetheless broader than Burridge's "spiritual level." The idea of the "spiritual" level would seem to Little and Twiss to universalize a "mystical" *type* of religious object beyond the other dimensions of human experience, while their criterion of "special distinctiveness" only requires that the religious object be in some way set off from everything else. Similarly, to locate the special function of religion in the transcending of the moral would be for Little and Twiss only one way to resolve the problems of interpretability.[5]

Burridge does indicate a range of relationships between the religious and the moral. In a "stable" period, the beliefs about power will be conceived as "underpinning" the moral order; the latter will be "grounded" in the former. Burridge does not mean to imply that the moral is derived or deduced from the nonmoral. Indeed, in its "protectionist and conservationist aspects," religion is "largely a consequence of moral awareness." Yet the religious level does far more than reinforce conventional, status quo morality. It likewise fosters an awareness of the possibilities of transcendence and unilateral action. It is from the perspective of the spiritual that man can "find, refine, defy, escape, alter, or [ultimately] transcend a given morality."

Burridge does not offer a detailed theory of these various relations. The Tangu provide primarily an example of maintenance and transcendence. The belief that unacknowledged and unexpiated wrongdoing has as its consequence a sickness leading to death provides a motive for the maintenance or protection of the moral order. (Non-reciprocal sorcerers also cause sickness and death, as do Dinka witches, who are completely removed from the moral order.) Such a belief is also an *interpretation* of suffering and death. But beyond the grave as a ghost a man can be *fully* non-reciprocal, as is his destiny:

> Tangu recognized that a conscience wholly subservient to morality was only for small men. As a ghost was itself non-reciprocal, so a man should preserve the non-reciprocal in his conscience if he was to realize his full potential as a man.

It would be instructive to examine in detail the other types of relation between a "given morality" (a set of particular rights and duties based on the criterion of reciprocity) and religious belief.

Whereas for Burridge the spiritual level can transcend the moral, for Lienhardt's Dinka the ultimate conditions of man's life are tied more closely to a moral perspective. The religion of the Dinka serves, in the terminology of Little and Twiss, to resolve the prob-

[5] Both Little and Twiss and Burridge have to face the sorts of misgivings about "comparative" work raised by some anthropologists, e.g., E. E. Evans-Pritchard, "The Comparative Method in Social Anthropology," in *The Position of Women in Primitive Societies and Other Essays in Social Anthropology* (New York: Free Press, 1965), pp. 13–36.

lem of interpretability, in particular the presence of suffering and death. Not only are particular unexpiated misdeeds punished through divine agency by sickness or death, as with the Tangu, but labor, sickness, and death as general conditions of man's state are due to an original act of "self-gratification" through which men are separated from God. Lienhardt compares the Tangu myth to the Genesis story of Adam and Eve. The primeval act is a paradigm of the basic wrongness of unwarranted self-assertion over against the spirit of mutual helpfulness which the Dinka prize. While it is not necessary to reunite oneself with the primeval nonmoral state pictured in the myth of origin, through prayer and sacrifices one must regain nearness to God as the final condition of happiness.

God is thus a judge for the Dinka, but he does not legislate the basic norms of their moral order. Lienhardt says that the Dinka "trace" their "social order" to the divinity, presumably as its creator, but its norms are seen as emanating from and endorsed by their ancestors. Nor are particular offenses or any "propensity" towards them the result of the original fault. Lienhardt even suggests that the norms of the Dinka are a "product" of their society, but, reminding us of a methodological point made by Little and Twiss, he does not say whether the Dinka themselves refer to social unity as a justification of particular injunctions, e.g., prohibitions against incest, certain sorts of homicides, etc. One does get the impression, however, that the Dinka *independently* recognize the rightness of their norms. Thus misery seems somehow intrinsic to wrong acts themselves, quite apart from religious censure and social punishments. One should also note that although the divinity is not seen as a legislator, the reference to ancestors would be interpreted by many as a religious belief (the Dinka also have clan divinities which Lienhardt takes as symbolic of social identity). The relation of norms to the ancestors reminds one of the "underpinning" or "maintenance" function to which Burridge draws our attention.

II

The second set of essays characterize and interpret major traditions within Judaism and Christianity. They do not attempt to be exhaustive studies, but to present certain analyses of important strands in these traditions. Studies of the relation of religion and morality in Eastern traditions should, of course, be done, but we have deliberately limited our volume, with the exception of the essays by Burridge and Lienhardt, to Judaism and Christianity. The essays included here address several of the most recurrent questions discussed in religious literature in the West, e.g., the moral attributes of God, and the "autonomy" of morality.

What, then, is the relation between religion and morality in those religious traditions which have dominated Western culture? James M. Gustafson thinks it makes sense to say that according to conventional modern definitions, God is understood in Judaism and Christianity to have a "moral" will. He finds that in Western religious literature moral and religious concepts are intertwined. It is hard to see how many of these concepts could be disentangled without doing violence to the intentions of the various users. Theological concepts such as sin, repentance, and righteousness, include what would be regarded in recent philosophical usage as both religious and moral features.

Yet it should be noticed too that Gustafson is uneasy about such conventional definitions. He speculates on whether one can readily identify the precise definitions of religion and morality. Given conventional definitions, certain concepts he elucidates include both. Should one then go on to ask about the status of the conventional definitions? If there is such interlacing in certain religious traditions, are doubts thereby cast on the viability of a general quest for the necessary and sufficient conditions of any morality? An insistence that all properly moral concepts are detachable from a religious framework, for example, is thus hardly obvious and requires argument. Can those who label one set of concepts "moral" and another "nonmoral," and consign all religious ones to the latter, answer the charge of arbitrariness? Little and Twiss presumably would agree with Gustafson that some concepts include both religious and moral elements. They would claim, however, that one *can* formulate convincing "reconstructive" definitions of religion and morality, on the basis of which one can separate the religious and moral elements of a concept for purposes of analysis.

Louis Jacobs is less hesitant than Gustafson to apply modern distinctions to historical materials. In such an application one need not, he contends, systematize unduly or import definitions misleadingly. He thinks that both biblical and rabbinic literature assume the "autonomy of morality" with overall clarity and persistence. Nowhere, he claims, is the "good" simply identified with the "will of God." The welter of moral obligations found in such literature are taken by the writers themselves to be self-justifying. No support from religious beliefs and experiences is strictly required. Whether a reader agrees with Jacobs' thesis depends partly on issues of historical-literary interpretation. In short, one might ask whether the literature under scrutiny speaks with the single voice he attributes to it. In any case, Jacobs makes clear that in Judaism one's relation to God is necessarily linked to one's treatment of human companions. Refusal to love others frustrates the divine will and flaws the religious relation.

In the first section of his essay Eric D'Arcy considers some of the reasons why Catholic moral theory has been on the whole rather insulated from English-speaking culture and philosophy. He laments this state of affairs and thinks that it is very much in the interest of Catholic moral theorists to pay far more careful attention to modern Anglo-American philosophy and not only to Franco-German existentialism and phenomenology. D'Arcy undertakes in a second section to identify some of the major principles and beliefs which represent the bulk of Catholic thinking on the autonomy of morality. According to him, Ockham and Biel held that "right" means and only means "commanded by God."[6] In contrast, Aquinas held that God commands certain actions because they are right; right in a sense independent of the fact of God's having commanded them. D'Arcy thinks that Aquinas' view (as he represents him here) is normative for the Catholic tradition.

Indeed, D'Arcy goes on to argue that the Christian religion and

[6] We will use the term "Ockhamistic" to indicate the position D'Arcy and later Robert Adams link with William of Ockham. On Biel, however, see Heiko Obermann, *The Harvest of Medieval Theology* (Cambridge, Mass.: Harvard Univ. Press, 1963). Moreover, what position Ockham actually held is a matter of dispute. Helmar Junghans, *Ockham in Lichte der Neueren Forschung: Arbeiten zur Geschichte und Theologie des Luthertums*, XXI (Berlin and Hamburg: Lutherisches Verlagshaus, 1968), has a useful review of recent interpretations of Ockham. See esp. Philotheus Boehner, O.F.M., *Collected Articles on Ockham* (St. Bonaventure, N.Y.: Franciscan Institute, 1958), pp. 151–54; and William of Ockham, *Philosophical Writings*, trans. with an intro. by Philotheus Boehner, O.F.M. (New York: Bobbs-Merrill, 1964), pp. xlviii ff.

morality are connected by what he calls "natural" rather than logical necessity. Christianity possesses three "salient characteristics" (H. L. A. Hart's phrase in another context) which are so closely tied to it that the relation to morality cannot be merely contingent. (1) A moral element is an integral part of the message of Christianity, in continuity with Judaism. Such an element does not necessarily constitute a part of "religion" as such. (2) In light of concepts like sin and redemption in Christianity, immorality is viewed as an offense against God and not only another human being. (3) A Christian doctrine of God includes an account of his "holiness." To hold that God is "worthy of worship" is to grant that human beings are able to distinguish justice and iniquity in independence from and prior to special revelation. Worship then is not coerced by superior power whose exercise is a matter of inscrutable fiat, as if the decalogue might be replaced by its opposite.

For the general position taken by Gustafson, Jacobs, and D'Arcy, there appears to be at least no *theological* violation of the "naturalistic fallacy," the attempt to define "moral" or "right" in exclusively nonmoral (including, on this usage, religious) terms. However, it is important to note that when Jacobs, for instance, refers to the "autonomy of ethics," which in his view is not violated in Judaism, he refers not so much to the logical character or *form* of rightness, which might render it incapable of any purported *definition*. Rather, he contends that in the Jewish tradition the *content* of rightness is not exhaustively defined by "commanded by God," but includes such basic notions as justice. The point applies also to Gustafson, and even to D'Arcy. While D'Arcy points out that his view assumes some form of cognitivism,[7] his major theme is that the content of rightness is not equivalent to "commanded by God." The rightness which characterizes God's nature includes "above all justice, mercy, and fidelity to his word." Furthermore, it has a deontological element, for God forbids "some actions whose wrongness is

---

[7] Roughly, "cognitivism" or "descriptivism" refers to those theories in which a moral judgment is held to ascribe a property, while "noncognitive" or "nondescriptivist" theories deny that a moral judgment is reducible to any set of properties. Noncognitive theories may of course differ crucially among themselves, so that, for example, the role of a moral judgment is held to express an emotion of the speaker or induce it in the hearer; or to prescribe a course of action applicable to anyone so circumstanced. See W. K. Frankena, *Ethics* (Englewood Cliffs, N.J.: Prentice-Hall, 1963), chap. VI.

not determined by their consequences but by the nature of the acts themselves."

D'Arcy does not tell us what sort of cognitivism he would defend. One wonders, for example, whether he would find that the following view, which Robert Adams contrasts with the "divine command" theory, reflects his own Thomistic position: "[T]he divine command theory is distinguished from alternative theological theories of ethical wrongness, such as the theory that facts of ethical rightness and wrongness are objective, nonnatural facts about ideas or essences subsisting eternally in God's understanding, not subject to His will but guiding it." If D'Arcy did accept this account, he would be accepting a definism, albeit in terms of "nonnatural" or nonempirical "facts."[8] The crucial question is how one should interpret his quotation from Aquinas: "Morality is based primarily on God's *wisdom*. It is his wisdom that establishes creatures in their proper relationship with each other and with him: and it is precisely in that relationship that the essence of the creature's moral goodness consists." Should one take "wisdom" and "proper relationship" here in a nonmoral sense, or, as it appears, do these concepts already include "moral" content?

It is uncertain then on what metaethical basis D'Arcy, Jacobs, and Gustafson would defend the sort of content they identify with "moral" or "right." Their point is not that no definition, theological or otherwise, can or should be given, but they counter the Ockhamistic alternative by claiming that according to a certain definition of the content of "moral," God's will is a moral will. According to their view of tradition, rightness is not, as a matter of content, to be defined exhaustively and without remainder as "commanded by God."

One should also ask about the notion of "religion" which these authors use. While all three distinguish the religious from the moral —the former has to do with the relation of men to God and the latter with relations between men—it is interesting to note that they interpret the religious relationship itself in moral terms. Because God is a moral being, to break the moral law is to commit an offense

----

[8] Definism is a version of cognitivism, where the moral term is analyzable in terms of other facts. See Frankena, *Ethics*, pp. 80–81. By "nonnatural" Adams simply means nonempirical; he does not of course intend to suggest the undefinable or unanalyzable predicate posited by G. E. Moore.

against him. Gustafson even notes that in one strand of Christian thought, where a focus on God as a "transmoral" *summum bonum* displaces worldly concerns, the claim is made that only with God as supreme end can one properly order one's values and relations with other men.

Thus religion for these authors appears not to signify, as it did for Burridge, a level of experience or reality beyond the sphere of morality. Jacobs, for instance, attempts to give an interpretation of Søren Kierkegaard's *Fear and Trembling* which will bring it within Judaism's view of God as a moral being. However, his interpretation is at variance with the traditional one, which takes Kierkegaard to say that religious duty can or even must come into conflict with moral duty.[9]

The issues about a position like Kierkegaard's seem to Gene Outka more complex, however, than either Jacobs' interpretation or the more usual one appear to recognize. A more elaborate analysis is required to determine which conflicts are verbal, which substantive. In the first place, Outka thinks it is important to question some of Kierkegaard's own contrasts between the religious and the "ethical." Moral action-guides as such need not be limited, for example, to the distinctive consequentialist and Hegelian features of the ethical set out in *Fear and Trembling*. In considering a characterization of the ethical which is not confined to these features, Outka concentrates on prescriptivity and universalizability, among the conditions widely canvassed in recent philosophical discussion. He tries to show, for instance, that certain salient features of the Abraham episode are allowed to be repeatable in principle. One should be wary, therefore, of sweeping comparisons of the episode with every sort of crime performed in the name of religious inspiration. Suppose one agrees that Kierkegaard's account of the duty to obey God violates neither prescriptivity nor universalizability. The issue which then arises is whether these two conditions are jointly sufficient as well as severally necessary to bring such a duty under the "moral" umbrella. Indeed, Little and Twiss treat prescriptivity and universalizability—or in their terminology, "generalizability"—as characteristics

---

[9] For a contemporary version of this view, see D. Z. Phillips, "Moral and Religious Conceptions of Duty: An Analysis," *Religion and Understanding*, ed. D. Z. Phillips (Oxford: Blackwell, 1967).

of religious as well as moral action-guides.[10] They also propose, however, to add an "other-regarding" characteristic to moral action-guides.

A closely linked issue thus concerns Kierkegaard's refusal to oppose Abraham's obedience to God and his love of Isaac. Apart from obedience to God, Kierkegaard avers, Abraham cannot "love" Isaac. Does such a refusal cast doubt on an account of other-regard which confines it to considerations of mundane welfare alone? Little and Twiss argue that the conflict between types of action-guides in Kierkegaard's interpretation of the Abraham-Isaac story hangs on the question of this-worldly welfare; since religious duty can call for a sacrifice of welfare in this sense, it cannot qualify as other-regarding. They indicate their awareness of the possibility that the "real" welfare of affected parties may be redefined in light of religious criteria, but they argue that "welfare" has a relatively fixed core of this-worldly conditions. One might agree to limit the concept of *welfare* in this way and still object to a like confinement of *other-regard*. Perhaps some generic term is warranted, like "well-being," which could encompass various other-regarding criteria, including final destiny or a relation to God as well as welfare. Kierkegaard treats love as other-regarding care which (a) in no way rules out concern about mundane welfare; yet (b) includes other criteria of "well-being," e.g., communion with God; and (c) allows for conflict between (a) and (b), with mundane welfare in such cases assessed as a subordinate good to the end of communion with God.

Finally, as we noted earlier, Kierkegaard insists upon the supremacy of obedience to God which is absolute rather than *prima facie*. Outka attempts to locate the final, irremovable sense to be given to this supremacy, where obedience to God may continue to override our ordinary antecedent moral judgments. One may well ask whether his formulation is the most felicitous for what Kierkegaard has in mind. But whatever definitional boundaries one draws

[10] Little and Twiss prefer generalizability since it does not suggest that the criterion must be extended to all men, as "universalizability" might. The requirement that "a recommended AG must apply to any similar person in *similar* circumstances, and for the same agent in all relevantly *similar* situations" can be applied to a particular "ingroup," and not necessarily to all mankind. Some philosophers, however, use universalizability in such a way that it does not exclude particularistic moralities. Cf. W. K. Frankena, "The Concept of Morality."

between religious and moral duty, Outka tries to show that Kierkegaard will not relinquish the following decisive contention (which presupposes a certain view of the relation between God and the world). Human beings could judge an action to be wrong—antecedently, in the sense of temporally before—but God may command it, and they would have to change their minds. In furtherance of the end of communion with him, it is fitting that *God* "is free to alter the normal moral obligations which persons justifiably commend to one another." Dispositional openness is enjoined because persons are not in a position in relation to God to furnish themselves with an absolute veto against the possibility of being wrong.

The essays by Gustafson, Jacobs, and D'Arcy, in any event, argue that God is a moral being, where moral rightness has a certain definite content independent of God's commands. Not only do they give little or no attention to the Ockhamistic position as an alternative for Jews and Christians, but they exclude other possibilities, at least by implication. D'Arcy, for instance, not only argues for the Thomistic over the Ockhamistic alternative, but in his characterization of God's "holiness" takes a position conspicuously different from that of Rudolf Otto. While in its "earlier stages," holiness referred to "separation, distance, differentness," or to a "power surpassing the human and the terrestrial," D'Arcy finds a third element, "moral perfection," which he believes "has become uppermost in English and . . . in many other languages of Christian culture." Otto protested against this view of the holy (for D'Arcy, the linguistic usage confirms a proper interpretation), claiming that there is not only a "rational-moral" aspect of the holy, but also a nonmoral nonrational "numinous" element. The latter is present, according to Otto, in the Christian as well as in other religious traditions.

Whereas D'Arcy sees an evolution in the idea of the holy to the point where the moral predominates, Otto stresses its nonmoral aspect. Service or obedience is a proper response to the *numinous* aspect of the divine, in contrast to Gustafson, Jacobs, and D'Arcy, for whom God's authority rests on his *moral* perfection. For Otto, as for the traditional interpretation of Kierkegaard in *Fear and Trembling*, the relation to the divine can be ultimately independent of "moral" considerations. The problem of "interpretability" is answered, paradigmatically in the case of Job, in terms of man's relation to the numinous. Thus although Little and Twiss treat the

religious response to sacred authority as nonmoral, one could argue
that a definition of religion should allow for divine authority to be
characterized as "appropriate" either in moral or nonmoral terms.

Indeed, as John Reeder shows, Otto himself tries to preserve both
the moral and the nonmoral aspects of the holy by linking the two
in several ways. Not only can we attribute moral qualities to the
holy, but there is a relation of "schematization" between the moral
qualities and the numinous aspect of the divine, a relation we know
in some sense as a "synthetic a priori." Furthermore, in a posthumously published essay, *Freedom and Necessity,* Otto even claims
that the numinous understood as "value" is the "ground and source"
of "moral value." Over against any view in which the purely religious is taken to override the moral as if the two were utterly distinct, for Otto the numinous can override the moral, but *as* its
ground and source. Furthermore, Otto holds to the logical autonomy
of morality. He would deny the Ockhamistic position that right
means—that is, is logically equivalent to—commanded or willed by
God. Furthermore, he explicitly denies the view that the meaning of
moral rightness men recognize is the product of the "contingent" or
arbitrary will of the divine. He regards the view that "good is good
because God wills it" as a misleading exaggeration of the numinous
aspect of the holy. While Otto, like Burridge, sees an aspect of the
divine which in some sense transcends the moral, morality not only
retains its independence, but is firmly linked to the numinous, which
is its ground and source.

The difficulty with Otto's position, in Reeder's opinion, is that the
bridges Otto builds between the numinous and the moral, culminating in the "ground and source" theme, are borrowed from the conceptual realm. Otto's central thesis, of course, is that the numinous
cannot be conceptualized in any terms. Strictly speaking, on Otto's
thesis one could not conceptualize the sort of relation in which the
numinous stands to the moral, other than to say that it cannot be
conceived in moral terms. To say that the numinous is *nonmoral* is
only to say that it cannot be conceived in moral terms. One is not
entitled to *assert* either that the numinous is "indifferent" to morality, *or* that the numinous is its ground and source. Either type of assertion would be a covert attempt at conceptualization. In *Freedom
and Necessity,* however, Otto does not claim that the ground and
source relation has conceptual validity; rather, he rests his case on

"feeling." The issue then becomes one of epistemology: how can feeling yield a non-conceptual insight?

Instructive comparisons may thus be drawn between the views of Gustafson, Jacobs, and D'Arcy on the one side, and Kierkegaard and Otto on the other. Moreover, the view that the content of rightness is not exhaustively defined by "commanded by God" possesses an affinity to the beliefs of the Dinka, as Lienhardt interprets them. According to Lienhardt, although the Dinka, "if pressed," would say that God (a sky god), as the creator of men, is in some sense the author of the social order, nevertheless, "moral teachings are seen as a product of their society, and are sanctioned by ancestral approval." While the deity is seen as the creator, moral principles are not defined simply as what he commands. Lienhardt finds the content of Dinka morality to be quite similar to a kind of utilitarianism, in which moral rules are justified by reference to the happiness and harmony of members of the social group. On the other hand, Burridge's view of the way the "spiritual" can transcend or conflict with the "reciprocal" or "moral" reminds one of themes in the writings of Kierkegaard and Otto.

III

The final essays by philosophers address several important types of issues about the relation of religion and morality in a Western context.

The arguments William K. Frankena develops are directed against the sort of view which D'Arcy identifies with Ockham and Biel, and thus his arguments could be taken as negative support at least for the Thomistic alternative D'Arcy espouses. Frankena contends that any proposal to define "right" exhaustively in terms of obedience to God's will founders. Although he says one cannot foreclose the issue with the "open question" argument, he claims nevertheless that to propose the definition is in effect to accept the principle that it is right, or one ought, to obey God. Thus Frankena seems to imply that in such a proposal "right" or "ought" has a meaning which is *independent of* obeying God. If one cannot, logically cannot, give an exhaustive definition of "right," since any definition one proposes reflects or expresses a moral principle, the definition must incorporate some meaning independent of "commanded by God." It is no longer an *exhaustive* definition. Frankena does not explain here what it is about the logic of "right" that makes this meaning independent. To support the claim that any proposed "definition" of "right" reflects a moral principle, one would go on to specify the meaning or aspect of the meaning of "right" which is reflected or expressed in it.

Frankena considers other kinds of possible relations between religion and morality as well, to ascertain whether they might involve logical dependence of a sort. He finds it plausible to contend, for example, that in order for a belief to be justified, one must show a logical entailment from some more basic view of man and the universe. Yet he thinks it is muddling to define religion so broadly that all ultimate views or concerns about the universe—theistic, humanist, and atheistic—effectively fall under it. Victories won by such terminological inflation are empty ones. The interesting issue for him is whether logical dependence follows from a theistic view and to this his answer is no.

However, in his reference to Mill at the end of his essay Frankena suggests that there may be a "larger sense" of "proof" or "justification" which would allow the theologian to claim that certain facts might be *sufficient* to "determine the intellect to give its assent" to a proposal that "right" be defined in theological terms. Though not strictly entailed in a logical sense, it might be "reasonable," he observes, to claim that if God is love, we ought to love.[11]

In contrast to Frankena, Robert Adams argues for a "modified" form of the classic divine command theory. On the Thomistic alternative, "what is right and wrong is independent of God's will" and "God always does right by the necessity of His nature." So it is "logically impossible" for God to command what is wrong, e.g., cruelty for its own sake. For the unmodified divine command theory, however, it is not logically impossible for God to command cruelty

[11] Paul Ramsey takes up a possibility Frankena discusses in another essay, namely, that one could make a normative metaethical proposal without presupposing a normative *moral* judgment. See Frankena, "On Saying the Ethical Thing," *Proceedings and Addresses of the American Philosophical Association,* 39, 1965–66 (Yellow Springs, Ohio: Antioch Press, 1966), pp. 21–42. Reprinted in *Philosophy Today,* No. 1, ed. Jerry Gill (New York: Macmillan, 1968), pp. 250–78. See Ramsey, "The Case of the Curious Exception," *Norm and Context in Christian Ethics,* eds. Gene Outka and Paul Ramsey (New York: Scribner; London: SCM Press; 1968), pp. 120–25.

for its own sake. Since "right" means in an exhaustive sense, commanded by God, it would be wrong not to practice cruelty for its own sake if God commanded it.

Some believers, Adams maintains, do use "wrong" to mean "forbidden by God," so that if God commanded cruelty for its own sake, it would be wrong not to practice it. But he and others do not use it this way, and his modified theory is an attempt to account for their use. It would seem that he both reports a view and argues that it is defensible (the classic divine command theory was not a report, Adams claims, of what everyone meant by "right" and "wrong"; it referred only to the discourse of believers).

On the modified theory, "wrong" means in part "contrary to God's commands," but certain conditions are assumed, namely, that God has the loving character which one believes him to have. If God did command cruelty for its own sake, then Adams would not hold either that it would be wrong to disobey or wrong to obey—his concept of wrong, he holds, would " 'break down' " if God so commanded. God's loving is a presupposition for the "applicability" of the concepts of right and wrong. Adams prefers to put the thesis this way rather than to make God's love part of the meaning of "right" and "wrong" ("wrong" would mean "contrary to the commands of a *loving* God"). The former keeps the point clear that for the believer, even on the modified theory, "right" and "wrong" refer to God's will, not to his love.

Thus even on Adams' modified theory the believer is a "nonnaturalist objectivist" in his metaethic. That is, "x is wrong" refers to a fact which is objective of any human being, and that fact cannot be "stated entirely in the languages of physics, chemistry, biology, and human psychology." For the divine command theory, modified and unmodified, the crucial point is that ethical facts are facts about the will and commands of God. However, the modified divine command theorist does not claim that " 'wrong' and 'contrary to God's commands' have exactly the same meaning for him." There is "some little difference" in meaning. Both a favorable attitude to God (based on his loving nature) and a reference to the fact of his command are necessary for the believer's concept of right and wrong to work. Thus, on the modified theory, the believer values some things independently of God's commands. Values, however, according to Adams, do not necessarily "imply or presuppose judgments of ethical right or wrong." Therefore, the modified command theory only presupposes independent valuations, not a "conception of ethical right and wrong . . . independent of . . . beliefs about God's commands." Yet such valuations are "involved in" or "even necessary for" a divine command conception of right and wrong; where a favorable valuation of God breaks down, the concept "breaks down."

How should one construe such a modified theory? Adams seems to keep the theological or metaphysical side of the Ockhamistic position, while he modifies the metaethical. That is, he makes very clear that in unity with Ockham, it is logically possible that God could command unloving things, e.g., cruelty for its own sake. The beliefs that the believer has about God, e.g., that he is loving, are taken to be "contingent truths." According to Barth, Adams claims, God is gracious to men, i.e., loving, but he was free not to be so. Nonetheless, Adams adds that for Barth, God has "committed Himself irrevocably in Jesus Christ" to be gracious. Thus it would be "unthinkable" that God would command what is cruel for its own sake, although it is logically possible. Insofar as God is believed to be loving, the tradition does not provide for the possibility that God would command cruelty for its own sake. God, for Ockham, was "unalterably opposed to any such practice," so that the "logical possibility . . . doubtless did not represent in Ockham's view any real possibility."

Yet what does God's irrevocable commitment mean? Is God no longer free to be unloving? If so, is it the law of non-contradiction which limits him, or is his commitment itself a moral obligation? If the belief about God's loving nature only reflects a contingent truth, then God could command differently. The issue here is what "unalterable" or "unthinkable" could mean if God is free to be other than loving.

On the metaethical side, however, it is clear that Adams wants to modify the Ockhamistic theory. While the meaning of "right" is defined as "commanded by God," independent valuations are the conditions for the applicability of such a definition. According to Adams, if God did command an unloving action, the believer's concept of right and wrong would break down. Presumably the believer must have "commanded by God" as the definition of "right," and if he is prevented by virtue of the sort of thing God has commanded, then the believer has no concept of right, or at least he is prevented from applying it. The believer accepts such a definition of "right" and "wrong," Adams notes, at least partly because of the valuations he holds. He values God's loving beneficence and feels grateful toward him. If the valuations change, i.e., if God should turn out not to be loving, then this reason at least for accepting the definition of "right" is no longer valid. Presumably what keeps the believer from accepting a new definition of "right" is the other sort of reason which prompted him to accept the original one, namely, religious "awe." The believer evidently is not prepared to accept any use of right and wrong which does not come "clothed in the majesty of a divine authority."

Thus, in contrast to Frankena, for whom to accept the "definition" of "right" as "commanded by God" presupposes or is tantamount to accepting the "moral" principle that it is right or one ought to obey God, for Adams one is moved to accept a definition of ethical rightness partly because of "valuations." Such valuations would not be presupposed in one's definition in the way a "moral" principle would be for Frankena. The valuations might be the presuppositions for the applicability of the concept of ethical rightness, but it would not *in its meaning* presuppose them.

In the end, however, one might ask how much practical difference remains between Frankena and Adams, since for the latter the believer may give priority to his "valuations" should God command something which offends them. The believer's "positive valuation of . . . doing *whatever* God may command is not clearly greater than [his] independent negative valuation of cruelty." By making valuations a part of the conditions for equating God's command with right and wrong, Adams may in effect accept the position Frankena proposes, where independent judgment—for Adams, of course, valuational judgment, not, as with Frankena, moral judgment per se—seems logically prior to accepting God's command as a *moral* duty.

In Donald Evans' essay predominant attention shifts from logical to psychological issues. Evans develops an account of "responsive freedom" through an examination of a recent creed of the United Church of Canada. He elucidates three responses to divine activity distinguished in the creed. First, kinds of divine activity are characteristically but not exclusively linked to kinds of attitudinal responses, which are " 'fitting' or 'appropriate' . . . because of an internal connection of meaning between response and activity," e.g., creativity and trust, reconciliation and joy, renewal and gratitude. These attitudes are "basic," in that they are "pervasive" in a temporal and spatial sense. "Basic trust," for instance, "provides continuity and inner harmony for a life as a whole" and "extends all inclusively to whatever it is that pervades the whole cosmos, giving it some unity." Second, there is the response of receptivity. Although it is an attitude, it is the "precondition" of the others. The other attitudinal responses presuppose that God is acting in a man, but receptivity is "what allows God to act in a man"; "God cannot act in a man unless the man permits it." Receptivity is not a matter of "earning" grace or "doing" something to which God responds, it is "a matter of letting go, permitting. . . . It is not willful exercise of one's existing powers or ability. It is allowing oneself to be empowered, enabled." Third, there are the practical responses of "witness" and "moral action." The latter includes love and service to others (including a proper love for self), expressed in part through the search for justice in society.

Moreover, the creed reflects the inner life of believers. The interaction between God and man pictured in the creed is believed to occur in and upon the psyches of men. Thus, says Evans, to examine "connections of meaning" is also to examine "connections between psychological states and events." The thrust of Evans' essay is the claim that the sort of interaction which the creed affirms is not incompatible with moral freedom, at least with the notion of freedom Evans calls "responsive." According to Evans, "some religious convictions . . . are compatible with moral freedom, where this freedom is understood to be 'responsive' rather than 'willful.' . . . On such a view, freedom increases rather than decreases when an agent is receptive to the (non-authoritarian) influence of another agent and to the depths within himself which are beyond his direct control." Evans contrasts this responsive freedom with a notion of willful freedom which is a "power to do what one wills, a power exercised over others so as to reduce their power over oneself, which reduces one's own power; or it is a power over oneself, an ability to use at will various physical and intellectual skills which one has acquired."

Although Evans' discussion falls within the classic genre of debates about the compatibility of grace and moral responsibility, his picture of the self and the divine activity is thoroughly modern. He sees men imprisoned by their "defensive sources of security," in a world which seems "hostile and indifferent," where "death seems to represent an ultimate cosmic untrustworthiness." Through the divine activity, however, "the defenses are dropped [and] in the new security provided by the divine activity and the attitudinal responses, a man accepts and respects not only his own fundamental needs and wants, but also those of others." God then "liberates men from domination by destructive and enslaving elements within themselves so that men can become creative and free." Although Evans does not formally label man's condition as "sin," his picture of the self appears to be a contemporary theological equivalent. Facing an untrustworthy world, men react in anxiety and defensive self-isolation. Seeking to protect themselves, they defeat themselves. God, if men are receptive, allows them to trust, to find their security in him, and therefore to drop their devices of self-defense and to achieve true fulfillment for themselves and others. For Evans belief in a trustworthy spiritual power resolves the problem of "interpretability," in the terminology of Little and Twiss, in a way which has intellectual, attitudinal, and behavioral dimensions. Whatever "mystery" the creed suggests, the God to whom men respond not only in moral action but in worship and witness is, like the God of Gustafson, Jacobs, and D'Arcy, a moral being, whose intention is to secure the well-being of men.

Evans seems to claim, then, that for a man to be liberated, he must achieve a certain psychological state, one of "basic trust" and the other attitudes. For Evans the alternatives are stark (a critic might begin his challenge at just this point): either one has a *basic* trust or one cannot, in a psychological sense, be other than anxious, defensive, alienated. Furthermore, one cannot help oneself but one must allow oneself to be helped by God, who works in one's depths and through other men.

However, one need not acknowledge that basic trust implies any religious belief. As believers may "unconsciously resist" God's activity, so atheists and agnostics can be "unconsciously receptive" to God and manifest basic attitudes and correlative moral responses. Such men have "implicit faith." According to the believer, God is at work wherever there is "liberation." However, Evans holds, no religious belief is necessarily implied even in an attitude of basic trust, for example: "Basic trust . . . may continue even when it seems that there is nothing in which to trust. . . ." Unlike an ordinary attitude, where beliefs are implied in a clear and rigorous fashion (e.g., "In saying, 'I trust John,' I imply that I believe that John is trustworthy"), no belief is necessarily implied in a basic attitude. In regard to basic trust, a "minimal believer can deny that any *positive* belief is implied, and a skeptical agnostic can deny that any belief at all is implied." One is logically free to reject *any* implication. Of course, if it could be shown that Evans' distinction—between ordinary attitudes which do imply beliefs and basic attitudes which do not—cannot be sustained, then he would have to claim that if an unbeliever did have *basic* trust, defined to mean trust toward a spiritual power at work in the universe, the unbeliever would have to admit the implication. If he admitted it, but did not affirm it, he would be irrational, as Evans himself admits.

On Evans' view as it stands, the unbeliever with basic attitudes is saved from their implications and the believer is not forced to assume an "Apologetic" stance: "Don't you see, you have basic attitudes which imply a belief in a trustworthy power." On the one hand, Evans thinks it is necessary to have certain attitudes which for the believer are correlated with explicit beliefs. However, he does not want to exclude the possibility of unbelievers having these attitudes, nor does he want to claim that their attitudes must imply religious belief.

Evans also quite clearly does not wish to claim the logical dependence of morality on religion, at least in the form of a definition of rightness in terms of what God does or wills. God exhorts men to love, as well as enabling them to do so (through God's power, men can become loving persons), but the "ought" of love is not based on the fact that it is commanded by God. In this sense love is a "criterion for what counts as divine. . . . [R]eligious convictions partly depend on moral convictions (though in a dialectical and dynamic way which is remote from Kant's account of religion and morality)."

Evans opposes what he calls the "is-then-ought" theory of moral judgment, at least in its pure form. On this view, to have moral freedom, one must examine the bare facts and then proceed to make a moral judgment. Evans favors some version of an "onlook" theory according to which one assumes "broad commitments" which link is and ought and specify "obviously appropriate" ways of acting. Faced with a situation, one decides that x is sufficiently like y to treat x as y should be treated: one "looks on" x as y. Thus one's prior commitments affect one's selection of relevant facts. Evans does not intend to argue that one's freedom to adopt one or another onlook is in any way limited. In a section on moral vocabulary, he makes clear that his claim is restricted to two points: (1) acceptance of a moral framework affects one's assessment of the relevant facts; (2) moral freedom does not require that one refrain from accepting such a framework prior to viewing the facts.

There does appear to be one sense in which Evans limits the epistemological autonomy of morality. Although love is the criterion of what counts as divine, he also claims that "a man does not already know what love is, and hence what divine activity is, prior to being receptive; he understands only to the degree that he is receptive." And at another point he writes, "Yet theology is not . . . made redundant to morality, for a man does not *adequately* understand by his own unaided powers what the terms mean ('love,' 'service,' etc.). He grows in understanding as he responds to the divine activity. . . ." This last statement is probably most indicative of Evans' basic position. It is not that a man has no notion of love before he understands himself to be in relation to the divine activity, but he does not understand adequately or fully what love is until he understands God, for God is the epitome or perfection of love.[12] (Would Evans claim that the unbeliever who is unconsciously receptive to God can *know* the full meaning of love, although he does not trace his understanding to God, or to Jesus as the paradigm of divine love?)

One should note, finally, that for Evans an understanding of the full meaning of love is not the result of a "revelation" of God's "will," as one might expect in some theologies. The "primary image" in the creed is not that of a "monarch" who reveals his will, or that of a "master craftsman, designing and making artifacts [including man]. . . ." The creed substitutes for either of these older models the image of men "responding" to the divine activity. Hence to "do

[12] See Evans on learning the paradigmatic meaning of terms like "love," "patience," and "fatherhood" from divine revelation, including references to Jesus, who rendered the paradigmatic faith-response to God, in "Barth on Talk about God," *Canadian Journal of Theology*, XVI (1970), pp. 175–92.

God's will" is to affirm oneself and others in receptive response to God.

Thus the creed mirrors a recent theological climate which has sought to avoid both the classical Protestant ethics of obedience to God's will and the Roman Catholic natural law ethic based on the idea of God as a designer.[13] Kierkegaard's account of the "knight of faith," for example, seems more akin to a divine command-human obedience scheme. Even if one agrees with Outka that the obedience to God in question may be interpreted in a way that does not violate one important sort of agent-autonomy, that the knight of faith must freely yield to God's command and independently make it his own, still, on the side of the agent's response, Kierkegaard appears to place greater stress than Evans on decision, and the struggle to obey in the midst of suffering. The agent is called upon passionately to appropriate a command which is issued, more than to discover or be receptive to non-authoritarian influences of other agents and within his own interior depths.

Evans has to face, in any event, the problem of the meaning and truth of language about God, whether expressed in terms of his "will," his "purpose," or his "activity." Indeed, it is precisely the problem of affirmations about God which the final essay, to which we now turn, raises so acutely.

In the two lectures printed here (with their lecture style preserved intact), R. M. Hare does not present arguments for the logical or epistemological autonomy of morality. Nor does he pursue the question whether men can "free" themselves, in Evans' sense, without the activity of God. Hare assumes that since Kant, one can insist on the "autonomy of morals—its independence of human or divine authority." One "can have a rational morality without the orthodox God, and cannot have one with him." He would hold, evidently, that if one defines God in moral terms, as on the Thomistic alternative, then moral considerations remain logically independent of his command, indeed of his existence. What concerns Hare es-

[13] Some philosophers of religion and theologians prefer to attempt to reinterpret older images, rather than abandon them for new ones, e.g., Paul Tillich in *Morality and Beyond* (New York: Harper, 1963), and Rudolf Otto in *Freiheit und Notwendigkeit* (Tübingen: Verlag von J. C. B. Mohr, 1940). Cf. Ian Ramsey on not taking "God's will" in an anthropomorphic sense: "Moral Judgments and God's Commands," *Christian Ethics and Contemporary Philosophy*, ed. Ian Ramsey (New York: Macmillan; London: SCM Press, 1966), pp. 168–69.

pecially are the first and second of the three traditional virtues of faith, hope, and love. For Hare it is not the hope that virtue will be rewarded or even that happiness will be coincident with virtue, but a "faith" that moral striving is not pointless.

Hare begins by examining the problem of the believer who has encountered the attack that if his beliefs are empirical assertions, they are false; and if they are not such assertions, they are meaningless. The latter point rests on the claim of the "Sophisticated Unbeliever" that "if the utterance was to express an assertion, there had to be something which, if it occurred, would constitute a disproof of the assertion." Hare, however, points out to the perplexed believer that not "all meaningful utterances" express "assertions in this [empirical] sense" and that "[t]here are, moreover, beliefs which are not beliefs in the truth of assertions, in this narrow sense. . . .'"

As an example of such a belief, Hare presents the belief of the scientist that nature is susceptible of "explanation" according to "causal laws." The scientist does not *know* there is such explanation —nothing could ever falsify his belief—but he has "faith" that his effort to explain is not futile. Just so, Hare contends, the Christian believer has traditionally held " 'the *hope* that this way of life is not vain or pointless. And this hope would be futile if the world were not ordered in a certain way.' " The believer also holds certain genuine empirical beliefs, for example, that people will generally respond positively to one's attempt to live according to an ethic of love, although there are exceptions. For Hare this is a factual belief, although it is "often expressed in terms of the working of the Holy Spirit in men's hearts." However, the sort of religious belief which is parallel to the scientist's is quite different. It is not an assertion in an empirical sense, but may be one "in some less restricted sense." The scientist whose hypothesis fails, does not give up his belief "that there are laws to be discovered." This is not an empirical assertion but "in another sense the belief is surely factual; it is 'about the world.' " Just so the Christian believer holds that his morality is not pointless; "the moralist has to have the faith . . . that it is possible to find, moral 'policies' . . . which are not pointless. . . . [N]o practical morality could do without an ample faith that events will not frustrate its ends." This faith is not simply a *prescription* not to give up hope, for if we lost it, we would have changed "our view about what the world was like."

Hare proposes, then, to add to the thesis of Braithwaite—that, in Hare's words, religion is "morals helped out by mythology"—the element of "faith that saves moral endeavor from futility." But no more than Braithwaite would, does Hare mean to claim that this faith can be retained in the form of traditional belief in the providence of God. Although faith and hope in the divine providence are ways Christians have expressed their assurance that moral endeavor was not futile, Hare rules out both what he calls the "contranatural" and the "transcendental" sense of the "supernatural." He distinguishes between propositions about "contranatural" events which are "perfectly meaningful empirical propositions," and statements about the transcendental which are not. The believer, when he decides under the impact of science that his contranatural beliefs are false, may try to substitute beliefs in "transcendental entities and events." But according to Hare, these are "idle" and hence statements about them are meaningless. The "existence or non-existence" of a transcendental deity makes no difference either to what is the case or what we ought to do—"His transcendence logically rules this out." When Hare affirms that he believes in "divine providence," he means "that matters are so ordered in the world that there is a point in trying to live by the precepts to which Christians subscribe."

Thus Evans' claim, for instance, that there is a trustworthy spiritual power at work in the world would be for Hare either contranatural and false, or transcendental and empty. Evans does not say in his essay here whether his belief is falsifiable, but elsewhere he does put the believer's claim squarely in the category of a falsifiable assertion.[14] Because Hare would regard such a claim as false, he bases his hope on a faith that moral striving will not be proven futile, i.e., the attempt to realize a moral policy in *this* world is not in vain. Evans' creed affirms that death does not represent an "ultimate cosmic untrustworthiness," whereas the problem of "interpretability" Hare raises is limited to this world.

[14] In an essay on "Scientific and Religious Assertions," Evans claims that while in several ways religious assertions are not testable by empirical observations, insofar as one believes that God *acts* in "depth experiences," "this specific connection involves a causal claim. . . ." According to Evans, if all such convictions "could be accounted for by reference to nondivine sufficient conditions, then faith in an actively self-revealing God would be falsifiable." Evans thinks that such falsification is not possible in practice, but it is in principle. *Science and Religion*, ed. Ian G. Barbour (New York: Harper, 1968), pp. 128–32.

Although Hare does not equate morality with Christian morality, he does seem to say that any moral person, Christian or otherwise, "still needs to have" faith that his striving is not futile. The "good man . . . can hardly pursue [his moral ideals] unless he has faith in the possibility, as things are, of realizing them." But what does Hare mean by "needs to have" and "can hardly pursue"? At other points, he uses the phrase "has to have" and claims that no morality "could do without" such a faith. Hare does not pursue very far here whether the connection between faith and morality is necessary, reasonable, assuring, fruitful, or some other kind. From the vantage point of the principal issues discussed in this volume, do the expressions above refer to a point of logic or psychology? It would appear that Hare must mean the latter, for it seems logically possible to pursue moral policies in the face of one's belief that they are pointless. If he means that it is psychologically necessary to have such a faith in order to continue striving, he could be challenged on empirical grounds. Does everyone, or do even most people, find such a faith psychologically necessary? In short, are there those who share a similar view of morality, but lack the hope that virtue will triumph?

If one did accept Hare's thesis that such a faith is essential in some sense for morality, what would one say about the logical status he claims for it? Some philosophers would challenge his view of the scientist's "faith" in nature's susceptibility to causal explanation. A critic would try to bring Hare's own specific notion of faith—in the non-futility of moral striving as an assertion of faith, about the world but not falsifiable like ordinary empirical beliefs—into the class of empirical beliefs Hare identifies, such as the belief that most men will respond positively to one's attempt to live the Christian life. As Hare notes, although such a belief is often interpreted in terms of divine activity, the presence of the Holy Spirit in men's hearts, it can be taken as an empirical claim, albeit one hedged with many qualifications and exceptions which make falsification unlikely. The belief in divine providence, the critic might argue, should be analyzed in precisely this way, instead of claiming a special status for it. It, too, shorn of contranatural or transcendental claims, expresses an empirical assertion about the consequences of our actions in light of the way the world is, an assertion which, although difficult, and even perhaps practically impossible to falsify, is nevertheless falsifiable in principle, unlike Hare's "faith."

Finally, Hare contends that on the whole it is less misleading to call his position "Christian" than "humanist." It is interesting to note his observation that in a meeting at Oxford at which Braithwaite spoke, believers thought Braithwaite a Christian and unbelievers did not. The former, Hare remarks, "showed a very sound feeling for what is essential to Christianity. . . ." For Hare, Christian morality and a non-supernatural faith that moral striving is not futile are the essential elements of Christianity. Hare seems to stand then in the tradition of those who have tried to find a viable "essence" of Christianity in the face of science. Moreover, he stands in the Kantian tradition, where religion is treated primarily in relation to morality, the tradition against which Otto and his followers reacted.

PART I

Definitions of Religion and Morality

BASIC TERMS IN THE STUDY OF RELIGIOUS ETHICS

David Little and Sumner B. Twiss, Jr.

I. INTRODUCTION

The study of religious ethics stands in need of conceptual and methodological clarification. This essay is an attempt to meet the need by proposing definitions for the basic terms "ethics" and "religion," and by indicating a method of study that is, hopefully, more rigorous and consistent than most approaches.

Though definitional activity is difficult, especially regarding the notions of morality and religion, much of the literature has been unnecessarily misleading. Max Weber, who made an enormous contribution to the investigation of religious ethics, was uncharacteristically confusing when he wrote: "To define 'religion,' to say what it *is*, is not possible at the start of a presentation . . . Definitions can be attempted, if at all, only at the conclusion of the study."[1] Unless one is prepared to offer *some* specification of the term "religion," it is impossible to see how he could begin to conduct a study of comparative religious behavior.[2] In fact, Weber does assume certain defining characteristics for distinguishing religious from legal, customary, and other sorts of behavior.[3] For some reason he is less explicit about

[1] Max Weber, *Sociology of Religion* (Boston: Beacon, 1963), p. 1.

[2] This is, of course, what Weber undertakes to do in his comparative study of religion.

[3] Talcott Parsons seems close to an adequate summary of Weber's assumptions about the meaning of religion when he writes: "A crucial point in Weber's theory is that there is no known human society without something which modern social scientists would classify as religion. Every society possesses some conceptions of a super-natural order, of spirits, gods or impersonal forces which

definitions in this case than he is in his use of no less complex terms such as "ethics"[4] and "law."[5]

In a recent comparative anthropological study, *Morals and Merit*, Christoph von Fürer-Haimendorf is similarly unclear with respect to the concept of morality. "Philosophers are not agreed on the definition of morality, and no sensible anthropologist will want to intrude into a debate in which the best brains of the past fifty or sixty generations have been engaged without reaching a definite conclusion. Yet," he continues, "no one can live in a primitive or any other society without realizing that certain activities seem to be regarded as morally neutral while the exercise of an individual's choice in other activities is subject to moral assessments. . . ."[6] Again, the matter of defining basic terms is not optional. Because he uses the word "moral" throughout his study, as he does in this passage, to differentiate "certain activities" from others, Fürer-Haimendorf is responsible to explicate and defend his definition. His failure to attend to definitions, not only with respect to "morality," but also to "religion" and "law," produces some confusions that mar an otherwise useful work.[7]

There are many other examples of careless use of basic terms in social scientific literature. John Milton Yinger, in *The Scientific Study of Religion*, contends that it is "possible and desirable to define [religion and morality] in independent terms and separate them analytically."[8] But though he discusses the relationship of religion and morality, he supplies only the vaguest specification for morality, and his use of religion shifts. "Morality," he says, "is concerned with

---

are different from and in some sense superior to those forces conceived as governing ordinary 'natural' events, and whose nature and activities somehow give meaning to the unusual, the frustrating and the rationally impenetrable aspects of experience" (Introduction, *Sociology of Religion*, p. xxviii).

[4] Max Weber, *Theory of Social and Economic Organization* (New York: Oxford Univ. Press, 1947), pp. 129–30.

[5] Ibid., p. 127; *Max Weber on Law in Economy and Society* (Cambridge, Mass.: Harvard Univ. Press, 1954), p. 17; cf. the editor's, Max Rheinstein's, comments on Weber's definitional procedure in the Introduction, p. lv.

[6] Christoph von Fürer-Haimendorf, *Morals and Merit: A Study of Values and Social Controls in South Asian Societies* (London: Weidenfeld & Nicolson, 1967), p. 9.

[7] Fürer-Haimendorf often distinguishes religion from morality, and gives much evidence that the peoples he is studying make such a distinction. Nevertheless, one is never quite sure precisely what the differentia of each concept are for him.

[8] John Milton Yinger, *The Scientific Study of Religion* (New York: Macmillan, 1970), p. 51.

the relationship of man to man,"[9] though that is too inclusive to be of much help. Religion, on the other hand, "is concerned with the relationship of man to some higher power or idea."[10] That attribute is not only rather inexact, in itself, but neither is it part of his "operational definition of religion" he supplies earlier.[11] Yinger makes another passing attempt to clarify his concepts when he asserts that "the distinction [between religion and morality] is in terms of the authority and the sanctions that are attached to the codes [of each]";[12] however, this sentence is hopelessly cryptic without explication and defense.

Alexander MacBeath has demonstrated how muddled is Bronislaw Malinowski's understanding and application of the concepts religion and morality. At one point Malinowski tells us that "all the morality of primitives is derived from religious belief,"[13] but at another place he contends that the ordinary rules of individual and social morality among primitive peoples "in no way have the character of religious commandments . . . but [are] provided with a purely binding social force." Such inconsistent usage can be traced to insufficient precision in defining terms as well as to careless argumentation.

Social scientists are not the only culprits. Philosophers who undertake to write about the relation of religion and morality, and who ought to be able, if anyone is, to clarify basic concepts for descriptive and comparative study, often produce the most disappointing results. This is true of William Warren Bartley's recent book *Morality and Religion*.[14] In the opening paragraph, Bartley states:

> I propose to begin by assuming, as others have done, that there is some such thing as morality and some such thing as religion, and I shall take as my first task the clarification of what would be involved in the inter-dependence of these two things.[15]

[9] Ibid.
[10] Ibid.
[11] Ibid., p. 33.
[12] Ibid., p. 51.
[13] Quoted by Alexander MacBeath, *Experiments in Living* (London: Macmillan, 1952), pp. 308–9. Moreover, Malinowski is given to oversimplifying other of his basic terms, as, for example, in the case of his definition of law. See Leopold Pospisil, *Anthropology of Law* (New York: Harper, 1971), pp. 30–31.
[14] (London: Macmillan, 1971). This is an exceedingly disappointing volume.
[15] Ibid., p. 1.

It is hard to see how one can trace relationships between two concepts, particularly concepts as complex as religion and morality,
without first specifying what the concepts mean. Given the diversity of viewpoint regarding the understanding of these terms, we
are hardly at the point where we can *assume* definitions!

Aside from conceptual shortcomings, there are substantial methodological confusions in much of the literature. In the first place,
social scientists, and particularly those of the "functionalist" school,
often muddle the study of comparative ethics by failing to indicate
when they are offering sociological or psychological explanations
for the existence of a code of conduct, and when they are examining
the beliefs and reasons the practitioners themselves aver for behaving as they do. Fürer-Haimendorf's account of the moral practices
of a group of Polynesian food-gatherers is a good example. On the
one hand, the islanders, according to Fürer-Haimendorf, believe
that violations of the moral code will evoke supernatural retribution
as well as public condemnation. On the other hand, he informs us
that infringements are likely to be disapproved of because they will
"disturb the harmony of the group."[16]

It is impossible to tell from the context whether the second proposition is something the islanders themselves affirm—something they
would offer as a reason for opposing violations of their code—or
whether it is Fürer-Haimendorf's own explanation as to the "real,"
though unconscious, reason that the islanders hold the beliefs they
do. Though the two possible readings are not mutually exclusive, it
is important to be clear whether a belief is being reported or an explanation advanced. This equivocation is not peculiar to Fürer-
Haimendorf.[17]

A second methodological difficulty is the lack of clarity about the
distinction between "descriptive" and "normative" ethics. Broadly,
the former is an empirical and analytical account of a given person's
or group's moral code. The latter is the advocacy and defense of a
particular moral position. For instance, Fürer-Haimendorf does not
always keep firmly in mind the difference between these two tasks.
Having asserted that the anthropologist "must confine himself to

[16] Fürer-Haimendorf, *Morals and Merit,* p. 33.
[17] See John Ladd, *Structure of a Moral Code* (Cambridge, Mass.: Harvard
Univ. Press, 1957), pp. 46–47, for a discussion of further examples.

describing" different systems of morality, Fürer-Haimendorf goes on to claim that

> any value-assessment he may be tempted to make will ultimately depend on his own ideological background and personal predilections. For it seems that we cannot measure and judge morals by absolute, scientifically determined standards but can only evaluate the moral norms of one society by comparing them with the moral system of another. In this process of comparison the essential features of the individual systems may be exposed and clarified, but an element of subjectivity in the value judgements appears to be an inescapable feature of all our thinking about morality.[18]

Though Fürer-Haimendorf shows no sign he is aware of the point, it is obvious that his claim about the subjectivity of moral evaluations is a normative claim, as is his statement that comparative study is inherently evaluative. These contentions require independent defense, and in no way follow from the nature of the descriptive tasks he recommends. Presumably, one may engage in useful descriptive work, whether he shares Fürer-Haimendorf's subjective relativism or not. The literature manifests too many examples of a similar carelessness in jumbling descriptive and normative arguments.[19]

II. CONCEPTUAL AND METHODOLOGICAL ORIENTATION

It is our belief that John Ladd's study *The Structure of a Moral Code: A Philosophical Analysis of Ethical Discourse Applied to the Ethics of the Navaho Indians*,[20] while not without its limitations, provides an admirable starting point for rectifying some of the conceptual and methodological confusions we have mentioned. As we shall make clear, we depart from Ladd at several critical points. Also, we develop further than he does some of his suggestions for the study of descriptive and comparative religious ethics.

To begin with, Ladd is aware that in order to engage in the study

---

[18] Fürer-Haimendorf, *Morals and Merit*, p. 228.

[19] See Paul W. Taylor, "Social Science and Ethical Relativism," *Journal of Philosophy* lv/1 (January 2, 1958), pp. 32–44, and Ladd, *Structure of a Moral Code*, pp. 322–28, for discussion of, and objections to, this sort of jumbling.

[20] See Note 17.

of comparative ethics, "we must decide upon some reasonably exact criterion of what is to be taken as ethical."[21] His approach to the definitional task is, in keeping with trends in analytic philosophy, to focus upon the language of ethics, or ethics as a form of discourse. "Ethical ideas and thoughts are always in principle communicable because they are formulated in the language of the society concerned."[22] The question, then, that Ladd puts, is what defining characteristics distinguish an ethical utterance or statement from other statements. His conclusion is as follows: "A moral statement . . . will be defined as 'A statement expressing the acceptance of a prescription for conduct which claims superiority and which is regarded as legitimate.' "[23] An ethical statement, by contrast, "is either a moral statement or a statement made in connection with one; for example, in justification of it."[24] (For Ladd, ethical statements are generally *reflective* responses to moral statements, usually in defense of them.)

Shortly, we shall advance our own definition of morality that is in certain respects similar to Ladd's. In elaborating and defending it we shall go over in detail some of the same ground Ladd goes over in discussing his proposal. We may, therefore, defer comment on the substance of the definition, though a few remarks are in order about the general task of defining—particularly in regard to open-textured words like "morality" and "religion."

The sort of definitions we seek are equivalent to Carnap's and Hempel's notion of *explication* or *rational reconstruction.*[25] Such

21 Ibid., p. 42. A recent book by John H. Barnsley, *Social Reality of Ethics: The Comparative Analysis of Moral Codes* (London: Routledge, 1972), is one of the few studies in this field that takes Ladd's approach seriously in proposing a definition of morality. Barnsley's sensitivity to recent philosophical discussions, together with a very useful survey of sociological and anthropological work in the field, make this a valuable book. Nevertheless, we are not satisfied with Barnsley's proposal for a "formal definition of morality." He also gives a rather confusing and incomplete account of the "elements of a moral code." (See esp. chaps. 2 and 3.)

22 Ladd, *Structure of a Moral Code,* p. 19.

23 Ibid., p. 85.

24 Ibid.

25 C. G. Hempel, *Fundamentals of Concept Formation in Empirical Science,* Vol. 2, no. 7, *International Encyclopedia of United Science* (Chicago: Univ. of Chicago Press, 1952), pp. 11–12; cf. Ladd, *Structure of a Moral Code,* pp. 44–45.

definitions provide clear and precise concepts of morality and religion, reinterpreted from ordinary usage, for use within comparative religious ethics. The general canons for a well-formed and properly asserted definition, including "formal" and "literary" requirements, are obviously applicable, and need not be stated.[26] Those canons peculiar to reconstructive definition within a comparative context, include the following: 1) that the definition permit reformulation of a large part of what is customarily expressed by the terms in ordinary usage (the proposed definition, when used within the natural community, must not be counter-intuitive to the members of that community); 2) that the definition permit the formulation of testable hypotheses, which may, if possible, have explanatory and predictive force; 3) that the definition have the capacity-in-principle to permit the development of a comprehensive and rigorous theory; and 4) that the definition possess cross-cultural applicability and thereby avoid the "fallacy of ethnocentricity."[27]

We are naturally aware of the standard objections that are raised against the quest for precise definitions of apparently imprecise terms. First, it is sometimes argued that vagueness and inconsistency are intrinsic to the customary usage of many natural language terms, and, therefore, the search for "true" analytic definitions is hopeless.[28] Second, and related to the first objection, is the generalized application to ordinary language of the Wittgensteinian notion of family resemblances. This point of view holds that any search for "if and only if" definitions is often misguided, since such an approach too easily assumes that there are distinctive generic properties for concepts like morality and religion. It recommends instead that we "look and see" whether there are any such generic properties by observing the use of a term in different contexts, and it goes on to suggest that rather than generic properties one is likely to find vaguer "family resemblances" among uses—now one set of common properties link-

[26] These canons are collocated, formulated, and denoted as "rules for complete definition" by H. S. Leonard, *Principles of Reasoning* (New York: Dover, 1967), pp. 608–16.

[27] This parenthetical, though not unimportant, point is heavily emphasized by M. E. Spiro, "Religion: Problems of Definition and Explanation," in M. Banton, ed., *Anthropological Approaches to the Study of Religion* (London: Tavistock, 1966), pp. 86–87.

[28] See Hempel, *Fundamentals of Concept Formation*, pp. 9–10.

ing two uses, now another, but no one necessary, ever present set of defining characteristics.[29]

Third, it is sometimes contended that terms like "moral" have been used indiscriminately in a persuasive manner by the natural language community, that is, without responsible presentation and justification.[30] Such usage has led both to inescapable confusion over the meaning of the term, and to a predominantly emotive use of the term. Given this state of affairs, definitional controversy is not fruitful.

Our basic response to all three objections is to advocate following Wittgenstein's counsel that we first of all "look and see" the use to which concepts like morality and religion are put, and come to our own conclusions whether they have "core meanings" or not. While we remain skeptical that any "true" or "if and only if" definitions can be found, we are confident we can identify some common attributes of the concepts of morality and religion that, for purposes of comparative work, are more determinate than the second objection would lead us to expect, and less exclusively emotive in content than the third objection suggests. Incidentally, the family resemblance approach may itself be inadequate in failing to specify where one "family" (e.g., morality) begins and another (e.g., law) ends. Overlaps and similarities *ad infinitum* seem to result in a large "family" indeed, making specific discourse about a particular phenomenon difficult, if not impossible.[31]

It is not without interest that in a field bordering closely on our own, the comparative study of law, much creative attention is recently being given to the definition of "an analytical concept of law that can be applied cross-culturally."[32] According to Leonard Pospisil, anthropologists have gradually come to realize, much as we

---

[29] See L. Wittgenstein, *The Blue Book* (New York: Harper, 1964), pp. 17–18, and *Philosophical Investigations* (New York: Macmillan, 1967), pp. 66–71. See also R. Bambrough, "Universals and Family Resemblances," reprinted in G. Pitcher, ed., *Wittgenstein: The Philosophical Investigations* (Garden City, N.Y.: Doubleday, 1966), pp. 186–204; and J. Kovesi, *Moral Notions* (London: Routledge, 1967), pp. 22–23.

[30] See C. L. Stevenson, "Persuasive Definitions," reprinted in *Facts and Values: Studies in Ethical Analysis* (New Haven: Yale Univ. Press, 1963), pp. 33–54.

[31] See Kovesi, *Moral Notions,* pp. 22–23, for a convincing attack on the "family resemblances" approach.

[32] Pospisil, *Anthropology of Law,* p. 40.

have, that comparative analysis of social phenomena cannot proceed without clear conceptualizations. Moreover, despite opinions to the contrary, it appears possible to formulate a relatively determinate set of attributes of the concept law that can "serve as criteria for a more exact delimitation of the law's boundaries and for separating legal phenomena from other, non-legal social categories."[33]

Having helped to specify what constitutes a moral code in the first place, Ladd makes two methodological advances in studying such codes. First, he clearly separates the task of causal investigation from the task of analyzing the mode of moral reasoning or justification employed by a given group. Second, he carefully identifies the latter task as the primary activity of descriptive ethics, and brackets off from the descriptive analysis of moral reasoning all normative considerations. As Ladd and we understand it, descriptive ethics is "a scientific meta-theoretical inquiry into the ethical discourse of a specified informant or group."[34] Thus, to engage in *comparative descriptive ethics* is to describe and compare the patterns of moral reasoning employed by the members of two or more designated groups to justify the respective moral codes of those groups.

Ladd's procedure, as applied to the moral code of the Navahos, provides an instructive model of analysis, but we are compelled, for our own purposes, to depart from it somewhat. Ladd's method, which he labels "the method of hypothetical reconstruction," is particularly adapted to the analysis of the moral codes of groups who are presently in existence. The method aims at proposing hypotheses about the content and form of moral reasoning prevalent in a given group, and then on the basis of those hypotheses, predicting what sort of moral judgments members of the group will make. Finally, it aims at testing those predictions by means of interviewing an informant, who may be taken as representative of the group. In this way, it is possible to verify scientifically, the "hypothetical reconstruction" of the code that the analyst advances. Obviously, such a procedure requires the presence of a living informant to whom one may apply the appropriate tests.

There are two reasons why, in the study of religious ethics, we do not restrict ourselves to Ladd's interview technique. First, we are

33 Ibid.
34 Ladd, *Structure of a Moral Code*, p. 30.

concerned to analyze the moral and religious codes for which there are no longer any available "informants," such as the code of the primitive Christians. Second, while it is perhaps true that in the case of contemporary religious and moral codes, the most reliable scientific method is Ladd's direct interview procedure conducted by a sophisticated investigator, it is also true that the comparative ethicist can perform an indispensable preliminary activity by learning how both to utilize secondary literature and to develop his own secondhand intuitions so as to formulate significant *hypotheses* regarding the structure and content of a particular code. As a matter of fact, given time and resources, sometimes the most a comparativist may hope for is the generation of plausible hypotheses. He therefore ought to know how to do the job well.

Since we wish to include historical materials in our analysis, over and above Ladd's interview technique, we are thrown back upon something like the "verstehende" or "interpretive" method, associated with Weber and others. Despite Ladd's disparaging comments about the method,[35] it provides for his basic distinctions between explaining social action causally, and investigating the "meaning system" or the "internal structure of cultural values" by which a given group justifies its action. This sort of investigation will involve, much as for Ladd, developing a "reconstruction" or "ideal type" of a hypothetical pattern of "intended meaning" according to which a group understands its behavior, and then attempting to verify the reconstruction against the relevant literature produced by the group, and/or by the relevant secondhand accounts of what the group believed. We are of course aware that the results of such a procedure are hard to verify rigorously: that is an unavoidable impediment in most intellectual historical inquiry.

III. DEFINITIONS OF "MORALITY" AND "RELIGION"

In keeping with our introductory remarks regarding the canons for producing a "reconstructive" definition of morality and religion, we begin by systematically "reformulating a large part of what is customarily expressed by the terms in ordinary usage," here and there

[35] Ibid., pp. 40–41.

suggesting how our proposed definitions can be put to work in cross-cultural analysis.

A. MORALITY. Before specifying and elaborating our proposed definition, it is necessary to draw attention, in a preliminary way, to certain minimal and intuitively obvious features of what we commonly understand by the concept moral. Firstly, we take it that morality "functions"[36] to guide the conduct of persons and human groups, in such a way that it constitutes an "institution," or a shared system of expectations for regulating behavior. Secondly, we take morality as an action-guiding institution having, in an important sense, to do with *relational action,* that is, with the mutually interacting and impinging conduct of persons and groups. Though there may be exceptions, generally speaking, something counts as a moral directive when it fulfills the "restrictive condition . . . that it can be adopted as a means of initiating or preserving or extending some kind of cooperation or social activity between human beings."[37] In other words, morality, among other things, provides a way of responding to what we call the "problem of cooperation" among self-interested, competing, and conflicting persons and groups.

Obviously, these two general and minimal conditions, while important in our common understanding of morality, are, as they stand, neither sufficiently refined, nor do they satisfactorily distinguish morality from other sorts of action-guiding institutions, such as law, etiquette, and religious ritual. We therefore turn to our specific definition.

We take a *"moral statement"* to be a *"statement expressing the acceptance of an action-guide which claims superiority, and which is considered legitimate, in that it is justifiable and other-regarding."* This reconstructive definition is schematized in the following heuristic conceptual diagram of a moral action-guide (MAG). The diagram below will structure and clarify our elaboration and defense of this definition.

First, we distinguish the two primary aspects, the prescriptive and the authoritative. With respect to the *prescriptive component,* we use the term "action-guide" (AG) rather than the more usual

[36] See J. Kemp, *Reason, Action and Morality* (London: Routledge, 1964), p. 193, for a convincing and sophisticated discussion of the "function" of a moral code.

[37] Ibid., p. 196.

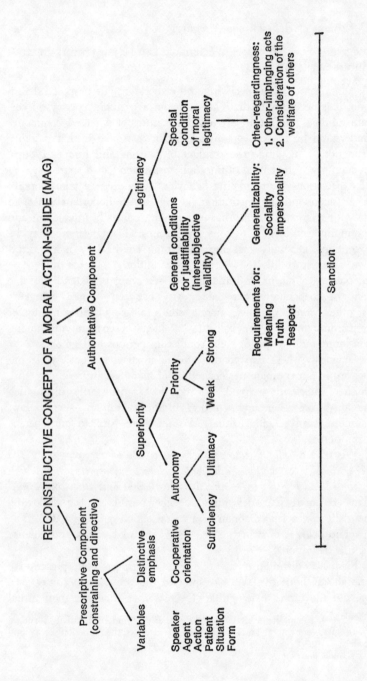

RECONSTRUCTIVE CONCEPT OF A MORAL ACTION-GUIDE (MAG)

Prescriptive Component (constraining and directive)

Variables

Distinctive emphasis

Speaker
Agent
Action
Patient
Situation
Form

Co-operative orientation

Sufficiency

Ultimacy

Autonomy

Superiority

Priority

Weak   Strong

Authoritative Component

Legitimacy

General conditions for justifiability (intersubjective validity)

Requirements for:
Meaning
Truth
Respect

Generalizability:
Sociality
Impersonality

Special condition of moral legitimacy

Other-regardingness:
1. Other-impinging acts
2. Consideration of the welfare of others

Sanction

expressions of "rule," "principle," "prescription," "judgment," "demand," etc., so as to employ the most inclusive term we can find. "Action-guide," thus, may refer to rules, principles, prescriptions, imperatives, commands, counsels, advice, fables, parables, etc., insofar as they are used to guide behavior and attitudes within the "moral form of life," as we define it.

Furthermore, the prescriptive component is singled out in order to emphasize that a MAG is both constraining and directive in regard to a certain course of action. It "constrains" in the sense that it demands that a certain action be done (or an attitude toward the action be held), whether or not the agent desires to do that action.

Moreover, the MAG tells the agent what to do, how to act, to whom, in what circumstances, etc. (the "variables" on the diagram), and in this sense "directs" him to the performance of a certain action.

The *authoritative component* of a MAG, or what is sometimes called "the special authority of morality," has frequently been identified as a distinctive characteristic of a MAG by philosophers and social scientists alike.[38] We do not depart from this tradition, except perhaps in our particular analysis of the authoritative component. Following Ladd, this component may be broken down into two broad logical features—*superiority* and *legitimacy,* each of which is in itself an internally complex category.[39] In general, "superiority" refers to the *autonomy* and *priority* of a MAG, two features which identify the prerogative which MAGs are often thought to have over nonmoral AGs. The "autonomy" of MAGs marks the recognized fact that MAGs can only be sufficiently and properly justified for independent, moral reasons (the apparent circularity here will disappear when we examine the feature of legitimacy). The autonomy of a MAG rests, of course, upon the logical requirement that no moral conclusions could be derived from premises which themselves do not contain a moral element. In brief, the autonomy of a MAG can be specified by the conjunctive features of its sufficiency —i.e., once a MAG is accepted for moral reasons, no further (nonmoral) justification is needed—and its ultimacy, i.e., a MAG cannot in principle be justified on nonmoral grounds.

[38] For examples, Ladd, *Structure of a Moral Code,* pp. 101–7; E. Durkheim, *Sociology and Philosophy,* trans. D. F. Pocock (Glencoe: Free Press, 1953), chap. 2, pp. 35 ff. Cf. Barnsley, *Social Reality of Ethics,* pp. 37–41.

[39] Ladd, *Structure of a Moral Code,* pp. 102–7.

The other aspect of a MAG's superiority, its priority, indicates that MAGs tend to take precedence over other, nonmoral AGs. However, priority may be asserted with varying degrees of strength; there may be "strong" and "weak" priority. Strong priority means that MAGs *always* take precedence over *any* conflicting nonmoral AGs. Weak priority signals a more modest understanding: although MAGs may be understood to have a *prima facie* priority over nonmoral AGs, in the sense that no MAG can always be ignored or subordinated without losing its status as a *moral* AG, *sometimes* nonmoral AGs can take precedence over *some* MAGs under specified conditions.

This reference to variations in degrees of priority identifies an issue in the study of comparative religious ethics of the utmost importance. Although many philosophers assume the truth of a view in favor of priority in the strong sense, such an assumption seems doubtful when looked at from the viewpoint of those religious positions which describe a tension, if not a direct conflict, between "moral duty" and "religious duty."[40] On such positions, it is by no means obvious that the moral always overrides the religious, for in such cases it is not merely a tension or conflict between two AGs, but also a conflict between two sorts of justification, for example, between an ultimate "other-worldly" commitment and a human "this-worldly" obligation. Insofar as they tend to conceive of all nonmoral AGs as necessarily subordinate to the "supremacy," "ultimacy," "finality," etc., of MAGs, many philosophers overlook the "supremacy," "ultimacy," "finality," etc., of some of the AGs accepted by religious people.[41] In order to do justice to the apparent tension between different sorts of authoritative AGs, we suggest that priority in the weak sense represents the more appropriate understanding, particularly for the comparative study of moral *and* religious codes.[42]

The second main feature of the authoritative component of MAGs —*legitimacy*—is a crucial part of our reconstructive definition. This feature grounds the notion of the "special authority" of MAGs,

[40] Cf. B. Leiser, *Custom, Law, and Morality* (Garden City, N.Y.: Doubleday, 1969), pp. 95–96.

[41] Cf. W. A. Christian, *Meaning and Truth in Religion* (Princeton: Princeton Univ. Press, 1964), pp. 60–77, 210–37.

[42] Leiser, *Custom, Law, and Morality*.

and it provides the rationale for why MAGs have a claim on "superiority" in relation to nonmoral AGs.

Our elaboration of this feature is tied to certain assumptions implicit in the minimal functional account of morality we introduced above—namely, that morality regulates human conduct so that cooperative living is possible. It seems obvious that such guidance is mainly achieved by means of discursive, or otherwise symbolic, communication among men, which permits AGs to become formulated, promulgated, and effective. In short, the development and use of language, along with other forms of communication, is a necessary condition for social life and its patterned regulation.

Further, it seems clear that to engage in practical discourse, or discourse over recommended courses of conduct, is not only to utter and to adopt AGs, but it is also to be prepared to *give reasons* in justification or legitimation of a recommended AG. We suggest that MAGs are like other AGs in entailing legitimation, but that, in addition, they involve a special condition of legitimacy, which distinguishes *moral* justification from other sorts of justification. At this point, our task is: 1) to elucidate the general presuppositions underlying the activity of practical justification (the "general conditions for justifiability"); and 2) to adduce the criterion which specifies the distinctiveness of moral justification (the "special condition for moral legitimacy"). The first set of criteria is presupposed by any sort of practical justification, and establish necessary, though not sufficient, conditions for moral legitimacy. The second criterion supplies a sufficient condition for moral legitimacy.[43]

The general conditions of justifiability are observed by analyzing the way in which men give reasons to justify their conduct. To begin with, the fact that justification is a *public* activity is demonstrated by its dependence on linguistic communication; for language, by its nature, is public and social. If a person adopts the public and social institution of language in order to discuss with other persons what policies of action ought to be pursued, he thereby enters into a discursive situation in which he is prepared, or at least willing, to

[43] Kemp, *Reason, Action and Morality*, pp. 194–97; W. K. Frankena, "The Concept of Morality," reprinted in G. Wallace and A. D. M. Walker, eds. *The Definition of Morality* (London: Methuen, 1970), pp. 146–73; see esp. pp. 156 ff. See also our extensive discussion of Frankena's proposal, below.

proffer his own reasoning, as well as to consider and appraise the reasoning presented by others.

There are certain "rules of the game" underlying such a discursive situation, which must be assumed to be "universal": the discourse must be intelligible, it must be applicable to the real world, and it must presuppose a certain self-understanding on the part of the participants.[44] In order to communicate intelligibly, each participant must adhere to customary rules of linguistic usage, and must, at least implicitly, accept certain common rules of logic.[45] Without such presuppositions, no intelligible discourse and practical argumentation (including deliberation and justification) are possible. In addition, certain empirically oriented truth-conditions for assessing claims of truth and falsity, probability and improbability, etc., must be made in order for the participants to discuss the practical applicability of a proposed policy to the real world, and some rules of inductive logic must be operative, accepted and observed by the participants. Finally, in order for the discursive activity to have any point and to accomplish its practical aim of persuasion, each participant must make certain presuppositions about himself and others. He must assume that he, as well as his partner, constitutes a "center" of sentience (desire and interest), thought (conception and valuation), and agency (decision and action). Without these presuppositions, there would be no point in offering reasons to others for their independent appraisal, in considering the "weight" of arguments, and in attempting to persuade or convince another regarding a recommended course of action.

We may call each of these three sets of discursive rules, respectively, the requirements of "meaning," "truth," and "respect." It will be noted that each of these requirements, in turn, presupposes the concept of intersubjective validity. That is, the requirements of meaning, truth, and respect make possible the proposal, considera-

[44] This presuppositional approach is inspired by R. S. Peters, *Ethics and Education* (Glenview, Ill.: Scott, Foresman, 1967). See the fascinating and very important essays by Martin Hollis, "Reason and Ritual," and Steven Lukes, "Some Problems about Rationality," reprinted in Bryan R. Wilson, ed., *Rationality* (New York: Harper, 1970), pp. 221–39 and 194–213. As Hollis puts it, "Native logic must either turn out to be a version of our own or remain untranslatable. . . . If the natives reason at all, then they reason as we do" (p. 232).

[45] Cf. I. M. Copi, *Symbolic Logic* (New York: Macmillan, 1967), pp. 36, 42–43, for nineteen basic rules of inference and theorems of replacement.

tion, and appraisal of intersubjectively valid assertions, or claims which can in principle be understood, assessed, and perhaps finally accepted by all the participants. In short, this concept of intersubjective validity, incorporating the requirements of meaning, truth, and (minimal) mutual respect, is necessary for discursive activity to be engaged in at all.

The last of the general conditions of justifiability we shall consider is the "condition of generalizability," which, following Ladd, is our adaptation of the much discussed concept of "universalizability." Before elucidating this condition, there are two preliminary questions to be addressed: 1) why choose "generalizability" over the more common term "universalizability"? 2) why should "generalizability" be treated as a general condition of justifiability (as we treat it) and not as a special condition of moral legitimacy?

1) We favor "generalizability" mainly to avoid confusion. In normal philosophical discussion "universalizability" is used in such a way as to exclude the practical reasoning of many non-Western and preliterate people. Such people propound a "particularistic" or "in-group" morality, one that is restricted and applicable only to the members of that society, and not extended, as, for example, in the Judeo-Christian and Western secular traditions, to "all men." Insofar as a non-particularistic morality in this sense is built into the prevalent understanding of "universalizability," we prefer "generalizability." It illuminates the justificatory activity of a wider range of societies than the "culture-bound" concept of universalizability.

2) It seems clear that AGs other than moral ones involve the condition of generalizability. For example, Pospisil includes among the four attributes of a legal decision, what he calls "an intention of universal application" (though, from his discussion, the phrase "generalized application" appears to cover better what he means, especially in connection with the particularistic tribal societies he mentions).[46]

> [N]ot only does a legal decision solve a specific case, but it also formulates an ideal—a solution *intended* [his italics] to be utilized *in all similar situations in the future* [our italics]. The ideal component *binds all other members of the group* [our italics] who did not participate in the case under consideration.

[46] Pospisil, *Anthropology of Law*, pp. 78–81.

The [legal] authority himself turns to his previous decisions for consistency.[47]

If Pospisil is right with respect to a legal action-guide (LAG), and his discussion is most persuasive, then the condition of generalizability can hardly be a special condition of moral legitimacy.[48]

Moreover, if we may adapt an argument made by R. M. Hare, it appears that it is in the logic of the word "ought" in its typical uses, that generalizability is required, rather than in the special logic of the word "moral," which is but one of the typical uses of "ought."[49] In other words, an AG involving "ought" cannot possibly be justified unless the utterer is able, on demand, to generalize it (in the sense yet to be specified). If Hare is correct about this, and he seems to be, then not only are LAGs necessarily generalizable, but that very wide range of action-guiding language employing "ought"-forms is as well. This claim, if true, further undermines any basis for considering generalizability as a special condition of moral legitimacy.

Turning now to the concept of "generalizability" itself, we find it can be formulated in various ways. One formulation of the concept puts it that an AG is generalized only if *it holds for every agent* who is under the same sort of circumstances as specified by the AG. This we call the "sociality" interpretation. A second version, often denoted as "the generalization principle," "the principle of impartiality," etc., asserts that a recommended AG must apply to any *similar* person in *similar* circumstances, and for the same agent in all relevantly *similar* situations. This can be called the "impersonality" or "impartiality" interpretation.

These two interpretations seem to specify what it means to generalize an AG.[50] And we are suggesting that generalizability is one of

47 Ibid., p. 80.
48 See John Rawls, *A Theory of Justice* (Cambridge, Mass.: Harvard Univ. Press, 1972), pp. 130–36, for a discussion of the insufficiency of the condition of generality in distinguishing "what we intuitively regard as the moral point of view."
49 See R. M. Hare *Freedom and Reason* (New York: Oxford Univ. Press, 1965), p. 37.
50 We have purposefully excluded still a third interpretation of generalizability, namely the condition of reversibility. (See, for example, K. Baier, *The Moral Point of View* [Ithaca: Cornell Univ. Press, 1958], pp. 200–4, for a discussion.) According to this interpretation, an AG is generalized when an agent looks at the results of an AG from the point of view of the recipient or patient. Ladd

the necessary requirements for justifying most, if not all, AGs. We come now to a consideration of the "special condition of moral legitimacy," namely, that MAGs are in some peculiar sense "other-regarding." This is the most controversial portion of our reconstructive attempt, but also the most crucial, and, we believe, the most original. We wish to argue that other-regardingness plays an important role in a large part of our use of the term "moral," and, on the strength of the comparative evidence we have, is also relevant in identifying specifically "moral" action and deliberation in cultures other than our own.

To begin with, the concept "other-regarding" needs careful scrutiny, for its use is equivocal not only in common parlance, but also in philosophical discussion. There are at least two senses of the term that need to be distinguished and reflected upon. They are brought out in the following passage from an essay by William Frankena, in which he designates an "other-regarding" condition as necessary, alongside other "formal" criteria (prescriptivity, universalizability, and "perhaps also supremacy"), for there being a morality.[51]

> X has a morality or moral AG only if it includes judgements, rules, principles, ideals, etc. which 1) concern the relations of one individual to others, 2) involve or call for a consideration of the effects of his actions on others (not necessarily all others), not from the point of view of his own interests or aesthetic enjoyments, but from their own point of view.[52]

Frankena's two specifications correspond to two different ways in which we use the word "regard." The second sense presupposes a personal subject or agent *who is able to consider and be aware of* the effects of his actions on someone else, whereas the first sense is non-subjective and means only that there is *a relation* of some sort

---

(*Structure of a Moral Code*, pp. 272, 305) finds no evidence that reversibility is universally present; therefore "considerable difficulties arise in the application of this [interpretation] to anthropology, since so many moral codes would have to be ruled out" (Barnsley, *Social Reality of Ethics*, p. 34). Nevertheless, there seem good grounds, on the evidence, for including the weaker form of generalizability (some combination of our two interpretations, mentioned above). As Barnsley puts it: "moral prescriptions must be considered equally binding upon oneself, and others. In this sense, they may be said to be impersonal or social." This weaker form of generalizability "makes possible some type of genuine consensus or dissensus over moral principles" (p. 45).

[51] Frankena, "The Concept of Morality," p. 155.
[52] Ibid., p. 156.

between one individual and others, whether the people involved are aware of the relation or not. In the first sense, "regard" means "has a bearing on" or "impinges on." In the second sense, "regard" means "considers" or "attends to."

Now, we contend that *both* of these senses of "regard"—the non-subjective as well as the subjective sense—are active in our understanding of other-regardingness, though not in the same ways as Frankena does. Let us sort out these two senses as we understand them. 1) We follow Frankena in suggesting that MAGs are, so to speak, "other-impinging," in our first sense of regard. But we mean by this term something more than Frankena appears to by his phrase, "concerns the relations of one individual to others." Frankena's designation is too vague, and misses an important point about our common understanding of what constitutes a *moral* problem. The point is effectively made by Eric D'Arcy when he speaks of "moral-species" terms as representing a class of human acts that "are so significant for human existence and welfare" as necessarily to be the object of moral reflection. This class of acts includes such things as "murder," "mayhem," "rape," "perjury," "calumny," and the like.[53] As a general rule, such acts "impinge upon" others in a quite special way: they have direct and usually dramatic effects upon the existence and/or welfare of another person(s). This point about "moral-species" terms is fortified by G. J. Warnock (though we do not necessarily subscribe to all that Warnock seeks to draw out of it): "[T]he limits [of *moral* evaluation] are set somewhere within the general area of concern with the welfare of human beings. . . . [T]he relevance of considerations as to the welfare of human beings *cannot,* in the context of moral debate, be denied . . . it *is* so, simply because of what 'moral' means."[54]

This understanding of other-regardingness as involving that class of acts which impinge directly and dramatically upon the welfare of another human being entails some specification of the term "welfare." We prefer "welfare" to the broader notion of "interests" because it designates a subclass of "interests," namely those associated with health, security, "basic need for survival," and the like. While it is undoubtedly true that there is "an extensive penumbral fringe

[53] Eric D'Arcy, *Human Acts* (Oxford: Clarendon, 1963), pp. 25–39.
[54] G. J. Warnock, *Contemporary Moral Philosophy* (London: Macmillan, 1967), p. 67.

of vagueness and indeterminacy" about what constitutes welfare—
certainly in cross-cultural terms, nevertheless, it seems true that the
"notion of 'the welfare' of human beings surely has, as one might
put it, a perfectly clear and determinate core or centre."[55] There
are certain actions, policies, and conditions of life which are, the
world round, conceived as being opposed to human welfare, such
as the promotion of suffering or human debilitation or impairment as
ends in themselves. There are other actions, policies, and conditions
of life which are universally understood to enhance the welfare of
any person, such as the promotion of health and security. This determinate core or center of the meaning of "welfare" is no doubt the
result, as Kluckhohn says, of the fact that

> all cultures constitute so many somewhat distinct answers to
> essentially the same questions posed by human biology and by
> the generalities of the human situation. Every society's patterns
> for living must provide approved and sanctioned ways for deal-
> ing with such universal circumstances as the existence of two
> sexes; the helplessness of infants; the need for satisfaction of
> the elementary biological requirements such as food, warmth,
> and sex; and the presence of individuals of different ages and
> of different physical and other capacities. The basic similarities
> in human biology the world over are vastly more massive than
> the variations.[56]

It is useful, further, to distinguish the concept of welfare, as one
class of interests, from the concept of "happiness," as another. The
two subclasses can be distinguished by at least two differentiating
characteristics: first, happiness concepts connote the achievement
of certain attitudes toward life, while welfare concepts are, as we
pointed out, more concerned with the provision of "material" conditions necessary to maintain life. Second, happiness judgments are
"agent-specific" in the sense that happiness necessarily involves the
personal experience and awareness of the agent, while welfare judgments have, as we have suggested, a relatively "fixed core." They are
more in the nature of "objective" necessary conditions for human
life, and less dependent upon subjective appraisal and experience
than are happiness judgments. It has been suggested in an illuminat-

---

[55] Ibid., p. 69.
[56] Clyde Kluckhohn, "Education, Values, and Anthropological Relativity,"
in *Culture and Behavior* (Glencoe: Free Press, 1964), p. 294.

ing metaphor that "happiness" is the "flower" of morality.[57] Correspondingly, "welfare" may be viewed as the "seed stock" of morality.

Our suggestion is that MAGs bear a special and indispensable relation to welfare concepts in two respects: first, there is a relatively fixed range of AGs that in all societies come to be regarded as "superior" and "legitimate" (according to one or another pattern of justification)[58]—namely, the "moral-species" terms that rule against indiscriminate cheating, stealing, or violence within the ingroup.[59] While a moral code is not exhausted by attention to acts of this sort, such acts are of basic importance, which is to say that they are "highly stringent" relative to other AGs. It seems, then, that whatever else it is, "moral reasoning" is indispensably concerned with this fixed range of welfare-oriented acts.

Second, there is often a range of highly stringent AGs to be found in a society that is not intuitively connected in any direct way with the basic welfare of human beings, as we have designated the notion. Nevertheless, on reflection, such AGs, in the minds of the adherents, do bear directly on matters of basic welfare. For example, the Navahos consider the following taboo to be highly stringent: "A man must not look at his mother-in-law and she must not look at him."[60] The *reason* given for complying with this taboo is that, if it

[57] Cf., for example, G. H. von Wright, *The Varieties of Goodness* (London: Routledge, 1963), p. 88. On the discussion of "welfare" and "happiness," see B. Barry, *Political Argument* (London: Routledge, 1965), " 'Good' and 'Welfare,' " pp. 187–90; S. I. Benn and R. S. Peters, *The Principles of Political Thought* (New York: Macmillan, 1965), "Criteria of Need," pp. 162–70; A. R. Louch, *Explanation and Human Action* (Berkeley: Univ. of Calif. Press, 1966), "Need," pp. 70–79; K. Nielson, "On Moral Truth," in N. Rescher, ed., *Studies in Moral Philosophy* (*American Philosophical Quarterly Monograph Series*, no. 1, 1968), pp. 9–25; R. S. Peters, *Ethics and Education*, "The Consideration of Interests," pp. 91–102; A. Quinton, "The Bounds of Morality," *Metaphilosophy*, 1, 3 (July, 1970), pp. 202–22; N. Rescher, *Distributive Justice* (Indianapolis: Bobbs-Merrill, 1966), pp. 28–30, 98–101; W. G. Runciman, *Relative Deprivation and Social Justice* (Berkeley: Univ. of Calif. Press, 1966), pp. 260–73; S. B. Twiss, Jr., "Critical Notes on 'Theology and Happiness,' " *Reflection*, 67, 3 (March, 1970), pp. 12–16; G. H. von Wright, *The Varieties of Goodness*, pp. 86–113; Warnock, *Contemporary Moral Philosophy*, pp. 54–61, 66–72.

[58] We do not treat the matter of justification in this paper, but in a later and more complete version we shall give the subject considerable attention.

[59] See Kluckhohn, *Culture and Behavior*, p. 294; cf. his discussion of "ethical universals" in "Ethical Relativity: Sic et Non," esp. pp. 276 ff.

[60] Ladd, *Structure of a Moral Code*, p. 230.

is violated, the offender will "go blind" or "will not be very strong and [his] body will be weak all over." Illustrations of this could easily be multiplied.

We emphasize that while the concern with "other-impinging," welfare-oriented acts is not the whole of morality, it is sufficiently intrinsic to be regarded as a "special condition" of moral reasoning.

2) The importance of the second sense of "regard"—as "to consider" or "to attend to"—in the process of justifying a MAG is suggested by Frankena's second stipulation of what it means to have a morality. But his formulation misses the mark. If we were to abide by Frankena's specification that a MAG exists only if it includes judgments, etc., which "call for a consideration of the effects of [one person's] actions on others . . . not from the point of view of his own interests . . . but from [the other's] point of view," then it would seem we would have to rule out, for example, the Navaho code as a morality.

Ladd describes the process of moral evaluation among the Navahos as follows:

> Every evaluation reflects the *evaluator's* interest in the actual past or anticipated effects of the action *on him personally.* . . . In effect, the grounds for evaluation are something like: 'That is bad, because it will bring trouble (to me),' or 'that is good, because it will help (me).'[61]

And it is clear that the Navahos are not alone in their apparently egoistic pattern of justification.[62] What seems lacking among the Navahos, and apparently among other groups as well, is not so much a consideration of the effects of one person's actions on others, but a consideration of effects *from the other's point of view.* If "other-regarding" means taking the other's point of view, and if that understanding, in turn, is a requirement of what it means to have a morality, then all such "egoistic" systems are nonmoral systems.

Incidentally, it is just because the "other-regarding" requirement, as Frankena defines it, seems to be lacking from the Navaho code, that Ladd drops it out altogether as a defining characteristic of the concept moral, and relies simply upon prescriptivity, superi-

[61] Ibid., p. 305.
[62] See Fürer-Haimendorf, *Morals and Merit,* and MacBeath, *Experiments in Living,* for what strongly appears to be further evidence of "egoistic systems" formally similar to the Navaho code.

ority, and legitimacy. In our judgment, both Frankena and Ladd take unnecessarily extreme positions in this matter. Frankena defines "other-regarding" (in the second sense) over narrowly. Ladd, for his part, throws out the baby with the bath by overlooking evidence he himself supplies that lends support to at least one form of the other-regarding condition. To quote Ladd:

> The basic factual belief which united egoistic premises with altruistic conclusions is that the welfare of each individual is dependent upon that of every other individual in the group. What is good for the individual is good for everyone else, and what is good for everybody is good for the individual.[63]

Or, as Ladd puts it elsewhere, there is a "general Navaho presumption that the welfare of others is a *necessary condition* of one's own welfare" (our italics).[64]

There are grounds here for concluding that in the Navaho justificatory scheme, taken as a whole, the welfare of others is in fact regarded—that is, is considered or taken account of—if only assumptively and somewhat indirectly. And Ladd's use of the phrase "necessary condition" indicates that consideration of the other's welfare is not a casual matter, even if it is not at the center of Navaho moral reasoning. Thus, while Frankena's formulation is too narrow to allow for the rather ulterior character of the other-regarding concern among the Navahos, Ladd's disinclination to attend to other-regardingness as a special feature of moral justification appears unwarranted by his own evidence. Our expectation is that among other "egoistic" systems, the same sort of indirect attention will be given to the welfare of others in the justification of MAGs.

Our general conclusion, then, is that Frankena's specification of the two senses of other-regardingness needs to be revised as follows:

> X has a MAG only if it includes (together with prescriptivity, superiority and legitimacy, as discussed) judgments, etc. which 1) concern acts that impinge on the welfare of others, and 2) involve, in the justification of AGs, *some* consideration of the effects of the actions of one person on the welfare of others.

Before proceeding to our explication of religion, it is necessary to

---

63 Ladd, *Structure of a Moral Code*, p. 304.
64 Ibid., p. 296.

tie up two loose ends. First, a word about the role of "sanction" within the reconstructive concept of a MAG. Are sanctions necessarily attached to MAGs? If so, what function do they have, what form do they have, and how are they related to the other conceptual components of MAGs? A strong and typical view of the role of sanction in morality is expressed by H. L. A. Hart, as follows:

> A further distinguishing feature of morality is the characteristic form of moral pressure which is exerted in its support . . . with morals the typical form of pressure consists in appeals to the respect for the rules, as things important in themselves. . . . So moral pressure is characteristically . . . exerted . . . by reminders of the moral character of the action contemplated and of the demands of morality. . . . Emphatic reminders of what the rules demand, appeals to conscience and reliance on the operation of guilt and remorse, are the characteristic and most prominent forms of pressure used for the support of social morality.[65]

Hart takes the position that the concept of moral sanction (pressure) is a necessary and prominent feature of a MAG. According to his view, moral sanction is not merely empirically necessary to sustain a given morality, but also conceptually requisite to the notion of morality. It is, however, possible to accept this latter claim without ascribing such primary conceptual importance to the moral sanction as Hart does. For what is moral sanction, other than the psychosocial manifestation (the obverse or negative side) of a MAG's (positive) authoritativeness? The concept of moral sanction itself cannot be understood without reference to the superiority and legitimacy of a MAG. Therefore these latter components are those which deserve primary conceptual emphasis—they provide the point, the rationale, for the concept of moral sanction. Thus we agree with Hart's functional and conceptual explication of the notion of moral sanction, but hesitate to ascribe it such predominance. Rather, for us, moral legitimacy explains and justifies moral superiority, which, in turn, granted certain facts about human nature, gives rise to and explains the emergence of moral sanction and its role.

A final, though by no means unimportant, point to observe about the logical features of the proposed reconstructive concept of moral

[65] H. L. A. Hart, *The Concept of Law* (Oxford: Clarendon Press, 1961), pp. 176–77.

is that they are appropriately characterized as "formal" in nature (as contrasted with "material"). That is, each feature and all the features conjunctively considered neither specify nor imply any substantive (moral) principles or code of conduct. This claim holds true even for the condition of consideration of others' interest, insofar as this latter feature only specifies a necessary sort of justificatory appeal involving the general range of welfare-type concepts, without definitely stipulating the precise content of such concepts. We view all such criteria, at least for our reconstructive proposal, as "formal" in the sense indicated (i.e., as devoid of substantive or normative content).[66] This approach helps to ensure that the reconstructive proposal satisfies canon #4, (see p. 41, above) thereby avoiding ethnocentricity and promoting cross-cultural applicability.

B. RELIGION.

It is true that definitions of "religion" are notoriously open to debate.[67] But there is no need to throw up our hands in despair and then proceed to study religious ethics without knowing what we are examining. In proposing our own definition, it is again useful to consider, as we did in analyzing the concept moral, certain minimal and commonly understood "functional" features of religion. We can acquire a preliminary understanding of what religion is all about by examining what it does in the context of human life.

We take it as widely assumed that religion "functions" to resolve certain distinctive problems in the lives of individuals and social groups. These problems are experienced as anxieties about certain

[66] See W. K. Frankena, "Recent Conceptions of Morality," in H.-N. Castañeda and G. Nakhnikian, eds., *Morality and the Language of Conduct* (Detroit: Wayne State Univ. Press, 1965), pp. 1–24; and "The Concept of Morality."

[67] See, for example, Rem B. Edwards, *Reason and Religion* (New York: Harcourt, 1972), chaps. 1, 2. Cf. essays and discussion on "The Problem of Attempting to Define Religion," *Journal for the Scientific Study of Religion*, II, I (Fall 1962), pp. 3–35; Christian, *Meaning and Truth in Religion*, chaps. 3, 4; Christian, "A Definition of Religion," *Review of Religion*, 5 (1941), pp. 412–29; Spiro, "Religion: Problems of Definition and Explanation," esp. pp. 87–106; Roland Robertson, *The Sociological Interpretation of Religion* (Oxford: Oxford Univ. Press, 1970), pp. 34–51; Clifford Geertz, "Religion as a Cultural System," in Banton, ed., *Anthropological Approaches to the Study of Religion*, pp. 1–46; Frederick J. Streng, "Studying Religion: Possibilities and Limitations of Different Definitions," *Journal of the American Academy of Religion*, XL, 2 (June, 1972), pp. 219–37.

"boundary situations" in human life and experience, and they are encountered at at least three points: 1) in trying to make sense out of the obstinate inexplicability of the natural world, its existence and purpose, its processes and events; 2) in trying to cope with the obdurate presence of human suffering and death; and 3) in trying to live with and manage the irresolvable ambiguities and puzzles inherent in human conduct. For convenience, these problems may be designated as *problems of interpretability*.[68] These problems, religion's problems, pose radical challenges or "ontological anxieties" in face of man's inclination to view the world and life as rationally comprehensible.

Religion copes with these problems in three ways: conceptually, emotionally, and practically. These three approaches to resolving the problems may be denoted as "religion-making characteristics." They consist, respectively, of adhering to a cosmology, expressing certain attitudes and emotions, and acting in certain prescribed ways. The first characteristic, cosmology, indicates that religion attempts to formulate and propound ideas of the general order of existence which provide perspectives or authoritative world views for handling those deeply disturbing concerns of life that cry out for interpretation. Secondly, these perspectives evoke certain attitudes, dispositions, and emotions which tend to counter the ontological anxieties mentioned. And, finally, these perspectives and attitudes combine to specify certain kinds of practical activity, such as rituals and ceremonials, which in their turn tend to reinforce the authority of the world view and the attitudes evoked.

In short, the three religion-making characteristics converge to produce and sustain religious persons or groups by resolving their anxieties over the problems of interpretability. Obviously, there are important causal connections among these characteristics. But while these characteristics are conceptually important and their interrelationships causally significant, they are not yet sufficiently refined to

[68] Though this phrase is our own, the problems mentioned are identified by Weber and many of his followers; see Weber, "Social Psychology of the World Religions," H. H. Gerth and C. W. Mills, eds., *From Max Weber* (New York: Oxford Univ. Press, 1958), pp. 267–301; Talcott Parsons, *Religious Perspectives of College Teaching in Sociology and Social Psychology* (New Haven: Hazen Foundation, 1952); Geertz, "Religion as a Cultural System"; Robert Bellah, "The Sociology of Religion," reprinted in *Beyond Belief* (New York: Harper, 1970), pp. 3–17.

distinguish religion from other similar phenomena, such as "grand" personal and social philosophies of life like existentialism and Marxism.

In attempting to define "religion" many scholars focus their attention almost exclusively on the emotional and practical religion-making characteristics. The general trend of their analyses goes something like this: religions and religious persons can be sufficiently characterized or defined by identifying the essential religious emotion and the essential religious practice. These two supposedly indispensable features of religion have been designated, respectively, as "sense of the sacred," "awe," "*mysterium tremendum et fascinans,*" on the one hand, and "worship," "piety," "devotion," on the other.

However, using such notions to define religion is objectionable on many grounds. First, the world's religions exhibit a considerable variety in their emotional expression and behavioral practice, and this diversity is not acknowledged by these notions as they are usually developed. A related objection is that using such notions to define "religion" begs, at the outset, questions as to whether all religions do in fact possess certain common emotional and behavioral features. Such questions require careful empirical inquiry, not premature settlement by arbitrary stipulations. A third objection is directed to those scholars who claim that these notions are intended to cover emotional and behavioral diversity. In fact, the narrow connotations of these terms are bound to generate confusion by de-emphasizing, rather than highlighting, the significant differences among religions. Finally, of course, it may be charged that such definitional approaches do not adequately account for all three religion-making characteristics. Whatever happened to the cosmological feature of religion? In light of these considerations, among others, we feel that whether there is a distinctive religious emotion and distinctive type of religious behavior should be left as an open question by our definitional proposal.

We contend that any adequate definition of "religion" must take into account all three religion-making characteristics, while at the same time allowing for the empirical diversity of each. We take a *"religious statement"* to be *"a statement expressing acceptance of a set of beliefs, attitudes, and practices based on a concept of sacred authority that functions to resolve the 'ontological' problems of interpretability."* The conceptual diagram below will help to structure and clarify our elaboration and defense of this definition.

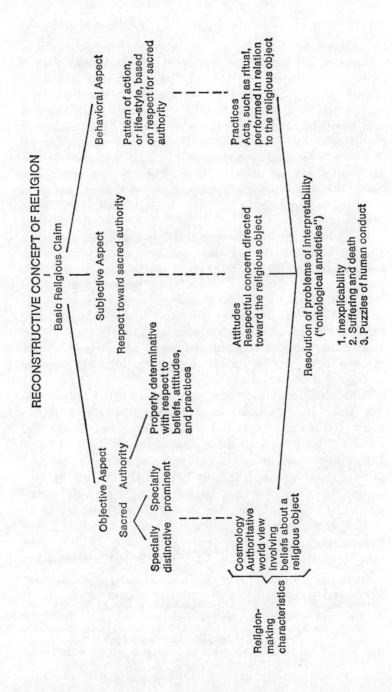

RECONSTRUCTIVE CONCEPT OF RELIGION

Basic Religious Claim

Objective Aspect

Subjective Aspect

Behavioral Aspect

Sacred Authority
Respect toward sacred authority
Pattern of action, or life-style, based on respect for sacred authority

Specially distinctive

Specially prominent

Properly determinative with respect to beliefs, attitudes, and practices

Attitudes
Respectful concern directed toward the religious object

Practices
Acts, such as ritual, performed in relation to the religious object

Cosmology
Authoritative world view involving beliefs about a religious object

Resolution of problems of interpretability ("ontological anxieties")

1. Inexplicability
2. Suffering and death
3. Puzzles of human conduct

Religion-making characteristics

We begin by indicating what we understand by the notion of "acceptance," as contained in our definition. To "accept" a set of beliefs, etc., is, implicitly at least, to affirm what we call a "basic religious claim."[69] Religious beliefs, attitudes, and practices are organized in "sets" or systems which comprise, however loosely, a conceptual framework, and such frameworks, in turn, yield basic claims that ground the fundamental convictions of various religions.[70] A particular framework, together with its basic claim, may be variously articulated and elaborated formally in scriptures, creeds, treatises, informally in liturgies, hymns, manuals, sermons, sayings of prophets, and symbolically in sacred stories, legends, myths, forms of art, etc.

By analyzing the logical nature of this type of claim, we believe we can articulate an acceptable definition of "religion" which touches base with the religion-making characteristics. We can begin this analysis by pointing out the obvious: a basic religious claim is the central belief of a religion's cosmology. It orients the perspective or world view of the religious believer. And it does this by combining three logically related aspects which correspond to the three religion-making characteristics. The objective aspect corresponds to cosmology, the subjective aspect to attitudes, and the behavioral aspect to practices. Let us take each in turn.

A basic religious claim makes an assertion about a religious object. This claim has two obvious components. It refers to a religious object, and it characterizes that object in some way. Clearly, the referent of the claim is an object which is the focal point of a religious belief system or cosmology. From a phenomenological point of view, this object may take many forms. It may be a quality (e.g., wisdom, love), a relation (e.g., harmony, unity), a particular natural entity (e.g., sun, earth, sky, river, animal), a particular human individual or group (e.g., king, the dead), nature as a whole, a pure form or realm of pure forms (e.g., Good, Truth, all Ideas), pure being (e.g., One, Being Itself, Ground of Being), a transcendent

---

[69] This term is a modification of Christian's term "basic religious proposal." Christian's discussion of "the logical structure of religious discourse" is most illuminating, and, to some degree, lies behind our argument in this section. See *Meaning and Truth in Religion*, esp. pp. 19–34, chaps. 7–9.

[70] Ibid., n. 13, p. 109, gives the following examples: "The God and Father of our lord Jesus Christ is the maker and ruler of all things," or "nirvana is the True State," or "We find the meaning of life by living in harmony with Nature."

active Being (e.g., Allah, Yahweh, God). These phenomenological categories are not exhaustive, but they are sufficient to indicate the variety of possible religious objects, thereby pointing to a complex variable in the fields of religious inquiry.

A basic religious claim not only refers to an object, but also characterizes it in some way. That is, a basic religious claim predicates one or more attributes, functions, or both, of an object. Its main assertive point is, of course, that its characterization is true.[71] Phenomenological inquiry provides a wide variety of such predicates, for example, "holy," "worshipful," "ultimate," "supreme," etc. Yet it should be noted that every such characterization has three logical features in common. First, every basic claim asserts a special distinctiveness for its object, by distinguishing it from everything else. Second, every basic claim ascribes a special prominence to its object, both in ontological and axiological terms. Third, every basic claim ascribes a high degree of authority to its object in terms of its relevance to the life of the religious subject.

Other students of religion have studied certain of these features in one way or another. But none has reflected very deeply on them, and none has noted that taken together they constitute a coherent structural specification of any religious object. As our proposal, we are contending that a careful conceptual analysis of the logical features of a basic claim in its objective aspect enables us to construct a formal model, if you will, of a religious object. That is, by carefully investigating the logical features of a distinctive type of claim, we can reconstruct the concept of a religious object and then go on to reconstruct an acceptable definition of "religion" by analyzing the other two aspects of a basic religious claim.

A basic religious claim presupposes, according to our definition, that the religious object is considered to be or to have "sacred authority," a phrase that requires special attention. By the adjective "sacred," we suggest two things about the way the religious object is regarded. First, it is taken to be *specially distinctive* in the sense that it is "set apart" or "marked off" from everything else in the world, thus constituting a "scope of reality" that is *to some degree beyond the control of human beings.*[72] This dimension of sacredness is

[71] See Ibid., chaps. 2, 12.

[72] This stipulation obviously raises the question of how "magic" is to be defined in relation to "religion," since one of the common designations of magic

sometimes characterized as the "transcendence" or "otherness" of the religious object, though these particular terms have their own difficulties for broad comparative purposes.[73] Nevertheless, this condition is extremely important. It is as relevant, for example, to the sharp distinction drawn in Theravada Buddhism, as well as in various forms of pantheism, between "illusion" and "reality," as it is to the notion of "holy people" and "ghosts" held among the Navahos, or to analogous beliefs widely found among other non-literate peoples.

Second, a religious object is taken as "sacred" in the sense that *special prominence* is attributed to it in the world of human experience. That means that religious objects are of unusual significance in relation to what human beings consider important. In other words, religious objects have a palpable bearing on the existence and values of human beings.

In addition to presupposing these two aspects of the notion of "sacredness," a basic religious claim also presupposes that the religious object is "authoritative" for the religious subjects. By "authoritative" we do not mean simply "having power or force," though such capacity is present in the activities of certain "sacred authorities" in some cultures. We mean, more broadly, that the religious object is acknowledged as being in some degree *properly determinative*

---

is instrumental manipulation or control over the sacred entities. The precise relation of magic to religion must remain an open question for us, although we are sympathetic to Goode's proposal that they be seen as related to each other on a continuum, rather than as completely separate from each other. This would mean, tentatively, that religion and magic are similar in that "they both deal with non-human forces, sometimes called sacred," as Goode puts it. William J. Goode, *Religion Among the Primitives* (Glencoe: Free Press, 1951), p. 50; see pp. 50–55. On the other hand, among other distinctions, magic would be distinguished from religion by its greater emphasis upon human control over the sacred entities. All this, however, remains open to further reflection and investigation.

[73] For example, Rudolf Otto's emphasis on the "otherness" of the divine as a defining characteristic of religion seems to have been construed rather too much in Western religious terms. Ninian Smart in *Philosophers and Religious Truth* (London: SCM Press, 1969), pp. 120–21, argues that "the sense of the fearful otherness of the deity [has] no place in [Theravada Buddhism]. . . . Hence, though Otto's analysis is extremely important, and illuminates a great area of religious experience and practice, it does not really cater successfully for mysticism." Nevertheless, Smart does admit a rather looser sense of "transcendence" as characterizing "some degree of unity" between contemplative and prophetic religion (p. 124).

with respect to the beliefs, attitudes, and practices of the religious subject.

This determinative function may be conceived in at least two ways. In one case, the religious subject is normatively controlled by the religious object's performances, such as commands, and/or actions—e.g., supernaturally initiated "mighty acts" with good or bad consequences for human life. This type of authority is especially operative in portions of Judaism, Islam, and Christianity, as well as in many non-literate religions, with their conceptions of personal and impersonal supernatural forces. In another case, for example, in Theravada Buddhism, versions of pantheism, and the like, the subject may appeal to the religious object as normative for his attitudes, decisions, and actions.

Finally, it is our contention that religious subjects *refer* to some conception of sacred authority in order to resolve the problems of interpretability, as we sketched them above. Part of what it means to say that a religious object is "sacred" in the sense of being of "special prominence" in human affairs is that the object is taken to bear in a momentous way on the "ontological" anxieties of human beings, namely the problems of inexplicability, suffering, and death, and the puzzles of human conduct.

Incidentally, we consider our definition, as elucidated so far, to be superior to certain other proposals, such as those of Paul Tillich,[74] William Christian,[75] and Melford Spiro.[76] Though there are differences between Tillich and Christian, they both would build a condition of "ultimacy" or "primacy" into what constitutes a religious object. But stipulating such a condition as necessary seems decidedly counter-intuitive, according to common usage. It seems we would want to call the "ghosts" and "holy people" of the Navahos "religious objects," even though they are *not* considered "ultimate," by the Navahos, as Tillich would require, nor are they

[74] "Religion is the state of being grasped by an ultimate concern, a concern which qualifies all other concerns as preliminary and which itself contains the answer to the question of the meaning of our life." Tillich, *Christianity and the Encounter of the World Religions* (New York: Columbia Univ. Press, 1963), p. 4.

[75] "A religious interest is an interest in something more important than anything else in the universe" (*Meaning and Truth in Religion*, p. 60).

[76] "I shall define religion as an institution consisting of culturally patterned interaction with culturally postulated superhuman beings" ("Religion: Problems of Definition and Explanation," p. 96).

considered "more important than anything else in the universe," as
Christian would seem to require. In contrast, these "supernatural
powers" are considered "sacred authorities," as we have specified the
term. This same application fits a broad range of religious objects
whose authority is no less sacred for being restricted.

On the other hand, Bentham's Utilitarian "pleasure principle"
could be regarded as "ultimate" for him, as "something more important than anything else in the universe," and therefore appear
to qualify as a religious object, on Tillich's and Christian's definitions. Moreover, the principle "functions to resolve the problems of
interpretability." Nevertheless, it is patently odd to refer to Bentham's
principle as a religious object. The reason it is odd, we suggest, is
that while the principle is "authoritative" (in our second sense),
and even "of special prominence," it cannot be understood as constituting a "scope of reality" that is to some degree beyond the
control of human beings. Therefore it does not comply with at least
one of our conditions of "sacredness."

Spiro's stipulation of "superhuman beings" as the necessary condition of a religious object is far too restrictive. In classical Theravada Buddhism, there is no conception of a "superhuman being,"
and yet its basic religious claim refers, as we suggested above, to an
object—namely, Nirvana—that complies with our conditions of "sacred authority," and accordingly qualifies as a "religious object." This
attribution appears intuitively correct.

We have, then, been able to identify and characterize a key variable of "religion"—sacred authority—by analyzing the objective aspect of a basic religious claim. But our inquiry does not end here,
for there are two other aspects of the basic claim which are relevant
to our analysis, namely, the subjective and behavioral aspects. First,
a basic religious claim implicitly maintains, or contextually implies,
that its characterization of the religious object calls for an appropriate response from the religious subject, both attitudinal and behavioral in nature. Second, a basic religious claim implicitly maintains,
or contextually implies, that its characterization authoritatively illuminates the subject's perception of the facts of life, as well as affects his general life-style. Both implications refer to the subject's
attitudes and behavior, and both have close logical ties with the
objective aspect. For convenience, we may designate the implications regarding the religious subject's thought, attitudes, and emo-

tions with respect to the religious object, as the basic religious claim's *subjective aspect,* and the implications concerning patterns of behavior, dispositions to action, and life-style, as the *behavioral aspect.*

The subjective aspect may be simply described in terms of a very general concept, respect. Because of the religious object's sacred authority, along with its concomitant features of illumination and appropriate response, the religious subject adopts a general attitude of respect for the object. The concept of respect employed here is very formal. It merely indicates that the subject takes the object seriously, that the object "merits" attention, and "claims" a determinative relevancy to life. As used here, respect does not imply any unique emotions or thrills.

The behavioral aspect also may be described in general terms which beg no empirical questions. This aspect is also based on the religious object's character and implications noted above. It refers simply to the dispositional correlate of the attitude of respect: the tendency of the subject to take serious account of the religious object in patterning his life, and to take account of it in a manner appropriate to its specific qualities and character.

The relations among the three aspects of a basic religious claim should be clear enough. From a conceptual point of view, the objective aspect grounds the subjective and behavioral aspects. The parallel between these aspects and the three religion-making characteristics should also be clear. The objective aspect corresponds to cosmology, the subjective to attitudes, and the behavioral to practices.

The question which now presents itself is whether religions, or rather basic religious claims, imply AGs of a distinctive type. Phrased in another way, the issue is whether conceptions of sacred authority yield any distinctive AGs. In the light of the previous discussion, an affirmative answer is indicated, since basic religious claims, as we suggested, call for appropriate attitudinal and behavioral responses on the part of their adherents. We contended that part of what it means to acknowledge a religious object as authoritative is to regard it as "in some degree properly determinative with respect to the beliefs, attitudes, and practices of the religious subject." For convenience, we may call the contextual implications regarding the attitudinal and behavioral aspects of a basic religious claim "religious action-guides" (RAGs). The central question now

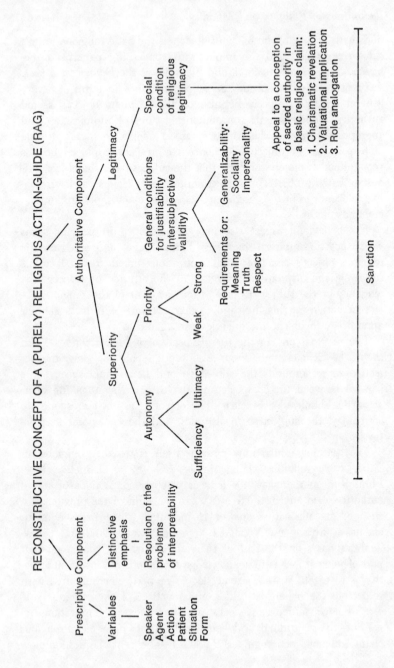

RECONSTRUCTIVE CONCEPT OF A (PURELY) RELIGIOUS ACTION-GUIDE (RAG)

facing us is, what is the logical character of these RAGs, and how are they related to MAGs?

Inasmuch as we have already developed an extensive terminology with regard to the concept of a MAG, we will employ that apparatus for discussing RAGs, noting, of course, important nuances and significant differences, and introducing new notions wherever necessary. Since RAGs are, by definition, AGs, we do not need to rehearse the prescriptive component, as discussed above. The authoritative component of RAGs, however, is another matter entirely. Certain of its features may be handled with dispatch, but others call for careful discussion. Those features which parallel our analysis of a MAG include a RAG's superiority over non-religious AGs. The earlier discussion of autonomy and priority carries over to RAGs, although the distinction between "strong" and "weak" priority signals an important issue which will be discussed below.

The second main feature of the authoritative component of RAGs —legitimacy—is the locus of important differences between MAGs and RAGs, and particularly at the point of the special conditions of legitimacy for each type of AG. We must therefore attend to the special condition of religious legitimacy.

To begin with, religious legitimacy involves a justificatory appeal to a conception of sacred authority, the object of a given religion. In order to understand the logical character of this justificatory appeal, it is necessary to explore the ways in which AGs may be derived from a basic religious claim. We suggest at least three distinctive types of derivation (though there may be others): 1) "charismatic" revelation; 2) valuational implication; and 3) role analogation. Before we elucidate these types of justification, it should be noted that they are by no means mutually exclusive with regard to any one religion.

1) "Charismatic," or authoritarian, revelation refers to that type of justification which involves the issuing of commands, edicts, orders, etc., by the sacred authority to the obedient religious subject. The means of revelation may be many, but the logical operation of the justification is the same: having accepted the charismatic authority of the religious object, the subject "awaits his orders from on high." In short, "Do x because the religious object says so."

2) Valuational implication refers to that type of justification in which the religious subject adopts an evaluative standard, identified

with or implied by the religious object, makes value judgments with reference to this standard, and then derives his RAGs from these value judgments. This type constitutes a complex category because of the variety of ways in which AGs may be derived through evaluative reasoning. Examples include: "Do x because the consequences produce results in conformity with the 'sacred' standard"; "Do x because x is itself in conformity with the sacred standard"; etc. Despite the variety, the logic of this justification is determinate and distinct from the first type, insofar as the religious subject "reasons" to his RAGs.

3) Role analogation refers to that type of justification in which the religious subject derives his RAGs not through evaluative reasoning but rather by examining the implications of his relationship to the religious object on the analogy of a human relationship. The subject discerns his RAGs by getting clear on the implications of the role relationship with the religious object. Examples are easy to come by: "To be a slave is to attempt to please one's master. You are the slave and God is the master. Therefore, you ought to attempt to please God." The same sort of reasoning applies in the case of all the many role images found in religious literature, such as father-son, author-creature, benefactor-beneficiary, promisor-promisee, etc.

Having briefly exemplified the special condition of religious legitimacy (as some form of appeal to a sacred authority), we turn now to the question of the applicability of our distinction between the special condition of religious legitimacy and the special condition of moral legitimacy. Specifically, the problem before us is whether or not RAGs are necessarily other-regarding, in the senses we have specified the term, and therefore, whether RAGs are, after all, intrinsically moral, as might be argued.

It may seem, at first blush, that insofar as RAGs are formulated in response to the problems of interpretability, they involve a relation to and consideration of the welfare of persons and groups, and, as a result, ought to be counted as fulfilling the other-regarding condition. Such a conclusion, however, flies in the face of the extensive empirical evidence we have of a divergence, and sometimes of an outright conflict, between AGs that are justified with respect to a sacred authority (RAGs), and AGs that conform to all our conditions of morality (MAGs). Such a divergence is amply documented, for example, by Fürer-Haimendorf,[77] though the following instance is particularly striking, paralleling, at the non-literate level, the famous opposition drawn by Søren Kierkegaard between RAGs and MAGs,[78] or, in his terms, between "the religious" and "the ethical." Fürer-Haimendorf's example describes a situation "when the demands of a god conflict with the tenets of accepted morality."

> Thus there is a tradition that the men of Purka clan were once faced by their clan-gods' demand for human sacrifice, but rather than comply with this gruesome command they rushed to the nearest river, and threw the sacred whisk symbolizing the female clan-deity into the water, and hence have performed the sacrificial rites only with the symbol of the male god who accepts the sacrifice of a goat and a cow.[79]

What is most interesting about this passage is, as in the case of Kierkegaard's discussion, that *the conflict between the two sorts of AG is over the consideration of human welfare, as we have described that notion.*[80] In other words, what locates the point of tension in both cases, is precisely the question of other-regardingness. It appears intelligible, then, to have an AG which is *religiously* legitimate, but which in no sense conforms to the special condition of moral legitimacy.

Of course, we are not unaware that there are many cases in which RAGs are formulated not so much in disregard of the benefit or harm to others caused by the action, but in the belief that the "real" welfare of affected parties is properly redefined in supernatural terms, and that the goal of a RAG supported by such a belief is, thus, "really" other-regarding, even though the action works against the "this-worldly" welfare of the affected party. Providing such a RAG meets all the other criteria of a MAG, might it not be correctly considered equivalent to a MAG?

Our response is negative, since, as we have argued, the concept

---

[77] *Morals and Merit*, pp. 31, 43, 95, 140–41, 213, 216. Cf. Ladd, *Structure of a Moral Code*, p. 268; and MacBeath, *Experiments in Living*, p. 326.

[78] Søren Kierkegaard, *Fear and Trembling* (Garden City, N.Y.: Doubleday, 1955), pp. 64–77. This is Kierkegaard's famous discussion of the "teleological suspension of the ethical" in face of the overriding duty to obey God, which is the point, according to Kierkegaard, of the story of Abraham and the near sacrifice of Isaac in the Old Testament.

[79] *Morals and Merit*, op. cit., p. 146.

[80] See pp. 22–29, above.

of welfare incorporated in our definition of morality appears to have a relatively "fixed core," which includes such "objective" conditions as physical survival, bodily and psychic health, security from arbitrary violence, and the like. It follows that the RAG in question does not meet the condition of other-regardingness constitutive of the concept moral, and therefore cannot be considered equivalent to a MAG.

We wish to make two remarks about our conclusion, however. First, saying that such a RAG is not "fully" a MAG is not invidious. It implies nothing whatsoever about comparative evaluation. Second, we realize that we are opening ourselves to the charge of arbitrariness. Our rebuttal is that boundaries must be drawn somewhere, if meaningful inquiry is to get started, and we feel our boundaries have a strong ring of plausibility to them.

Still another "boundary line" problem in distinguishing RAGs from MAGs concerns the issue of priority, referred to here and there along the way. It involves a tension or conflict between two AGs, each of which, based on its own distinctive type of justification, claims superiority in terms of autonomy and priority. It is our contention that both RAGs and MAGs possess the conceptual features of superiority. How, then, are we to go about settling which is "really" and "finally" and "ultimately" superior? We argue, at least for the purposes of comparative religious ethics, that this is an improper question. Why should we be required to settle it in abstraction? Is it not sufficient that we have provided definitions of morality and religion which are clear enough to enable us to identify the points of tension and conflict? We contend that both MAGs and RAGs possess, *prima facie*, at least, priority in the weak sense, which means that either one can be overridden in specific circumstances and for "good reason" without being deprived of its title to presumptive superiority or "weightiness." Having dealt with the matter of priority in this relativistic way, we suggest that the question of whether RAGs or MAGs take precedence can only be resolved on a case-to-case basis. It is an empirical matter.

If someone charges that we have left our definitions ambiguous, incomplete, and wishy-washy, we must deny the charge. Indeed, to try to settle the issue of priority in abstraction involves, we suspect, normative argumentation, and a persuasive use of terms. Examples are not hard to find, as for example, in Tillich's discussion of the superiority of religious commitments.[81] But, as we said at the beginning, we have methodological scruples about confusing normative with descriptive activity.

We conclude that the criterial distinctions and overlappings between RAGs and MAGs, as we have indicated them, are of the greatest importance in identifying many of the central issues involved in the study of comparative religious ethics.

With these elaborations of the crucial differentia of basic terms behind us, we are at last in a position to comment on what is supposedly our central concern, namely, "religious ethics." We need to examine what an AG looks like that *combines* the features of both RAGs and MAGs. In a word, we need to exhibit the anatomy of what we may call a religious-moral action-guide (R/MAG) and a moral-religious action-guide (M/RAG).

Actually, these AGs that combine the features of religion and morality can quite easily and predictably be diagrammed as shown below.

The mark of both a M/RAG and a R/MAG (to be distinguished in a moment) is the *dual character* of the prescriptive and authoritative components and subcomponents. With respect to the prescriptive component, the matter of the variables requires no special comment, though in the case of the distinctive emphases it will be noticed that a combined AG can be understood as addressing both the problem of co-operation and the problems of interpretability. One example from the New Testament will suffice to illustrate this sort of synthesis:

> Let each of you look not only to his own interests, but also to the interests of others. Have this mind among yourselves, which you have in Christ Jesus, who, though he was in the form of God, did not count equality with God a thing to be grasped, but emptied himself, taking the form of a servant, being born in the likeness of men. And being found in human form he humbled himself and became obedient unto death, even death on a cross. Therefore God has highly exalted him and bestowed

[81] Paul Tillich, *Dynamics of Faith* (New York: Harper, 1958), p. 12; cited in Edwards, *Reason and Religion*, p. 9. "In true faith," says Tillich, "the ultimate concern is a concern about the truly ultimate; while in idolatrous faith preliminary, finite realities are elevated to the rank of ultimacy." This is clearly a *normative* stipulation, closely related to Tillich's own particular theological point of view.

RECONSTRUCTIVE CONCEPT OF A MORAL/RELIGIOUS
ACTION-GUIDE (M/RAG) OR A RELIGIOUS/MORAL ACTION-GUIDE (R/MAG)

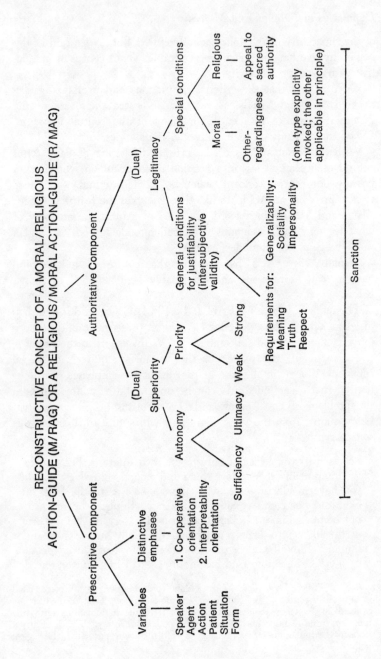

on him the name which is above every name, that at the name of Jesus every knee should bow, in heaven and on earth, and every tongue confess that Jesus Christ is Lord, to the glory of God the Father.[82]

This generalized AG, regarding treatment of others, involves a concern for the problem of co-operation, as well as making certain claims about the ultimate meaning of life and death.

By briefly examining the authoritative component, we can discover the point of distinguishing a M/RAG from a R/MAG. A M/RAG is an AG which is explicitly viewed by an individual or group as religious (that is, it is justified by means of an appeal to a sacred authority, and also meets the conditions of superiority). At the same time, the AG satisfies both the general conditions of justifiability and the special condition of moral legitimacy.

Consequently, although it may be taken by its proponent as a RAG, it can in principle be comprehended as a MAG on autonomous moral grounds. Within the Christian tradition, for example, AGs that are taken by believers *both* as commanded by God *and* as the practical conclusions of natural-law reasoning would be obvious examples. Conversely, a R/MAG is one which is explicitly viewed as a MAG by its proponent, yet it can in principle be comprehended as a RAG on autonomous religious grounds. Though the matter must be determined empirically, it may be there are examples of this sort of combination in the case of "secularists" and "humanists" who, in fact, turn out to base, or at least to support, their MAGs on religious grounds which they have left unexamined. Thus both formulations, M/RAG and R/MAG, seem necessary for proper descriptive and comparative studies in religious ethics.

[82] Philippians 2:4–11.

LEVELS OF BEING

K. O. L. Burridge

The brief for this essay is a discussion of the relations between religion and culture. What is attempted is a breakdown of these two terms by developing, within a different perspective, a working definition of religion presented elsewhere,[1] that religion and religious activity are to be found in "the redemptive process indicated by the activities, moral rules, and assumptions about power which, pertinent to the moral order and taken on faith, not only enable a people to perceive the truth of things, but guarantee that they are indeed perceiving the truth of things." What I propose is, first, an explication of this definition; then an examination of it in relation to certain life crises and institutionalized confession among a New Guinea people, Tangu; and finally some remarks on the broader implications of the argument.

I

The definition is qualified by "working" because it is not so much a definition *of* religion as *about* religion and how to find out about religion. Exploratory, it defines a problem for research and investigation rather than coming to a conclusion, and provides a way of talking about religion and religious matters that need not be entirely ethnocentric. Anthropologists in particular have to assume that there is some range of experience, thought, and activity in another cul-

[1] Kenelm Burridge, *New Heaven, New Earth* (Oxford: Blackwell, 1963), p. 6.

ture that properly deserves the label "religious."[2] To do otherwise seems an indefensible limitation and, as has often happened in the past, we are apt to find that while we have religion other peoples merely have superstitions. More importantly, rejecting the positive view is to reject the principle involved in it: that despite the difficulties involved there can, ultimately, be some meaningful communication between one culture and another. If we are to examine the ways in which religious activities relate to other aspects of life, we must accept religion as a universal in human affairs and so define it that it becomes accessible to investigation.

Given, then, that there is something in another culture which can be called "religion," anthropologists are bound by professional canons to use empirical data in their descriptions, analyses, and inferences about the nature and content of any particular religion. Moreover, they can only move toward that kind of language which tells the reader, almost intuitively, that the concern is with religious affairs, after they have become familiar with the ways of life, experience, and categories of thought of a strange culture. The same principle of discovering the religious life as it is secreted in the interstices of the culture leads us into the rejection of definitions which depend on a "belief in spirits" or a "belief in the supernatural." For although anthropologists have worked with such *a priori* definitions for many years, and many still do, the word "belief," a key and multivalent term which, in English, includes conviction as well as frank doubt, becomes positively misleading when used of another, especially non-literate culture. What is a matter of empirical fact and general experience in one culture may not be in another, and to reject the authentic experience by placing it in a category which, in context, looks very like "superstition" is to evade the very problem being investigated. Similarly, unless rigorously defined, as, for example, in Christian theology, or by contextual usage, words such as "spirits" and "supernatural" are subject to gross misuse and lead to misunderstanding rather than understanding. The taxonomy of cross-cultural experience is necessarily rough, and we have to make do with such words as we have. But given that the development of any subject consists to a large extent in alternately opening and

[2] For a contrary view see Werner Cohn, "Is Religion Universal: Problems of Definition," *Journal for the Scientific Study of Religion*, II (1962), pp. 25–33.

closing particular categories, it seems useful now to reopen some
that had seemed closed.[3]

If it can be said, as it often has been, that religion underlies or
pervades every aspect of life in a primitive culture, it is as useful to
assert that that which underlies or pervades anybody's life is what we
mean by religion. Such an assertion may seem to lead into strange
territory in relation to, for example, atheists or agnostics. Yet there
seems no good reason why we should not try to look at ourselves and
our subcultures in the same way as we regard others. Far from wid-
ening the meaning of religion into the meaningless, it forces us into
the ontology of a culture, obliges us to seek out the relations between
different kinds of experience, and enables us to perceive in these
relations what is essentially religious even though, at times, they
may appear as "godless."

The definition speaks of "assumptions about power." And for our
purposes the word power includes all the manifestations of particular kinds of power identified by a culture. These may be the wind,
thunder, lightning, flood, storm; political or economic powers; powers
of persuasion, oratory, humor, wit, creativity, or destruction; powers
of intellect, imagination, technology, speech, sex—any kind of
power, whether wielded by man or otherwise. While I would argue
that religion is concerned with all kinds of power, it seems particularly concerned with powers regarded as peculiarly beneficial or
dangerous, creative or destructive. Each culture selects, from the
variety of powers it has succeeded in identifying, particular kinds
of power which it regards as more important than others. Indeed,
within any culture not only can the identified powers be arranged
in a hierarchy of importance, but it is usual to find that lesser powers
are derived from, or are refractions of, or are explained by, greater
powers. That is, there is often an integrated and hierarchical relationship between the identified powers. Some of these identified
powers seem in fact to be, and are represented as, external to man
himself. Other kinds of power, also represented in the culture as external, may seem to an outside observer to coincide or correspond
with particular burgeonings in man's inner condition—his varieties
of fears, impulses, and desires. Often an internal experience fixes

[3] For a recent and stimulating reopening in another context in the North
American literature, see Robin Ridington, "The Inner Eye of Shamanism and
Totemism," *History of Religions*, X, no. 1 (August 1970), pp. 49–61.

on, and is then imaged in, an external manifestation of power; and an interplay between the experience and its image may generate a third image, which, in turn, may bring a further experience into awareness. Sometimes the nature of a power, the occasions of its manifestations, and its effects are fairly well known and controllable. Even so, it is a religious concern. At other times the nature of a power is not well known, its manifestations are unpredictable, and the effects not controllable. Again, such a power is the concern of religion. While it is through an apparent ongoing and developing interplay between sets of overt effects or outward manifestations, and their apparent sources of causes, that particular powers are identified and their natures approximated or determined, once identified the potentials of powers become the "assumptions about power" of the definition. In this view "God" is an assumption about power, and so are the "devil," "Art," "Science," or "Survival of the fittest" . . . Each gathers into itself particular kinds of knowing, doing, affecting.

The process of classifying sets of effects and relating them to their apparent sources, a diagnostic process, is a process of ordering. Concerned with power, religion is also concerned with ordering the different kinds of identified powers. From this ordering comes some kind of control, a control that does not necessarily entail a manipulation. And even though there will be animals, things, and phenomena which do not quite fit into the order, which are "interstitial" and therefore regarded as special,[4] particular manifestations of powers no longer appear wholly random. Yet the ordering would be futile if it did not, first, reflect the truth of things and, second, guarantee the truth of things.[5] So long as the total lived experience harmonizes with its conceptualization or ordering, so long does the latter reflect the truth of things and guarantee the truth of things. As experience again and again validates the assumptions, so do the latter come to guarantee the validity of experience. It sometimes occurs, however, that for a particular individual there may appear to be a discrepancy or dissonance between his experience and the ordering which his culture provides. Considering his experience in

[4] Compare Mary Douglas, *Purity and Danger* (London: Routledge, 1966), esp. pp. 29–40.
[5] Cf. Godfrey Lienhardt, "Religion," in *Man, Culture and Society*, ed. H. L. Shapiro (New York: Oxford Univ. Press, 1956), p. 327.

relation to the ordering, he may consult with others. More often than not what results from this is the discovery either that the experience has been misinterpreted, or that the ordering has been misunderstood. But this does not always happen. Sometimes the lived experience is so vivid, or the discrepancy between the lived experience and the ordering so pointed, that nothing except a reordering will satisfy. Upon informing others, the individual may be regarded as mad or eccentric. He may be tolerated, exiled, killed, or put into a lunatic asylum—depending on how others see the effects of his discovery on themselves. If on the other hand the discrepancy and the suggestions which are made in relation to the reordering are such that others find that their own lives yield just such a discrepancy, and that the reordering—implying new assumptions—achieves a correspondence or harmony between assumptions, faith, and experience, or that the reordering implies kinds of experience which are coveted, then the traditional ordering of power is likely to yield to a new ordering.

In any culture within a given stable period the assumptions about power will be found in, and thought of as underpinning, accepted rules or conventions of conduct. These rules constitute the moral order, a normative system of rules which discriminate between right and wrong action. Yet the assumptions which guarantee the truth of things are such because they command a consensus as to the fit between life's experience and its ordering or conceptualization. And although there is always interplay between assumptions and moral rules, the one qualifying the other, in the stable situation it is perhaps fair to say that the moral rules are grounded in the assumptions, in faith. As the aberrations of particular individuals, discrepancies between the "is" and "ought" or "might be" can be handled. In a literate culture, where the assumptions are formulated authoritatively, a change in assumptions usually tends to lag some way behind a changing or broadening experience and the adoption of informal moral rules. If it lags too far, then the formulated experience it represents is in danger of being cast aside. In fact, in the Western or Christian experience, reformulations of assumptions and moral rules have been a continuing characteristic. The "is," "ought," and "might be" suffer continual readjustment. In a non-literate culture, relatively isolated from other cultural influences, the lag is almost imperceptible. But when a non-literate culture is exposed to, for example, the complex apparatus of a highly industrialized society, then the culture and its moral order break down. Nor can they be renewed until, following a period of grave unrest and a series of reformulations, experience, moral rules, and assumptions about power reach a new harmony.[6] Ultimately, man falls victim to his reach for what seems a truth.

It could be argued, perhaps, that even if there were no faith, no assumptions about power, something like moral rules would arise from the fact that man lives in community. Without some subtraction from what, for the moment, may be supposed to be the sovereign will and purpose of the individual, community life would be impossible. Baboons, for example, live in troops, and there appear to be inarticulate rules and conventions of behavior by which they order their lives within the troop. A lone baboon would be a dead baboon. In order to survive, baboons must live in troops, baboons are conditioned by troop life, and their modes of behavior are explicable in terms of instinctual responses to a variety of pressures. Nor can there be any doubt that similar kinds of instinctual pressures and responses also operate in man. But man differs from baboons in that, among other things, neither he nor his forms of society can be understood in the simplistic terms of "survival" and "instinct." Man is measured by, and may only be understood in terms of, his grasp of the truth of things, the articulate thought by which he comprehends his awareness of truth. Man's biological survival is intimately bound up with, but subordinate to, his awareness of the truth of things. His rules for living in community and creating and maintaining the cultural environment in which he thrives are articulate, rationalized. And however instinctive or impulsive his actions may be, they are referred to what is articulate. Man's prime activity consists in articulating and rerationalizing his rules so that they may accord with his perceptions of the truth of things—even though, from the vantage point of another time or space, these truths may be perceived as mistaken or deliberate falsifications. If there are times when he seeks to loosen the rules so as to give instinct, impulse, and self-willedness relatively free play, there are other periods when instinct, impulse, and self-willedness are remorselessly crushed. And although

[6] For examples see Vittorio Lanternari, *The Religions of the Oppressed* (New York: Mentor, 1960/65); Peter Worsley, *The Trumpet Shall Sound* (London: MacGibbon and Kee, 1957/68).

one might say that changes in permissible kinds of behavior and experience were "nothing but" the rationalizations of responses geared to biological processes, the important point is that when man acts he thinks, articulates, and rationalizes, and that both before and after he acts the action is referred to articulate rules. Lacking this there could be no religion. Religion has to do with the ways in which man, seeking the truth of things, articulates his total experience and conditions of being as they are revealed to him or as he reveals them to himself. Hence the difficulties of comparative religion, hence the necessity for going to the raw experience for which the rationalization is a shorthand clue to the truth, and then attempting an analytical rerationalization.

Man's experience of being, in which baboons and other animals have an albeit inarticulate share, is conditioned on one level by millions of years of biological space-time. At this level and even though baboons are conditioned to "community" life, individual baboons will seek to evade the "rules," will "cheat," attempt to "take advantage," exempt themselves, assert themselves over against the "community." And they are brought to order by the reactions of others in the troop. The same impulses are present in man and he too is brought to order by the reactions of others in the community. At quite different levels of space-time, however, man enjoys, first, a generalized cultural experience measurable in thousands of years; and secondly, a moral experience which is subject to change and which rarely persists in all its particulars for more than a few generations. While the cultural equipment and capacities may remain fairly stable, their organization in relation to moral discriminations may vary considerably. The former are but the raw stuffs which man orders by making them subject to articulate rules, and which he reorders as his experience grows, changes, or widens. At the cultural level man is able to symbol, to communicate via a medium. But he is not necessarily moral. He becomes moral when, in rationalizing his instincts, impulses, and cultural capacities, he is articulately aware of his discriminations between right and wrong. Yet these discriminations are rarely totally inter-consistent, are subject to the exigencies of a changing consensus, and do not remain invariable. And the total dynamic involved in the ways in which individuals seek to discharge, or evade or defy—redeem—their obligations to each other in relation to the normative moral rules is the "redemptive process" of the definition.

The word "redemptive" is used advisedly. The very fact that the English language does not provide a synonym as adequate to the situation is instructive. Since it seems necessary to open avenues of experiential content, the evocations of the particularities of salvationist religion may be temporarily suspended or held in the back of the mind. At the same time, the use of "redemptive process" enables us to penetrate the relevance of salvationist religion in a comparative sociological context. It is a phrase whose content is discoverable in the activities, moral rules, rationalizations, images, concepts, ideals, and categories of a particular culture; and it can be seen as the process by which individuals collectively seek to order and interrelate or integrate the various contexts and levels of their being and experience. And though, within this redemptive process, the relations between the three levels of being mentioned—the animal, cultural, and moral—seem to depend mainly on perceptions of harmony and consistency, it is these very perceptions which, acted out, provide the redemptive process with its dynamic. What man can articulate about his animal experience is derived from, and reflected in, his cultural and moral experience. His observations of the natural world yield insights into his own psycho-physiological nature and moral experience. In turn, the moral experience is projected into the natural world and into animal and cultural capacities. In all, this complex interplay is the environment from which, humanly speaking, conscience is derived, and in which we can most adequately observe its formation and development.

If in one, ethnocentric sense conscience is given by, and ultimately answerable only to a power identified as God or the Divine, its most pertinent observable field of operations lies within the constraints of normative moral rules. And these, in the spirit of Kant's imperative, are based upon reciprocal obligation. This is the debt to which every individual is born, his price of survival in community, a debt and price which he has to redeem. The larger and more complex the community, the more complex the developments of this primary reciprocity. Like for like is translated into a variety of conventions of equivalence, particular rights and privileges are joined to prescribed duties and obligations. If in a literate culture most of these rights and obligations are to be found in written or codified form,

many are not, and in a non-literate culture they only become evident
to a stranger after he has observed and participated in the activities
pursued by the culture, after he has made an entry into the various
idioms of rationalization. Yet in no culture that we know of is the
possibility of unilateral action, whether by man, deity, or natural
or meteorological agent, not admitted. If man could, animal-like,
have his affairs regulated for him, there would be no need for conscience. As it is, the fact that man is morally aware is largely due to
his perception of the existence of the unilateral or non-reciprocal
and random or capricious both in himself and in the world around
him. Shorn of this and the rules and rationalizations which, in ordering the known and controllable, set apart and confine the non-
reciprocal, random and capricious, conscience and morality could
only be programmed and instinctual, animal-like. Indeed, it is precisely when he is confronted with that whose onset, progress, and
effects he cannot control, or which his system of order cannot accommodate, that man may perceive a flaw in his design of the truth
of things. Then, as the ordered bounds blur in flux, he may move
into that central core of the religious life, the level of the "spiritual."

Despite differences of vocabulary, idiom, and cultural content,
literate theologies indicate a substantial area of common ground
when describing the mystical or "spiritual" experience; and we know
that this common ground is shared, to some extent at least, by non-
literate peoples. Yet we are not so much interested here in what the
varieties of the "spiritual" experience or mystical ecstasy are—though
we may provisionally and minimally identify them as rooted in a
harmony of personal feeling and experience with outer conditions
through which the limitations of time and space and social context
are overcome and a truth perceived—as in the relations these kinds
of experience bear to other, more accessible kinds and levels of experience. If as a rough approximation we may say that a "spiritual"[7]
experience combines into a unity what would otherwise be quite distinct contexts of experience, we also have to add that it is one of the
sources whereby an existing moral order is confirmed or changed.

The working definition implies, as indeed anthropological experience bears out and our own religious insist is or should be the case,
that what is called religion is not a compartmented set of activities

[7] In quotation marks because while the provisional identification would
command some agreement, the varieties of expression might not.

which operate once a week on Sundays—that is religion at its most forced and artificial—but is (or should be in a particular way to a religious) present in everything we do. The sociology or anthropology of religion, whether in our own society or elsewhere, is always at the level of a "people's religion" and is to be discovered in all that is said, done, and experienced. To break the barriers of distinct vocabularies of discourse and so make contact with the intellectual refinements of theology, an anthropologist must attempt to discover and interrelate the experiential content of particular rationalizations. For our purposes here it is possible to abstract from the matrix of man's total condition the categories of culture on the one hand and the biological or animal or natural on the other. Considering the cultural animal we can discern certain articulate rules, conventions, and discriminations which order or organize the animal and cultural capacities, and which we call the moral order. The ways in which these rules are encountered and manipulated constitute the redemptive process. But moral order and so redemptive process are dependent on a continuing search for the truth of things, one of whose sources we have identified as the "spiritual" experience. In this view religion becomes a *unitive* category which, in spelling out the relations between animal, cultural, moral, and "spiritual," tells us about the dynamic entailed in the redemptive process. Whether we derive the word religion from *religare*, to bind or hold back, or from *relegere*,[8] to collect together and so to recollect, ponder, think intensely about, both etymologies taken together evoke the wider essentials of any religion: the existence of rules which regulate community life; a set of assumptions about power, the nature of man, his society, and the environment; that thought which, grounded in experience, addresses itself articulately to the rules and assumptions in relation to the truth of things, and reveals itself in action.

II

We may now turn to examine briefly and in outline the crises of birth, puberty, and death among Tangu, a New Guinea people. What is being sought are the links between what might otherwise be simply existential, biological, or physiological events, the assump-

[8] E. A. Worms, "Religion," *Australian Aboriginal Studies,* ed. Helen Shiels (Melbourne: Oxford Univ. Press, 1963), p. 241.

tions and rationalizations that man-in-culture makes about the
events, the moral rules by which he orders the events, and finally,
that level of being which we think of as the "spiritual" life.

Tangu lived[9] by hunting, foraging for wildstuffs, and the cultivation of a variety of root crops, coconut and sago palms. They
were settled in ridge-top villages in a generally forested and hilly
environment where thunderstorms, floods, and earth tremors are
frequent, and where the only mammals apart from man were the
pig and a species of rat. Village and forest were contraposed categories. The first was the center of culture, where men and women
were bound by morality; the second, where nature ruled and wild
things roamed. Cultivated fields were, in a sense, man's victory over
nature and the wild and nonmoral. Safety lay in village and cultiva-
tions. The forest was dangerous. The social system was characterized
by a generally competitive but ordered egalitarianism in which each
individual was taken to be the best judge of his own best interests
as he participated in activities concerned for the most part with the
exchange, barter, and trading of foodstuffs, artifacts, and valuables.
Reciprocity and equivalence in transactions were the rule. Com-
plaints about breaches of equivalence were frequent. Claims and
counterclaims were properly, that is morally, resolved in public assembly, and improperly or nonmorally resolved by resorts to underhand and secretive measures. Like all peoples whose community
relations are directly reflected in, and measured by, transactional
relations, life was heavily accented toward the moral, and individuals developed a keen and critical sense of the wrongdoings of others.
Though the roles and tasks of the sexes were sharply distinguished,
and male and female evoked opposed values, in both cases the opposition was complementary. Young children of both sexes were associated with women, and so with female values. Growing boys and
girls associated themselves with fathers and mothers respectively.
Unmarried youths and maidens formed a group much unto themselves though they were expected to help with household tasks. Since
the transactional activities which formed the core of social life
were based upon hard work in field and forest, and organized by
relationships deriving from marriage, being married and active and
healthy were prerequisites to being fully involved in community

[9] Because the focus here is on a traditional life that has all but disappeared, I
forego the conventional ethnographic present and use the past tense.

affairs and gaining relative status and prestige. Though widows were always valuable helpers in the households of their daughters, and to that extent took an active part in the activities leading toward a transaction, old men and widowers were forced into peripheral roles which, if they did not entail complete exclusion from community affairs, implied a minimal involvement in the complex of reciprocal transactions that made up the greater part of community life.

In each village there were managers or entrepreneurial initiators who organized transactional activities, and who took the leading part in community affairs. Other men, "ordinary" men, who might by hard work and shrewdness themselves become managers in time, attached or allied themselves to managers to form co-operative groups. While these alliances were generally temporary, shifting with the contingencies of life, perceived advantages and disadvantages, and the ambitions of the more able, they were rationalized in terms of the kinship idiom. Co-operating adults were regarded as siblings, and exchanges were carried out across the marriage bond, between affines. Sexual relations between brother and sister were regarded as incestuous. Marriage between first cousins or the members of co-operating households was not allowed, but was enjoined between classificatory matrilateral cross-cousins or the children of households in competitive exchange relationships. Friendship was a category distinct from kinship. But while the son and daughter of a pair of friends might marry, and so create kin, friendships, though maintained by reciprocities, were explicitly outside the competitive reciprocities engaging those whose relationships were expressed in the kin idiom. While friendship and kinship determined what kinds of obligations were owed to whom, the obligation initiated could also determine whether the kinship or friendship idiom was more proper.

In most villages, too, there were men who, with their wives and children, opted out of the competition for relative status entailed in the exchanges between affines. They were known as "rubbish" men. While they did not positively contravene the ideals and rules of the culture, they were scorned for their general disengagement from competitive transactional activities. For these were considered to reveal not simply the best qualities of manhood but the meaning of morality. In this respect "rubbish" men relinquished claims to true

manhood. Managers, because their morality was continually tried
and tested in transactional and organizational activities, were regarded as ideal types. Contraposed to the managerial ideal was the
sorcerer, best thought of as a category or label looking for the man,
manager or otherwise, who appeared to be defying the rules of reciprocal obligation and equivalence, who cheated, who resorted to
underhand and secretive or magical measures to gain his ends, who
did not submit his claims to trial in public assembly, who was an
adulterer, prone to promiscuous sexual activity, who could and did
kill or cause sickness in another. The bare outlines of the redemptive
process were and are discoverable in the activities and interactions
of managers who obeyed, manipulated and might transcend the
rules; "ordinary" men, who obeyed the rules as best they could; "rubbish" men, who did not put themselves to the test; and sorcerers, who
evaded, defied, or broke the moral rules.

In their thought about the birth of a child, Tangu held that a
woman had within her a "germ of being" which was capable of becoming a human child if it was "fed" by the husband. This "germ of
being" was associated with the menstrual blood, and the "food" with
which the husband "fed" (the same word is used of ordinary food
and feeding) the "germ of being" was "milk" (again the same word
as in relation to other milky stuffs) of the penis, or semen.[10] Only
by being continually thus "fed" by the woman's husband could this
"germ of being" develop into a human child. That is, casual sexual
intercourse and random or promiscuous sexual activity (as in a
sorcerer) were distinguished from the sustained and continuing
moral relationship between husband and wife that was required to
create a human child. Or, human beings were required to be born
out of a moral relationship brought about by the categories enjoining
and barring marriage—if, we might add, they were to enter moral
being. Myth adds a further dimension. For in this idiom the "germ
of being" is represented as the child of parents who have just
started to make a new garden. While the parents busy themselves
with their several tasks, however, a hawk takes the baby boy, soars
over the hills of Tangu, and deposits him in its nest in the branches

[10] Kenelm Burridge, *Tangu Traditions* (Oxford: Clarendon Press, 1961),
pp. 84, 375.

of a wild almond tree. When the baby cries (to be born?) the hawk feeds him milk from its penis.[11]

Among Tangu breast nipple and penis were associated: both have erectile properties and produce a milky fluid. So that the experience of feeding a newborn babe from the breast was projected into the feeding of the embryo with the "milk" of the penis. In relation to man, birds were thought of as free-movers for whom nature provides abundantly. And because women were not considered fully morally responsible, but were thought of as being themselves, acting and reacting according to their natures as though animals (albeit cultural animals), whereas men were held responsible and should act the part of a man, birds expressed the female principle. Yet in certain contexts in myths males are also figured as birds. This yields the value "free-mover with or in or through responsibility," which, when checked through the gamut of Tangu culture, remains firm. The hawk, therefore, conjoins male and female principles and conveys the message of birth through the co-operation of man and woman, and the union of responsibility with freedom-of-being or being-in-nature. If Tangu see birds not so very differently from ourselves, the fact that the hawk soars should bring a number of features to mind. In a man the sexual act is accompanied by a sense of soaring, of the earth slipping away beneath. For a few brief moments the limitations of time and space seem overcome, and a man is not simply as a bird but as a hawk, a positive and commanding force. In Tangu tradition, too, as the rain fructified the soil and enabled a "germ of being" in tuber, coconut, or sago palm to proliferate or sprout suckers, so did the semen "feed" the "germ of being" in the womb. And as thunder and lightning herald or are accompanied by rain, so was the flowing semen accompanied by an explosion and streaks of light in the crown of the head.

Imagery or metaphor, the interplay between levels of being and experience is clear. Through this interplay, an animal act, copulation, was transformed into a moral act, itself invoking a relationship determined by the constraints of marriage. The possibility of a "spiritual" experience, a harmony between inner and outer conditions, was provided by embedding the creative sexual act in a context which included animal being, the exterior world of nature, the

[11] Ibid., pp. 374–99.

cultural capacity to symbol, and normative moral contraints. Just
as the sensation of soaring, of a flight out of time and space, is frequently used among ourselves to describe a mystical or "spiritual"
experience, so it was with the Tangu hawk. But among Tangu the
hawk was not, as it might be among ourselves, necessarily a separate,
differentiated image. It was tied fast to the moral relationship of
marriage, to the biological experience of the sexual act, to other in-
terrelated events in nature such as thunder, lightning, rain, soil,
and germinating plants. To put it lineally, something like a "spiritual" experience, a preparedness to be or act in terms of man's total
condition, becomes possible after first making the passage from the
animal to the cultural and moral, and then reaching back through
and within the moral via the cultural symbol to an awareness of the
animal and world of nature in order to transcend the moral. Distinguishing and maintaining the cultural and moral over against
nature and the animal is certainly one part of religion. Without that
distinction man would not be human. But the truth of things demands the discovery of the whole man—not by blurring the distinction (as it might be with the use of drugs) but by transcending it.
Which is only possible if the distinction is first recognized.

Puberty was regarded by Tangu as a transformation analagous
to birth. Like birth (invested with symbols of non-reciprocal or
unilateral powers such as hawk, thunder, lightning, rain) puberty
was an irreversible physiological event. While girls were expected
to make the passage naturally, like animals, according to their natures, and received little or no ritual treatment, boys, about to enter
an ambience of moral responsibility where they would be directly
held to account for their words and actions, particularly in relation
to transactions, were treated with great care. This concern was related to the notion of the *gnek*.[12] In traditional times men, but not
women so far as could be ascertained, were considered to be pos-
sessed of a *gnek*, a word which may be loosely translated as mind or
soul or conscience. The active verbal form, *gnek'gneki*, means to
think, ponder, recollect. Thought to be seated in the head, the *gnek*
survived death and was the active source of moral responsibility. As
we shall see, during confession it was the *gnek* that was active. At

[12] Ibid., pp. 175–91.

puberty a boy had, as it were, a "germ" of a *gnek*, an undeveloped *gnek* which had to be brought out into the world as a *gnek* capable of growing into full maturity and moral awareness.

Before puberty, boys accompanied their fathers and learned from them, in a generally permissive ambience, the skills required of a male. And, since fathers also talked to their sons in more general vein, telling them anecdotes, stories, and myths, sons gained from their fathers a general knowledge and "philosophy" of life's fortunes and exigencies. But a father had little disciplinary authority over his son. This was vested in the mother's brother. When a boy was recalcitrant, the mother's brother was summoned to threaten and admonish. Where the father was kind and patient, the mother's brother entered the tutorial role irritated and abrupt. On reaching puberty, however, just when he was beginning to resent the hitherto amicable relationships with his father, a boy entered a clubhouse where, after strenuous educative procedures and ordeals under the supervision of mother's brothers, he was eventually circumcised, again by a mother's brother.[13]

Now, although only males were allowed into the clubhouse, and its membership was wholly male, at the level of myth the building and membership—the collectivity of men in union—were represented as a "male womb," a male thing with the female property of being able to give birth. Again in myth, the building of a clubhouse was associated with mother's brothers figured as birds (males with a female aspect). Among these birds was the hornbill, a large and fierce-looking but otherwise gentle bird with a frightening and protuberant beak. When nesting, pairs of hornbills seek out a convenient hole in a tree. Having prepared the nest together, the female lays its eggs. But the male bird, walled up with mud and clay in the nest by the female, incubates the eggs. The male bird, that is, was associated with an otherwise generally female task. Correspondingly, the role of the mother's brother in the clubhouse was to "incubate" his sister's son so that when he emerged from the clubhouse he might be born into moral responsibility. As circumciser the mother's brother was, as it were, both cutting the umbilical cord and removing the boy from the womanly state of animal and natural being in order to bring him into a state of moral being.

[13] Ibid., pp. 170–75.

Before puberty young boys went naked. After circumcision they wore breechclouts, a binding in of the vehicle or instrument, as Tangu saw it, of promiscuous sexual activity. When, after circumcision and clad in a breechclout a lad emerged from the clubhouse, his body, and particularly his head, the seat of the *gnek,* were rubbed down with a mixture of red ocher and pig fat—like a newborn baby certainly, but also something more. A wild almond tree about to fruit and fruiting is reddish; blood is red. When initiating an arrangement or relationship, Tangu offer each other betel nut, pepper, and lime to chew; chewing this mixture produces quantities of red spittle. In myth this red spittle emerges as a curative and creative element, blood is life or life-giving, and the wild almond about to fruit takes us back to the babe fed by the hawk. Moreover, the pig fat was not simply a medium for the ocher, but a preface for what was to come: a circumcision feast centered on a pig donated by the father of the newly initiated lad. In myth, father teaches son a series of technical skills, and also "enters into"[14] a pig so that son may kill it. When the pig is killed its flesh becomes men, the intestines become women, and son, sitting down and pondering (*gnek'gneki*) says: "It was my father who made the land as it is, who made men, who gave them a language so that they could speak, who taught them to understand one another, who brought men and women together in villages. . . ."[15] Though it is not certain that the pig of the myth and the pig of the circumcision were positively identified with each other, it seems probable that it was so. Either way we may notice the importance of thought and articulate language as father's gift to his son. Language, thought, and technical skills, cultural capacities, were, so to speak, the semen which, fed into the clubhouse, the "male womb," combined with the activities of the mother's brothers to bring a lad into the arena of moral responsibility.

While the arrangements for, and thought about, puberty show how what might have been—and was in the case of girls—an existential physiological event, was given moral relevance, father's entry into a pig re-emphasized man's total condition. On the level of day-to-day experience father was morally responsible, provided food and shelter for his wife and children, "fed" the "germ of being" in the womb of his wife, brought son to the point when, under the tutelage

14 Ibid., p. 397.
15 Ibid., p. 386.

and disciplinary authority of mother's brothers, he became morally responsible. Nevertheless, if only because son could never repay father for his gifts, nurture, and training, or revenge himself on father if the latter evaded his responsibilities, the relationship between father and child was non-reciprocal. At the level of myth the images of a soaring hawk, thunder and lightning, rain, and fruiting tubers reveal that no child was thought of as being born of and into culture and morality simply. The business of making a child represented an accommodation of the reciprocal and moral with the non-reciprocal and animal. Father's gifts to his son were figured as being dependent on some quality or property of father entering or reaching into the animal condition, as a hawk at birth, into a pig which had to be killed at puberty. And in the context of clubhouse and puberty one part of the message is, clearly, that the animal (pig) in man must be "killed" if culture and morality are to be maintained. The idea that continuity of culture and morality through the generations is or was largely contained and preserved in the father-son relationship is also evident. On the other hand, underlining the value of the non-reciprocal, there is the thought that there is or was a quality in man, particularly as father, which could and should transcend the space-time limits of culture and morality by entering the animal—and "spiritual"—condition if culture and morality were or are to continue to be maintained. These ideas become more explicit in the context of death. For when father died his *gnek* survived in the form of a ghost to his son.

Though women seem always to have been considered as "natural beings" or as "animal-like," their close association with gardens, both in myth and in life, reveals them as cultural animals rather than wild animals. Traditionally without a *gnek,* upon death a woman was thought to re-enter animal nature. She assumed the form of a rat—the only other mammal, man and pig aside, in traditional Tangu experience which is to be found in gardens and villages but is only rarely encountered in the wild forest. But since it was men's active engagement with women through marriage that brought them fully into the field of transactional reciprocities, the complementary relationship between male and female figured the moral and reciprocal. Men by themselves or in relation to each other without the mediation of a woman could and did figure the non-reciprocal and self-willed. A man could be as hawk, or as pig. Men hunted in the forest, where they encountered the non-reciprocal and self-willed, because they themselves could be non-reciprocal and self-willed. Hence the importance of revealing the female aspect when attempting to transform a headstrong lad into a being aware of moral responsibility. Nevertheless, because a man could be self-willed and non-reciprocal he should, in Tangu terms, realize his potential by being more than simply obediently moral: this sort of man was a very "ordinary" or "rubbish" man. A real man, a man-ager, was expected to do better than that by, on the whole, trans-forming, transcending, or actively maintaining the moral order through an exercise of his capacities for non-reciprocity and self-willedness. And again, the field in which these capacities found their source was largely contained in the father-son relationship.

When a father died the relationship with son continued as father appeared or manifested himself to son mainly in dreams, or dream-like situations, but also in the context of what would otherwise be normal waking life. To Tangu this was, and to a large extent still is, a simple fact of life. Sons have encounters with dead fathers or, as we might say, with their ghosts. And though encounters with a ghost were generally considered to take place when son had something on his mind, particularly when he was considering alternatives in re-lation to transactional obligations, they might occur when nothing, on the surface, seemed toward. But a ghost was entirely self-willed and non-reciprocal. After father's death the non-reciprocal relation-ship between father and son maintained itself, albeit in a higher key. Within the context of an encounter with a ghost a son might seek advice or even upbraid the ghost if misfortunes had been oc-curring. But the ghost, under no obligation to comfort or give good advice, might be oracular or aggressive or sly or admonishing or en-couraging or deceptive or whatever. So that while a ghost did not necessarily provide son with a direct and positive assurance, so far as the encounters must have entailed a conversation between the self and otherness, and so extensive probings into personal circum-stances, fears, and motives, son was preparing himself for a wiser and more adequate handling of his environment and social relation-ships. While managers were considered demonstrably capable of handling the ambiguities of the ghostly relationship, "ordinary" men and "rubbish" men were clearly not as adept. A ghost forced a man to think, use his *gnek* and engage the redemptive process, or, as we might say from another viewpoint, wrestle with his conscience. If we ourselves tend to think of conscience as a "still and inner voice," Tangu tended to think of it as contained in a continuing relationship between father and son, and then in an entity thought of as external to the self.

Though birth, puberty, and death, physiological or animal events, were the chief occasions on which Tangu reminded themselves of their total condition, they also recognized a series of further transformations which, after the first "moral parturition" at puberty, occurred as a man entered more and more fully into the range of opportunities and temptations offered by the culture.[16] But we cannot go into these here. It suffices that in spite of these opportunities the emphasis was always on the maintenance of moral relationships. Marriage steered a man into the active moralities entailed in transactions and, as children were born, nurtured, and put into the clubhouse, gave him the opportunity to become aware of himself in the wholeness of his being. But while the circumstances of daily life sufficed to keep most men engaging the redemptive process within the rules most of the time, limited resources, advantage, and ambition entailed a choice of priorities in meeting obligations. Then it was that a ghost forced a man to take stock, reflect, make and act on a decision which could not be unequivocally moral. If the relationship with a ghost could drive a man to cowardice on the one hand, or into defiance of the rules on the other, it could also impel him into braving the consequences in public assembly or even transcending a present morality by introducing new rules which commanded consent. Tangu recognized that a conscience wholly subservient to morality was only for small men. As a ghost was itself non-reciprocal, so a man should preserve the non-reciprocal in his conscience if he was to realize his full potential as a man.

III

The word "confession" is used here to describe the procedure whereby, on certain occasions, Tangu think about and recall (*gnek'-*

[16] Ibid., pp. 427–40.

gneki) their past activities, and then recount them to particular persons who may bruit it abroad that such has been done. If, in a traditional context, contrition was present, it was implicit and understood rather than explicit. Currently, after nearly fifty years of exposure to Christian (Roman Catholic) teaching, contrition may be presumed. But it should be made clear that during the period of fieldwork the Christian and traditional forms of confession coexisted, and that while contrition is necessary to the former it did not appear as necessary to the latter.

Thinking about and recalling past activities, particularly transgressions of the moral rules, might occur on a number of occasions: during a thunderstorm, after an accident or unusual or strange experience, after an encounter with a ghost, on seeing a large snake, when facing a wild boar, after an earthquake or tremor, when incapacitated or sick, in almost any circumstances, one might say, when a man found himself confronted by the actual or potentially non-reciprocal. But articulating and communicating the thoughts to another rarely took place outside a context of sexual misdemeanor, encounters with ghosts, sickness, and death. Discovered sexual misdemeanors did not require confession: they were dealt with by more direct procedures, forcefully and reactively. A well-executed and undiscovered adultery might, but need not, occasion confession. Yet because there was the possibility that the act, failing discovery and so reaction by members of the community, might itself react on the perpetrator in the form of sickness, the wiser course was to confess to an old man or a friend before the sickness came. The friend or old man, standing outside the complex of competitive reciprocal obligations involving those whose interrelations were expressible in the kin idiom, would tell others what had been done. The covert act, undiscovered, covertly confessed, covertly bruited abroad, remained covertly acknowledged. No further action was taken in a direct sense, though several kinds of overt acts might flow from the affair. An undiscovered incestuous sexual act, or sexual intercourse within the sweetheart relationship,[17] would almost certainly bring on a severe sickness if undiscovered and unconfessed. Again, the confessor was an old man or a friend who apprised other members

---

[17] The sweetheart relationship was one between a male and a female which included joking, bawdiness, petting and breast play, but specifically not sexual intercourse or marriage.

of the community that a confession had been made. Thus even if a sexual misdemeanor was not immediately confessed, the probable ensuing sickness would provide the context for confessing it later. And sickness incapacitated a man, prevented him from working and honoring his obligations, retarded and might ruin his prospects in the competition for status. No man with managerial ambitions could afford to be sick for long, and those who achieved managerial status were men who were not subject to recurring sicknesses.

The principle of reciprocity, derived from the more general experience of transactional obligations, was, as has been noted, qualified by the unilateral or non-reciprocal, by experiences with animals, natural phenomena, and men acting alone or in concert without the mediation of the female principle. Inhering in the relationship between father and son, even after father had died, non-reciprocity was also typical of the sorcerer. While some sorcerers might be persuaded into reciprocity, the ultimate and definitive quality of a sorcerer was that he was non-reciprocal. Men who were thought of as sorcerers were generally considered to have had irresponsible fathers, and the sons of irresponsible or unpleasant or odd or strange fathers, or of immigrant fathers, were generally thought to have something of the sorcerer about them. As the agents of non-reciprocal action, sorcerers were thought to be responsible for most sorts of trouble, particularly adultery. And "trouble" in Tangu meant anything that could vitiate a current set of reciprocities. Adultery, because it endangered the principle of marriage upon which reciprocities were based, was regarded as especially heinous. Still, the most important focus of a sorcerer's activity, which was linked directly to confession, was the sickness which seemed to be leading to death. For though Tangu had their ways of treating a variety of minor ailments, the question in their minds when the sickness was serious, particularly when it involved continuing diarrhea, was which of the two principles, reciprocity or non-reciprocity, was at work and whence its source. The first step, presuming reciprocity, was to elicit a confession from the sick man and announce the admission of fault. If, then, the patient recovered, it became clear that the cause had been traced. Confession nullified the power causing the sickness whether the power had been set in motion by a human or non-human agent. But if the sickness continued, then either a full confession had not been made, or a sorcerer was responsible and might be going through to the kill. The presumption of reciprocal action began to be qualified by the suspicion that unilateral action was in train. Hence it became necessary to extract further confessions, and from the circumstances revealed by them to find out who might have had a motive for causing the sickness. Enforcing a counter-confession from a suspect by threats and beatings might bring about the recovery of the victim. If it did, victim (or patient) and sorcerer engaged in a compensation exchange. If, however, the victim died, then the guilt probably lay elsewhere outside the community, and it became necessary to fix the guilt more securely and take a life for a life.

There is no need here to go into the full details of sorcery detection and its consequences.[18] It suffices that, traditionally, confession was related directly to the reciprocities characteristic of the moral order. The fact that Christian Tangu engage in both Christian and traditional modes of confession shows not simply that actively maintained reciprocities are still a lively concern, but that the Christian mode cannot deal either with the sorcerer or with the kinds of reciprocity in which Tangu involve themselves. Since Christian confession entails secrecy and a relationship between a man and God which, despite the offices of an intermediary, requires that the custodian of conscience shall be, mainly, the individual self, it bypasses the reciprocities that are and were all-important for Tangu. Given the possibility of unilateral action, for Tangu it was necessary, first, to exhaust the possibilities of a man having brought misfortune and sickness on himself through a prior transgression. Sickness and death, that is, were in most cases taken to be the results of moral lapse, and the therapy was thought to lie in both a particular and more general reassertion of the moral condition. But this reassertion of the moral condition, be it noted, was occasioned by an experience of the non-reciprocal and unilateral. The idea of sorcery, whether or not a sorcerer could be identified, was as essential to the maintenance of a moral order based on transactional reciprocities as the fact that a particular man could be thought of as a sorcerer.

Lacking the evidence of what a Christian might call "true contrition," it is not easy to perceive in the traditional Tangu mode of confession any reach into the "spiritual" life. On the other hand confession should not be regarded as a procedure in isolation. As father

18 Burridge, *Tangu Traditions*, pp. 124–55.

"fed" the "germ of being" in his wife, so his initial training of son fed the moral embryo; as a child was born of woman, so was a moral being with a conscience born of the mother's brothers in the club-house. As conscience was born of the clubhouse and shaped by the reciprocities of the transactional life, so, reversing the syntax and procedure, father as ghost imbued son's conscience with a quality of the unilateral and non-reciprocal. But the development of conscience was not unambiguous. The boys who grew into sorcerers had had the same treatment as the boys who grew into managers, and managers and sorcerers, equally, had encounters with ghosts. And though the quality of conscience must have depended to a large extent on the relationship between a man and his father's ghost, and this relationship must have, in turn, depended on the father-son relationship in life, confession provided the possibility of a more absolute test. For in confession a man was invited to break the barriers of time and space and, confronting himself in all his aspects, reveal himself to his fellows and himself. That this invitation was rarely accepted without reservations is only human. What is important is the provision of an opportunity to seize upon a truth through whole-ness of being.

IV

The ways in which religion is related to other aspects of culture has received masterly treatment from the pens of Fortune, Evans-Pritchard, Lienhardt, Turner, Geertz, Douglas,[19] and others. Here, taking a leaf from Teilhard de Chardin, the main concern has been to sketch, very briefly and simply, the relations between distinct categories of experience and levels of being. Discovered on the level of the collective and normative, in the articulate transformation and bringing together of different kinds of experience as they are

[19] Reo Fortune, *Manus Religion* (Philadelphia: American Philosophical Soc., 1935; and (Lincoln: Bison Books, Univ. of Neb. Press, n.d.); E. E. Evans-Pritchard, *Nuer Religion* (Oxford: Clarendon Press, 1956); and *Theories of Primitive Religion* (Oxford: Clarendon Press, 1965); Godfrey Lienhardt, *Divinity and Experience* (Oxford: Clarendon Press, 1961); Victor Turner, *The Forest of Symbols* (New York: Cornell Univ. Press, 1967); *The Ritual Process* (Chicago: Aldine Pub., 1968); Clifford Geertz, *The Religion of Java* (London: Free Press, 1960); Mary Douglas, *Purity and Danger* (London: Routledge and Kegan Paul, 1966); *Natural Symbols* (London: Crescent Press, 1970).

expressed in institutionalized life, these relations may be rationalized by an observer as interdependent. At bottom, however, each separate feature, seemingly "just so" or arbitrary, appears as rooted in an appropriateness seized upon by the human (Tangu) imagination when contemplating its condition. And it is the appropriateness of what is "just so" or arbitrary that yields itself to the continuing appetite for the truth of things—even though such truth may, in the end, be mistaken or misconceived.

Given man's common biology or animality; much common ground in what is meant by a "spiritual" life or experience; and that the physiological processes at work during a "spiritual" experience are probably very similar if not identical; animal man and "spiritual" man would seem to be interdependent, and this irrespective of the varieties of culture and morality that happen to exist. Yet this is simply to restate the burden of most myths of origin: that before culture and morality intervened man was in paradise, a free-mover not subject to articulate rules, at one with the Creator and All-being. But culture, and particularly morality, have intervened. It may be possible to shrug them off for a while with the aid of drugs, but not on the whole to transcend them. If it is the business of religion to maintain culture and morality, and particularly morality as distinct from culture, it is also its business to reveal how, as ultimate conclusion to the redemptive process, the animal and cultural and moral may be distinguished, harmonized, and then transcended in full awareness of the dictates of each so as to gain the level of the "spiritual."

From an anthropological point of view religion, particularly in its protectionist and conservationist aspects, is largely a consequence of moral awareness, of knowing that we can discriminate between right and wrong, of knowing that we can and do organize these descriminations into a system. The dynamic and creative elements, on the other hand, are provided by the symboling and imagery which belong first to culture and then to morality. Moreover, since the capacities for symboling and imagery are freely associative and imaginative, no particular set of moral constraints can keep them in thrall for long. Indeed, unqualified by the imaginative act and perception nourished by culture, morality of itself would bar any access to the "spiritual" life. The germ of religion is typically contained in the possibilities of transcendence evoked by the culturally determined images of, say, hawk, thunder, lightning, rain, and germinating crops; in the performance of the creative sexual act within a moral relationship; or in the confession which, going beyond a review of the self in relation to a set of normative moral discriminations, is able to appreciate the self in relation to the constellations of meaning attaching to, for example, father, hawk, pig, clubhouse, death, and ghost. But such fleeting "spiritual" experiences are followed by a return to life in time and space, a re-engagement of the redemptive process. And since there are varieties of morality and culture, redemptive processes and the modes and objects of transcendence also vary.

Integrated with a relatively closed community bound together by densely knit ties of reciprocal obligation, confession in Tangu was directly related to reciprocities. But in the relatively open, moneyed, and complex communities of Christendom it would be quite impracticable to relate confession directly to reciprocities: the social order requires that confession be between the individual self and God, with or without an intermediary. If in the one case a man is overtly invited to come to terms with his fellows, but must ultimately come to terms with himself, in the other he is asked to come to terms with himself and his God, a formula which includes relationships with his fellows so far as it is possible in the conditions obtaining in an open society. Because more closely bound to God and the self than to one particular and readily ascertainable group of people, the Christian environment probably provides more opportunities for the "spiritual" life than did the Tangu. On the other hand, held fast by a morality rooted in clearly defined networks of reciprocal obligation as Tangu were, they were allowed interaction with a ghost. Through the circumstances of the relationship with a ghost, one may charitably think, Tangu were permitted a glimpse of that higher, divinely ordained moral law from which, in a platonic sense, Christians opine that particular moralities are derived, and to which such moralities should aspire. Though even among ourselves, where the ties of relationship in life were sufficiently dense, a dead person will continue to exist as some sort of presence evoked by words spoken or a shaping situation, the point of the Tangu ghost is not simply that it can be directly related to the maintenance of moral obligations, but that the ghost itself was non-reciprocal. While it may be the case that closely woven relationships cannot be broken by death, so that a ghost or presence fills the gap left by the dead person, and this, in turn, confirms the suspicion of an afterlife or state of being other than the animal, cultural, or moral, what is more pertinent is that strong moral bonds breed conscience, and conscience seeks a custodian. If this custodian is located only in the reactions of fellow humans, then man is forever held fast to the moral. The Tangu ghost may have kept most men within the bounds of a current morality. But while it enabled some to defy morality it also enabled others to transcend it or re-create morality in a new image. A new or higher or more developed morality could be born of perceptions of the relevance of the currently non-reciprocal.

While in most literate and developed religions it is an explicit purpose, open to all, to overcome limitations of time and space and transcend the cultural and moral in order to achieve a "spiritual" condition, in non-literate societies such a purpose is generally implicit. It is left to those with particular insights, such as the shaman or seer, to provide the example. In both cases, however, it seems more opportune to achieve or show forth the "spiritual" condition—the harmonizing into a unity of hitherto distinct categories of experience—when normative moral values are in question rather than when they are firm and axiomatic. Gautama Buddha, Jesus, and St. Francis, for example, lived and worked in times of acute stress. The challenge of new ways and competing moralities had put hitherto trusted moral norms in disarray. To the exclusive community of Jews, threatened by the Roman hegemony, Jesus brought a teaching that transcended the old Mosaic law: "Love God through loving your fellow men. Let your morality extend to all, let their moralities extend to you, then you will see God." As "The Christ" he epitomized the condition to be achieved through his teaching. As "The Buddha," Gautama epitomized a similar condition to be achieved by quite different means: "Expunge desire." If this can also mean "expunge love" (in the Christian life-affirming sense), it should be remembered that Gautama seems to have lived at a time of confused social conditions with no hegemony in sight, when a guarded withdrawal from the flux of moralities would, in retrospect, seem to have been appropriate. A soldier who had played his part in the frequent wars between petty Italian states, St. Francis went into the wild, where, it is said, he communed with the birds. He then transformed the comradely loyalty and affection of a soldier for his fellows into a love of all men through service to them.

A few examples cannot make a case. Nevertheless, they suggest lines of investigation which might be fruitful. Is it possible to find a common denominator in the lives and teachings of the prophets, saints, and founders of world religions, or in the activities of those who have inspired so many "nativistic" or "messianic" movements among the simpler peoples, such that it will enable us to say something pertinent not so much about culture, morality, and the "spiritual" in themselves as about the relations between them? In a literate culture the student has a wealth of experience at his command. The conditions are there, one might say, for becoming wholly self-aware, for systematically setting out along the path to the "spiritual" state. But while in India, for example, the first step to the "spiritual" life is a withdrawal from caste and normative morality, and the same is substantially true of most non-literate communities, a Christian could only accept this temporarily and reluctantly. If there is a very real sense in which it can be said that each achievement of the "spiritual" state is a fresh one, uniquely conceived and achieved, it must be allowed that each self-conscious reach into animal and instinctual being must make use of, and be accomplished through, the cultural and moral environments in which it finds itself. The unique is born of, and is rendered intelligible by, that which is collectively expressed and general.

Mainly through the works of Max Weber and R. H. Tawney, and also because, in the West, "religion" appears as conveniently compartmentalized and separate, we have come to think of "religion" and "culture" as significant variables. The thrust of this essay is to suggest they are not. If we accept "religion" as a unitive category, implying the bringing together into an acceptable harmony of different kinds and contexts of experience, each of which has something to do with the exercise of power; and if we separate the cultural capacities from normative morality, holding them in a context which includes the animal and "spiritual"; then we allow for that crucial spontaneity and spark in human affairs which, in spite of rulers, governments, propaganda, and bureaucracies, really decides men's fates. Further, what has here been called the redemptive process, an operational or investigatory notion, allows us a wider and empirically accessible context within which to follow a dialectical interplay between the known, ordered, and controllable on the one hand, and the unpredictable, quirky, or truly mysterious on the other. On the basis of the observations in this essay, let us suggest—as hypothesis —that since a normative morality seems both bar and pathway to the "spiritual" life, the more rigid and axiomatic the former, and the more closely it is tied to transactional life and economic exigencies, the harder it is to transcend, and the more compelling grows the urge to defy, question, or destroy that moral order so that, with doubt, the conditions for formulating a new morality may be attained. Where morality is tied to transactional life and economic exigencies, animal or instinctual man is distanced, and, particularly under urban conditions, that necessary and intimate acquaintance with and awareness of nature and the wild is stultified. The imaginative and symboling capacities of cultural man are held on a tight rein; social situations together with their rules, symbols, and images are neatly ordered, set apart, strictly compartmentalized; opportunities for a creative interplay between different levels of being and contexts of experience are restricted, throttled back.

Still, human beings are neither bees nor ants. Imagination and outer conditions are continually engaged, awaiting the spark of an appropriate conjunction between what had hitherto seemed separate and distinct. Sometimes, grasping the opportunity perceived, individuals will take themselves off to a more congenial environment. Or they may found a new sect which will provide the environment they want. Or, rejecting the pain and labor of reformulating morality, much the same ends may be achieved temporarily and artificially by the use of drugs. Or again, what seems a peculiarly apt relationship between the moral order, one's own circumstances, and an imagination linked to particular desires can be managed through astrology, or a deft use of tarot cards and similar oracles. But there is no need to specify each of a myriad modes of attempting to find, refine, defy, escape, alter, or transcend a given morality. What is important is the conceptual realization of the religious life as an ongoing process that continually modifies a normative moral order by repeatedly bringing together within a unitive framework different contexts of experience and levels of being. As an empirical problem the heart of the matter seems to be contained in the discovery of the processes whereby a given normative morality, necessarily based on reciprocal obligation, is either being continually modified by being forced to come to terms with that which is not reciprocal and cannot be denied, or is rejected in favor of more radical change because such modification seems impossible in relation to experience. Alternatively, to pose the same problem in the form of a question that assumes our levels of being: What are the opportunities, in a particular culture, for allowing the animal and instinctual in man to be realized and imaged in the outer conditions of nature and society such that articulate thought and moral discrimination may seize the moment and allow themselves to be carried into the truth of things?

MORALITY AND HAPPINESS AMONG THE DINKA

Godfrey Lienhardt

Twenty years ago the Dinka[1] had only slight and indirect contact with foreign moral teachings. Though there were several Christian missions and some schools among them, their literate pupils were so few, in proportion to the large population widely dispersed over a territory with poor communications, that they could have carried only faint echoes of foreign instruction to the majority, who in any case would hear them only if they corresponded to Dinka ideas.[2] Transhumant cattle-herders by choice, but cultivating near their permanent settlements as far as sharp seasonal alternations of flooding and drought permitted, most Dinka then wished for no other way of life than their own. Few of them were or really cared to be literate, and though they took occasional advantage of the cheaper luxuries available in little scattered townships, they finally held the whole apparatus of urban living in contempt. To say of any kind of behavior that "it is what is done in town" or "it is not what they do in our Dinkaland" was usually to condemn it.

The Dinka were thus very conscious that they had a moral code

[1] The Dinka are a Nilotic people of the Southern Sudan (now in the Democratic Republic of the Sudan) who, at the time of my visits in the late 1940s, may have numbered up to 1,000,000. Rebellion, and then civil war and military occupation, have since assailed the life I knew, and Dinka, some highly educated in the modern way, have been scattered far from their own homeland. But the Dinka are tenacious of their own values, and one generation of misery and strife is not likely to have weakened much of the traditional morality here described.

[2] The fact that many European visitors have singled out for praise the high moral standards of the Dinka suggests, however, that these principles corresponded at many points to those assumed in "Western" tradition.

of their own, superior in their view to that of others as was the traditional way of life which validated it. In legal discussions, in a vast range of songs, and in much ordinary conversation, they represented and reflected upon the moral qualities of persons and situations; and their leaders—masters of the fishing spear, I have called them, after the sacred spears which are their symbols of office—and other elders were renowned for their moral subtlety as for their eloquence[3] in homiletics. But Dinka were not of course academic students of their own ethics, and those in other societies who study ethics and religion may care to know how far their own interests in morality and happiness are reflected in the lives and thought of such a people.

We may well begin by examining the Dinka myth which explains why human life involves misery, and especially the misery of death.[4] It is even of some interest that such a question, implying as it does an intellectual confrontation of the only life men can have directly experienced with certain purely ideal possibilities, should arise in its different forms among so many peoples of the world. In the Dinka myth, God[5] created in the beginning a man and a woman, and the earth was so near to the sky that men on earth could easily reach God in the sky by a rope which stretched between them. Sickness and death were unknown, and a single grain of millet was sufficient for a day's food. God forbade them to pound more than this single grain; but the woman wanted more food, and began to pound more grain with the long-handled pestle the Dinka use. In doing so she struck God, who withdrew above and sent a finch to sever the rope which once had allowed man easy access to him. Therefore man has since had to work hard to get his food, and death and sickness, unknown when God and man were near together, are his lot.

[3] The early traveler John Petherick, though presumably working through interpreters, comments on this eloquence and gives examples of a Dinka chief's speech (which sounds even now entirely authentic) "clothed in words of which many in the enjoyment of civilization and education might be proud." *Egypt, the Soudan and Central Africa* (Edinburgh and London: W. Blackwood and Sons, 1861), p. 424.

[4] I have discussed this myth at some length in Lienhardt, *Divinity and Experience: The Religion of the Dinka* (Oxford: Clarendon Press, 1961). It is inevitable that this and some other parts of that book should be recapitulated in the present article.

[5] In other writings I have preferred to call the Dinka sky-god "Divinity" for reasons given in the book mentioned, but in the present context the meaning of the word "God" is not misleading.

Christian or post-Christian moral philosophers and theologians
may rightly see in this brief myth an analogy with the story of the
Fall and its consequences. Its plain meaning to the Dinka is that the
ultimate evil, death, became the lot of all mankind as a result of an
act of disobedience to God's command on the part of the first woman;
that the many forms of human weakness from which mankind suffers are the result of a separation from God following "man's first
disobedience"; and that nearness to God is a condition of human
happiness in its most general form. As is amply evident in their religious practice, Dinka believe that in order partly to escape the unhappy consequences of that original fault, God must on occasions
be brought nearer to men by prayer and sacrifice.[6]

Yet, if the Dinka myth be examined in the light of what has been
regarded, in popular Christian theology at least, as the meaning of
the Fall, some differences become apparent. First, as other Dinka
mythological information makes clearer,[7] man's original closeness to
God, though giving freedom from death and labor, could not be
represented in the Dinka context as a state of supreme bliss. Although the daily pounding of grain is perhaps the most wearying
task that women have to perform, it is an accepted condition of having plenty to eat, and where real hunger is often a major cause of
suffering and death, women certainly prefer to pound as much as
they can when it is available in order to provide plenty, than to produce a mere sufficiency. Hence although in Dinka terms the first
woman did wrong in disobeying God because she was "greedy" (and
the Dinka expression here, *kok myeth*, involves perhaps a milder
sense of disapprobation), she was also doing what any Dinka would
now approve in an industrious wife.[8] There is no suggestion of her
weak collusion with a force of evil. Nor would the Dinka story bear
that emphasis on the virtue of obedience in itself which some Christian exegesis has drawn out from the story of the Fall. Certainly the
Dinka explicitly believe that men should conform to God's will, and
further that women and children should be obedient; but in their
extremely democratic society obedience for its own sake, subordination of one person to another, is not an accepted necessity of social

[6] Lienhardt, *Divinity and Experience*, chap. 1.

[7] Ibid.

[8] Dinka emphasis on death *and toil* as being the prime consequences of the
woman's act, however, accord very well with those of the actual text of Genesis.

order.[9] People may "hear the words" of other people, and if they agree with them, act accordingly, but no man is expected to take orders from any other. So the entire subordination of man to God represented in the myth is not an unambiguously happy state. Freedom from arduous toil and death denied man satisfactions considered at the present time to be necessary and legitimate.

And although one of the Dinka's very greatest sources of happiness is their cattle, deeply associated as will be seen with the pleasures of artistic creativity, of courting, marriage, procreation, and progeny, they have no important role in this myth. I cannot say that no Dinka would suppose that there were cattle at that time, but the logic of the story is that one grain of millet a day was all man was allowed, and hence the milk and cattle products essential to Dinka diet, consumed with conviviality and produced from all the enjoyment of pastoral tasks which contrasts with the dull necessity of cultivation, play no significant part. There is another Dinka story of the origin of death, less common in my experience than that related, in which God tells the first man that people will die for a month, and then return. Man rejects this offer on the grounds that if this were to happen the people would be too numerous for the cattle. Here their traditional life with cattle is to be preferred to immortality. Cattle and the pastoral life would be essential to any state of complete bliss that the Dinka could imagine. In fact they do not imagine any such state since as we have seen the place where the first man and woman lived was something less than an earthly paradise, and there is no Dinka idea of heaven. The nearest Dinka equivalent to an earthly paradise would be rather their imagined land of permanently lush pastures, "the pastures of Lual Aghony," than the home of their first parents.

Nevertheless it is plain from their myth that the Dinka, as far as can be known independently of any foreign teaching,[10] hold that men still suffer for an original offense which divided them from God. From this, as from the sin of Adam and Eve, unhappiness and evil

[9] The Dinka might well say with Paul Valéry: "Then where did the idea originate that man is free, or the opposite idea that man is not free? I am not sure whether it was philosophy or the police who began it." Paul Valéry, *Reflections on the World Today*, trans. F. Scarfe (New York: Pantheon, 1948), p. 48.

[10] It is possible of course that there may have been far earlier connections with biblical lands, but if that were so this myth has certainly been fully incorporated into Dinka belief and not superimposed on other beliefs inconsistent with it.

followed, and they believe that the intervention of God and the gods is still necessary to deliver them from some of the consequences of that offense. God also is represented most importantly as bringing judgment[11] upon men for their misdeeds, especially for those which do not readily come to light; and death, sickness, or serious misfortune prompt them, with the help of diviners, to examine their consciences to discover what they or close relatives have done wrong in the past. But no more in fact than in the story of the Fall are the actual detailed immoralities of mankind itemized as direct results of their separation from God, and their mythological explanation of human weakness and mortality could serve as a theological and anthropological basis for moral principles different from their own. These, and the proportions in which the Dinka see them, emerge rather from the particular form of their social order, which in the myth is still undefined. Though if pressed, Dinka would trace that order, like all that is, to God, their custom and its virtues are more immediately endorsed by human tradition, by their ancestors. Thence, rather than direct from God, comes Dinka morality, and indeed their religious beliefs themselves are what the ancestors have defined and handed on.[12] Moral teachings are seen as a product of their society, and are sanctioned by ancestral approval.[13] Thus though, for example, incest among the Dinka is a serious offense, and exogamic prohibitions cover a wide range of kin, the story by which they account for frequent marriage of first cousins among the Arabs does not suggest that the Arabs are always committing incest, *akeeth,* but explains why there is *no* incest among them, "incest" here being regarded as a matter of Dinka definition.

Of all the qualities and activities of human beings which in Dinka are "bad" or "wrong" (the single word *rac* can carry both meanings) what is translatable as "witchcraft" (*apeth* and *roth*) is in a category

[11] Here the Dinka confirm to a considerable extent Newman's view that in "natural" as distinct from "revealed" religion the major attribute of God (for him suggested by "Conscience") is retributive justice. John Henry Cardinal Newman, *An Essay in Aid of a Grammar of Assent* (Garden City, N.Y.: Doubleday, 1958).

[12] So the main cults of the Dinka are concerned with the divinities of their clans, and in them members of a clan pray to God, the ancestors, and the clan divinities together in the phrase, "You of my father . . ." Other peoples are thought to inherit and rely on the particular strengths of their own forebears.

[13] Thus a Dinka moral philosopher would probably, like Aristotle, see "ethics" as a branch of political science.

of its own.[14] Other evils can appear as relative, so that, for example, even incest is in practice regarded as more or less reprehensible according to its specific circumstances, as are the other cardinal offenses later discussed. But witchcraft is an absolute evil,[15] the summation of all serious vices. The last point is of some importance, for if witchcraft were simply regarded by the Dinka as a single vice comparable, for example, with unjustified homicide, Dinka moral notions would appear to be further from those usually discussed by professional philosophers than they in fact are. In the word *apeth*, the most insulting condemnation that one Dinka can apply seriously to another, are concentrated all the characteristics of a person who hates and is hateful to his fellowmen, through envy, malice, and licentiousness in all their various forms. One must add immediately that "witchcraft" is not in fact among the Dinka an obsessive daily source of worry, and to highlight anthropologically their concern with it would be to present their moral life in entirely wrong proportions. It is as a theoretical construct, rather than as the constantly suspected attribute of actual persons, that it bears on Dinka notions of morality. Witches are the embodiment of malice and envy, which they direct towards their neighbors' cattle and children in particular. They "eat" peoples' good looks, making them thin, or bald. They are associated with night, darkness, concealment of person and motive; they are held literally to foul the homestead, the source of domestic happiness and peace, and are agents of sickness and death.

Dinka emphasis on these characteristics of witches tells us something about the social and moral order to which they aspire and (in that Dinka themselves regard witchcraft in their own society as the practice of a few individual deviants) may indicate that they recognize the binding force that order effectively has over the majority. For much that the Dinka most value both morally and materially can be deduced by contrast from the basically simple acts of wickedness they attribute to witches. Their harmfulness to cattle sets them against almost everything the Dinka love. Cattle are ob-

[14] For a fuller account see Godfrey Lienhardt, "Some Notions of Witchcraft Among the Dinka," *Africa*, XXI (1951), pp. 303–8.

[15] It is recognized that there may be more or less virulent witches, and "witch" may be a term of joking abuse. Moreover, one born with witchcraft may not use it, or use his power against malign witchcraft. But witchcraft itself is always evil.

jects of poetic contemplation, their colors and movements a constant
delight to the Dinka imagination.[16] They are a necessary adjunct
to courting since their beauty enhances that of their owners. They
are exchanged for women in marriage, when they enable a man to
set up his own homestead, and their transfer legitimizes his children.
Those children will stand by him throughout his life, bury him de-
cently, and then keep his name alive in the lineage as a link in his
turn with their earlier ancestors and the divinities. The constant
generation and regeneration of their clans and lineages represents
a very great moral good to the Dinka,[17] and witches who injure
cattle and children, spoil courtship, and foul the homestead, attack
that good at its foundations, where ideas of moral duty and individual self-fulfillment coincide.

In a different category from that of witchcraft appear a number
of serious offenses grouped together under the term *adumwom*,
translated by Father Nebel as "sin";[18] and that they should be so
grouped does indeed show that the Dinka have an indigenous conception of such differences between kinds of wrongdoing as theologians and lawyers discuss. The offenses comprised in this category
stem not from envious malice, as with witchcraft, but from self-
gratification in defiance of basic moral rules. They are incest, adultery, homicide in certain circumstances, deliberate indifference to
prohibitions on injuring the totemic emblems of the clan, theft in
certain circumstances, disposing improperly of a beast consecrated
to the clan divinity and denying their rights to people too weak to
assert their own. All these offenses are thought to bring their own
retribution in the form of sickness or death to the offender or his
kin, and require restitution or expiation. Without this, their painful
consequences follow inexorably, and they differ in this from wrong-

---

[16] I have described this at length in *Divinity and Experience,* and some
aspects of it in "Dinka Representations of the Relations Between the Sexes,"
Studies in Kinship and Marriage, ed. I. Schapero (London: Royal Anthropological Institute, 1963), pp. 79–92.

[17] Dinka are divided into clans united by descent in the male line from their
original ancestors, and further subdivided into lineages, which are groups within
the clan formed on the same principle. Each clan has its divinities, whose emblems are selected natural or social phenomena which must be respected. Thus,
for example, a clan with the giraffe divinity respects giraffes by refraining from
injuring them.

[18] Fr. A. Nebel, F.S.C., *Dinka Dictionary with Abridged Grammar* (Verona:
Missione Africane, 1936).

doing in general, *awoc,* in which the notion of having made a mistake, of having failed to do right and in this sense having done wrong, plays a greater part.

Although it would be held in general that it is God who punishes these offenses, Dinka also recognize that the misery of guilt and anxiety is intrinsic to them. Those who have done wrong in these ways cannot be happy, since their "hearts," to which the affections and joy and grief are referred, are constantly troubled until they have made amends. The notion that wrongdoing is its own punishment, irrespective of any social penalties that may be imposed, is here thus clearly acknowledged, for traditionally among the Dinka there was no possibility that any of these offenses could be judicially punished.

The offenses mentioned have in common either the privacy in which they are committed or the fact that they are publicly indefensible or both, and all are serious infringements of the rights of others, whether men or divinities. To consider incest first, the Dinka rule is that intercourse between those who can trace relationship by descent on either the paternal or the maternal side, is in principle forbidden. In fact circumstances alter cases, and where the relationship is considered by the elders to have become distant, a ceremony may be performed in which a living beast is cut apart longitudinally, symbolizing the dividing of the living unity of the lineage or clan to which those who wish to marry belong. Also, since agnatic relationship may extend more widely than individuals always know, they may, as it were, take a chance, and have intercourse without first consulting those who would know better about the degree of their relationship. This is regarded as relatively inculpable, and again the ceremony of division is performed to cancel the kin relationship retrospectively. But in either case, public account must be taken of the liaison; otherwise misfortune and death, especially in childbirth, are its inevitable consequences. In general people have a duty to marry outside the descent groups of their parents. They have no right to have sexual relations with those they have no right to marry. And they could not marry a kinswoman, according to the Dinka rule, with bridewealth cattle, when a wide range of kin contribute to the cattle handed over by their kinsman, for they would also have a right to share in the cattle received at the marriage of that kinswoman. It would be completely wrong for the cattle merely to circulate within the same kin group, the bridegroom giving cattle from which he had a right to receive a share back. So incest would directly undermine both the integrity of the clan and lineage, and the exogamic rules maintaining the relations between different clans and lineages within the wider community. To break the exogamic rules is to "sever the back of the lineage," as the Dinka say, and is the very type of offense which involves its own punishment, since by committing it the offenders deny themselves the moral benefits which clan and lineage integrity are held to confer. Children are taught as early as the age of seven or so the dangers of playing with relatives of the opposite sex, and begin to learn that incest has dire automatic consequences.[19] The very word for it, *akeeth*, is also the word for those consequences, in particular a skin disease akin to leprosy, through which it reveals itself.[20]

All the other offenses commonly comprised in the category of *adumwom* similarly strike in one way or another at the central principles of Dinka communal order. Adultery (not premarital intercourse, which if discreetly contrived is not condemned) is a kind of theft, and some say that a man who commits it will be killed by a lion, lions also being associated with theft.[21] It clearly invades the lineage through its smallest component unit, the family, and if unconfessed would make nonsense of the incest prohibitions.[22]

Theft, which all observers assert to be very rare among the Dinka, strikes at the mutual trust which a people whose homesteads are open to all must place in one another. According to my information it stands with intimacy with related girls as an evil Dinka children are early taught to shun. If a Dinka wants something from another, he asks for it, and since openhandedness is counted a great virtue he may not uncommonly get it. "He is a very good man—he gives to people" is perhaps the commonest expression of approbation.[23] To take something by stealth goes against the whole spirit of giving,

19 See also Lienhardt, "Dinka Representations."

20 Whether or not intercourse with a distant relative should be regarded as incestuous is sometimes judged by whether the disease is contracted.

21 Lions are of two kinds, one being that which seizes cattle, called *cwer*, the word also for thieves.

22 Hence, as I am reminded by my friend Mr. Isaiah Majok Akoc, adulterers suffer ostracism and may even be forbidden to visit their own sick children.

23 Even very poor Dinka fear to refuse something to still poorer people when they beg. Dr. Francis Deng provides a Dinka proverb which sums up the virtue of giving: "What is given circulates, what is consumed is wasted."

and appears therefore worse, even, in the context of Dinka life than in societies where personal property is more tenaciously held on to and protected. So theft, like the other offenses committed secretly, is thought to trouble the heart of the thief, until eventually some sickness or misfortune is attributed to it and it has to be openly acknowledged and redressed. To take or borrow openly even without the owner's permission, is a different matter, and to seize cattle from foreigners or distant political communities is not theft but a commendable exercise of valor. There are thus distinct words, with different moral overtones, for thieving, taking, and seizing in a raid.[24]

Homicide of any kind demands a rite whereby the killer protects himself from being haunted by his victim, and is thus recognized as inevitably troubling the conscience. But moral condemnation of homicide varies with its nature. To kill in war, or in the prosecution of a feud—acts performed openly on behalf of the clan, lineage, and political community—may be a positive duty. To kill a stranger without this social justification, or to go further than duty demands in slaying, or in mutilating the corpse (in order, for example, to remove the bracelets of the dead, a theme of several Dinka stories)[25] are wrongs which continue to disturb the conscience until some sickness frightens the offender into bringing them into the open and atoning by sacrifice. Killing a member of the local political community is particularly to be avoided, as the convention that clubs, not spears, should be used in local fighting suggests. Homicide may also entail blood vengeance perhaps leading to feud, always a great evil for the whole community. A series of Dinka proverbs expresses the necessity of preserving peace between those who are most closely linked, either by kinship or by local contiguity: "Better enmity in the bush than enmity in the home"; "Better hatred between neighbors than hatred between half brothers"; "Better hatred between half brothers than hatred between full brothers"; "Better enmity with foreigners than enmity at the fireside"; "Better enmity in the cattle camp than enmity within the lineage." The other grave offenses—injuring the totemic emblem of the clan or failing to give

[24] Respectively *kwal* or *cwer, loom* or *nyai,* and *pec.* European justice was at variance with that of the Dinka in attempting to treat cattle raiding and killing in the feud as culpable in the same way as theft and willful murder.

[25] Father Nebel records a case in which leprosy was attributed to such an act of mutilation. A. Nebel, *I Dinca Sonó Cosi* (Bologna: Museum Combonianum 21, 1968), p. 187.

the clan divinity its dues—are clearly denials of the moral duties and demands of clanship, of which the clan divinity is the symbolic expression, and in this respect compare with incest.

I have said that these offenses are not itemized as direct results of man's initial separation from God, nor have I ever heard it suggested that men's propensity for them (as in the Christian theology of Original Sin) comes from that event. There is no myth or legend which incorporates God-given commandments against them, though all Dinka would say that they are "what God has hated" and that unless the offender makes amends their consequence must be death. The sickness which finally prompts him to do so is in fact a sign of that approaching death which by his own act he has brought nearer to himself and his family. Hence, in focusing the guilty conscience upon death, these offenses do recall man's separation from God and in sacrifices God is again asked to come nearer to men to help them in their weakness.

So it is that the Dinka myth of the origin of death, in which no moral teaching is given by God, and these graver offenses against an ancestral moral code, have in common the theme of division and alienation leading to death. By an original small act of self-gratification, man separated himself from God and death followed. By the offenses mentioned—incest, adultery, unjustified homicide, theft as defined, injustice especially to the weak, and disregard of the clan divinity—all alienating the self-gratifying individual from the moral unity of the group—death follows similarly.

Here we may see why witchcraft is in a different category. The imaginary figure of the witch is the very type of individual alienated by his or her *nature* from society, and actively subverting its moral values. Witches, Dinka may say, are "people of the boundary" (*koc akeou*), the reference being to the boundary between homesteads, and indicating therefore in this context people outside and separated from the homely center of affection, co-operation, and mutual respect. Since then it is their very nature to be evil, when speaking of witches Dinka sometimes seem to imply that they belong to a different species from ordinary human beings.[26]

Hence witchcraft is different from the grave offenses called *adum-wom*, which disturb the conscience—the heart—of the offender. For

---

[26] Similarly it is held that there are some people who are not really men but lions, who prey on men and cattle.

he, unlike the witch, wishes to remain within the moral universe from which he has separated himself by an aberrant act of self-gratification, and his only hope of escaping death is in openly performing the prescribed rites of atonement. Similarly in the myth discussed earlier, man's original act of individual self-gratification separated him from God, with whom he still tries by sacrifices to remain conjoined when he fears suffering and death.

It is not necessary to accept the extreme Durkheimian proposition of an identity between a god and a society to see an analogy between the alienation of the individual wrongdoer from the collective values of his community, and the original alienation of man from God, both leading to death. The Dinka's basic social groups, based as they are on kinship and descent, are indeed more correctly viewed as "communions" than as "groups," for they are united (an adequate translation of a common Dinka expression) in their clan divinities and their unity thus has a religious integrity and sanction. So it is not only the wrongdoer himself who may suffer for his offense. For the Dinka, the sins of the fathers, especially in the lineage, may certainly be visited on the children, a belief which makes any idea of posthumous rewards and punishments in a heaven or a hell irrelevant, since according to them retribution always follows wrongdoing in this life. If the father sins and the son becomes sick, the father himself is thereby punished. It is from such a communion of kin, and especially of agnatic kin, that those who do wrong in the way mentioned excommunicate themselves, as the first man and woman excommunicated themselves from God.

So although, as I have said, the Dinka do not systematize their morality in abstractions, there appears in their moral commentary and practice a congruence between ideas of "goodness" and "happiness," and of unity and union, on the one hand, and between "badness" and "unhappiness" and division and disunion on the other. That Dinka would express this congruence more concretely is not in question: they express it in their own way.[27] At the simplest level

[27] To this extent Malinowski's attempt to enroll the Trobriand Islanders (as a non-literate people) in the then fashionable attack on metaphysics may mislead philosophers. But his reference to "such harmless adjectives as good and bad, expressing the savages' half animal satisfaction or dissatisfaction in a situation" being "sublimated into 'Goodness' and 'Badness' [to] create whole theological worlds and systems of Thought and Religion," is perhaps clearly a flamboyant

it is evidenced in songs where, for example, a common theme is that of a person who complains that his people injure him with their malicious gossip (usually about his love affairs) and reflects on his isolation. To have no kin, and thus be cut off from that central communion, is recognized as one of the greatest sources of misery, or again (another common complaint in songs) to remain unmarried when all one's age-mates are setting up their own homes is to be divided from the group to which one had belonged,[28] an unhappy anomaly. The sacrificial reparations which those who have offended in the ways earlier discussed are required to make involve "atonement" in its etymological as well as its theological sense, the at-one-ment with the divine and with Society.

And also the very structure of Dinka clans and lineages, which form the basis of their moral and political communities, corresponds to this association of "good" and "happy" with unity, and "bad" and "unhappy" with disunity. It is in the nature of lineages to divide and subdivide into smaller morphologically similar segments formed on a common agnatic genealogical principle; but the opposition and division between these lineages at lower levels of segmentation is complemented by their union at a higher, so that, for example, those who are divided as the descendants of two brothers are united as descendants of the father of those brothers. On the maternal side too, though genealogical connections are not so long remembered as on the paternal, division by descent through males is balanced by what is often regarded as the closer union of those descended from one woman.[29] That these transcending unities are seen as a higher good is suggested by the fact that in prayers members of different lineages of the same clan may assert to augment their power that "they are one, not two." The cutting apart of a beast to counteract incest is a symbolic statement of the original integrity of the exogamous group to which the guilty couple belong, the living body of the beast standing for that integrity which forbade congress be-

oversimplification. Bronislaw Malinowski, "The Problem of Meaning in Primitive Languages," C. K. Ogden and I. A. Richards, eds., *The Meaning of Meaning* (New York: Harcourt, 1946), pp. 296–336.

[28] Age-mates are morally integrated with one another by initiation.

[29] All Dinka descent relationships can be categorized by those who are related through men and those who are related through women. Those most clearly united are those related on both principles.

tween them.[30] In the rites for concluding a blood feud a living beast is also sundered, but in this case transversely. Here the parties to the feud have divided the wider political community by polarizing loyalties within it, but the integrity of that community does not derive directly from common ancestry, as does the integrity of the exogamous group. Dividing the generative organs would not therefore be symbolically significant.

Dinka political and religious leadership also is based upon the ideal congruence between "goodness" and "happiness," and unity and concord. The ideal Dinka community, both at the domestic and political levels, consists of families, or lineages, living in harmony in the relationship of mothers' brothers and sisters' sons to one another, where "your mother's brother's family is put together with your father's," in the Dinka expression. Thereby separate and potentially hostile descent groups have come to share a common life, and are bound in a particularly intimate affection, by the marriages between them and the children those marriages have produced.

The mother's brother has ideally (and in my experience often in fact) a role of kindly and dispassionate authority. So it is that the Dinka "masters of the fishing spear," priest-chiefs around whom and around whose lineages Dinka political communities are formed, are often referred to as *naar wut*, "maternal uncles of the cattle camp [tribe]."[31] For their people, they are mediators and reconcilers, both between different sections of their communities and between their communities and God. When they "put their words together to make one word" (again, a Dinka expression), their people are united, strong, and prosperous.[32] With "many words," on the other hand—with lies, contradictory reports, half-true gossip, divided interests and motives, all summed up as *aliap*, the vice perhaps most frequently condemned by Dinka—"the country is spoilt."

And still more influential than ordinary masters of the fishing

[30] As I have said, the beast is divided longitudinally, and it is particularly stressed that the genitalia should be so divided. This does not suggest the separation of the penis of the man from the vagina of the woman, but the division of the generative organs from which their own relationship prohibiting intercourse derives.

[31] This is discussed more fully in *Divinity and Experience*.

[32] ". . . according to the adage 'Two come together'; for two people have a greater power both of intelligence and of action than either of the two by himself." Aristotle, *Nicomachean Ethics*, trans. J. E. C. Welldon, p. 246.

spear have been outstanding individuals, for the most part from priestly clans but also supposed to be directly inspired by God, who have succeeded in uniting members of previously hostile political communities in opposition to foreign intrusion. Such prophets, credited with an insight into the human condition greater than that of other men, and in whom a higher wisdom is thought to be combined with a more inclusive sense of human community, embody the highest form of virtue. And it is consistent with their position as agents of atonement (again in the etymological meaning of the word) that the greater priest-chiefs of the Dinka should be represented as having overcome the ultimate divisiveness of death by voluntarily entering the grave towards their end while life yet remains in them. Hence their interment rites are made the occasions of collective expressions of happiness, whatever the private grief their people may feel.

The Dinka expressions for "a happy man" or "a good man," simple evaluative terms as they are, thus raise many questions about the particular form of Dinka society and religious belief. A Dinka who has committed a grave offense cannot be a happy man, for he is alienated from that part of himself which accepts the dominant mores of his people. A man may indeed be unhappy, on the other hand, if he himself is blameless, but here again the root of unhappiness is conflict with others or with circumstance. In either case, Dinka moral philosophy, in this respect has much in common with that of Aristotle:

Unanimity then appears to be political friendship, and indeed it is often so described, as it touches the interests and concerns of life. Such unanimity can exist only among the virtuous; for they are unanimous both in themselves and in their relation to each other.[33]

[33] Ibid., p. 296.

PART II

Traditions in Judaism and Christianity

RELIGION AND MORALITY FROM THE PERSPECTIVE OF THEOLOGY

James M. Gustafson

INTRODUCTION

How are religion and morality distinguished from each other? How are they related to each other? Authors who, for various reasons and out of various interests, have dealt with these two questions have long recognized that they can be framed as different sorts of questions. If one asks how religion and morality have been related to each other historically, one's approach to the basic questions will be different from that of a person asking what the logical relation is between propositions stipulated to be distinctively religious and those stipulated to be distinctively moral. An historical approach needs to be refined into several possible attacks. One is to address significant religious texts to see what relations are asserted, assumed, or consciously developed in these writings. What is the relation in the Torah? In Amos? In the Johannine letters? In Rabbi Hillel? In the *Pirke Aboth*? In Augustine's *Morals of the Catholic Church*? etc. What have religious leaders believed and taught to be the relation? Indeed, the question has to be raised whether some of them even made a distinction.

Another way is to address the question of what consequences for human action and historical events certain religious movements have had. To illustrate this in its broadest, and least refined terms, one can ask what has the influence of Judaism been on the morality of Western culture? To work this out in social-historical refinement requires many judgments about what the "connections" are between religion and culture, how one sort of phenomenon is related to (or is a part of) another sort. I suppose that the historically oriented sociology of religion of Max Weber is an example of this approach— and that the Weber corpus is a good place to begin to study both the possibilities and the difficulties of this way of working. In a sense what is pointed toward in this paragraph is a sociological relation of religion and morality.

Still another way, continuing to use historical materials, is to examine the actions, in so far as they can be known, of individual agents to seek to understand how morality and religion are related. Here the use of biography and autobiography are particularly important. One asks not only, for example, what did Gandhi, or Tolstoy, or Jesus, articulate the relation to be, but what does it appear to be in their less self-conscious expressions, and in their actions.

There is no need to expand the illustrations. The sorts of questions asked are amply treated in other essays in this volume. I wish only to set a context in which the particular interests of this essay can be located. My principal query, and the general interest which gives direction to this essay, can be approached by stating some sorts of "wondering" I have done in response to contemporary philosophical essays on religion and morality.

I wonder what happens to the way in which the question of the relation of religion and morality is framed if one looks at some of the beliefs about God that have been influential in the course of the development of Judaism, Catholicism, and Protestantism. For example, what happens to the framing of the question if it is affirmed that God's will is a moral will, whatever other sorts of adjectives might also qualify it? What happens if in writing about God's "moral will" in one way or another, the religious authors referred not only to God's will as his purposes or intentions, but also to the sorts of things he activates as an agent in the course of human affairs? If God is One, in Western religious beliefs, and if he is (in some sense) sovereign, and if his will is a moral will, and if all that occurs is (again, in some sense) dependent upon him, can one readily distinguish between a "religious" and a "moral" obligation? Between a religious and a moral relationship (or response) to God? If goodness is attributed to God—in giving his gifts of life to the world and man, in sustaining and restoring human life—and if that goodness is (in modern distinctions) both moral and nonmoral, does man's gratitude to God require deeds that are moral and religious at once?

Why is it that "sin" in both Judaism and Christianity cannot be exhausted simply by using "moral wrong"? While some figures and movements in Western religion stress sin as primarily "lack of trust" in God, why do even they always assume that this lack of trust is related to doing things that are morally wrong? While others stress sin as "morally wrong acts," why do they always assume that one is to repent before God for what he has done? Similarly, why does "grace," however it is primarily used, universally include forgiveness for doing moral wrongs, and almost universally include an empowering to do what is morally right?

Sin is used as a qualification not only of specific acts, but of moral agents as well; not only are deeds sins, but men are sinners or sinful. Why is this? The sinful agent seems to be one whose morally wrong acts are "rooted" not only in his moral capacities (whatever these might be) but also in his basic orientation or disposition toward God. Why have religious persons and thinkers thought in these terms? Can religion and morality, men in their religious "consciousness" and in their moral "consciousness," be easily and readily distinguished?

Similarly, "righteous" is used to qualify not only specific acts of persons, but also to qualify persons themselves. Western religious texts are replete with designations of certain persons as "righteous" men. The righteous man is, at least in many instances, not merely the morally admired person who obeys the moral rules, but he is also a person of commendable piety, or a person whose relation to God, as well as whose deeds, are "right." Is it merely logical confusion that leads to this sort of view? Or is there in the theology and anthropology (in a philosophical sense) of Judaism and Christianity some basic affirmation which requires that religion and morality be bound together in a particularly tight way?

Also the figure of the "saint," the admired holy man, is usually one who receives such appellation not only because of his piety, but also because of his morality. Can piety (as religion) and morality be readily distinguished? Both Jewish and Christian religious literature of an "edifying" sort are guides to the cultivation of virtues, and do not draw sharp distinctions in all instances between "religious" and "moral" virtues, but instead assume not only that one sort might support the other, but also that they are in some sense united. I have in mind such Christian classics as Thomas à Kempis, *Imita-*

tion of Christ, William Law, *Serious Call to a Devout and Holy Life*, Ignatius, *Spiritual Exercises*, John Bunyan's *Pilgrim's Progress*, and also Jewish classics such as the fifteenth-century treatise, *Orchot Tzaddikim* (The Ways of the Righteous), and Moshe Chayim Luzzato, *Mesillat Yesharim* (The Path of the Just).

I wonder how the assumption in this literature—that one cannot readily distinguish between man's moral and religious capacities—is correlated with the Western religious beliefs about God's will being a moral will.

Religions all involve outlooks toward the future, as well as orientations from the past—not only in grand historical and even cosmological terms, but also with reference to individual and personal life. Jewish and Christian thinkers, and ordinary believers, have looked forward to the coming of a Messiah, or to the Reign or Rule of God which will bring with it peace and justice, love and harmony among men. Or, cosmologically, they have believed that all things come from God and return to God, and, in some cases, that there is a *telos* in nature and in history which is bound to be fulfilled. These future-oriented notions are never totally devoid of moral overtones; in serving the God whose reign is to come one is to do morally right deeds, to prepare the way with anticipations of that coming by seeking justice and peace among men. Can one easily separate religion and morality when the orientation of one's intentions is toward God, whose reign is a moral (whatever else it is) rule?

Or individuals are admonished to be directed toward the fulfillment or salvation of their own souls. Morally wrong deeds (sins) jeopardize this; morally right deeds, if they do not secure it with certitude, at least are expressions of a proper outlook toward God. In St. Augustine's view, for example, to love God and to love the city of God above all things is to be reoriented in one's moral life in a way that meets better the moral well-being of the world. Can the religious and the moral be separated easily in such a view? In the Letter to the Ephesians, the Christians are admonished, among other ways, in the following: "For be very sure of this: no one given to fornication or indecency, or the greed which makes idols of gain, has any share in the Kingdom of Christ and of God" (Eph. 5:5, New English Bible). Does the threat about the future, stated in "religious" reward terms (or can we say they are only "religious"?), mean that the admonitions against fornication and greed are not really "moral" admonitions in this case, since they are so closely tied to what some would call "prudential" (and therefore not moral) calculations?

These "wonderings" might find themselves fixed on a statement of Flavius Josephus, written about A.D. 96 in a treatise he wrote in defense of Judaism. With reference to Moses, Josephus wrote, "And the reason why our lawgiver in his legislation far exceeded all other legislators in usefulness to all, is that he did not make religion a part of virtue, but had the insight to make the various virtues parts of religion; I mean justice, fortitude, self-control, and the mutual harmony of all things of the members of the community with one another. All our actions and studies and words have a connection with piety towards God, for our lawgiver has left none of these things indefinite or undetermined."[1] Note that not just the virtues, but all human actions "have a connection" with piety. Josephus' statement can be broadly applied to Christianity as well.

Traditionally, then, Judaism, Catholicism, and Protestantism (these are the only religions I feel competent to comment on; Islam clearly ought also to be included) have not separated religion and morality. The arguments, of course, are about what that "connection" is, since there seems to be some distinction between morality and piety. The question of whether one can be "moral" without being "religious" is not a central point of dispute in major historical texts of these religions. The Noachic commandments have traditionally been assumed to be binding on all men, not just on Jews: they include both more distinctively religious and more distinctively moral prohibitions—against idolatry, incest, murder, profaning God's name, robbery, and eating parts cut from living animals; also included is a more positive requirement—to form instruments of justice. Christians have from earliest times, in one way or another, used notions of "natural law" to indicate that morality is grounded in human nature, and not just in historical religious tradition or in "revelation." The issue is whether, within Jewish and Christian religious communities, morality and religion can be as easily separated as some modern distinctions find possible. It is the thesis of this paper that there is a coherence, or correlation, between 1) the theological assertions that God a) is sovereign and b) his will is

[1] *Against Apion,* excerpted in N. N. Glatzer, ed., *The Judaic Tradition* (Boston: Beacon, 1969), p. 141.

moral; 2) the view of the person as responsible to this God and thus
not readily "separated" into moral and religious capacities, dispositions, and behavior; and 3) the view that the destiny of the world
and of individual persons, the orientation toward the future, is directed toward this God. I am not, in this essay, interested in making
a theological defense of this view for purposes of justifying religious
morality. I do wish to make the case that discussions of the relation
of religion and morality which attend to particular historical religions, those dominant in Western culture, should take into account
the theological premises of those religions, and that if they do, the
distinction (not to mention separation) between the two is more
difficult to make than appears to be the case in some discussions.
Concretely, it is not as easy to distinguish between "religious" and
"moral" assertions, obligations, human capacities, and ends, as one
might wish for it to be from an interest in logical analysis. In the
Western religions, their documents, their histories, and the experiences of their communities, religion and morality are joined together,
intertwined, commingled, indeed in some instances and respects
even unified. Further, because of this commingling and unification,
the concept of morality itself evades the precise definition and usage
that philosophers often seek. It is a richer (or perhaps looser), or
more complex one in traditional Western religious discourse than it
is in some other contexts.

In the end, it might be that some philosophers might simply view
religious texts as confused and confusing, or they might impose distinctions on the texts in such a way as to make explicit distinctions
which they deem to be implicit in the texts. And, in the end, some
religious thinkers might judge the philosophical distinctions to be
artificial and inappropriate with reference to Western religious
views of life, or views of the world. Some might even resist pressing
the questions of the relation of religion and morality, for as practical
as well as speculative thinkers, they do not see what beneficial effects
for life and action are forthcoming from such an enterprise. As one
who has long sought to gain more clarity in the "moves" made in
theological ethics, I have no sympathy for such rejection. But as
basically a religious thinker, working in the Western religions, I
find it necessary to deal with the claims of texts in a sympathetic,
as well as critical manner.

THEOLOGICAL ASSERTIONS ABOUT GOD'S WILL AS A MORAL WILL

In the controversy over the relation between is and ought, between "fact" and "value," it has been asserted over and over that one cannot derive an ethical conclusion from a factual premise, unless there is built into that premise already a value or normative element. If this matter can be transposed into the sphere of theology in relation to ethics, it might be framed in the following way. Statements about God (statements of belief in the indicative mood) cannot be premises for ethical statements—referring to commands, rules, moral ends (begging the deontological-teleological questions), or moral virtues —without normative elements or values being built into these theological statements. With reference to what is dominant in the Jewish, Catholic, and Protestant traditions, there is no embarrassment about this being the case. Moral qualities are attributed to God: God is just, or (though some might find it "looser" as a moral term than *just*) God is love. Further, many statements about God are statements about his "activity," and the sorts of things God does are, at least in a loose sense, moral. In some instances, he *judges* the unrighteous, and indeed punishes the unjust, as he also rewards the just. Or he seeks the "well-being" (which at least some philosophers would admit to include moral aspects) of his people. Other statements about God refer to his purposes for man and creation, and again some of these are moral in a strict sense, and others include aspects which many persons would call moral. Thus, Western religions not only provide reasons for being moral—men ought to be moral out of gratitude for the goodness of God in his gift of life, for example—but the very understanding of God, the ultimate power on whom all in some sense depends, includes specifically moral aspects; thus religion and morality are intimately bound together. It is the purpose of this section of the essay to establish the warrant for this generalization from selected but typical religious texts, and to indicate what inferences can be drawn from this with reference to the framing of the basic questions addressed in this volume. I am, to reiterate a point made in the Introduction, not interested in showing that to be moral one must be religious, but rather in showing that men who have been and are religious, in the context of Judaism and Christianity at least, find morality to be entailed (perhaps even in the strict logical sense) by their religion.

Three sorts of materials from the Scriptures shared by Jews and Christians can be cited to show that God's will was believed to be a moral one. They are a) materials which attribute moral commands to Yahweh in the context of his Sinai covenant with Israel; b) materials which attribute God to be the indictor and judge who condemns not only religious idolatry, but also immorality; and c) materials which attribute moral significance to events in which God is the purposive agent, so that it can be said that God's "activity" is moral activity. In an article which has the scope of this one, these materials cannot get the sophisticated historical or analytical development that they ought to have; no fundamental injustice to them is done, however, with regard to present purposes.

MORAL COMMANDS OF GOD

The Torah, the first five books of the Bible, by the time it was canonized, according to critical scholarly opinion, had several major source documents and redactions. Its most widely known sections are those which contain the Ten Commandments, Exodus 20, and Deuteronomy 5. In each case, they are prefaced by statements that God spoke them. Whatever are the actual historical origins of the commandments, it is clear that in the belief of the community both "tables" of the Decalogue have divine authority. The point to be stressed here is not that one can distinguish between "religious" and "moral" commandments, but rather that the "moral" commandments, like the "religious" ones, are part of the expressed will of God.

In the great "Holiness Code" of Leviticus, judged to be the latest source document of the Torah, one finds a detailed account of the commandments attributed to God. In the nineteenth chapter there is an excellent example of the admixture of what in modern distinctions are moral and religious rules. The opening of the discourse gives a general command, together with a theological justification for it, and for the subsequent specific commands: the Lord orders Moses to speak to the community, "You shall be holy, because I, the Lord your God, am holy." What follows are commands against idolatry, ritual or cultic laws (what cultural anthropologists might call taboos), rules of harvesting which benefit the poor and the alien, and precise moral rules of conduct. A sample of this admixture will show how "moral" and "nonmoral" rules both are grounded in God's "holiness."

You shall not steal; you shall not cheat or deceive a fellow-countryman. You shall not swear in my name with intent to deceive and thus profane the name of your God. I am the Lord. You shall not oppress your neighbor, nor rob him. You shall not keep back a hired man's wages till next morning. You shall not treat the deaf with contempt, nor put an obstruction in the way of the blind. You shall fear your God. I am the Lord. You shall not prevent justice, either by favoring the poor or by subservience to the great. You shall judge your fellow-countrymen with strict justice. You shall not go about spreading slander among your father's kin, nor take sides against your neighbor on a capital charge. I am the Lord. You shall not nurse hatred against your brother. You shall reprove your fellow-countrymen frankly and so you will have no share in his guilt. You shall not seek revenge, or cherish anger towards your kinsfolk; you shall love your neighbor as a man like yourself. I am the Lord. You shall keep my rules. [Lev. 19:11–19a, NEB]*

In this quotation, a number of the commandments of God are unambiguously "moral" even in the most restrictive use of that term. Some of them could be described as instances of specifications of formal notions of justice, such as the command to judge one's countrymen with strict justice. Equals are to be treated equally, and all of one's countrymen are "equal." Neither greatness nor poverty are relevant substantive qualifications which would require unequal treatment. To each his due; thus the hired man's wages should not be withheld until morning. In addition to ideas of formal justice, one might also use the general notion of respect for persons, and read some of these commands as substantive specifications of that principle. "You shall not treat the deaf with contempt, nor put an obstruction in the way of the blind." The text indicates rules about attitudes: one is not to nurse hatred, or cherish anger.

Obviously it did not occur to the compiler of the code to distinguish "religious" commands from "moral" commands in the text. Indeed, the Decalogue's two "tables" are more easily distinguished in their texts than are the religious and the ethical here. Commands not to profane God's name and to fear God are interspersed among the more distinctively ethical commands. It is not unfair to the text

* All biblical quotations in this article are from this translation.

to read all of these as specifications of the general command, "You shall be holy." Nor is it unfair to see the theological justification for that general command to be also a justification for the subsequent specifications: "You shall be holy, *because* I, the Lord your God, am holy." The members of the community are obligated to keep the more distinctively moral commands not because (or at least, not *only* because) an ethical justification can be given them, such as principles of formal justice, or of respect for persons. Rather they are obligated to keep them because they are God's will. They are in accordance with God's nature as holy. This holiness is not simply an otherness which inspires an awesome response; it is also a moral holiness. An infraction of the moral rules is an offense against God. It would logically follow, as it does historically, that the word *sin* refers not only to a moral wrong, but to a relationship of disobedience to God, and that recompense for moral wrongs includes not only consequent duties to the offended person, but duties to God. It also follows logically—and historically—that a right relationship to God is expressed not only in cultic practices, but also in adherence to the moral commands. Righteousness includes a moral aspect, although it cannot be reduced to its moral aspect.

God is not only the moral lawgiver in the Scriptures shared by Jews and Christians; he also makes moral indictments—he is the moral judge. The language of arraignment or indictment is found in a number of the prophetic books that came out of the interpretation of political and social events in the period in which the kingdom established by David is threatened, divided, and finally conquered. One long example of such can be found in the visions "received by Isaiah," and recorded in the first five chapters of the book designated by his name. The prophet speaks the judgment of the Lord; it is the Lord who is the judge. In 3:13ff., the text reads:

> The Lord comes forward to argue his case
> and stands to judge his people.
> The Lord opens the indictment
> against the elders of his people and their officers.

He warns, he cajoles, he promises punishment; he specifies the wrongs for which the offenders will be judged.

What sorts of deeds are subject to the indictment and judgment of God? It is clear that they include both what modern analysts would call "moral" and what they would call "religious" misdeeds. In 1:4 the prophet begins:

> O sinful nation, people loaded with iniquity,
> race of evildoers, wanton destructive children
> who have deserted the Lord,
> spurned the Holy One of Israel
> and turned your backs on him.

The root evil is, no doubt, that of spurning and turning their backs on the Holy One of Israel. It is even clear that proper cultic practices are not sufficient to meet their obligations to God; 1:11ff. begins, "Your countless sacrifices, what are they to me?" and the rhetorical power continues to pour scorn on the merely cultic. The section ends with moral admonition in 1:17:

> Cease to do evil and learn to do right,
> pursue justice and champion the oppressed;
> give the orphan his rights, plead the widow's cause.

The arraignment continues with many items that are offensive to the Lord. Some are clearly "religious"—the land is filled with idols, for example. Others are more clearly "moral": 3:12, "Moneylenders strip my people bare, and usurers lord it over them"; 3:14, "the spoils of the poor are in your houses"; 5:8, "Shame on you! you add house to house and join field to field until not an acre remains, and you are left to dwell alone in the land"; 5:22-23, "Shame on you! you mighty topers, valiant mixers of drink, who for a bribe acquit the guilty and deny justice to those in the right." Indeed, it is interesting to note that the indictments are made in descriptive language; they are accounts of events and behavior which are, in a sense, factual. But as in many other moral indictments, it is assumed that the behavior which is described is clearly morally wrong, in this case a violation of God's moral will. It is not necessary for the prophet to announce in God's name which moral principles and rules have been violated by the described behavior. The hearer, even if he is unaware of the religious moral background of these words, can easily infer what the implicit "commands" are under which men are indicted.

Again, it is clear that God's will is a moral will, and that violations of justice are deemed worthy of his wrathful judgment. Turning from the Lord is turning away from his moral law, and disobedience to his moral law is turning away from the Lord. Indeed, adherence to the "religious" requirements of sacrifices, festivals, and prayers is not sufficient to avoid the judgment of God. It is not possible to separate religious and moral obligations, for both have one source, and to fulfill the moral obligations is to be faithful to God. He is the moral judge, and to be free from his wrath requires a morally righteous life.

The notion of God's activity being in part a moral activity, or activity in which the moral and the religious cannot easily be divided, has roots in the prophetic literature. It finds modern development in recent Protestant theological ethics, and to two of those we shall turn subsequently. A thorough survey of biblical material would demonstrate that the community believed God acted for the immediate benefit of the people (he brought them out of bondage in Egypt, for example) as well as acted against their immediate interests in order to chastise them. Some passages are couched in the language of a declaration of intention on God's part, such as one in the visions of Isaiah. In 1:24ff., for instance, the "word of the Lord, the Lord of Hosts, the Mighty One of Israel" is:

> Enough! I will secure a respite from my foes
>   and take vengeance on my enemies.
> Once again I will act against you
> to refine away your base metal as with potash
>   and purge all your impurities. . . .

The political and military struggles of the Kingdom of Judah were read by the prophets to be events in which God's purposive action was the most significant meaning. Jerusalem had turned away from its Lord; it had been guilty of unfaithfulness to him—both "religious" and "moral" infidelity. The destructive armies of the enemies were the executioners of God's indignation against his people. For example, the prophet Ezekiel, speaking "the words of the Lord God": "I am handing you over to those whom you hate, those who have filled you with revulsion; and they will make you feel their hatred" (Ezek. 23:28–29). The enemy is the agent of the judgment of God; defeat in battles is retribution for the sins (moral and religious) of the nation.

This theme of God's activity has been developed in recent Protestant theological ethics. Its treatment there surely appears to some philosophers to be a confused and confusing one with reference to the distinctions which are the themes of this book. Yet from one Christian theological standpoint, there is no lack of intellectual integrity, coherence, and consistency in what appears to be indiscriminate running together of religious and moral language, of theological and ethical concepts. Two American theologians can serve as examples of the theme of "God's action" as it pertains to ethics. They are Paul Lehmann and the late H. Richard Niebuhr. Both serve to illustrate the main point of this section, namely that the presence of certain theological principles makes it difficult to draw sharp distinctions between religion and morality.

In the case of H. Richard Niebuhr, one has a theological principle of a monotheistic sovereign God who is the only absolute, and who is the ultimate good, and who "acts" in and through all actions and events that persons experience. Thus the primary principle for persons is one of responsibility to God. "Responsibility affirms: 'God is acting in all actions upon you. So respond to all actions upon you as to respond to his action.' "[2] Niebuhr distinguishes this from theological ethics of teleological and deontological types. "Monotheistic idealism says: 'Remember God's plan for your life.' Monistic deontology commands: 'Obey God's law in all your obediences to finite rules.' "[3]

The scope of ethics in such a theological view is broad in comparison with some current restrictive usages and practices. It necessarily includes theological and religious elements. The sovereignty of "the One beyond the many" implies that there are no human actions which are without implicit if not explicit relations to the purposive activity of God in human events. For the religious person, the one who has explicit confidence in and loyalty to God (Niebuhr's explication of the idea of faith), there is a particular vocation, namely, to interpret his actions and interactions in the light of what can be known about God's action. Because he eschewed "natural theology" for epistemological as well as religious reasons, Niebuhr (as an admittedly culturally relative religious person) had to use the Jewish-Christian "story" for his understanding of God's action. Thus, to get

[2] H. Richard Niebuhr, *The Responsible Self* (New York: Harper, 1963), p. 126.
[3] Ibid.

a clue to what sorts of actions God is engaged in, the theological ethician has recourse to the events recorded in the Scriptures, and to the interpretations of them in the subsequent tradition. Current human situations are interpreted in the light of the sorts of purposes men have deemed God to have in the past, including his purposes for the future. This interpretation occurs through two media, it seems to me; one is generalizations gleaned from the biblical story so that God's purposes can be said to be "creative," "governing," "judging," "redeeming," "reconciling," etc. Thus the practical questions for men are framed: what might God's judging and reconciling actions be in one's relations to his family, or in relation to the struggles between blacks and whites in our society. The other medium is drawing historical analogies between past events in which men believed God was acting and present events. Thus Niebuhr could write an article during World War II on "War as Crucifixion," just as black theologians now use the exodus of the Hebrew people from Egypt analogously in relation to current events to show that God's activity is "liberating" activity.[4]

The confluence of what for other purposes can be distinguished as religion and as morality makes such distinctions difficult in this instance. The goodness of the Sovereign One is moral and nonmoral goodness (as distinguished by many philosophers); man's sin is both absence of confidence in God and absense of fidelity and loyalty to him and his purposes (religious and moral); reconciliation, as a characteristic of God's action, has ends or consequences which are more inclusive than moral ones (in a restrictive usage), and yet always include the moral. Man responds in his actions not merely to finite, and therefore relative, beings, but he is also accountable to "the One beyond the many." Since, in an ultimate sense, nothing occurs apart from God's action, every human action is at least an implicit response to God. Since God's actions, in an ultimate sense, have a unity, and since this unity includes the "moral" and the "religious," it is not possible to separate religion and morality in such a theological view.

The other American theologian who has written a major book on ethics which rests on a theological principle of God's action is Paul Lehmann. Lehmann's view is much more Christocentric than

---

[4] See James Cone, *Black Theology and Black Power* (New York: Seabury, 1969), p. 44.

Niebuhr's; for him ethics done in a Christian context is *"the reflection upon the question and its answer: What am I, as a believer in Jesus Christ and as a member of his church, to do?"*[5] In outline form the structure of the task which follows is this: First, in view of a theological principle which Lehmann develops about God's activity, the first practical question is: "What is God doing?" In a sentence that is surely puzzling to moral philosophers, it is clear what the source of the answer to that will be. *"Christian ethics . . . is oriented toward revelation and not toward morality."*[6] Second, on the basis of a process of theological generalization from a doctrine of Christ, that question is answered, "The focus of divine activity is what God in Christ has done and is doing in the world for the humanization of man,"[7] or as he states in a number of places, the focus is on what "God is doing to make and keep human life human." The human, we can note here, has normative content, part of which is developed from the term "maturity." Thus other sentences which might puzzle philosophers: ". . . *Christian ethics aims, not at morality, but at maturity. The mature life is the fruit of Christian faith. Morality is a by-product of maturity.*"[8] And "maturity *is* the integrity in and through interrelatedness which makes it possible for each individual member of an organic whole to be himself in togetherness, and in togetherness each to be himself."[9]

The third step, then, is to answer the question, "What am I to do?" The answer is that I am to conform my action to God's action; I am to do what is human, or humanizing. A fourth question follows, namely, "How do I know what God is doing?" In part its answer is that, having a theonomous (to be contrasted with autonomous and heteronomous) conscience, one is "immediately sensitive to the freedom of God to do in the always changing human situation what his humanizing aims and purposes require."[10]

Of most interest for this essay is the notion that God is doing "humanizing" work in the world. As was noted, the basis for this understanding is distinctively Christian in its theological content, though

[5] Paul Lehmann, *Ethics in a Christian Context* (New York: Harper, 1963), p. 25.

[6] Ibid., p. 45.

[7] Ibid., p. 316.

[8] Ibid., p. 54.

[9] Ibid., p. 55.

[10] Ibid., p. 358.

it is also affirmed that men can be doing what God's purposes require apart from explicit Christian faith and belief. To say that
wherever "humanization" is occurring in the world God is purpos-
ively acting, is not unfair to Lehmann. The "human" is a normative
term, and while the definition of maturity quoted above is the most
explicit content given to the term, this is sufficient to indicate that
actions which flow from maturity will be moral, i.e., humanizing. If
ambiguities in Lehmann's statements can be bracketed for our purposes, one can line out the bare bones of a theological ethical argument. God is active, and his activity is moral, at least in a loose sense.
Man is enabled to be sensitive to this activity, and to be, in a sense,
its agent. God also enables man to have this sensitivity through life
in the Christian community. (This part of the thesis I have not included previously.) Thus when one is doing moral activity, is he
doing "religious" activity? Not in the sense that no distinction could
be drawn between worship, for example, and civil rights work. But
in the sense that all moral activity is ultimately God's activity, there
is a religiously significant quality to all morality. And in the sense
that the principle characteristic of God's activity is humanization,
all "religious" activity (activity in accordance with God's activity)
has moral significance. Presumably even worship could be justified
in part on the grounds that it is humanizing.

The analyses of God as lawgiver, as indictor and judge, and as
actor are made to establish the point that within the theological
principles characteristic of Judaism and Christianity, there is, if not
a unity of religion and morality, at least a confluence of them which
makes their separation impossible, and their distinction difficult.
This is not to deny that logical distinctions cannot be made for
analytical purposes, and that such analyses are useful and important. It is, however, to suggest that when one's point of orientation
is the theological claims made by historical Western religions, the
task is more complex than it is if stipulative or formal definitions of
religion and morality are used. Where religious belief posits as its
primary theological principle a sovereign God whose "qualities" are
both moral and nonmoral, whose will is both moral and nonmoral,
moral obligations to him are religious obligations, and moral actions
have religious significance. The concept of morality becomes difficult to pin down from this perspective, as does the concept of re-

ligion. Both have reference to beliefs and experiences which are richer and more complex than some definitions of each permit.

THE MORAL AGENT IN THEOLOGICAL PERSPECTIVE

Two further points which are implications of the theological perspective remain to be made. One pertains to religion and morality as they relate to the end of moral actions. The other, on which attention is focused here, pertains to the moral agent, as a religious and moral person. In both the Introduction and the previous section I have mentioned that Western religious notions of man as sinner, and his acts as sinful, involve both moral and religious referents, as do notions of man and his deeds as righteous. The principal thesis is that both in the ideas and practice of Western religions, it is not always easy to separate the religious from the moral dispositions. The same applies also to religious and moral consciousnesses and actions.

A vast theological and popular religious literature could be surveyed in order to make this point, from Scripture on forward through history. Not only sin and righteousness, but repentance, grace, sanctification, atonement, justification, and other important terms and their usages would lend themselves to study. Not only theological treatises, but books of spiritual guidance could be studied in Jewish, Catholic, and Protestant traditions—and not only books, but the articulated experiences of religious man. To be disoriented toward God is to be disordered in oneself, and disordered with others. To be disordered in relation to others is to be askew within oneself, and to be disordered toward God. Such general affirmations hold for wide varieties of specific accounts of the issues involved.

Selectivity is necessary, obviously, and two terms which are central to Western religions must suffice for this essay. One is sin, and the other is repentance. Only brief allusions to grace, renewal, and righteousness will be made, though they beg for elucidation.

Certain acts have been judged to be sins, or to be sinful, and agents are called sinners or sinful. Distinctions can clearly be made between deeds that are sinful in an exclusively religious sense, and others which are more weighted on the side of morality. The use of idols by the heirs of Moses is clearly a "religious" sin; yet as the notion of idolatry is theologically considered and developed, its implications for morality become clearer. It becomes the false absolutization of a value, which is "religiously" wrong because it displaces God, but it also has a morally bad consequence because it disorients a man's relations and deeds with reference to others.

Even treatises which make a *prima facie* distinction begin to move toward aspects of life where it is harder to hold them. In *Orchot Tzaddikim, The Ways of the Righteous,* a fifteenth-century Jewish treatise of moral and spiritual edification, the unknown author writes: "Sins are of two kinds. There are those between man and God alone. Blessed be He, such as Tefillin, Fringes, the Sukkah and similar commandments. And there are sins between one man and another." His subsequent illustration of failure to fulfill a positive precept in man's duties to God, however, involves what might be judged to be a duty toward other men in a way that the cultic failures first listed do not. "And if he has not been in the habit of giving charity, he should make a point from the time of his repentance and thereafter to give charity."[11] It is not unfair to comment that the failure to give charity is the failure to obey a commandment of God, and thus is a sin against God, but it is also to deprive other men of what they are due as a result of God's command, and thus is a sin against man, a moral wrong in a stricter sense. But the two cannot be separated.

A study of the words used in the history of Western religions to signify what often comes out in modern usage as undifferentiated sin shows the varieties of referents for the term.[12] In some places, both from Hebrew and Greek, the term "missing the mark," or "missing the way" is more precise; here, in a sense, sin is objectively making a mistake. In some instances the context is clearly legal, and a "sin" is a breach of the law. If the language of missing the mark or breach of law seems to be more at home in those experiences where there is a clear designation of what one is expected to do objectively, sin as rebellion is at home in the relations of father and son, and signifies a subjective and willful opposition to the normal expectation. Other terms suggest less culpability, and represent an erring or straying out of ignorance. This is a sufficient noting of the variety to make clear that historically, at least, terms which can be set in a theological context are also used in non-theological contexts, and

[11] *The Ways of the Righteous,* trans. Seymour J. Cohen (Jerusalem and New York; Feldheim, 1969), p. 489.

[12] See the section "Sin," translated from Gerhard Kittel, ed., *Theologisches Wörterbuch zum Neuen Testament,* in J. R. Coates, trans. and ed., *Bible Key Words* (New York: Harper, 1951).

thus the serious religious issues come to the surface when one asks whose "way" is being missed, against whom man is rebelling, from what paths he is straying. When the way, the rule, the path, is God's, the offenses involved are also offenses against him. The waywardness is not merely moral in character; it has religious significance as well.

It is this conviction that a moral offense is also an offense against God that marks the religious view of immoral persons as sinners, and of immoral acts as sins. The theological frame of reference for interpreting acts binds their religious and moral characters together. For example, in Christianity, St. Thomas Aquinas accepts one of St. Augustine's statements as sufficient to get to the heart of the matter, a view which (with some variations) Christians for centuries have learned in catechetical instruction. A sin is any "word, deed, or desire contrary to eternal law." For Thomas this could be worked out at one level by human reason: an act is evil insofar as it does not conform to its due measure, and its due measure could be ascertained by reason's account of the natural law. But at this level one has only a proximate rule or measure of conduct; at the primary level the rule or measure is the eternal law, "which is God's reason, so to speak." From a theological perspective, then, an act which is contrary to the orders of "nature" is also contrary to the order of God. Thus Thomas can make the following distinction: "The theologian considers sin chiefly as an offense against God, and the moral philosophers, as something contrary to reason."[13] While there is a "root" to man's propensities to violate the eternal law, and while man's natural disposition to act in accord with his nature can be severely wounded, the dominating view of sin in St. Thomas is violation of a theologically interpreted moral order.

In the major Reformation writers one has more emphasis on man as the sinner, on the root propensities which flow into deeds that are morally wrong. In Lutheranism, for example, sin was deliberately interpreted against "scholastic" doctrines, in such a way that it referred primarily to the "first table," the more "religious" part of the Decalogue. Melanchthon's "Apology of the Augsburg Confession" makes this point several times. With reference to the scholastics, he wrote:

Thus when they talk about original sin, they do not mention

[13] Thomas Aquinas, *Summa Theologica* I-II, q. 71, a. 6.

the more serious faults of human nature, namely, ignoring God, despising him, lacking fear and trust in him, hating his judgment and fleeing it, being angry at him, despairing of his grace, trusting in temporal things, etc. [Article II, 8]

We wanted to show that original sin also [in addition to con-cupiscence] involves such faults as ignorance of God, contempt of God, lack of fear of God and of trust in him, inability to love him. These are the first flaws in human nature, transgress-ing as they do the first table of the Decalogue. [Article II, 14][14]

The connection with morality is explicated in the corpus of Luther-anism in terms of bad trees bearing bad (immoral) fruits, and good trees bearing good (moral) fruits. It is the unfaith of the moral agent that is at the root of immoral acts; the ground of moral evil is a "religious" ground. To be sure, persons can use their reason to fulfill justice and do what is morally right from an objective moral standpoint, but men of faith work through love in such a way that their acts are not only morally righteous but also right in relation to God.

Calvin also sees sin as a "pravity and corruption of our nature, diffused through all parts of the soul . . . and producing in us those works which the Scripture calls 'works of the flesh.'" He views this, as does Luther, as being in accord with St. Paul's view of sin. "The works which proceed thence, such as adulteries, fornications, thefts, hatreds, murders, revellings," are the fruits of sin.[15] The relation between "sin" and the "fruits of sin" is described in other metaphors by Calvin; they are "like the emission of flame and sparks from a heated furnace, or like the streams of water from a never failing spring."[16]

The reformers were not oblivious to distinctions parallel to mod-ern ones. They made a distinction between the loss of "original righteousness" on the one hand, and its consequences for moral righteousness on the other, between sin and its fruits. They also distinguished in their views of salvation between the righteousness which men are freely given in relation to God through the work

---

[14] In Theodore G. Tappert, ed., *The Book of Concord* (Philadelphia: Muhlenberg Press, 1959), pp. 101, 102.

[15] John Calvin, *The Institutes*, bk. II, chaps. 1, 7, in the Allen trans. (Philadelphia: Westminster Press, n.d.), Vol. I, p. 274.

[16] Ibid., p. 275.

of Christ on the one hand, and a renewed capacity for moral righteousness on the other. In some instances their moves between the two referents of both sin and righteousness are clear and distinct, such as in Luther's sermon of 1519, "Two Kinds of Righteousness." There, as elsewhere, he speaks of "alien righteousness," "instilled in us without our works by grace alone," which "is set opposite original sin" on the one hand, and "proper righteousness" in which men "work with that first and alien righteousness" to live a "manner of life spent profitably in good works" on the other. This second righteousness is "the product" of the first, "actually its fruit and consequence."[17] In other instances, however, particularly in Luther's writings, terms are used in both a soteriological (doctrine of salvation) context and a moral context in an imprecise way.[18]

For purposes of this essay the insistence of Reformation theologians on an internal relationship, an intrinsic relationship, between the state of human life before God (both in "sin" and in "faith") and man's moral capacities and actions in relation to other men is important to stress. How this relationship was described varied, and, as we have seen, metaphors were frequently used.[19] But in the light of the theological principle of a sovereign God before whom all men stand, sin is both an offense against God and against man, and righteousness is a state in relation to both. What can be distinguished in terms of primary referents can never be separated, and both are always bound together from a theological point of view.

When one looks at admonitions to repent, or examines what acts of repentance, or a repentant posture, mean in the history of Judaism and Christianity, another area is opened in which the confluence of religion and morality is notable. The biblical books are full of admonitions to repent. Whether one is dealing with ancient legends

[17] Martin Luther, "Two Kinds of Righteousness," in J. Dillenberger, ed., *Martin Luther* (Garden City, N.Y.: Doubleday Anchor Books, 1961), pp. 88–89. The point is made more technically and complexly in the 1521 treatise "Against Latomus," *Luther's Works,* American Edition, XXXII (Philadelphia: Muhlenberg Press, 1958), pp. 136–260.

[18] Hans O. Tiefel, in his unpublished dissertation "The Ethics of Gospel and Law," Yale University, 1967, has provided the best analytical account I have read of what are *prima facie* confusions in Luther's use of law and gospel as both soteriological and ethical terms, pp. 6–117.

[19] My book *Christ and the Moral Life* (New York: Harper, 1968) focuses on this whole issue of the relation of Christian faith to ethics, and attends particularly in chaps. 3 and 4 to the moral agent.

of pre-Mosaic times, with the Law itself, with interpretations of the history of the people of Israel in historical or prophetic books, with John the Baptist, Jesus, or early Christianity, the theme is always strong. Traditions of penitence and penitential acts continue through various religious holy days, rites, and sacraments to the present day. Penitential prayers and psalms are a significant part of the popular religious literature of the West. Perhaps Psalm 51 is one of the most familiar:

> Be gracious to me, O God, in thy true love;
> In the fullness of thy mercy blot out my misdeeds.
> Wash away all my guilt
>   and cleanse me from my sin.
> For well I know my misdeeds,
> and my sins confront me all the day long.
> Against thee, thee only, I have sinned
> and done what displeases thee. . . .
>
> [vs. 1–4a]

The assumption in all views of repentance is that persons are morally and religiously culpable or accountable for their actions; they are (to use a word seldom discussed in contemporary moral philosophy except with reference to law) guilty. They are culpable not merely in the face of moral rules, or social mores, but are culpable before God. Thus the penitence that is consequent is expressed in relation not only to persons whose rights or well-being have been offended, but also to God. It is "against thee," that is, God, that men have sinned.[20]

Books of edification abound not only with exhortations to examination of conscience, but with procedures found effective to engage in such reflection. St. Ignatius of Loyola, in his *Spiritual Exercises*, develops ways in which the conscience is to be examined, and "Rules for the Discernment of Spirits." In William Law's *A Serious Call to*

---

[20] Prayers used by Christians can be cited to confirm this. For example, the Anglican prayer of General Confession reads: "Almighty and most merciful Father, we have erred and strayed from thy ways like lost sheep. We have followed too much the devices and desires of our own hearts. We have offended against thy holy laws. We have left undone those things we ought to have done; and we have done those things which we ought not to have done. . . ." A commonly used Lutheran prayer reads: "I confess to thee, Almighty and most Holy God, that I have sinned in thought, word, and deed, through my own fault, my own most grievous fault. I acknowledge my want of faithfulness in holy service, my want of discipline and obedience, my want of love. . . ."

a Devout and Holy Life, as in Puritan and other devotional writings, the examination of conscience is a primary step in the development of a life of virtue. *The Ways of the Righteous,* which has previously been cited, has chapters on various "virtues" and "vices" (much like Christian books of the same period), such as modesty, pride, love, hatred, joy, remorse, anger, graciousness, laziness, and generosity. Near the end one comes to a long chapter on repentance with extensive sections that also are similar to those found in Christian books: seven reasons why a man should repent early, seven things to be taken to heart to achieve complete repentance (for example, "Therefore a man who would repent must know the sins he has committed"), "twenty matters that are among the principal considerations in repentance" (for example, "take seriously the transgressions one has treated lightly"), twenty-four things which impede repentance (for example, hating to be reproved), four motivations ("The first is . . . because he has come to recognize his God"), six things which stir the heart, etc.[21] The chapter closes: "He who is a true penitent should seek to do good deeds, and to remove himself from thoughts of this world, and to strengthen himself in the counsel of God, Blessed be He, and to take shelter in His shadow. . . ."[22]

Many more writings could be cited to show that the religious person in the West measures his qualities of moral life, as well as his deeds, in relation to what he comprehends God's will to be. His obligations, even strictly moral ones, are obligations to God, and thus it is to God he owes repentance. In the practice of religious life there is a commingling of devotion to God and devotion to moral duty, of fear of divine wrath and a sense of culpability before the neighbor. "It is necessary," the Jewish writer tells us, "to make known to everyone that every man who wants to bring his soul towards attainment of good qualities [moral and nonmoral] must mingle reverence to Heaven with each and every quality. For it is fear of the Lord, reverence of God, that strengthens all our qualities."[23]

Finer distinctions between religion and morality could be drawn than those made by religious writers on subjects of sin and repentance, as they could be with writers like John Wesley or Schleier-

[21] *The Ways of the Righteous,* quotations from pp. 463, 465, 475, 497.
[22] Ibid., p. 553.
[23] Ibid., p. 15.

macher, who make great claims for a moral transformation as
a result of repentance and grace. A close analysis of possible distinctions is not the purpose of this essay. Rather, it is clear that the
moral agent, under the sovereign God whose will is moral, is seen
to have a religious-moral relation to God, to be a religious-moral
being, and thus he is guilty before God for his moral wrongs, he
repents to God, and what he expects from God is not only forgiveness but also a moral renewal. Stipulative definitions of religion
and morality that make them exclusive of each other, do not easily
fit the complexities of the historically developed theories of theological ethics, or the practical experiences of the overlap, if not unity,
of religion and morality, religious and moral consciousness, and
deeds.

THE ENDS OF MORAL ACTION IN THEOLOGICAL PERSPECTIVE

Ethics can be defined in such a way that the ends of action are excluded from consideration as part of the discipline; at least in some
more stringent forms of deontological ethics the ends are secondary
in consideration. Certainly it is difficult to validate the opinion that
Christian ethics are exclusively deontological, just as it is difficult
to defend the opinion that Christian ethics are exclusively teleological. Certainly the central tendency of Catholic Christian ethics has
been a teleological one; the fulfillment or realization of the propensity of individuals and communities toward their true nature and
common good has been a basic point. One issue often discussed by
moral philosophers in the past several decades is whether "good" is
a moral term, and if it is, what distinctions are to be drawn between
its moral and nonmoral uses. To those persuaded of the great importance of such distinctions, a major bloc of historical Christian
ethics will appear to be unsophisticated and crude, for the religious
life has been interpreted by many to be directed toward God as the
object of intentionality, toward a vision of God, and the love of God.

Orientation toward God as "the Good" has been judged to be of
importance not merely for piety, but for morality. If, as thousands
of Calvinists have been taught, "the chief end of man is to glorify
God and enjoy him forever," surely considerations of salvation and
eternal life supersede those of morality. And so it is; Christianity
(more than Judaism) has been concerned about the salvation or
redemption of man. But the primacy of this "religious" intention

has not ruled out the importance of morality. To have God as the ultimate object of intention does not rule out, but rather includes, moral ends. We have seen that repentance for sin and renewal by grace have moral referents. So it is that the love of God, or the vision of God, also has moral referents. Thus, acting to "the glory of God" is not limited to prayers of thanksgiving and hymns of praise; all of man's actions are to glorify God, including his moral actions.

There is no doubt that the influences of Platonic and Aristotelian philosophies have been great in giving shape to the structure of a major part of teleological Christian ethics. But the biblical texts are not without affinities to teleology. There are Psalms which join the vision of God with morality. Psalm 24:3–6 reads:

> Who may go up the mountain of the Lord?
> And who may stand in his holy place?
>   He who has clean hands and a pure heart,
> who has not set his mind on falsehood,
>   and has not committed perjury.
> He shall receive a blessing from the Lord,
>   and justice from God his saviour.
>   Such is the fortune of those who seek him,
>   who seek the face of the God of Jacob.

A moral life has significance in the religious quest to "see God."

It is just as fair to say that the religious quest to "see God," to seek after his Kingdom, to be oriented toward his future (to refer to a current theological theme) has significance for the moral life. A vision of the Kingdom of God which will come has provided both motivation and an understanding of "the good" for many religious persons. Just as prophets looked toward the "peaceable Kingdom," in which the lion and the lamb could lie down together, so modern writers in Christian ethics have seen a view of the highest good spelled out in Jesus' teaching about the Kingdom of God. They have sought to realize, or approximate, or anticipate, that ideal kingdom in present historical circumstances. It is to be a kingdom of justice, of love, of brotherhood, of peace and harmony. Orientation toward God as the end (*telos*) of man has been orientation toward the good of man; the good of man has surely included moral values as well as nonmoral values.

In sentences which must be odd to the minds of secular moral philosophers, K. E. Kirk, the late Bishop of Oxford, states the central thesis of his great historical and systematic study, *The Vision of God:* "It is suggested . . . that the doctrine 'the end of life is the vision of God' has throughout been interpreted by Christian thought at its best as implying in practice that the highest prerogative of the Christian, in this life as well as hereafter, is the activity of *worship;* and that nowhere except in this activity will he find the key to his ethical problems. As a practical corollary it follows that the principal duty of the Christian moralist is to stimulate the spirit of worship in those to whom he addresses himself, rather than to set before them codes of behavior."[24] Obviously, in Kirk, we have a more Catholic form of Christianity than a Protestant one, as, for example, we saw in Lehmann's dictum that Christian ethics aims at maturity rather than morality. In the Reformed theologian, morality is a by-product of maturity; in the Anglo-Catholic theologian, it is a by-product of worship, of contemplation, of orientation toward God.

In a sense the whole historical discussion is a commentary on the relations of the two parts of the love commandment to each other: "Thou shalt love the Lord thy God, and thy neighbor as thyself." The ways in which orientation toward God as the end (*telos*) of man in turn affects man's moral activity have been interpreted differently in Christian theological ethics. Susceptibility to an amoral mysticism is often, if not always, present in such views. If the highest good, the vision of God, is always a transmoral good (as it is in much of medieval Christianity), does not the fulfilled religious quest always carry men beyond the claims of the neighbor? If the eternal order is man's true home, does he not have to reject the temporal order to find his peace and his good in God? The duality of God and the world can be interpreted to imply a dualism between man's true and highest good to be found in God, and his temporal (including moral) good. Not every theologian who has written in this vein has succeeded in maintaining a significant relation between orientation toward God as the Good, and orientation toward the temporal moral good, between love of God and love of neighbor.

One claim made by St. Bernard of Clairvaux and others is that after contemplation (not likely to be the ultimate unity with God,

[24] K. E. Kirk, *The Vision of God: The Christian Doctrine of the Summum Bonum* (London: Longmans, 1931), pp. ix–x.

which St. Bernard doubted to be attainable "in this life"), one's love
for God leads to a zeal for righteousness (including morality) in
one's own life, and among men. Here the effect is upon one's volitional capacities, upon motivation in the sense of movement of will
as well as reasons for action. But there is another sort of effect that
is claimed. In his discussion of the love commandment in the first
of four stages of love, St. Bernard indicates that it is possible to love
the neighbor out of interest in oneself, and that while this is not
perfectly commendable, it does extend self-love to the common good,
and thus benefits the neighbor. "Nevertheless," he continues, "in
order that it may be perfect justice to love one's neighbor, it is imperative that it be referred to God as its cause. Otherwise, how can
he love his neighbor without alloy who does not love him in God?
He surely cannot love in God who does not love God. God must be
loved first, in order that one's neighbor, too, may be loved in God."[25]
It is the last sentence of the quotation which entices the intellect.
Several steps are involved in the wider context of the stages from
which this passage comes. For our purposes, it is interesting to note
that loving the neighbor for the sake of love of self issues in some
beneficial consequences. But it is a "lower" form of neighbor love.
The highest form of neighbor love is to love him in God. I believe
it is not unfair to interpret St. Bernard to indicate that one's neighbor love is morally "better" when he is loved in God. And to love the
neighbor in God requires that first one love God.

This, it seems to me, is a simple paradigm of a theological ethical
claim made in many different forms, particularly by Catholic theologians of a Platonic and mystical bent. Only in loving God first
and foremost, can one have proper love of self and of neighbor. Or
to make the point more formally, in becoming rightly related to God,
one becomes rightly ordered with reference to his own proper interests, and rightly ordered in relation to his neighbor.

St. Bernard echoes his great predecessor St. Augustine in this
line of thought. With reference to the love command, St. Augustine
wrote, "For he alone has a proper love for himself who aims dili-
gently at the attainment of the chief and true good . . . this is nothing else but God. . . ." "Now you love your self suitably when you
love God better than yourself. What, then, you aim at in yourself

[25] St. Bernard, *On the Love of God*, chap. 8.

you must aim at in your neighbor, namely, that he may love God
with a perfect affection. For you do not love him as yourself, unless
you try to draw him to that good which you are yourself pursuing."[26]
These quotations would not support my thesis unless "the chief
and true good" included the moral as well as nonmoral good.

That it does, for St. Augustine, can be seen from an earlier section of *On the Morals of the Catholic Church,* in which he develops
the consequences for the moral virtues:

> I hold virtue to be nothing else than perfect love of God. For
> the fourfold division of virtue I regard as taken from four forms
> of love. [He defines them]: that temperance is love giving itself
> entirely to that which is loved; fortitude is love bearing all
> things for the sake of the loved object; justice is love serving
> only the loved object, and therefore ruling rightly; prudence is
> love distinguishing with sagacity between what hinders it and
> what helps it. The object of this love is not anything, but only
> God, the chief good, the highest wisdom, the perfect harmony.[27]

The point is that love of God rightly orders the moral virtues toward
their true end, and therefore rightly orders man's relations and actions toward other men. For the good (moral and nonmoral) of all
is served when all are rightly oriented by love for God.

Jonathan Edwards, the greatest theologian in American history,
shared this Augustinian vision in which the nonmoral and the
moral aspects of the good were held together. Clyde Holbrook summarizes Edwards' theme, "What Edwards offered was a vision of
the spiritual universe in which a profound organic and aesthetic
harmony was what God aimed at as a desirable goal."[28] "True
virtue," Edwards wrote, "most essentially consists in *benevolence
to being in general.*" "It is that consent, propensity and union of
heart to being in general, which is immediately exercised in gen-

[26] St. Augustine, *On the Morals of the Catholic Church,* chap. 26. For St.
Thomas Aquinas' treatment of these issues, see *Summa Theologica,* II-II, q. 44
and q. 26.

[27] St. Augustine, *On the Morals of the Catholic Church,* chap. 12.

[28] Clyde A. Holbrook, "Edwards and the Ethical Question," *Harvard Theological Review,* 60 (1967), p. 168. See Roland DeLattre, *Beauty and Sensibility in the Thought of Jonathan Edwards: An Essay in Aesthetics and
Theological Ethics* (New Haven: Yale Univ. Press, 1968) for a fuller
secondary account.

eral good will."[29] It follows, for Edwards, "that true virtue must chiefly consist in *love to God*,"[30] and that properly ordered benevolence to other beings follows from the love of God. "And so far as a virtuous mind exercises true virtue in benevolence to created beings, it chiefly seeks the good of the creature; consisting in its knowledge or view of God's glory and beauty, its union with God, conformity and love to him, and joy in him."[31] Again, as in our previously cited writers, the moral life is understood primarily in terms of a proper fundamental orientation, in this case, benevolence to being in general. The chief end of man is to love and glorify God. By having this *telos*, one can be rightly oriented toward other beings.

In viewing God as the end of all man's life, it is still possible to distinguish between certain actions or virtues as being more weighted on the side of morality than are others, but the significance of moral actions is not exhausted by their moral consequences or their rightness. They are occasions in which one's vision of and love for God is expressed. And in one's contemplation of and love for God, one's moral actions find direction. The "good" life flows from love of "the Good." God is "the Good." His goodness is moral and "nonmoral." To love God is not only to be fulfilled in the goodness of spiritual beauty and happiness; it is to be rightly and beneficially (in moral senses) related to others.

CONCLUSION

I have not sought to justify the absence of clear distinctions in theological and religious texts. It goes without saying that the literature cited in this essay to show some ways in which morality does not have complete autonomy from religion in the West invites a more rigorous and refined analysis than it has received here. The modest purpose here is to show that from within a theological frame of reference, there are reasons why religion and morality are not two autonomous spheres of activity and experience, why theology and

[29] Jonathan Edwards, *The Nature of True Virtue* (Ann Arbor: Univ. of Mich. Press, 1966), p. 3.
[30] Ibid., p. 14. See also *Charity and Its Fruits,* sometimes published under the title, *Christian Love*.
[31] Ibid., p. 25.

ethics are not separable realms of ideas and languages. Thus, if in logical analysis of their relations, the analyst desires to deal with the claims of Western religions, he must take into account the theological principle of a sovereign God whose being has moral qualities and whose will is a moral will. He must take into account some of the implications of this principle for understanding the moral agent, and the ends of his action, as these have been developed in religious moral literature in the West.

Not only is there a commingling, and in some respects a unification of religion and morality in the pious texts and experiences of the Western religious communities. There is also a commingling of religious and moral references in many of the key concepts that have been developed in the theologies of these traditions, such as God, sin, and righteousness. The fact that philosophers cannot come to agreement on the definition of morality, on the distinctions between the moral and the nonmoral becomes clear even from a non-professional reading of pertinent literature. The concept of the moral is used in different ways by different groups of philosophers, and even by those whose work bears close resemblance to each other. In a religious and theological context a sharply limited definition of morality becomes even more difficult to develop.

THE RELATIONSHIP BETWEEN RELIGION AND ETHICS IN JEWISH THOUGHT

Louis Jacobs

This essay seeks to explore the relationship between religion and ethics as conceived of in the Jewish tradition. As in every other investigation of a great Jewish theme it must begin with the Bible, the source book of the Jewish faith, but the biblical writers were not systematic philosophers, so that it would be futile to examine the Bible in order to discover any kind of direct treatment of the relationship between religion and ethics. There are, in fact, no words for these concepts in classical Hebrew. What Zangwill said of the Rabbis of the Talmud is true of the biblical authors—they were the most religious of men but had no word for religion. Nor had they a word for ethics. The ethical injunctions in the Bible are numerous but nowhere in this book, or, better, collection of books produced over a long period, is there any consideration in abstract of the nature of ethics. Just and righteous conduct is urged with passion but Socratic-like discussions as to how justice is to be defined are totally absent. Yet, indirectly, the biblical viewpoint of the relationship between religion and ethics is stated clearly enough and can be detected without any attempt at reading into the texts ideas they do not contain.

It is as well to begin with the Decalogue. In six of the ten commandments ethical conduct is enjoined as a divine imperative: "Honour thy father and thy mother"; "Thou shalt not murder"; "Thou shalt not commit adultery"; "Thou shalt not steal"; "Thou shalt not bear false witness"; "Thou shalt not covet." (In the Bible and in the Jewish tradition generally the Decalogue is called the "ten words" not the "ten commandments" but this is irrelevant for

our purpose since they are obviously put forward as divine commands.) Although God commands them it is not implied that the
command is the reason for their observance, so that if God had commanded man to steal or to murder this would have been the right
thing to do. On the contrary, the commands are announced in such
a way as to suggest that they are already fully comprehensible to
man as the basis for living the ethical life. It is implied that man by
his nature knows that it is wrong to steal and right to honor his parents, so that what God is ordering him to do is to be true to himself,
to be a man, to be fully human. God, being God, so it is implied,
could not have commanded him to do wrong. Once God has commanded, however, the command itself is, of course, an additional
reason for its observance.

The Covenant Code is introduced with the words: "These are
the rules that you shall set before them" (Ex. 21:1). The famous
modern biblical exegete Ehrlich understands the words "that you
shall set before them" to mean "for their approval," i.e., that God
wishes the people to see that the laws He gives are fully in accord
with human nature and humans are bound to say "Amen" to them.
But even if Ehrlich's comment is too fanciful it remains true that
nowhere in the whole of the biblical record is there the faintest
suggestion that God imposes upon man arbitrary rules which must
be obeyed purely on the grounds that God so desires. The Deuter-
onomist states it explicitly: "Behold, I have taught you statutes and
ordinances, even as the Lord my God commanded me, that ye should
do so in the midst of the land whither ye go in to possess it. Observe
therefore and do them; for this is your wisdom and your understanding in the sight of the peoples, that when they hear all these statutes,
shall say: 'Surely this great nation is a wise and understanding people'" (Deut. 4:5–6). The "peoples," without the benefit of revelation, are quite capable of acknowledging the "wisdom" and
"understanding" inherent in the precepts. "And what great nation
is there, that both hath statutes and ordinances so righteous as all
this law, which I set before you this day?" (Deut. 4:8). The statutes
and ordinances are not recommended because they are in the law
but, so it is suggested: they are in the law because they are "righteous." (This is not to say, of course, that the Deuteronomic authors
held that the *sole* purpose of the observance of the laws was for the
"nations" to acknowledge Israel's wisdom.) An Abraham can even

plead with God Himself to practice justice: "That be far from Thee to do after this manner, to slay the righteous with the wicked, that so the righteous should be as the wicked; that be far from Thee; shall not the Judge of all the earth do justly?" (Gen. 18:25). The similar plea is put into the mouth of Moses: "O God, Source of the breath of all flesh! When one man sins, will you be wrathful with the whole community?" (Num. 16:22).

Writing at the end of the twelfth century, Moses Maimonides was close to the meaning of the above passages when he remarks:

> There is a group of human beings who consider it a grievous thing that causes should be given for any law; what would please them most is that the intellect would not find a meaning for the commandments and prohibitions. What compels them to feel thus is a sickness that they find in their souls, a sickness to which they are unable to give utterance and of which they cannot furnish a satisfactory account. For they think that if those laws were useful in this existence and had been given to us for this or that reason, it would be as if they derived from the reflection and the understanding of some intelligent being. If, however, there is a thing for which the intellect could not find any meaning at all and that does not lead to something useful, it indubitably derives from God; for the reflection of man would lead to no such thing.[1]

For the group Maimonides attacks it is an offense to suggest that the laws of God are "reasonable," for if they are then they are all too human. Only a law which humans would never arrive at by their own understanding has a right to be called divine. Maimonides attacks this as folly, as a sickness of the soul. "It is as if, according to these people of weak intellects, man were more perfect than his Maker; for man speaks and acts in a manner that leads to some intended end, whereas the deity does not act thus, but commands us to do things that are not useful to us and forbids us to do things that are not harmful to us." Maimonides relies on the verse in Deuteronomy we have quoted. Moreover, he applies the idea to all the precepts including the ritualistic taboos for which there is no evident reason. For Maimonides there is reason behind all these and it is man's task to discover what the reason might be, because the notion of God

[1] Moses Maimonides, *Guide of the Perplexed,* trans. S. Pines (Chicago: Univ. of Chicago Press, 1963), pp. 523–24.

ordering man to carry out purposeless acts is abhorrent to Maimonides' religious sensibilities.

According to the critical view, the Pentateuchal laws which "God spoke to Moses, saying," are the fruit of the people's sustained reflection on ethical conduct and of their ripe ethical experience. Thus, to give one example among many, when the older laws regarding inheritance were seen to be unfair to women, the "test case" of the daughters of Zelophehad (Num. 27:1–11) was constructed and read back into the times of the great lawgiver since this development of just legislation was seen as God's command: " 'Why should the name of our father be done away from among his family, because he had no son? Give unto us a possession among the brethren of our father.' And Moses brought their cause before the Lord. And the Lord spoke unto Moses, saying: 'The daughters of Zelophehad speak right: thou shalt surely give them a possession of an inheritance among their father's brethren; and thou shalt cause the inheritance of their father to pass unto them. And thou shalt speak unto the children of Israel, saying: If a man die, and have no son, then ye shall cause his inheritance to pass unto his daughter' " (vs. 4–8). In these instances the right course for man came to be seen as God's will for him and hence "given" to Moses by God.

In many of the Pentateuchal laws the reason for their observance is stated, a reason which appeals to man's innate ethical sensibility. "And a stranger thou shalt not oppress; for ye know the heart of a stranger, seeing ye were strangers in the land of Egypt" (Ex. 23:9). "If thou at all take thy neighbour's garment to pledge, thou shalt restore it unto him by that the sun goes down; for that is his only covering, it is the garment for his skin, wherein shall he sleep? And it shall come to pass, when he crieth unto Me, that I will hear; for I am gracious" (Ex. 22:25–26). "Thou shalt not have in thy bag diverse weights, a great and a small. Thou shalt not have in thy house diverse measures, a great and a small. A perfect and just weight shalt thou have; a perfect and just measure shalt thou have; that thy days may be long upon the land which the Lord thy God giveth thee. For all that do such things, even all that do unrighteously, are an abomination unto the Lord thy God" (Deut. 25:13–16). "Thou shalt not abhor an Edomite, for he is thy brother; thou shalt not abhor an Egyptian, because thou wast a stranger in his land" (Deut. 23:7).

The same theme is found constantly in the prophetic writings. If the good were simply identified with the will of God it would be tautologous to say, as the prophets do, that man should obey God's will *and do good*. "Will the Lord be pleased with thousands of rams, with tens of thousands of rivers of oil? Shall I give my first-born for my transgressions, the fruit of my body for the sin of my soul? It hath been told thee, O man, what is good, and what the Lord doth require of thee: only to do justly, and to love mercy, and to walk humbly with thy God" (Mic. 6:7–8). "Wash you, make you clean, Put away the evil of your doings from before Mine eyes, Cease to do evil; Learn to do well; seek justice, relieve the oppressed, Judge the fatherless, plead for the widow" (Isa. 1:16–17). The prophet Amos castigates Damascus, Gaza, Tyre, Edom, Ammon, and Moab for atrocities they have perpetrated, even though these peoples had received no divine law, the implication being that man is capable of discerning right from wrong by the natural light within him (see Amos, chaps. 1 and 2). Indeed, nowhere in the prophetic writings are the "nations" condemned for worshiping their gods, only for the ethical abominations such as child sacrifice associated with the worship. The very detailing of separate ethical offenses in prophetic admonition is itself proof of the contention that for the prophets each of these offenses is wrong in itself and they are consequently not covered by the blanket condemnation of disobedience of God's will.

> Oh that I were in the wilderness, In a lodging-place of wayfaring men, that I might leave my people, and go from them! For they are all adulterers, An assembly of treacherous men. And they bend their tongue, their bow of falsehood; And they are grown mighty in the land, but not for truth; for they proceed from evil to evil, And Me they know not, saith the Lord. Take ye heed every one of his neighbour, And trust ye not in any brothers; For every brother acteth subtly, And every neighbour goeth about with slanders. And they deceive every one his neighbour, And truth they speak not: They have taught their tongue to speak lies, They weary themselves to commit iniquity. [Jer. 9:1–4]

The autonomy of ethics is similarly adumbrated in the Rabbinic literature. It is implicit in the very classification by the Rabbis of the precepts into the two groups, "between man and God" (e.g., prayer, study of the Torah, wearing phylacteries) and "between man and his neighbor."

> For transgressions that are between man and God the Day of Atonement effects atonement, but for transgressions that are between a man and his fellow the Day of Atonement effects atonement only if he has appeased his fellow. This did Rabbi Eleazar ben Azariah expound: *From all your sins shall ye be clean before the Lord* (Leviticus 16:30)—for transgressions that are between man and God the Day of Atonement effects atonement; but for transgressions that are between a man and his fellow the Day of Atonement effects atonement only if he has appeased his fellow. [Mishnah, Yoma 8:9]

The idea is found in the Rabbinic literature that God Himself keeps His laws. The Greek saying that the law is not written for the king is quoted and it is said that a human king decrees laws for others but need not keep them himself, whereas God orders man to rise in respect before the aged and He did this Himself, as it were, out of respect for Abraham (Jerusalem Talmud, Rosh Ha-Shanah 1:3). The Rabbis give as examples of commandments "which if they had been written in Scripture should by right have been written": the laws concerning idolatry, immorality, bloodshed, robbery, and blasphemy (Babylonian Talmud, Yoma 67b). The third-century Palestinian teacher Rabbi Johanan said: "If the Torah [the law] had not been given we could have learnt modesty from the cat, honesty from the ant, chastity from the dove, and good manners from the cock who first coaxes and then mates" (Babylonian Talmud, Eruvin 100b). Gentiles, to whom the Torah was not given, could still be righteous and the righteous of all nations have a share in the World to Come (Tosefta, Sanhedrin 13:2). Stories are told of Gentiles who observe such obligations as honoring parents in a manner superior to that of the Jews (Babylonian Talmud, Kiddushin 31a). In this Talmudic passage the late second-century teacher Rabbi Hanina observes that if Gentiles who are not commanded to honor parents are so heavily rewarded for honoring them Jews who are *commanded* to do so will be rewarded all the more since one who does that which he is commanded to do is greater than one who does it without being commanded. The idea here seems to be that by a natural human propensity that which is commanded awakens rebellion. There is a need to kick against the traces. The verboten has its subtle allure. Man finds it easy to do the most difficult things except when these are in response to the call of duty. In any event it is clearly acknowledged that the moral life needs no religious spur to be effective. When God, it is further said in the same passage, began the ten commandments with "I am the Lord thy God" and "Thou shalt have no other gods," the nations of the world declared that He was "expounding for His own glory." But when they heard Him say: "Honor thy father and thy mother," they acknowledged the earlier commandments, i.e., they saw that even the first two were not for God's sake but for the benefit of man.

The nearest a strongly ethically orientated religion like Judaism comes to a complete separation between religion and ethics is in the following remarkable Talmudic comment (Babylonian Talmud, Kiddushin 40a):

> "Say ye of the righteous, when he is good, that they shall eat the fruit of their doings" (Isaiah 3:10). Is there then a righteous man who is good and a righteous man who is not good? But he who is good to Heaven and good to man, he is a righteous man who is good: good to Heaven but not good to man, that is a righteous man who is not good. Similarly, you read: "Woe unto the wicked man that is evil; for the reward of his hands shall be given unto him" (Isaiah 3:11). Is there then a wicked man that is evil and one that is not evil? But he that is evil to Heaven and evil to men, he is a wicked man that is evil: he who is evil to Heaven but not evil to man, he is a wicked man that is not evil.

Somewhat misleadingly, this is rendered by Montefiore and Loewe as: "One who is good towards God and good towards men is a good righteous man: and one who is good towards God but bad towards men is not a good righteous man. Similarly: one who is bad towards God and bad towards man is a bad bad man; one who is bad towards God but not bad towards man is not a bad bad man."[2] Montefiore remarks:

> In these strange words, the Talmud seeks to distinguish between the commands in the Law which are ordered by God, but which do not relate to our fellow-men, and those commands

[2] Claude Montefiore and H. Loewe, *A Rabbinic Anthology* (London: Macmillan, 1938), pp. 285–86.

which do relate to our fellow-men. The former set of commands are less weighty than the latter. Thus one might say, from this point of view, the Jew who violates the Sabbath, does not observe the Day of Atonement, etc. but who honours his parents, and is charitable, just and kind towards his fellows is "not a bad bad man," whereas he who does just the reverse, is "a not good righteous man."[3]

Loewe admits that the difficulty is a real one but suggests that the cause of it might be the deficiency in Hebrew of abstract terms. Actually, the Rabbis here use the terms "wicked" (*rasha*) and "righteous" (*tzaddik*) in the technical sense of what we would today call a man with religious feeling. They are, in fact, calling attention to the phenomenon that it is quite possible for a man to have a strongly developed religious or "numinous" sense but to be at the same time a thorough scoundrel so far as his ethical conduct is concerned. The passage contains no *ethical* judgment as Montefiore suggests it does. The meaning is brought out more clearly if, instead of "bad bad man," "good bad man," etc., we paraphrase: "bad irreligious man"; "good irreligious man"; "good religious man"; "bad religious man." At all events it is suggested here that one can speak of a man as having a strong moral character without him having any use for religion and the Rabbis are saying that such an assessment of human character need not be wrong since religion is one thing and ethics another, though, of course, for the Rabbis, Judaism demands both.

Before leaving the Rabbis it is perhaps worthwhile referring to Moritz Lazarus' rejection, in the name of the Rabbinic attitude, of von Hartmann's reproach that "theism may not suffer a moral principle above or beside the Divine Being." Lazarus quotes the Targum (the Old Aramaic translation of the Bible), which renders Genesis 3:22 as: "See, man is unique, knowing of himself good and evil" and he concludes:

> The moral principle is, indeed, not above and not beside the Divine Being; it is *in itself*. Precisely for that reason it is at the same time *in God*—in God in as much as he is the prototype of morality. To repeat: not because the principle is in God is it the moral principle, but because it is the moral principle, in itself and absolutely, therefore it is necessarily in God.[4]

[3] Ibid.
[4] Moritz Lazarus, *The Ethics of Judaism* (Philadelphia: Jewish Publication Society of America, 1900), pp. 130–31.

The medieval Jewish thinkers, influenced by Greek philosophy in its Arabic garb, began to think systematically about their religion. In the year 933 the great Babylonian teacher Saadia Gaon compiled his *Beliefs and Opinions,* in which he has a classification of the precepts of the Torah into the *rational* and the *revealed,* a classification much utilized by subsequent thinkers.[5] The rational precepts, which include the ethical, would be recognized as binding even without revelation. Revealed precepts (such as the Jewish dietary laws) are not irrational, there is a reason for them (a view which Maimonides followed, as above) but here obedience to God's will is more prominent. Obviously man would not know the revealed precepts without revelation. He would not wear phylacteries or refrain from eating pork if he were not *commanded* to do so, for how would he otherwise know that this is what God would have him do? But what need is there, asks Saadia, for revelation in connection with the rational precepts? If man can know them without revelation, if, in the terminology we use nowadays, they are autonomous and are to be kept because it is right to do so, not because they are enjoined in Scripture, why are they, in fact, revealed through the prophets? His basic answer is that revelation is required to avoid all uncertainty and for the precise details of how the rational precepts are to be carried out. Thus, for example, it is true that man would know by his own reason that it is wrong to steal but revelation is required in order to inform man how property is to be acquired. Saadia seems to be saying that without religion's precise teachings man's moral sense would still function but it would be confused in application. In Saadia's own words:

> A further example is that, although reason considers stealing objectionable, there is nothing in it to inform us how a person comes to acquire property so that it becomes his possession. It does not state, for instance, whether this comes about as a result of labor, or is effected by means of barter, or by way of inheritance, or is derived from what is free to all, like what is hunted on land or sea. Nor is one informed by it as to whether a sale becomes valid upon the payment of the price or by taking hold of the article or by means of a statement alone. Besides these, there are many other uncertainties pertaining to this subject which would take too long and would be too difficult to

[5] Saadia Gaon, *Beliefs and Opinions,* trans. S. Rosenblatt (New Haven: Yale Univ. Press, 1948), Pt. III, chaps. 1–3.

enumerate. The prophets, therefore, came along with a clear-cut decision for each instance. Another example is the question of the expiation of crime. Reason considers it proper, to be sure, that whoever commits a crime should expiate it, but does not define what form this expiation ought to take: whether a reprimand alone is sufficient, or a *malediction* should go with it, or flogging too should be added. In the event that the punishment take the form of flogging, again, the question is how much, and the same applies to the malediction and the reprimand. Or it is possible that no satisfaction will be obtained except by the death of the criminal. And again it might be asked whether the punishment should be the same for whoever commits a certain crime, or whether it should vary from person to person. Then the prophets came and fixed for each crime its own penalty, and grouped some of them with others under certain conditions, and imposed monetary fines for some. For these considerations, then, that we have enumerated and other such reasons, it is necessary for us to have recourse to the mission of God's messengers. For if we were to defer in these matters to our own opinions, our views would differ and we would not agree on anything. Besides that, we are, of course, in need of their guidance on account of the precepts prescribed by revelation, as we have explained.[6]

Strictly relevant to our theme is the acute analysis of Moses Maimonides (1135–1204) of Greek and Hebraic ethical ideals where these seem to be in conflict.[7] Who is the better man, asks Maimonides, the one who has no desire to do wrong or the one who wishes to do wrong or the one who wishes to do wrong but refrains by exercising constant self-control? The Greek thinkers appear to be saying that the better man is the one who has no desire to do wrong, no murder in his heart, no urge to take that which does not belong to him, no hateful or harmful thoughts. The Talmudic Rabbis, on the other hand, seem to be saying the exact opposite. The Rabbis seem to maintain that man should have a desire to sin and a man should not say that he would not do this thing even if it were not forbidden. For instance, the Rabbis maintain that a man should not say that it is impossible for him to eat forbidden food but he

___

[6] Ibid., p. 146.
[7] Moses Maimonides, *Eight Chapters* (New York: Columbia Univ. Press, 1912), chap. 6.

should rather say that he would like to eat it and wants to eat it only his Father in heaven had commanded him not to do so. Maimonides resolves the conflict by a neat (some have felt an over-neat) distinction between religious and ethical laws. The Rabbis are thinking of purely religious laws and here the element of obedience is paramount. The man who has no desire to eat forbidden food because, for example, he dislikes its taste does not abstain out of religious conviction and since the act itself is ethically neutral his abstention has no religious value. But the Greeks are thinking of ethical demands and the Rabbis would agree that to refrain from murder by exercising self-control is to fall short of the purpose of the ethical laws, which is to produce the good character the possessor of which has no wish to harm others.

Also relevant to our theme is the medieval discussion of the purpose of divine worship. Moses Nahmanides (1194–1270), for instance, in his *Commentary to the Pentateuch*, considers whether divine worship is for God's sake or for man's.[8] Nahmanides first quotes the Midrash (Genesis Rabbah 44:1) on the verse: "The word of the Lord is tried" (Ps. 18:31). The third-century Babylonian teacher Rab is quoted in the Midrash as taking the Hebrew word (*tzerufah*) translated as "tried" to mean "refining." Hence Rab understands the psalmist to be saying that the word of God refines, it has a purifying effect, and he concludes: "The precepts were given for no other purpose than to refine people. For what difference does it make to God whether the act of slaughtering animals for food is done at the neck or from the back of the neck? But the precepts were given only for the purpose of refining people." The meaning of Rab's teaching would seem to be that it is absurd to imagine that the deed in itself can have any significance for God but that it is the effect of the deed on the human character that God wants. The command to kill animals for food in this way rather than that, at the neck rather than from the back of the neck, has as its aim the inculcation of kindliness and compassion. By slaughtering the animal in the most painless way rather than by cruel methods, man's character becomes refined. Nahmanides quotes this passage because he sees in it the key to the Rabbinic understanding of the purpose of worship. By worshiping God, by obeying His laws, which all have

---

[8] Moses Nahmanides, *Commentary to the Pentateuch*, II (Jerusalem: Mosad, Harav Kook, 1960), pp. 448–51.

the effect of benefiting man and encouraging virtue, man becomes
more perfect, more God-like. God does want us to worship Him, as
it were, but it is not the act of worship in itself that He requires but
the effect it has on the human character. In Nahmanides' words:

> The benefit which comes from the observance of the precepts
> is not to God Himself, may He be exalted, but the benefit is
> for man himself, to keep him far from injury or from evil be-
> liefs or from ugly traits of character or to remind him of the
> miracles and wonders of the Creator, blessed be he, so that man
> might come to know God. This is the meaning of "to refine
> people," that they should be as refined silver. For the silver-
> refiner does not carry out his task without purpose but does it
> in order to remove all the dross from the silver. So it is with
> regard to the precepts. Their aim is to remove every evil from
> our hearts, to make the truth known to us, and to remind us
> of it at all times.[9]

It goes without saying, continues Nahmanides, that God does not
need for Himself the light provided by the lampstand in the Temple
or the meat of sacrifices or the fragrance of incense, but even when
He commands us to remember the wonders He wrought in Egypt
and that He created the world it is not for His benefit or advantage
only that we should know the truth, for our words and our recalling
these things mean nothing to Him.

Thus both Maimonides and Nahmanides from different angles,
and they are typical of medieval Jewish philosophical thought in
general, refuse to identify the good with the will of God. If God's
will can be spoken of at all in this connection, it is, according to
these thinkers, that man should strive to improve his character to
be a good man in the ethical sense.

Maimonides' discussion on the negative side found an echo centuries later on the positive side among the followers of the
nineteenth-century Lithuanian Musar movement, a movement
whose aim was to promote greater inwardness in the religious life
but with profound ethical concern. The Musar teachers encouraged
severe self-scrutiny; every one of man's deeds should be carefully
weighed to see if it accorded with the highest ideals of Judaism. The
opponents of the movement, and they were many, viewed this em-

[9] Ibid., p. 451.

phasis on introspection with suspicion, arguing that it cannot be wholesome for a man always to be taking his spiritual temperature. Be that as it may, the leaders of the movement considered the following question. The devout Jew prefaces the performance of a religious obligation with the declaration that he does it for the sake of God. (The actual formula for this is very late and is mystical in content but for the Musar teachers its mystical aspect was not primary. The important thing for them was that attention was being called to the performance of the obligation as an act of divine worship. The mystical formula is: "I am about to do this for the sake of the unification of the Holy One, blessed be He, and His *Shekhinah*" [= Divine Presence]. It is recited, for example, before donning the prayer shawl or the phylacteries.) Would this apply to the performance of acts of benevolence, to the precept: "Love thy neighbor"? The Musar teachers were divided on this point. Rabbi Zalman Dolinsky used to recite the declaration before he carried out any act of mercy. But Rabbi Simhah Züssel of Kelm argued that "one should fulfill precepts of this order out of natural feelings; they should stem from the natural benevolence of a kind heart," i.e., to invoke the concept of a religious duty here is to frustrate the purpose of the command of love. Rabbi Simhah Züssel gives an interesting turn to the verse: "Love thy neighbour as *thyself*": "Just as self-love is natural to man, requiring no calculations or special intentions, so should be his love for his fellows."[10] The man who has to have the intention of performing a religious duty before he can love others will never progress beyond the *I-It* relationship, to use Martin Buber's terminology, when what is called for is the *I-Thou*. The religious command to love others should be seen as a ladder to be kicked away once it has served as the means by which man attains to the heights to which it is directed.

One of the most powerful protests in modern times against the identification of religion with "human morality" in which the question of God and His commands have no place, is that of Søren Kierkegaard. Kierkegaard's *Fear and Trembling* is a commentary on the story of the binding of Isaac (the *Akedah*, "binding," as it is known in Jewish thought) told in the twenty-second chapter of the book of Genesis. Abraham is bidden by God to sacrifice to Him his

[10] On the views of these teachers see Dov Katz, "The Musar Movement," *Tenuat Ha-Musar*, V (Tel Aviv: Tzioni, 1963), pp. 138–39.

only beloved son Isaac. Abraham, in Kierkegaard's interpretation of the story, cannot be sure that God really wants this dread thing from him but, if He does, Abraham is prepared to carry it out. If it is really God's will then there must be a "teleological suspension of the ethical" and the deed must be done, but of this Abraham cannot be sure. And so he goes in "fear and trembling," ready to obey if need be but haunted all the time by the fear that he may be embarked on an act of sheer murder.

The chutzpa of a Gentile, Jews might protest, to write a midrash on "our" biblical narrative, but what a midrash it is! Only so gifted a writer as Kierkegaard could call attention so effectively to the heart of the ancient tale missed by both the philistine and the pious.

We read in those holy books: "And God tempted Abraham, and said unto him, Abraham, Abraham, where art thou? And he said, Here am I." Thou to whom my speech is addressed, was such the case with thee? When afar off thou didst see the heavy dispensation of providence approaching thee, didst thou not say to the mountains, Fall on me, and to the hills, Cover me? Or if thou wast stronger, did not thy foot move slowly along the way, longing as it were for the old path? When a call was issued to thee, didst thou answer, or didst thou not answer perhaps in a low voice, whisperingly? Not so Abraham: joyfully, buoyantly, confidently, with a loud voice, he answered, "Here am I." We read further: "And Abraham rose early in the morning"—as though it were to a festival, so he hastened, and early in the morning he had come to the place spoken of, to Mount Moriah. He said nothing to Sarah, nothing to Eleazar. Indeed who could understand him? Had not the temptation by its very nature exacted of him an oath of silence? He cleft the wood, he bound Isaac, he lit the pyre, he drew the knife. My hearer, there was many a father who believed that with his son he lost everything that was dearest to him in the world, that he was deprived of every hope for the future, but yet there was none that was the child of promise in the sense that Isaac was for Abraham. There was many a father who lost his child; but then it was God, it was the unalterable, the unsearchable will of the Almighty, it was His hand took the child. Not so with Abraham. For him was reserved a harder trial, and Isaac's fate was laid along with the knife in Abraham's hand. And there he stood, the old man, with his only hope! But he did not doubt, he did not look anxiously to the right or to the left, he did not challenge heaven with his prayers. He knew that it was God the Almighty who was trying him, he knew that it was the hardest sacrifice that could be required of him; but he knew also that no sacrifice was too hard when God required it—and he drew the knife.[11]

A distinguished Jewish theologian, the late Milton Steinberg, writes in fierce opposition to Kierkegaard's interpretation:

> From the Jewish viewpoint—and this is one of its highest dignities—the ethical is never suspended, not under any circumstance, and not for anyone, not even for God. *Especially not for God.* Are not supreme Reality and supreme Goodness one and co-essential to the Divine nature? If so, every act wherein the Good is put aside is more than a breach of His will; it is in effect a denial of His existence. Wherefore the Rabbis define sin as constituting not merely rebellion but atheism as well. What Kierkegaard asserts to be the glory of God is Jewishly regarded as unmitigated sacrilege. Which indeed is the true point of the *Akedah*, missed so perversely by Kierkegaard. While it was a merit in Abraham to be willing to sacrifice his only son to God, it was God's nature and merit that He would not accept an immoral tribute. And it was His purpose, among other things, to establish that truth.[12]

Steinberg has misunderstood Kierkegaard. To be sure, the story has a "happy ending"; the angel bids Abraham stay his hand. And Steinberg is right that God, being God, could not have commanded a man really to murder his son. Kierkegaard is fully aware of the "dread" in the whole episode. His point is rather that if Abraham had been convinced that it was God's will he would have done it because as "knight of faith" his ultimate aim, unlike that of "ethical man," is not subservience to the universal ethical norm but his individual relationship with God. Abraham is "ethical man" as well as "knight of faith." That is why he goes in "fear and trembling." In terms of our analysis we might put it that God wants man to be "ethical man" but this is because to be "ethical man" is part of that which is involved in the relationship the "knight of faith" has with his God.

[11] Søren Kierkegaard, *Fear and Trembling*, trans. Walter Lowrie (Princeton: Princeton Univ. Press, 1969), pp. 35–36.
[12] Milton Steinberg, *Anatomy of Faith* (New York: Harcourt, 1960), p. 147.

This leads to a possible solution to the question which now must loom very large. We have tried to examine how the tension between religion and ethics manifests itself in a particular religious tradition —the Jewish. If, as we have seen, it is a dominant theme in Judaism that religious motivation is not essential for leading the good life in the ethical sense, and if ethics is really independent of religion, what, then, is the connection between religion and ethics? The fundamentalist thinker might follow up the hint thrown out by Saadia that in revealed Scripture we have the precise details of how ethical norms are to be applied in concrete situations. But such a solution is not open to anyone who, under the influence of biblical criticism, cannot see the biblical laws as direct divine guidance of this kind. It might still be argued, as it should be, that there is sufficient wisdom in the religious classics of Judaism to provide help in the inquiry, but even so a subjective element enters into the picture to make Saadia's suggestion less convincing. What then are the religious associations of ethics? The answer is surely that for the believer religion provides life with an extra dimension, as it were. The religious man sees his ethical concern as part of his total relationship with his God. This should not be taken to mean that there is a conflict between love of God and love of man, as George Orwell did, for instance, when he pronounced that you cannot love both God and man. On the contrary, the love of man is part of what is meant by the love of God. In theological language, it is the will of the Father of mankind that all His children should love one another. But this in itself imparts a different quality to man's ethical strivings. Man has no need for the God hypothesis in order to appreciate the claims of the ethical side of human life. If he has to invoke his religion here he is remote from the good as religion sees it. But the religious man believed that God *is* and that His nature is such that every act of love and compassion makes for the fulfillment of His purpose, every act of cruelty and oppression for its frustration. Man is to live both horizontally and vertically, open to earthly needs and responding to them as any other ethical man would do, but with his religious beliefs to add to the scene the infinite glories of heaven.

This idea was emphasized especially by the Jewish mystics. There is, for example, a detailed treatment of our theme in the gigantic compendium of Jewish piety known as *Shenei Luhot ha-Berit* (The Two Tablets of Stone) by the German Kabbalist Isaiah Horowitz

(c. 1555–c.1630). At the beginning of the book under the heading "Creatures," Horowitz discusses the obligation to love all God's creatures and its connection with the other great command to love God.[13] The Babylonian Talmud (Sabbath 31a) tells a well-known tale of the master Hillel. A prospective convert to Judaism approached Hillel requesting the sage to teach him the Torah while he stood on one leg. Hillel replied: "That which is hateful unto thee do not do unto thy neighbor. This is the whole of the Torah. All the rest is commentary, go and learn!" The medieval commentators were puzzled by the tale. What of Judaism's purely religious obligations? The eleventh-century French commentator Rashi, whose commentary is printed in most editions of the Talmud, remarks that Hillel was either referring solely to the ethical precepts or that by "thy neighbor" he meant God. Horowitz uses this as a basis for his contention that in fact both loves—of the neighbor and of God—are really one since God is One and all is from Him. The love of the neighbor is part of the love of the God who created the neighbor. By loving one's neighbor one fulfills God's purpose. Horowitz adds a more mystical note. Since there is a divine spark in the soul of man, who is created in God's image, the love of one's fellow is quite literally the love of God.

Horowitz sums it up as follows:

> In the truth if you examine the matter carefully, you will find that the majority of the precepts depend for their fulfilment on the command to love one's neighbour. First there are all the precepts regarding alms-giving, leaving the forgotten sheaf and the corners of the field to the poor, tithing, honesty in business, the prohibition of usury and many others of a like nature. Then there are all the virtuous traits of character: compassion, kindliness, patience, love, judging others charitably, running to help them when they are in danger, not slandering them or bearing tales, not scorning them or hating them or feeling envious of them, not flying into a rage, not being over-ambitious, these and thousands of other virtues depend on loving one's neighbour and only thus can one become perfect by keeping both the positive and negative precepts. And even with regard to those precepts which have no connection with one's neighbour—the prohibition, for example of forbidden food and of

[13] Isaiah Horowitz, *The Two Tablets of Stone* (Jerusalem edition, 1963), pp. 44b–45b.

eating leaven on Passover—a man will keep them *a fortiori*. For if he loves his neighbour as himself how much more will he love God who loves him with an unqualified and true love, who is Lord of the universe and to Whom all belongs, blessed be He. So you see that the command "and thou shalt love thy neighbor as thyself" is the leg upon which the whole world stands. [There is possibly a hint at the Hillel story here in which there is a reference to "standing on one leg."] So you see that "and thou shalt love thy neighbor as thyself" brings about "thou shalt love the Lord thy God."[14]

Something of the kind would seem to be implied in the normative Jewish approach to this question. The love of other human beings and the ethical life in general are autonomous in that they justify themselves, requiring no support from religion. But there is a religious dimension to life and it has its effect on the whole of life. On the religious view it is God's concern, as it were, how man behaves towards his fellow and the love of the neighbor is the love of God.

[14] Ibid.

"WORTHY OF WORSHIP": A CATHOLIC CONTRIBUTION

Eric D'Arcy

This contribution cannot avoid presenting a somewhat Janus-like appearance.

Sometimes I must speak as a Catholic addressing others: for I have undertaken to summarize briefly the background of assumptions, of principles and beliefs which Catholic moral theory brings to the question under discussion in this book. That I shall do in Section II.

At other times, however, I must write as a Catholic priest who is a member of a typical philosophy department in an English-speaking civil university, addressing fellow priests who work in ecclesiastical institutions. For I welcome this opportunity to meditate a little on the fact that Catholic moral theory has never had deep roots in English-speaking culture, let alone in English-speaking philosophy; and to urge, indeed, that it needs to put down such roots. That I do first, leaving to Section III my own personal suggestions about the topic of this volume.

I

1.1 To begin with, one must remark that Catholic moral theory, as traditionally practiced, has been done largely within ecclesiastical institutions educating young men for the priesthood. These "seminaries" had indeed existed, especially in Germany, from the fifteenth century, but they became widespread as a result of legislation brought down by the Council of Trent (1545–63). Prominent in the education they provided was the study of Moral Theology. This was largely practical in intent, in particular preparing priests for their work in the confessional. But a systematic theoretical basis was provided, and this was, by and large, derived from the synthesis of Christian doctrine and Aristotelian philosophy made by the medieval Scholastics, above all St. Thomas Aquinas.

A series of papal decrees, beginning with the encyclical *Aeterni Patris* of Leo XIII in 1879, insisted that seminary teaching was to be done in the spirit, the conceptual idiom, the categorial framework, and the methodology of Thomism. The Code of Canon Law, which came into force for the whole Latin Church in 1918, stipulated:

> In studying rational philosophy and theology, and in teaching these subjects to seminarians, professors are to follow the method, the doctrine, and the principles of the Angelic Doctor [St. Thomas Aquinas] and hold them religiously.[1]

In the various versions of Neo-Thomism and Neo-Scholasticism that were actually taught, this commonly involved a distinction between "Ethics" and "Moral Theology." "Ethics" was commonly presented as a systematic moral philosophy done within the confines of what could be discovered by human reason unaided by divine revelation. "Moral Theology" was based on, and continuous with, this natural ethic, but incorporated within it the data of revelation, the teachings of Scripture, and the authoritative teachings of the Church.

One result of this was that one really needed to be familiar with the general apparatus of Thomism before being thoroughly capable of assessing many of its specific principles and claims. For instance, the Thomist ethic has commonly been presented as a Natural Law theory. There have of course been many different versions of what is called "Natural Law Theory." Many of them have been concerned with arguments in legal rather than moral philosophy. To my mind, this was to a considerable extent the interest of St. Thomas himself. However, insofar as modern Thomists have drawn on Natural Law theory to sketch an ethic, the version they used was a derivative of Aquinas' general metaphysic of actuality and potentiality. This led to a constant teleological strain in Thomist moral theory. For instance, the classical starting point was to cast about for the "End" of human life and, once having established it, to argue to the "Means" necessary for its attainment. These means came out

1 *Codex Iuris Canonici*, Canon 1366.2 (my translation).

as the items of an ethic: they might be virtues, or they might be morally good or obligatory actions. The same teleological strain was often apparent in arguments about the morality of particular kinds of action; considerations would be adduced to establish the "End" of a particular faculty, and from this inferences were made about the wrongness of certain kinds of action which ran counter to that end: e.g., the end of the faculty of speech was to communicate to others what was in one's mind; and from this, and a few connected principles, a sophisticated morality of truth-telling, lying, and mental reservation was inferred.

Such a basis for ethics immediately invites head-on objections from Hume's famous *No-Ought-from-Is* passage. To anyone familiar with that, perhaps the most celebrated of all paragraphs on moral theory written in English, the objection positively leaps to mind. But here is a point I really do want to stress: Hume's *Treatise* appeared in 1739; yet the centers of Catholic moral theory were so completely insulated from the barest commonplaces of philosophy written in English that book after book, text after text came out repeating the same schema (first, the ultimate End of man, or other subordinate Ends; hence, the "Norms of Morality") without so much as a mention of this familiar objection. Perhaps it would have been different if Hume's seminal paragraph had been sloganized in Latin as, for example, *Ab esse ad debere non valet illatio.*

In addressing myself therefore to my fellow-priests who work on moral theory in ecclesiastical institutions in the English-speaking world, I venture to beg them to turn their attention to the main problems of contemporary English-language, or "anglophone" moral philosophy.

1.2 For two facts are essential, if not exactly central, to understanding contemporary intellectual history; and they are altogether central to understanding the point I want to make.

First, the philosophical movement dominant in the English-speaking world lives and works in well-nigh total separation from that which predominates in the countries of Franco-German culture. In these latter countries the prevailing philosophical movement in recent decades has been that which descends from Kant and Hegel, as well as from Kierkegaard, through Phenomenology, into the different varieties of Existentialism. In the anglophone world, however, the dominant philosophical movement is that which has grown out of the enormous advances in logic pioneered by Frege, Russell, and Whitehead, and philosophized upon by Russell, Moore, and Wittgenstein. British philosophers have often been reluctant to accept a "label" for this movement, but Americans have not been so coy and have commonly called it "Analytical Philosophy." The position was summarized by Abraham Kaplan as follows:

> There is no doubt that the broad philosophical movement which I am loosely designating as "analytic philosophy" is far and away the most influential one in the English-speaking world. In almost every American university, certainly in the British ones, philosophy has virtually come to mean just this kind of enterprise. For the younger generation of students of philosophy, at any rate, the ideas of this movement are thought to be by far the most exciting and promising.[2]

To a large extent these two movements work in mutual isolation, and few practitioners of either pay even lip service to the philosophical value or relevance of the other.

Second, the leadership in modern Christian theology, Protestant and Catholic, has come in great measure from writers whose philosophical and general intellectual background is that of Franco-German cultural life.* If a theology is to be healthy, robust, and "incarnate," it must grow out of its practitioners' own intellectual matrix; and it is surely greatly to the credit of many of these theologians that they have been doing theology, and re-thinking and re-stating the Faith, in terms of the philosophical idiom and intellectual style of their own culture. This tends to be true of *moral* theology as well as of other departments.

Anglophone Catholic theologians have, in the main, been content to follow the lead of their Franco-German colleagues, address-

[2] A. Kaplan, *The New World of Philosophy* (New York: Vintage, 1961), p. 53.

* I use this awkward expression—rather than, say, "continental"—because I mean Germany, France, Switzerland, Austria, Belgium, and Holland. I do not suggest, of course, that there is a perfectly undifferentiated Republic of Letters running through these countries, with no distinctive characteristics according to language and nationality; but there is quite a Common Market of ideas, terminology, style, approach, and background which makes possible a great deal of "dialogue," as they love to say, even between those who disagree on many matters of specific doctrine or thesis.

ing themselves mainly to the theological issues and problems that are uppermost in the Franco-German world. Nobody would deny that many advantages have accrued from this. Anglophone theology has been jolted into new life. It has been enriched and enlivened in many valuable ways. In moral theology, in particular, a much richer vision of Christian moral life has been taking shape; fidelity to Christian morality is seen, not just as obedience to an external code of law, but even more as a response to the Spirit of Christ prompting from within. For the purposes of this paper, however, I would mention three drawbacks arising from the present situation.

1.31 First, there is the matter of *style*. One must not underestimate the importance of intellectual and cultural style in the effectiveness of a theological movement. If its language and manner and ethos, the categories in which and the temperature at which it works, are alien to a country's educated public, then it will tend to be without influence or effectiveness there. Anthony Kenny once remarked on the contrast between the style of a typical continental philosopher and that of Bertrand Russell, whom that philosopher was discussing. Kenny rendered one sentence thus:

> In opposition to the monistic confusion defended by absolute idealism, Russell set up the organic unity of multiplicity, loyally recognizing both the plurality of terms in their undeniable authenticity, and the linking-up of these terms by a system of real relations of objective metaphysical impact.[3]

In particular, Franco-German philosophers when compared with their anglophone contemporaries, commonly evince two characteristics: a heightened dramatic intensity; and a taste for abstractions.

As I have said, it seems to me that it is greatly to the credit of many of the Franco-German theologians that so much of their writing has its philosophical roots in the living philosophical enterprise of their own countries. The style in which a great deal of their writing is couched is the style familiar to people who have been formed and educated in a milieu saturated with that sort of philosophical spirit. This is not just a tactic, a mere device cunningly adopted to "make themselves acceptable" or to "gain influence." Genuinely children of

[3] Review of *Il Pensiero di Bertrand Russell*, by Emmanuele Riverso, in *Mind*, 70 (April, 1961), p. 272.

their own culture, they find it quite natural to do theology in this terminology, conceptual schema, and philosophical idiom which is native to them. The term "Dialogue," which often seems like cant to educated anglophones, can be full of reverberations at more than one level for people in whose philosophical formation the Hegelian dialectic has been a pervasive element, and who are at home with Martin Buber's dialogic philosophy. For people familiar with Heidegger's philosophy of Being and Existence, Tillich's theology of God as "Ground of our being" and "Depth of our existence" has great immediacy and resonance; as has Schillebeeckx's theology of the sacraments as "Personal encounters with Christ" for those at home with philosophies of Existentialist Personalism. For people without such philosophical formation, however, such theologizing lacks the force of immediacy, and can seem to lack point. Even straightforwardly linguistic facts make it hard to bring home the full force of a doctrine of *I-thou* relationships to someone who first needs an explanation of what it is to *tutoyer*. Imagine reading a discussion of freedom and obligation in, say, *Mind* and coming across the following passage by a contemporary German Catholic moralist:

> Moral law indicates to man his true essence as his duty to perform, or in other words: through moral law man is confronted with his true essence, an essence to which he is unconditionally obliged, that creates obligation for him. . . . The unconditional "ought" is the form in which the creaturehood of a person is expressed. Existence under law is the necessary condition of the personal creature.[4]

This sort of thing is true, not only of the *philosophy* that a theologian uses, assumes, or draws upon. It tends to be true even of the general cultural background against which he works. A German theologian writing of the *People of God* as something more than the sum of the individual mortal human beings who belong to it, can count on all sorts of associations and resonances in the reader whose notion of *das Volk* has been formed by a tradition to which Goethe, Schiller, Hegel, Fichte (and Wagner?) made such contributions.

---

[4] Bruno Schüller, *Gesetz und Freiheit: Eine Moraltheologische Untersuchung* (Düsseldorf: Patmos-Verlag, 1966), pp. 11 and 19. English translation kindly provided me by Rev. W. Daniel.

A theologian writing in, say, Australia, can count on no such response.

To a large extent the distinctive features of this philosophical and theological style are perhaps the product of deeper and more pervasive cultural traits. Perhaps the sort of philosophy that takes root in a culture is as much the product as the cause of the people's characteristic cast of mind. The abstractness and the romanticism which German-language culture seems so naturally to produce are incurably alien to the typical educated anglophone. This persuades me that, quite apart from the prevailing interests of professional philosophers, there is little future in our countries for a theology written in the key of The Tragic Sense of Life. That theology will have to be transposed into a very different key before it can ever feed, let alone form, a sustained imaginative Christian vision of the world in us. For us, to adapt a phrase of Nancy Mitford, "No large abstractions, no vague mysticism, no fits of absence, little of the romantic yearning for the unknown."[5] Rather, our typical questions tend to be of the sort, "What does it mean?" "How do you know?" "Does it work?" "What difference does it make?" These are the questions equally of the trained professional doing philosophy, and of the man in the street hearing—or not hearing—the Gospel of Christ. Professor Vincent Buckley, who is so very much a child of the English literary tradition, wrote recently:

> Our task is to contemplate Christ and to work our way into his life, which means expanding our own imagination to reach into his imagination. Most non-Christians are as sick as I am of the language of "confrontation," "encounter," and "the man for others." They ask, "Is he real?", in a sense not entirely unlike the sense in which one might ask, "Is Blake real?" or "Is Hamlet real?"[6]

In 1970 the Holy See issued a new document on the education of students for the priesthood.[7] It insists that, in general, a seminarian's education be done within the context of his own national mentality and culture; and in particular, that his philosophical edu-

---

[5] Nancy Mitford, *Don't Tell Alfred* (London: H. Hamilton, 1960), p. 61.

[6] Vincent Buckley, "The Strange Personality of Christ," in *Quadrant*, XIV (Sydney: September–October, 1970), p. 21.

[7] *Ratio Fundamentalis Institutionis Sacerdotalis*, issued by the Sacra Congregatio pro Institutione Catholica (Rome: Typis Polyglottis Vaticanis, 1970).

cation take account of developments in philosophy in his own country. On these scores, if not on others, I should have thought that
Franco-German houses of ecclesiastical education have a long start
on their English-speaking counterparts. At all events, I see all this
as one drawback arising from the fact that anglophone theologians
are primarily involved in the world of Franco-German theology and
philosophy.

1.32 The second drawback is connected with the first: it concerns
the *topics under discussion.* Contemporary Catholic moral theologians
have very little interest in many of the most crucial questions being
asked by moralists in the English-speaking world.

Of course, there are many burning issues concerning morality
which are canvassed throughout the Western world. That is why it
is such a nuisance that theologians tend to discuss them in a style
so alien to ours; but with goodwill and effort one can come to see
what they have to say. One writer, Frederick Olafson—not a theologian—has attempted to bring the contributions of the two movements together at a point quite closely related to the central interest
of this collection of essays. In the case of Sartre at least Olafson has
set out to argue that

> It is both possible and worthwhile to disengage the elements
> of an ethical theory from the forbidding ontological terminology
> which the existentialists use and to restate them in terms that
> are intelligible to those philosophers who do not share this
> special "ontological" orientation.[8]

In connection with our own question—Is an action immoral because
God forbids it, or vice versa?—one might paraphrase Olafson by
saying that he sees Sartre as a secular Occamist, for Sartre and Occam alike turn upside down the thesis that

> value predicates have meaning by virtue of standing for ob-
> jective qualities or relations that are independent of our feelings
> or volitions.[9]

But for one thing, this does not apply to many Catholic existen-
tialists; and for another, Olafson's argument has drawn some atten-

[8] Frederick Olafson, *Principles and Persons* (Baltimore: Johns Hopkins Press,
1967), p. xiii.
[9] Ibid., p. 4.

tion within the world of Anglo-American philosophy, but very little within the world of Catholic moral theology written in English. The fact is, it is very hard to find moralists working in Catholic seminaries or colleges who contribute seriously to the moral, especially the metaethical, problems engaging the interest of analytical philosophers.

The most obvious example is that of the Naturalistic Fallacy. I have already remarked that Hume's No-Ought-from-Is argument was ignored by Catholic moralists. That state of affairs continued even after 1903, when Moore reformulated the objection and gave it the name by which it has gone ever since. It has dominated a great deal of this century's English-language moral philosophy; but you will be hard put to find so much as a mention of the term in the texts commonly in use in Catholic seminaries, or many colleges, in the English-speaking world. In preparing this essay I turned back to a number of books of moral theology and philosophy used in seminaries in the U.S.A., Australia, and Great Britain. Several of them were manuals of traditional neo-Thomist style and content; several were products of the renewal in moral theology that owes so much to writers like Gilleman, Häring, and Fuchs. In the latter group there were references to Authenticity, to Bad Faith, to the Creation of Values, and other questions of the day in Franco-German moral philosophy. In not one of them, however, did I find so much as a mention of the very term "Naturalistic Fallacy" even in a footnote discussion.[10] A recent collection of influential papers written in the United States, Britain, and Australia during the last three decades opened with the words, "The central problem in moral philosophy is that commonly known as the *is-ought* problem";[11] yet it did not appear as even a marginal issue in Catholic seminary or college textbooks. In 1956 Prior wrote:

> In our own time the perception that information about our obligations cannot be logically derived from premises in which our obligations are not mentioned has become a commonplace, though perhaps only in philosophical circles.[12]

[10] The same complaint holds true for much of the periodical literature. An important exception has been the Irish *Philosophical Studies,* published annually.

[11] W. D. Hudson, ed., *The Is-Ought Question* (London: Macmillan, 1969).

[12] A. N. Prior, *Logic and the Basis of Ethics* (Oxford: Clarendon Press, 1956), p. 36.

But it was a commonplace which, though calculated to "subvert all the vulgar systems of morality," especially the Christian, was ignored in Catholic institutions. For all the attention it received there, it would hold the field unchallenged. If it is no longer a commonplace, but a theory under dire attack, that is because of the work of writers in open universities.

The grounds for this complaint are by no means confined to meta-ethical questions. What Catholic moral theologian has seen the importance of Professor Anscombe's study of the *description under which* an act is performed? What interest has been shown by Catholic anglophone theologians in Mrs. Foot's powerful arguments against "Free-will as involving Determinism"? What have they made of Von Wright's arguments for Virtue as a key concept in moral theory? What contribution have they made to the debate about the relationship of Law to Morality initiated by Lord Devlin and Professor Hart, and seriously examined from a Christian point of view by Professor Basil Mitchell? If it is true that a theology to be healthy and robust needs philosophical roots in its own culture, this second "drawback" to which I think we must confess is a source of even greater disappointment than the first.

1.33 The third drawback concerns the *logic* in use. It can be summarized quite succinctly: contemporary theologians use an outdated logic. They have, with great profit, drawn on modern developments in several of the natural and social sciences; but they have failed to make any use of the enormous developments in modern logic.

For the professional this is an even more serious matter than the two just mentioned. The use of an alien style, and the concern with questions which are so often irrelevant to the interests of English-language philosophers, are things that detract from the theologians' work extrinsically. The fact that they use an outdated logic, however, weakens their work intrinsically.

Modern theology has drawn most fruitfully on many developments in modern science. For example, biblical scholarship has profited greatly by making use of the techniques and methods of scientific archaeology, anthropology, and linguistics. Moral theologians have made good use of developments in modern psychology and sociology, and many of them when tackling medico-moral problems inform themselves with great thoroughness on the medical and scientific aspects of the question. Unfortunately, however, theologians—anglophone as well as continental—have made practically no use of the enormous developments in modern logic; and this often gives their work a distressingly amateur, unprofessional appearance.

Greater advances have been made in logic in the last ninety years than in the previous twenty-three centuries. This is most spectacularly true, perhaps, with regard to formal logic; but it is true also to some extent of philosophical logic, and it is this especially which makes available immensely powerful tools for working on many theological problems in a far more sophisticated fashion than used to be possible. Some Protestant theologians, such as Professor T. F. Torrance, have shown to what effective and imaginative use these tools may be put. Unfortunately, however, Catholic theologians have on the whole remained ignorant even of the existence of such tools. Struggling with many problems which cry out for the most sophisticated logical instruments available, either they use logical tools which are comparatively primitive, or even fail to see that some of them are indeed problems of logic, rather than of epistemology or metaphysics. In Christology, for instance, a number of fascinating questions have recently been raised concerning the relationship of Christ's divine and human natures, and particularly the divine and human self-consciousness. Such discussions can seem to be pitched at a low level of logical rigor, however, when compared with Bernard Williams' examination of a parallel aspect of the mind-body problem in his paper "The Self and the Future."[13] At the heart of Christology is the problem, How can Jesus of Nazareth be at the same time literally divine and literally human? Studies of this problem could be greatly tightened by the use of such methods as those employed by Professor Strawson in examining the question, How is it that mental and physical predicates can be attributed to the very same thing?[14]; and by the use of the methods employed by analytical philosophers who have dealt critically with Strawson's account.

Professor Hans Küng in his recent book *Infallible? an Inquiry* struggled with a number of issues involving the logic of meaning, truth, and propositions; he speaks of a Greek rationalist notion of truth, commonly accepted in Christianity, which locates truth in propositions. Unfortunately, his account often seems somewhat un-

---

[13] *Philosophical Review,* 79 (April, 1970).
[14] P. F. Strawson, *Individuals* (London: Methuen, 1959), p. 3.

satisfactory through showing no acquaintance with the classics of analytical philosophy on such topics, summarized for instance in articles such as those of Lemmon[15] and Cartwright.[16] Dr. Hugo Meynell dealt very effectively with suggestions of this sort, put forward a little earlier, by drawing out the confusions that arise from a failure to distinguish between sentences and propositions,[17] ignorance of which well-known developments detracts somewhat from Küng's work. Professor Patrick McGrath drew attention to other confusions in the book which could have been clarified by some knowledge of modern logic.[18] Gabriel Moran's influential *Theology of Revelation* runs into similar difficulties. Puzzling over the "objectification of revelation," he treats the problem as if it were one only of metaphysics and epistemology, rather than primarily one of logic; and for help, he falls back on Hegelian metaphysics.[19] Had he seen the logical issues at stake, and had he drawn upon the work of the analysts in such fields, a very different treatment might have been achieved. Much the same sort of thing holds for Moral Theology. Analytical philosophers have made very useful examinations of the different logical statuses of rules, and of methods for deciding the appropriate *description under which* an act is to be morally evaluated. A study such as that of Van der Marck,[20] who is very keenly aware of the importance of settling upon the appropriate description under which an act is to be morally evaluated, falls somewhat short of the rigor which could have been attained had he been familiar with such analytical work. One sees something of how usefully such work can be brought to bear on Catholic moral studies by reading the versions of Natural Law theory put forward by Father Herbert McCabe[21] and Dr. John Finnis.[22]

15 E. J. Lemmon, "Sentences, Statements, and Propositions," in B. Williams and A. Montefiore, eds., *British Analytical Philosophy* (London: Routledge, 1966).

16 R. Cartwright, "Propositions," in R. J. Butler, ed., *Analytical Philosophy* (Oxford: Blackwell, 1962).

17 H. Meynell, "Shaking the Foundations," in *The Month*, March, 1970.

18 *The Tablet* (London), July 3, 1971.

19 G. Moran, *Theology of Revelation* (London: Burns, 1967), esp. chap. IX.

20 W. Van der Marck, *Love and Fertility* (London: Sheed, 1965), esp. chap. 2.

21 H. McCabe, *Law, Love and Language* (London: Sheed, 1968), esp. chap. 2.

22 J. M. Finnis, "Natural Law and Unnatural Acts," in *Heythrop Journal*, October, 1970.

The suggestion is sometimes made that we may at present be in something of a twelfth-century situation—the data being collected, the tools being forged: the bold, powerful, imaginative synthesis lying just ahead. But this hope may come true only if the best working instruments become a normal part of the apprentice theologian's tools of trade.

II

Next, I have undertaken to summarize a number of features of Catholic moral theory which provide a background to the specific problem tackled in this book. Some of these are points of content, some are points of conceptual idiom and method, the first is socio-pedagogical. Actually, the present time is an awkward one to attempt a summary even on this limited scale. A vigorous and rich renewal in Catholic moral theology began about 1930 and was in many ways further encouraged by the Second Vatican Council. Still, the new movement is not a repudiation of previous work, and it is possible to make a number of points.

2.1 Catholic teaching has always insisted that substantial fidelity to morality is a necessary condition of enjoying God's favor. This is not to say, of course, that it is a *sufficient* condition of this: that issue has been a topic of lively theological dispute since the time of Pelagius and Augustine, and this is not the place to rehearse it. Not sufficient, therefore; but *necessary*. Accordingly any systematic reflection on the Christian view of human destiny must concern itself with the question, What is involved in substantial fidelity to morality—whether that is referred to as the moral law, or moral duty, or a morally good life, or however? This immediately leads to a second point.

2.2 Catholic moral theology developed as a "scientific discipline" largely in the context of training clerical students for their future work as confessors. The background of this, of course, was Catholic belief in the sacrament of Penance. Christ's words "Whose sins you forgive they are forgiven and whose sins you retain they are retained" provide the scriptural background to the priest's work in the confessional. A central point in Christ's work of redemption was the reconciling of sinful man to God, and this is carried on in the life of the Church and the individual Catholic by his seeking pardon for his sins in the sacrament. Furthermore, not every sin alienated one totally from God. A distinction was made between venial sin and mortal sin. Only the latter broke one's loving union with God, and the strict obligation of confessing one's sins to the priest in the sacrament applied only to mortal sin. One preoccupation of moral theology therefore became a very thorough study of what actions or omissions did and what did not constitute mortal sin.

This preoccupation often became so exaggerated as to drive a wedge between "Moral Theology," which sometimes seemed to be a study of the bare minimum that a Christian could "get away with" without being alienated from God, and "Spiritual Theology," which was for the generous soul bent on the perfection of the Gospel. It led to the charge of "Legalism," which has sometimes provided an excuse for escaping intellectual rigor, but has often served as a useful label to sum up the opposite of what the renewed movement was seeking. Some of the ideals of the new movement are canonized by the recent Ecumenical Council: moral theology must be done scientifically; it must be based more directly on the teachings of Scripture; it must vividly portray the vocation of the faithful in Christ; it must bring home the obligation to bring forth fruit in charity, for the life of the world.[23]

2.3 Catholic philosophico-theological writers have commonly accepted a definition of philosophy which restricts it to those "truths which can be discovered by the light of unaided reason," i.e. without any appeal to the Scripture or revealed religion of any kind. In the background to this there lies an assumption that certain religious truths are, in principle, totally beyond discovery by the human reason unless God chooses to reveal them. Among these the most important is the doctrine of the Blessed Trinity, the doctrine that in the one living God there are three distinct and equal persons. It is interesting that when St. Paul gave some account of truths which are, in principle, completely inaccessible to human reason, he used a version of Privileged Access theory: "No-one knows the depths of a man, save his spirit within him; so also no-one knows the depths

[23] Decree *Optatam totius,* § 16.

of God, save his Spirit that is within him."[24] The Natural Law theory of morality held that moral truths are in principle discoverable by the human reason without the assistance of divine revelation. Admittedly, given the limited resources of human intelligence and time and dispassionate inquiry, most men find it morally impossible to arrive at them without some degree of error and imperfection, unless taught by God. However, my point here is that, by the self-denying ordinance imposed by this particular definition of philosophy, it was commonly held that purely theological concepts were not the business of philsophy. I should have thought that this was a great pity: that one needs to philosophize upon the data of theology and religion, without claiming to adjudicate on their truth or falsity, somewhat as one philosophizes upon the data of physics, without adjudicating upon their truth or falsity. At all events the upshot has been that a number of items in moral *theology* have not received the rigorous philosophical analysis which they need.

2.4 For a long time the Catholic Church has claimed infallibility for its teaching on faith and morals, given certain conditions. In 1870 the First Vatican Council explicitly credited this infallibility to the Pope, again given certain conditions. There was no suggestion that the Church as a whole or the Pope on his own received new revelations from God, and there developed quite an elaborate theology of how this infallibility was exercised. In every case strong appeal was made to scriptural foundations for any authoritative teaching. This is a large question and it is the subject of considerable discussion at the moment. However, the point to be made is that there has been a universal assumption of Objectivism and Cognitivism in Catholic moral teaching and theory. A claim to infallibility in some matter makes sense only if there are true and false, correct and incorrect, answers to the questions raised.

2.5 Catholic moral teaching always held that there was an intrinsic connection between morality and God. Morally good and virtuous actions, performed from good motives, were in accordance with God's will and God's law; immoral actions involved breaches of God's law and ran counter to his will.

[24] I Corinthians 2:11.

When it came to organizing the Christian moral life into an intellectual system, two systems tended to develop: one took as central Aristotle's four cardinal virtues, the other took the Ten Commandments. It is worth saying, however, that for many hundreds of years the background of Catholic moral teaching and preaching has been Aquinas' synthesis of the scriptural teaching concerning morality with Aristotle's ethical theory. Plainly two different models were entertained.

We are familiar with two different models for passing judgment on human performance. One is that of the law court: the court sets out to judge whether or not an action falls under some particular law; the judgment will say that the action in question was or was not illegal or criminal and so on. A different model is that of aesthetic judgment: the literary critic, the panel of judges in a painting competition or a music festival, even the sports writer—all these are engaged in passing judgment on various kinds of human performance, but in a way very different from that of the judge in a court of law. It would be naïve to think that they merely decided whether the novel or the painting or the performance they were evaluating fell under some law; their criteria are far more flexible; they are not so much judging the candidate under this or that law, as they are saying to what extent it embodies this or that ideal: and indeed their ideals are themselves often enlarged by the work which they are judging as the artist uncovers new potentialities of beauty and excellence. Now, the model frequently entertained by scriptural moralists was that of the law court; they saw a given human action as obeying or breaking God's law. Greek ethical theory was much more prone to follow the other model: an action, when the subject of moral appraisal, was often thought of less as obeying or breaking a divine law, than as satisfying or not satisfying more mobile and flexible criteria, as embodying more successfully or less this or that ideal.

St. Thomas Aquinas set out to synthesize these two sources of Western thought about morality. By and large he adopted the Aristotelian framework hinging on the four cardinal virtues of wisdom, justice, temperance, and fortitude, and he meshed into these the distinctive Christian virtues of faith, hope, and charity.

With the growth of a moral theology oriented towards the hearing of confessions the legal model tended to prevail. Furthermore, that model provided a very natural setting for preaching about such scriptural topics as the Last Judgment, and the mode of one's afterlife as being settled by a sentence handed down on the model of Matthew 26.

2.6 A traditional thesis has been, "Charity is the form of all the virtues." This is, of course, an Aristotelian-style version of St. Paul's "If I gave all my goods to feed the poor, if I gave up my body to be burned, but had not charity, it would profit me nothing."[25] The Aristotelian Doctrine of hylemorphism features in many places in the Thomist synthesis, and the soul itself is presented not as a complete Platonist psyche residing in a complete distinct body, but as the *substantial* shape or *form* of the human person. In somewhat the same way, the living presence of divine charity gave the distinctively Christian nature to human morality.

In recent years a powerful and promising movement in Catholic moral theory has set out to organize the anatomy of Christian morality around this central precept or value of *charity*. The pioneers were Gilleman and Häring, and Fuchs presented an outline for wedding this with one version of traditional Natural Law theory.[26]

2.7 There are, of course, many different versions of Natural Law theory. Twenty years ago Professor A. P. d'Entrèves showed how diverse they are, from the Stoics and Cicero through such well-known anglophone variants as that of Blackstone, so amusingly parodied by Bentham.[27] In a new edition in 1970, d'Entrèves discusses the modest contemporary version in Professor H. L. A. Hart's plea for the "core of good sense in Natural Law," arguing for a minimum content of Natural Law.[28]

It has become fashionable among a number of "new" Catholic moralists to speak as if Natural Law theory were discredited. Sometimes this seems to be simply the product of the reflex of hostility to anything that they consider to smack of "Legalism" or "Logic chopping." Sometimes, however, it is supported by arguments. Some of these

---

[25] I Corinthians 13:3.
[26] G. Gilleman, *Le Primat de la Charité en Théologie Morale* (Bruxelles: Desclée de Brouwer, 1954); J. Fuchs, *Le Droit Naturel* (Tournai, Belg.: Desclée, 1960); B. Häring, *La Loi du Christ* (Tournai, Belg.: Desclée, 1955).
[27] A. P. d'Entrèves, *Natural Law* (London: Hutchinson, 1951).
[28] H. L. A. Hart, *The Concept of Law* (Oxford: Clarendon Press, 1961).

may be brought to bear against the hylemorphic background of
Aquinas' Natural Law theory. Other arguments draw on anthropological data showing that there is a far greater diversity of moral
conviction and standard than was previously suspected: though it is
not always seen that such data do not of themselves tell one way or
the other against items of Natural Law. Not much troubled by these
trends among some Catholic moralists, two writers (cited above)
have deployed lines of argument which strike me as full of power
and promise for a contemporary version of Natural Law theory. That
of Dr. John Finnis, first sketched in the British *Law Quarterly Review* was developed in an article in *Heythrop Journal;* that of Father
Herbert McCabe, first given in the course of open lectures delivered in the University of Kent, has now appeared in book form.
Neither of them, alas, seems to have commanded much attention
from Catholic moral theologians working within clerical institutions.

2.8 Catholic teaching, like nearly all other Christian teaching, has
always seen an intrinsic connection between the morality of one's
life in this world and the mode of one's life in the next. However,
the nature of that connection has been variously represented. The
obvious presentation is that of the Gospel in, e.g., Matthew 26,
handed down like a verdict in court: the connection is then on the
model of Reward and Punishment. Another way of seeing the connection has roots in Aristotle and was given its classical statement at
the start of St. Thomas Aquinas' *Prima Secundae:* the connection
is that of Means to End, even that of Road to Destination. It is in
this latter approach that Aquinas' metaphysical bias becomes most
plain. His theory of act and potentiality is involved in explaining
the way that a morally good life in this world is a condition (necessary, not sufficient) of developing intrinsically into the sort of person capable (given supernatural elevation of his powers by grace)
of enjoying the presence and sight of God in the next. The connection is therefore less of the nature, "If you graduate from medical
school you can have a new Buick," than of the nature, "If you graduate from medical school you can become a good doctor." It is in the
elaboration of such views that one understands fundamental moral
principles of Aquinas such as, "Any action which runs counter to
natural inclination is evil."

Hence a morally good life in this world is not seen as being pursued simply for its own sake, as if "Virtue is its own reward." Nor is it seen as being pursued *merely* for the sake of reward, as if there were no intrinsic connection between the moral life in this life and the sort of life one enjoys in the next. Rather it is a matter of so living as to become such a kind of person as will be capable of enjoying that sort of life in the next world. It is not like the man who works long hours on a second job so as to get money for a holiday in Florida; it is more like the dedicated student of music who, after years of self-denying application, revels in Beethoven's last quartets. It is true that a life of substantial fidelity to moral law (or to "moral ideals" or "moral values," or to the central principle of charity), is difficult and toilsome: Christ himself left his followers in little doubt about that—"If any man would come after me he must deny himself, take up his cross daily and follow me." But in a variety of ways the New Testament casts about it for ways of saying that the sufferings of this time are not to be compared with the joy that is to come. Once again, however: the connection with the joy that is to come is illustrated less by the man lying on the beach at Miami, than by the person entranced by the quartets. In another metaphor, seeking to make the point that the connection is intrinsic, St. Paul says that a man will reap as he sows; if he sows seed only in the field of his lower nature, he will reap from it a harvest of corruption; but if he sows in the field of the Spirit, the Spirit will bring him a harvest of eternal life.

2.9 In medieval Catholic writing on the topic which preoccupies this volume, there were two opposed schools of thought, and they are well exemplified in two *loci classici*. The first is that of St. Thomas Aquinas:

> Morality is based primarily on God's *wisdom*. It is his wisdom that establishes creatures in their proper relationship with each other and with him: and it is precisely in that relationship that the essence of a creature's moral goodness consists. To say that morality is determined simply by God's will is to suggest that God's will may sometimes not follow order and wisdom; and that would be blasphemous.[29]

[29] *De Veritate* 23, 6.

The other view, often called "Moral Positivism," is given very clear expression in the following passage of Gabriel Biel:

> It is true that God cannot act against right reason. However, where actions outside himself are concerned, right reason is precisely that which he wills. It is not the case that something is right or just, and therefore God wills it; rather, God wills something, and therefore it is just and right.[30]

This view of Biel had also been that of his more famous master, Ockham, and is that to which I referred above in connection with Professor Olafson. One remembers that Wittgenstein considered it to be "the deeper view" in the debate. However, the position that I shall take lies on the same side of the fence as that of St. Thomas.

III

Against this background, then, I sketch a Catholic approach (no one particular position can claim to be *"the* Catholic answer") to the problem discussed in this volume. In summary, my own position is this: God forbids certain kinds of action because they are wrong, not vice versa; God commends, commands, or forbids certain kinds of action and certain frames of mind because he is essentially holy, and they are intrinsically good, or evil; the connection between morality and the Christian religion is therefore intrinsic and necessary, though a connection of natural, not logical, necessity. If I had to summarize my reasons in a single phrase, I should say that they are packed into the Christian's notion of his God as being literally and unreservedly *worthy of worship.*

3.1 To begin with, I suggest that the question *How is Morality related to Religion?* is more akin to the question *How is Law related to Morality?* than it is to the question *How is Religion related to Science?* This last question was canvassed at length especially in the aftermath of Darwin's great publications, and has evoked a number of worthwhile contributions even in recent years: say, in some of the better discussions on the work of Teilhard de Chardin. However, these discussions tended to be arguments about the way in

[30] *Collectorium circa IV Sent.,* I, d. 17, q. 1, a. 3, coroll. 1. Ockham gives his view in his Commentary on the Sentences: *In II Sent. 19 ad 3 et 4.*

which religion and science might be mutually illuminating (in recent years), or mutually antipathetic (in the earlier debates); they were not much concerned to inquire whether the connection between religion and science is intrinsic and necessary or simply extrinsic and contingent.

Such a connection has been explored with regard to law and morality in the discussions initiated by Lord Patrick Devlin in his celebrated Maccabean lecture.[31] Devlin held that the connection is necessary and intrinsic. Professor Herbert Hart, in his Harry Camp Lectures at UCLA,[32] and his Lionel Cohen lectures in Jerusalem,[33] argued that the connection is simply extrinsic. Hart admitted that morality had as a matter of historical fact influenced law; but this was a contingent fact, and the connection between the two was extrinsic only. This seems to be much more like our own question. Nobody doubts that religion has often exercised considerable influence on morality; the question is, Is there any *necessary* connection between them? My own answer is: In the case of the Christian religion, Yes: a connection of *natural* necessity.

3.2 Next, in view of the fact that I claim a necessary connection between morality and religion, it may be worthwhile to make three explicit disclaimers.

First, to hold that there is a necessary connection between morality and religion is in no way to be committed to holding that a person who does not believe in God cannot know many moral truths. It is not the case that without religion or religious belief one cannot know the difference between moral good and evil, moral right and wrong, or that one cannot push back the frontiers of these distinctions. Some of the great moral reformers, especially in the last two centuries, have been non-believers; on the other hand, many a believer has resisted moral reform. Maritain has remarked how, in drawing up the United Nations *Universal Declaration on Human Rights,* it was possible for people to reach a great deal of agreement as to what those rights are, though entertaining considerable philosophical and religious

[31] Patrick Devlin, *The Enforcement of Morals* (Oxford: Oxford Univ. Press, 1968).

[32] H. L. A. Hart, *Law, Liberty and Morality,* (Oxford: Oxford Univ. Press, 1968).

[33] H. L. A. Hart, *The Morality of the Criminal Law* (Jerusalem: Magnes Press, 1964).

differences about the way that those rights are to be vindicated.[34] Obviously I, as a Christian, believe that there is enormous value in having God's guidance on human morality, and as a Catholic I believe that that guidance is a continuing force available in the life of the Church. But I am anxious that this belief should not be exaggerated. On the one hand, even without belief in God, a great deal of moral truth can be known and the implications of established moral truths discerned. On the other hand, even with belief in God, and indeed even with belief in an authoritative living teacher of morals, a great deal of moral truth will yet remain unknown: "infallible" does not mean "omniscient." There are plenty of moral issues in dispute among Christians who accept an authoritative, even an infallible, guidance in morality. Furthermore Christians often quite fruitfully debate moral issues without explicit reference to God.

Second, to hold that there is a necessary connection between religion and morality is not to be committed to holding that only religious believers can perform morally good actions. It is not the case that without religion or religious belief one cannot act morally (how the unbeliever's actions can be supernaturally meritorious, is another question). Equally, it is not the case that believers can (or think that they can) become incapable of immoral action. Many an atheist is honest and chaste and reliable, unselfish, generous, and kind. On the other hand, many a believer has been dishonest and unjust, insensitive to the feelings of his own family or to the needs of the poor. This is of course a truism of Catholic morality and daily experience, but perhaps it deserves to be stated.

Third, the thesis that there is a necessary connection between morality and religion does not entail the thesis that any philosophical rationale of moral concepts is false if it does not make explicit reference to God. This disclaimer, as much as the first and second just stated, sits best with the view that morality is not determined merely by the will of God; for if immoral actions are immoral merely because God so wills it, merely because God legislates against them, it would be sheer coincidence if someone who knew nothing of God or his law happened to adopt the same views about particular actions as God did. If God's law against murder and treachery is simply like

[34] Jacques Maritain, *Man and the State* (London: Hollis & Carter, 1954), pp. 69–73.

the Irish or the Australian Government's laws against driving on the right-hand side of the road rather than the left, there is no reason why the morally minded atheist and the Christian should entertain the same attitudes concerning the immorality of murder and treachery.

3.3 A remark of Hart serves well to introduce my own thesis:

> It is a truth of some importance that for the adequate description not only of law but of many other social institutions, a place must be reserved, besides definitions and ordinary statements of fact, for a third category of statements: those the truth of which is contingent on human beings and the world they live in retaining the salient characteristics they have.[35]

Hart calls the logical status of such statements, "natural necessity," and I propose the same term to characterize the relationship between morality and the Christian religion. For, although they are not related by force of straightforward meaning and definition, there are three "salient characteristics" of the Christian religion which are so intimately connected with it and with morality that it would be quite inadequate to call their relationship one simply of contingent fact. These three characteristic features overlap considerably, but they are sufficiently distinct to enable one to treat them separately, and thus to argue cumulatively for the thesis.

3.31 First, there is the fact that the Christian religion, in continuity with the Jewish, contains strong moral teaching as an integral part of its message: "You wrong and cheat people—even your own brothers. Surely you know that the unjust will never inherit the kingdom of God: people of immoral lives, idolaters, adulterers, catamites, sodomites, thieves, usurers, drunkards, slanderers or swindlers will never inherit the kingdom of God."[36] Not all religions include moral teaching and moral demands; for this reason, my own thesis is put forward concerning one particular historical religion; it should therefore become plain why it seems to me a mistake to say what the relationship is between morality and "religion" as such.

Some Middle Eastern religions contemporary with the origins of

[35] *The Concept of Law*, p. 195.
[36] I Corinthians 6:9–11.

Judaism made *cultic,* but not *moral* demands on their votaries. Primitive religions commonly sought the favor of their god, and cultic details were often conceived less as a duty owed him than as means of flattering and wheedling him, and keeping him happy or at least quiet; they seem often to have been modeled on ways of keeping the Strong Man on one's side: paying tribute, showing gratitude, bringing gifts, providing amusement, offering fulsome praise. Moreover, worship often contained strong elements of magic, even further removed from a connection with moral obligation: if only one could hit on the right trick, discover the right formula, perhaps one could *compel* the god to do what one wanted. In any event, many religions saw the winning of a god's favor as the outcome of meticulously accurate or ingenious worship. It was not that kindness or faithfulness or truthfulness were the values which a god naturally, being divine, prized and would reward; the point rather was that in the details of magic and ritual one rested the precarious hope of humoring him. There were sometimes elements of this in Jewish religious history. Seeing that Yahweh had revealed to Moses the details of a cult that would please him, the great thing was to follow them meticulously; get the right priest to say the right words and make the right gestures in sacrificing the right victims.

This attitude was constantly rebuked in the Scriptures; at the heart of the six hundred and sixteen items of the Law was the Decalogue itself. Time and again the message was hammered home, "I desire mercy, not sacrifice"; the most elaborate ritual is useless without serious concern for morality.

> Your countless sacrifices, what are they to me?
> > says the Lord.
> The offer of your gifts is useless,
> > the reek of sacrifice is abhorrent to me.
> Put away the evil of your deeds, out of my sight.
> > Cease to do evil, and learn to do right.
> Pursue justice and champion the oppressed;
> > give the orphan his rights, plead the widow's cause.[37]

The lesson was vigorously continued, of course, in the Christian Gospel: "Go home and learn what the text means, 'I desire mercy, not sacrifice.'"[38] "People of immoral lives, idolaters, adulterers, cata-

[37] Isaiah 1:11, 13, 16, 17.
[38] Matthew 9:13.

mites, sodomites, thieves, usurers, drunkards, slanderers or swindlers will never inherit the kingdom of God."[39] Furthermore, the Gospel demands more even than morally correct external behavior; a constant theme is the demand for interior goodness of a piece with external behavior. It is a major theme in the Sermon on the Mount, which commands us not only to refrain from harming our neighbor, but also to love him; demands not only abstinence from unchaste action, but also chastity of heart.[40] The same theme is in evidence in Christ's condemnation of the lawyers and Pharisees: "You are like tombs covered with whitewash; they look well from outside, but inside they are full of dead men's bones and every kind of filth. So it is with you: outside you look like honest men, but inside you are full of hypocrisy and crime."[41]

3.32 Next, the notion of *sin* is central to the Christian religion, together with Christ's mission to *redeem* sinful man. Remove the notions of sin and redemption, and one is no longer talking about the Christian religion.

Of course, the word *sin* is sometimes used to mean simply an immoral act: an infringement of the moral code, as distinct from a breach of the law. If one student steals another's lecture notes on the eve of an examination, he may think of it simply as a breach of university regulations. No doubt it is that; but this is quite trivial compared with what it is in moral truth. Some time ago I saw a pharmacist interviewed on television; he said that selling unlicensed medicines was an offense against a particular State act of 1957; then he added, apparently as an afterthought, "And of course you might kill someone." Such examples are helpful to illustrate the distinction between the immoral and the illegal; and Lord Devlin in his Maccabean lecture used the word *sin* to characterize the immoral.

However, Christians have always used the term *sin* in a much stronger sense: to connote an offense against God and his holy Law. Some of the most profound Christian meditations have borne upon this. The mysterious fact that God gives man, not only a law, but also the freedom to disobey his law, has exercised many Christian

[39] I Corinthians 6:11.
[40] Matthew 5:20–48.
[41] Matthew 23:27–28.

thinkers since St. Augustine. An immoral life is not merely a failure to match up to noble human ideals: an immoral act is not *only* a violation of the dignity of the human person; sin, of its nature, affects our relationship with God. It has been argued, particularly in some recent writing, that it is comparatively trivial to speak of sin as an infringement of God's law; in its fullest connotations it describes the whole fundamental set of one's personality turned completely away from God towards some merely created good. Some Christians with an Existentialist background have spoken about the "fundamental option" taken up for God, or—in sin—against him. They have distinguished between those grave acts of choice which do, and those superficial ones which do not, constitute a person's basic orientation or a serious turning point in his life. They have sought connections between a man's sinfulness and the "mystery of iniquity" of which St. Paul wrote.[42] For our purposes, however, it is enough to note the Christian conviction that immorality is not merely an offense against the human person but also involves an offense against God and his law.

At the same time, the Old Testament often forbids—as sinful—actions which are not immoral; and it often commands—under pain of sin—actions which are not morally obligatory. Catholic moralists have traditionally distinguished between that which is *prohibitum quia malum* and that which is *malum quia prohibitum*. The term *immoral* applies only to those things which are *prohibita quia mala*. There is nothing intrinsically wrong in driving on the right-hand side of the road, but it is wrong to do so in Australia or Ireland because it is forbidden by law. On the other hand, it is also true that the law forbids one to maltreat or neglect one's children; but that is not what makes it wrong to do so. Similarly God does will that men should not be cruel or dishonest or unfaithful; but that is not what makes it wrong to be so. Needless to say, I am not denying that God forbids murder, injustice, lying, and adultery; I am saying that it is not *merely* his will that makes such actions wrong, as it is merely his will that we keep holy the seventh rather than the sixth or the eighth day; it is because they are wrong that he forbids them. Graham Greene said recently, "If you do not believe in a god who punishes, you will never take any human wrongdoing very seriously";

---

[42] II Thessalonians 2:7.

but such remarks would make sense to me only if applying to a law of God which was based on a recognition of how wrong wrongdoing is, and not on a capricious or petulant divine distaste for certain kinds of human personality and behavior. Once again facts such as these form such an integral part of Christian belief as to support the thesis that the relationship between morality and the Christian religion is one of natural necessity.

3.33 The same thesis seems to suggest itself even more strongly if we consider the place occupied in the Christian religion by its doctrine of God, and specifically of God's holiness.

Religions differ not only in the content of the beliefs about their god but also in the degree to which those beliefs have been articulated and occupy a central place in their teaching; to illustrate this, it is enough to contrast the place occupied by the doctrine of God in Mohammedanism with that which it occupies in Hinduism. Now, the Christian (as the Jewish) doctrine of God is highly developed, and utterly central to every other part of the Christian religion.

The point of that doctrine which concerns us here is that of God's *holiness*. Even a nodding acquaintance with classical and biblical literature illustrates the point. The Homeric gods are contentious, and devious and shifty in their quarrels; they are moody, capricious and inconstant in their amours, in their alliances, and in their dealings with men. But Yahweh, the God of Israel, is "Holy, holy, holy"; he loves justice and hates iniquity, "and holy is his name."

Scripture scholars, with the help of data from anthropologists, trace three stages in the development of the notion of the *holy*. First, the term *holy* suggests the notion of separation from ordinary things. Ordinary things may be used freely, even lightly; holy things belong to a sphere apart. Even in primitive religions this sense of the holy is powerful; it is from Polynesian sources that the word *taboo* came into English. This element is strong in the biblical notion of the holy; the Hebrew root *qadash*, from which comes the adjective *qadosh, holy*, originally denoted separation, distance, differentness. This element is recognized in such phrases as Karl Barth's description of God as *das ganz Andere*, the wholly Other. A second element in the notion of holiness is the possession of a power surpassing the human and the terrestrial, illustrated, say, in the mana-belief of some Melanesian peoples; they fear exceptional powers in certain plants and animals, and show a religious fear of superhuman energies in many places. This element also is present, of course, even quite early in the development of the biblical notion of God's holiness. But in it a third element develops: that of absolute moral perfection, comprising above all justice, mercy, and fidelity to his word. Yahweh, the God of Israel, loves justice and hates iniquity; there is a difference in kind between the goodness of the most innocent human being and the blinding, ineffable holiness of God, before a remote glimpse of which the greatest of the prophets cries out, "Woe to me, for I am a man of unclean lips, and I dwell in the midst of a people having unclean lips."[43]

It is the third of these elements in the development of the notion of the holy that has become uppermost in English and, I believe, in many other languages of Christian culture; and the antonym, *unholy,* is an antonym of it only in its moral connotation. In the approach to, and the mentality behind, cult and worship there is therefore a change of capital importance in the transition from the first and second to the third stage in the development of the notion of the holy. In the earlier stages there are the emotions of religious fear and emotion elicited by some sense of the *mysterium tremendum et fascinans,* and the holy one is worshiped because that may be the way to win his favor and keep him in a good humor. But an enormously significant development has occurred when he has come to be recognized as *worthy of worship.*

Hence the importance of the revelation that Yahweh, the God of Israel, "loves justice and hates iniquity." No doubt for one with direct insight into the nature of the only true and living God, that would be, with glaring obviousness, an analytic proposition. But to a people surrounded by all kinds of religions exacting rituals often marked by cruelty and sexual license, it is synthetic; it conveys information that takes a long time to digest; and the information induces reflection. If a god hated justice and loved iniquity, it might yet be *prudent to worship* him. But if, in addition to being divinely powerful, he loves justice and hates iniquity; if it is mercy he desires, more than sacrifice; if cruelty and injustice "are an abomination before Yahweh your God"; if he wants "justice to flow like water, and integrity like a stream that does not fail"; then, he is *worthy of worship.* According to Ockhamist principles, it would seem to be con-

---

[43] Isaiah 6:5. This summary is taken from W. Leonard, "The Sanctification of the Priest in Worship" in *Living Parish Week* (Sydney: Pellegrini, 1958).

ceivable that God could—*saltem secundum potentiam absolutam*—replace the Decalogue with its opposite: legislate for a way of life in which we were commanded to keep the sabbath day holy by torturing an infant to death; to dishonor our father and mother, to kill, to commit adultery, to steal, to bear false witness against our neighbor. Such a god might be able to force us to worship him; but he would not be worthy of worship.

The important revelation that Yahweh loves justice and hates iniquity presupposes that one can distinguish between the just and the iniquitous independently and in advance of that revelation. A number of unjust and otherwise immoral acts are itemized in the Pentateuch; it is assumed that they are known to be unjust and immoral; then, in addition, the important information is given that they are "abominations hateful to Yahweh your God."

This suggests, of course, some kind of cognitive metaethic. More specifically, it suggests the thesis, commonly held among Catholic moralists, that some kinds of acts are intrinsically wrong. This does not mean that there are some actions which are so heinously wicked that they could never be justified; rather, it means that there are some actions whose wrongness is not determined by their consequences but by the nature of the acts themselves. Such a thesis provides a natural background for doctrines such as St. Paul's: "One must not do evil that good may come." One must not lie, St. Paul says, even to promote the glory of God; to condone that would be to make good the slander of some of his enemies who attributed to him the view that one may do evil that good may come. They are wrong, he says, to attribute such a principle to him; but they are right in condemning the principle.[44] Aquinas comments on this as follows:

> Some people libelled the Apostles, quoting them as saying that one may do evil so that good may come. This would be the case if one were to lie in order to commend God's mercy and truthfulness. . . . A person deserves to be condemned if he does evil that good may come. Just as in syllogising one will not reach a true conclusion from false premisses; so one cannot hope to achieve a good end through evil means.[45]

This is one more example of the naturally cognitivist assumptions that Aquinas brings to moral theory.

[44] Romans 3:5–8.
[45] *In ad Rom., ad hunc loc.*

Here in quite acute form there is raised the problem of *description of action*. In performing "the very same act" a person may, in different circumstances, be doing different things: in signing his name, for example, he may be drawing a check, entering a contract, or giving his autograph to an admirer. Indeed, he may even be doing opposite things: issuing a death warrant or granting a reprieve. Often it is only after the appropriate act-description has been determined that one may proceed to the moral evaluation of the act. In traditional Catholic moral theology, the appropriate act-description was called (in Latin) the *obiectum* of the act. One may feel that there was not sufficiently detailed study of the *obiectum*, and insufficiently detailed criteria provided for distinguishing between the *obiectum* and the *finis*. But even if the distinction was not well enough articulated as a general philosophical doctrine, it was always clear that some descriptions or re-descriptions of action were logically inappropriate. Calvin said that the burning of the heretic Servetus was "really defending the truth." Salvator answered that to kill a man is not to defend the truth or to do anything else; it is to kill a man. Such a refusal to accept logically (and humanly) inappropriate descriptions is in keeping with the thesis of intrinsically wrong acts.

In contemporary philosophy the explicit study of descriptions of action was well-nigh pioneered by Professor Anscombe in her book *Intention*. She confines the study to that, although in other places she has made it clear that she believes a theory of description-of-action to be a prerequisite of the discussion of the morality of many actions. I myself have considered some of the implications for moral evaluation in my book *Human Acts*. Very interesting preliminary work for the next step, that of examining the morality of the act once satisfactorily described, has been begun by Herbert McCabe. For instance, in a review of Bishop Robinson's *Honest to God* he addressed himself in particular to the bishop's chapter on "The New Morality." As McCabe says, Robinson has given an account of Situation-Ethics, "a theory of morals according to which it is not possible to describe a human action which would be in every circumstance morally wrong. . . . It is a radical ethic of the situation, with nothing prescribed—except love."[46] McCabe suggests that such remarks will have meaning only if there are certain kinds of action

---

[46] Reprinted from *Blackfriars* in *The Honest to God Debate*, ed. D. L. Edwards (London: SCM Press, 1963), p. 178.

which are incompatible with the description "loving." He pursues this suggestion very fruitfully in his book mentioned above, *Law, Love and Language.*

One strong conviction among the Jewish people was that God is true to his word, both in the sense that one can rely on his promises, and also in the sense that one can believe what he says: that the possibility of his lying is incompatible with the perfection of his holiness. Professor Geach has argued that it is logically impossible that our knowledge that lying is bad should depend on revelation.[47] Plainly, truthfulness is one moral attribute of God on which those who accept a religion as divinely revealed are particularly dependent. If there is nothing intrinsically wrong with lying, if lying is evil only because God chooses to forbid it to his creatures, there is no reason for thinking that what Christians believe God to have revealed to them is true and worthy of acceptance. Indeed, given the Christian doctrine of the Trinity, one could imagine bizarre possibilities. If the holiness intrinsic to the divine nature does not necessarily exclude lying, and certain ways of treating persons, what is there to prevent the divine persons lying to each other, maltreating each other? One might reply: it is useless to lie to an omniscient person; it is impossible to maltreat an omnipotent person. But I should have thought that, given the Christian doctrine of God, the notion of such actions being performed would be seen as much more immediately incompatible with our concept of the divine holiness, than the notion of their being undergone would be with our concept of the divine omniscience or omnipotence. At all events, it will be clear that I see belief in God's holiness to be such a "salient characteristic" (in Hart's sense) of Christianity as to argue a relationship of "natural necessity" between morality and the Christian religion.

[47] P. Geach, *God and the Soul* (London: Routledge, 1969), pp. 119–20.

RELIGIOUS AND MORAL DUTY:
NOTES ON *FEAR AND TREMBLING*[1]

Gene Outka

One of the most striking concepts Kierkegaard considers is what he calls, in *Fear and Trembling,* the teleological suspension of the ethical. Some find it a troubling notion, others a pernicious one; certainly it has been the subject of wide controversy. I shall try to enter into the spirit of his enterprise and not rule it out of court in advance. Such an approach will be far from easy. Several of his moves are vexatiously difficult to chart with precision. The slender volume is, after all, as much a work of literature as of philosophy or theology. No matter. The issues he poses are serious, even if one finds some conclusions repellent or formulations obscure.

This essay concentrates on a single thinker, work, and episode in order to examine the complex character of the relation between religion and morality. The importance of more inclusive treatments of the relation is not in question. However, broad accounts often pay a considerable price for the high level of generality to which they aspire. Nuances may suffer neglect and assumptions go unidentified. I prefer to focus on one particular view.

A more substantive reason stands behind the choice of Kierkegaard for scrutiny. I want to examine one instance of a recurrent contention which the following statement nicely expresses:

Religious belief (of the kind we are now considering) brings on the stage, so to speak, an element that has absolutely no

[1] In writing this essay I have profited greatly from discussions with members of two graduate seminars, especially Philip Turner, John Hare, Jerome Hanus, and David Cain.

parallel, to which nothing is at all comparable, among the infidel's *dramatis personae*—namely, a being to which, in a quite unique sense, veneration is owed, which is uniquely an object of both love and fear, and above all to whose behests is owed, uniquely, *obedience*.[2]

The kind of religious belief held in *Fear and Trembling* exemplifies *par excellence* the effects of bringing a being on the stage who is uniquely the object of both love and fear. What occupies us here of course is the effect on morality. *Can* or *must* religious duty conflict with moral duty? Kierkegaard opts for the stronger contention: collision must occur. Yet precisely what is at issue in any insistence that conflict cannot be avoided remains unclear until the characterization of the two sorts of duty is examined. So my first task will be to sketch the major contrasts on which Kierkegaard insists (Section I). The sketch will be brief and yet detailed enough to put before the reader my admittedly disputable interpretation of some difficult texts and to prepare the way for what follows. I shall then go on to argue that at least two of the three contrasts to be identified depend upon a distinctive characterization of the ethical which is open to challenge (II–III). The challenge may be issued without going outside the province of "rational morality." That is, one may appeal to plausibly rational characterizations of the ethical which call into question Kierkegaard's insistence on a conflict in principle and suggest an excessively stipulative element in the account of the ethical that he offers.

Even if one finds the challenge convincing, not all of his case for conflict is thus rebutted. It is uncertain whether the remainder can or should be, and difficult to sort out the disagreements which are verbal and those which draw blood. The controversies revolve largely around the well-worn but troublesome and complex topic commonly referred to as the "autonomy of morality." Will it do to say that in the end God's commands are either heteronomous or redundant? The question is far from a straightforward one. I shall try to distinguish certain senses of autonomy and ask which of them Kierkegaard appears to accept or reject (IV–V). I shall then go on to speculate on the wider considerations and attendant difficulties which dispose a religious thinker like Kierkegaard to fear redundancy more

[2] G. J. Warnock, *The Object of Morality* (London: Methuen, 1971), p. 141.

than heteronomy, if in certain respects one is compelled to choose. Why is complete understanding of divine commands out of place (VI)? Are there then no limits to what God can command (VII)? How does God issue commands and how are they known (VIII)? Finally, I shall summarize the minimal claim which remains congruent with Kierkegaard's program but is perhaps more modest, where obedience to God *can* conflict with our antecedent judgments of right and wrong (IX).

I

In the twelfth chapter of Genesis it is recorded that Abraham receives the promise that in him and his descendants all the families of the earth will be blessed. Abraham believes the promise, and continues to expect its fulfillment, even during the long years when Sarah his wife remains barren. Isaac is born to them in their old age. The episode on which Kierkegaard concentrates is found in the twenty-second chapter, where once again, and decisively, Abraham is tried. God tests him by a command to take Isaac to the land of Moriah and give him there as a burnt offering. Abraham does not hesitate, though everything now seems inexplicably lost. He knows it is God who imposes the trial, yet he cannot see its point, for it appears to contradict, and annihilate, all that has gone before. When he arrives at the appointed place, he builds an altar, lays the wood on it, and binds Isaac. He is stopped only after he draws the knife: when his readiness to obey is beyond dispute. "The angel of the Lord" intervenes: "Do not lay your hand on the lad or do anything to him; for now I know that you fear God, seeing you have not withheld your son, your only son, from me." Abraham lifts his eyes, sees a ram trapped in a thicket, and gives it as a burnt offering in place of Isaac. The promise to him is then reiterated, "because you have obeyed my voice."

Kierkegaard's treatment of the story is regarded by many as highly idiosyncratic, of interest mainly to those concerned with his personal biography or the intellectual history of the nineteenth century. They often cite a common interpretation by biblical critics that the purpose of the narrative in light of the "happy ending" is to repudiate human sacrifice. The most one should say is that Abraham simply performed a wrong act with a good intention. God tests his affections perhaps, but not his scruples. Some go on to offer a progressive account of revelation, which stays slightly ahead of the moral level of the people to whom it is given. Certainly not everything is clear from the narrative, though certain interpretations have no basis in the text. Whether Kierkegaard's should be consigned to the latter category is contestable. Some scholars think his treatment catches more of the original sense than, say, a progressivist view.

I shall not attempt to assess the exegetical controversies. Nor shall I consider the multiple commentaries on the *Akedah* in the Jewish tradition.[3] I shall have to bypass also the lively discussion among scholars of Judaism on Kierkegaard's treatment. Some are severely critical; others defend him and claim to find interpretations very like his own in certain strands of the Midrash.[4] I shall concentrate on *Fear and Trembling* and pause only for piecemeal comparisons of Kierkegaard with Aquinas and Kant on several issues.

Kierkegaard views Abraham as a paradigmatic "knight of faith" and accordingly endeavors—under the pseudonym, Johannes *de silentio*—to draw out a range of concepts which inhere, he thinks, in the story and serve to characterize the relation between religious faith and morality. Let us begin with the "double movement of the spirit."

Abraham executes two movements simultaneously. The first movement, which is a necessary condition for the second, Kierkegaard calls "infinite resignation." Each person can make this movement by himself; no assistance from others is required. The yearning for such assistance is in fact a corruption. To permit oneself either to be governed by the opinions, expectations, or wishes of the "crowd," or to be content to justify one's actions before some public tribunal which examines only the perceptible results, is precisely to fail to resign the "finite." Someone who enters the cloister, Kierkegaard observes,

[3] See, e.g., Shalom Spiegel, *The Last Trial*, trans. Judah Goldin (Philadelphia: Jewish Publication Society of America, 1967).

[4] His critics include Joseph H. Gumbiner, "Existentialism and Father Abraham," *Commentary*, 2 (February, 1948), pp. 143–48; Marvin Fox, "Kierkegaard and Rabbinic Judaism," *Judaism*, 2 (April, 1953), pp. 160–69; Milton Steinberg, *Anatomy of Faith* (New York: Harcourt, 1960), pp. 130–52. Those more sympathetic include Emil L. Fackenheim, *Quest for Past and Future: Essays in Jewish Theology* (Bloomington: Ind. Univ. Press, 1968), pp. 52–65; Jacob L. Halevi, "Kierkegaard and the Midrash," *Judaism*, 4 (Winter 1955), pp. 13–28; Halevi, "Kierkegaard's Teleological Suspension of the Ethical–Is It Jewish?" *Judaism*, 8 (Fall 1959), pp. 291–302.

may have made the movement of infinite resignation, though it may seem to others a lamentable waste of talent, a sacrifice of some promising secular career, and it may contribute nothing of discernible consequence to the general welfare.

As a prelude to the case of Abraham, consider another example from Kierkegaard. A young man, a "knight of infinite resignation," falls in love with a beautiful princess. His love is so single-minded that "the whole content of his life" is defined by it; so complete that every level of his consciousness is pervaded with it. Yet when he assesses the actual prospects of union the results are mercilessly discouraging. Naturally more cautious types, who are cunning in worldly matters and always hedge their bets, advise him against further indulgence of his wish. His love seems doomed to be unhappy; and other alliances, they urge, are fully as respectable, with greater promise of realization. Still he holds out; he refuses to disperse his energies superficially in all directions. He is capable of an almost pure intensity and concentration. Though each remembrance of her brings him pain, none is quickly forgotten by plunging into a new round of involvements. Now what occurs? His wish is pressed inward and the love is kept young. Yet he ceases to want or need any further visible contact with the princess. He expresses his love "spiritually" by infinite resignation; that is, he posits in the depths of his inner life, in the constancy he wins there, an "eternal validity" to the love, even as he waives any actual claim to it.

> Love for that princess became for him the expression of an eternal love, assumed a religious character, was transfigured into a love for the Eternal Being, which did to be sure deny him the fulfilment of his love, yet reconciled him again by the eternal consciousness of its validity in the form of eternity, which no reality can take from him.[5]

In this process he comprehends the "deep secret" that in order to love another in such a way, one must be sufficient unto oneself. He comes to affirm a like validity to his own deepened and purified inner consciousness as such, which persists irrespective of external changes and social status. If the princess is similarly able to make the movement of infinite resignation—to do so is open to man and

[5] Søren Kierkegaard, *Fear and Trembling,* trans. Walter Lowrie (Princeton: Princeton Univ. Press, 1969), p. 54. Hereafter cited as FT.

woman without distinction—there will be a profound and permanent agreement between them, though they remain separated forever. If external circumstances alter and the barriers are removed, they will be capable of beginning just as they would have had they been united at the start.

Kierkegaard appears therefore to think that infinite resignation is a movement any agent can train himself to make, but that he must perform it finally by himself. Negatively it requires that he genuinely relinquish the need for further actual interventions (he does not have to talk with the princess just once more) or an interest in worldly vindication as a final outcome (he does not expect that he will get the princess after all, though of course he will rejoice if this takes place). Positively it involves an awakening to sublime levels of inner awareness; one "feels the lofty dignity assigned to every man." By resignation one gains one's "eternal consciousness" and faith presupposes it.

> The infinite resignation is the last stage prior to faith, so that one who has not made this movement has not faith; for only in the infinite resignation do I become clear to myself with respect to my eternal validity, and only then can there be any question of grasping existence by virtue of faith.[6]

Grasping existence by virtue of faith is the second of the two movements. It is perhaps this second movement which the person who enters a cloister has yet to make. In the case of the young man, if he is a "knight of faith," he executes the first movement exactly as before. He faces the actual impossibility of union without fanciful flights and hollow daydreams; and he waives his claim. Yet beyond all such sober analysis, beyond anything in fact ascertainable by hardheaded rationality and yet different from the merely improbable or unforeseen, he makes a second movement still more remarkable. He says, "I believe nevertheless that I shall get her, in virtue, that is, of the absurd, in virtue of the fact that with God all things are possible."[7] Johannes *de silentio*, who confesses that he is no knight of faith, finds this second movement unattainable. For such "mystical soaring" he is too heavy. When he contemplates it he

[6] Ibid., p. 57.
[7] Ibid.

becomes giddy, yet he admires it without reserve. The greatest person is the one who can perform both movements.

Kierkegaard sees such a double movement in Abraham, though additional considerations make his case far more complex. The first movement is performed by waiving his claim to Isaac. Kierkegaard insists on the sincerity of Abraham's renunciation. The final outcome of the story must not be entertained precipitously, for God must not be "swindled" out of the first movement of infinite resignation. Abraham's agony is genuine. Indeed, his situation has peculiar pathos, because of its additional religiously defined features. Abraham experiences more than a love which awakens sublime inner awareness of a status exceeding the transiency of the everyday, but the actual realization of which he must give up. He confronts a divinely imposed trial, an explicit command which seems bitterly discontinuous with his prior faith in the promise as well as his love for his son. What can the point of such a command, in Abraham's case in particular, possibly be?

> All was lost! Seventy years of faithful expectation, the brief joy at the fulfilment of faith. Who then is he that plucks away the old man's staff, who is it that requires that he himself shall break it? Who is he that would make a man's gray hairs comfortless, who is it that requires that he himself shall do it? Is there no compassion for the venerable oldling, none for the innocent child? And yet Abraham was God's elect, and it was the Lord who imposed the trial.[8]

Kierkegaard dwells relentlessly on the pain of the trial. Abraham's suffering is unrelieved until the very end and yet throughout he does not cease to believe or refuse to obey.

Abraham's faith includes but also exceeds obedience to this specific command, whatever it costs him. For he makes the second movement as well. While ready to sacrifice Isaac, he believes he will get him back "by virtue of the absurd," for, as in the young man's case, with God all things are possible. Abraham believes "nevertheless"—after all human calculation has ceased—this will not come to pass or a new Isaac will be given him. The knight of faith receives again what he has honestly renounced; he makes the "movements of infinity" and then the movements of "finiteness." Kierkegaard relishes

8 Ibid., p. 34.

the irrational character of this second movement. One exists in such a fashion that resignation of the finite expresses itself as complete harmony with it.

The knights of the infinite resignation are easily recognized: their gait is gliding and assured. Those on the other hand who carry the jewel of faith are likely to be delusive, because their outward appearance bears a striking resemblance to that which both the infinite resignation and faith profoundly despise . . . to Philistinism.[9]

This second movement is indeed paradoxical and its implications unclear. Is one *assured* of always getting Isaac or the princess back provided that the resignation is genuine? Would any such assurance not limit God's freedom? And has the wheel come to such a full circle that the significance of the first movement is placed in jeopardy? Fortunately I do not have to try to answer such questions here. The critical movement for present purposes is the first.

Let me bypass for now Abraham's religious perplexities concerning the point of the command, given the earlier promise, and attend instead to that particular part of the finite which Abraham is asked to suspend. Kierkegaard calls it the ethical. In the Kierkegaardian literature as a whole one can distinguish various senses of the ethical, some of which are more allied to the religious than others.[10] In *Fear and Trembling* he seems to have a Hegelian version especially in mind and holds out for the possibility of a conflict in principle between religious duty and this sense of moral duty. I shall try, however, to avoid as much as possible intramural questions about Hegel's own philosophy and Kierkegaard's specific attacks on it, and concentrate at present on certain general contrasts between the religious and the ethical put forward in this work.

One interpretation of the contrast can be mentioned at the out-

[9] Ibid., p. 49.

[10] The "main forms of the ethical" in Kierkegaard's corpus are summarized in the editors' notes to *Søren Kierkegaard's Journals and Papers*, 1, ed. and trans. Howard V. Hong and Edna H. Hong (Bloomington: Ind. Univ. Press, 1967), pp. 530–32. Different characteristics of the ethical are sorted out by Harold Ofstad, "Morality, Choice, and Inwardness," *Inquiry*, 8 (Spring 1965), pp. 33–73. One example among many in which the ethical and the religious are held to be deeply allied is the following from *Stages on Life's Way*, trans. Walter Lowrie (New York: Schocken, 1967), p. 400: "the ethical desires to be separated from the aesthetic and from the outwardness which is its imperfection, it desires to enter into a glorious alliance, and that is with the religious."

set, because it is so widely held, but it should then be largely set aside. Kierkegaard is often thought to be distinguishing Abraham's higher duty from what might be called ethical philistinism. Abraham's integrity is tempted by established public opinion. He violates the canons of respectability and offends those who take as authoritative the moral opinions of their class and circumstance. The levels of dread and conflict he knows are out of the reach of prosaic temperaments who are content to abide by conventional rules of their historical epoch.[11] There is clearly something in this interpretation; the general timbre of *Fear and Trembling* makes it intelligible, and in a vague impressionistic sense, partly correct. Throughout his writings, Kierkegaard attacks what he thinks is the passionless, materialistic, bourgeois society of the nineteenth century, with its simpleminded hedonism and insolent confidence that it knows what religious faith is, that attainment of faith is an easy, unremarkable affair. But taken as a rigorous and comprehensive characterization, this interpretation does not suffice. Kierkegaard also insists that to be a "tragic hero," for instance, requires courage and may violate conventional moral opinions, and yet does not involve a suspension of the ethical. The suspension envisaged is not synonymous with an attack on philistinism or customary morality.

Let me attempt then to characterize the contrasts in more formal and precise terms. A necessary condition of the ethical to which even the tragic hero may intelligibly conform—and which really serves to illuminate his predicament and justify the steps he takes— has to do with the results of actions. One properly ethical test of rightness and wrongness is held to be a consideration of consequences. This test applies to the ethical in all of its gradations. Kierkegaard cites as examples three tragic heroes who for the sake of a given requirement for societal cohesion make appalling sacrifices. Agamemnon in his role as commander-in-chief finds he must offer his daughter; Jephthah does the same as he saves Israel by a vow he cannot later repudiate; Brutus honors the sanctity of law by punishing the guilty, even when one such party is his son.[12] A

---

[11] See, e.g., Geoffrey Clive, " 'The Teleological Suspension of the Ethical' in Nineteenth-Century Literature," *The Journal of Religion*, XXXIV (April, 1954), pp. 75–87. He links Kierkegaard with other nineteenth-century figures such as Hawthorne, Melville, Dostoyevsky, Tolstoy, Ibsen, and Strindberg.
[12] FT, pp. 68–69.

modern man may recoil from a particular requirement and still allow that the action in question in a certain social context is defensible with unusual courage displayed and a grandeur achieved. The duties of the tragic hero are understood and sympathized with because they are justified by virtue of their effects: the people are saved, the idea of a state is maintained, and so on. Tragedy may be unalterable in the conflict of obligations affirmed to be good in themselves, and the depth of the suffering may seem bizarre to those for whom conventional moral opinions are authoritative, but the action nevertheless is not "temporally" pointless. Its aim may be finally appreciated by all, even when they disagree or are themselves unable to approach similar heights. Security for the tragic hero is found in such universal comprehensibility.

This security means secondly that ethical judgments are held to be universally communicable in principle. Even the hero can justify no "final" concealment; when challenged he is obliged to offer publicly cogent arguments to support his action. Here one confronts Kierkegaard's problematic references to the "universal."

> The ethical as such is the universal, again, as the universal it is the manifest, the revealed. The individual regarded as he is immediately, that is, as a physical and psychical being, is the hidden, the concealed. So his ethical task is to develop out of this concealment and to reveal himself in the universal.[13]

It is arguable that the "universal" has several meanings in *Fear and Trembling* which are not logically equivalent, but to attempt to show this now in detail would be to digress. I shall be content to introduce two possible senses in which the ethical as the "universal" might be said to forbid concealment. The first is the more familiar in that it is linked to contemporary discussion about the universalizability test. To pass this test, one must grant as a logical requirement that any judgment he makes in a particular situation of moral choice he must make about any other situation which is similar in the morally relevant respects. One cannot make an arbitrary exception on one's own behalf but must accept that what is sauce for the goose is sauce for the gander. That is, the reasons one gives to justify one's actions must be applicable to anyone so circumstanced. In this sense the agent when challenged is obliged to offer publicly cogent argu-

[13] Ibid., p. 91.

ments; he is logically prevented from acting on principles which he is unwilling to see similar persons act on in similar circumstances. Whether the suspension of the ethical in *Fear and Trembling* must be interpreted as suspending this requirement, explicitly or by implication, is a question I shall consider later. I think, however, that a second sense in which the ethical forbids concealment is a more likely reading of some very difficult passages. The second sense, which Kierkegaard finds in Hegel among others, seems to refer to the universal as having a certain metaphysical status vis-à-vis the individual agent rather than as a logical requirement (in the sense just noted). Here the demand for universal communicability seems to presuppose a single coherent structure which the "reason" can penetrate and explain. What is required of the agent is that he understand his own nature in terms of its place in the structure, the "universal"; this alone will rightly allow him to determine what he may and may not do. He is accountable to the structure and should see himself in every respect as coextensive with it. To act ethically is to conform to the structure and give reasons intelligible in relation to it. On this view, "as soon as the individual would assert himself in his particularity over against the universal he sins."[14] To rule out final concealment is one means of abolishing such particularity.

A final characteristic of the ethical is that it requires no direct and active reference to God, nor does it lead to a personal relation with him.

> It is a duty to love one's neighbor, but in performing this duty I do not come into relation with God but with the neighbor whom I love. If I say then in this connection that it is my duty to love God, I am really uttering only a tautology, inasmuch as "God" is in this instance used in an entirely abstract sense as the divine, i.e. the universal, i.e. duty. So the whole existence of the human race is rounded off completely like a sphere, and the ethical is at once its limit and its content. God becomes an invisible vanishing point, a powerless thought, His power being only in the ethical which is the content of existence.[15]

It is this characteristic perhaps which Kierkegaard finds most worrisome. He aspires to move his reader to what he takes to be a decisive

14 Ibid., p. 65.
15 Ibid., p. 78.

relationship with God. One may well be troubled by the obscurity of his account of the relation between the tragic hero who achieves a more lofty realization of the ethical and yet also appears at points to be identified with the knight of infinite resignation who, as we saw, relinquishes everything finite—including the ethical as the "content of existence." If, however, this obscurity is ignored, it seems clear that Kierkegaard wants above all an account of religious obligation which is anything but tautological; one in which God is certainly more than an invisible vanishing point.

Let us see how he characterizes Abraham in contrast to the ethical as it has been identified thus far. To begin with, Abraham is held to accomplish nothing whatever in the form of socially beneficial results. Taking Isaac to Moriah seems a private venture devoid of long-range societal objectives, where he himself is tried and examined. As the young man cannot do what he does for the sake of getting the princess after all, so the pivot in Abraham's case remains the personal trial and not what he achieves or endeavors to achieve on behalf of any surrounding community. He is bereft of the security to be found in universal comprehensibility; his action appears "temporally" pointless. The stress on a personal trial is positively associated with Kierkegaard's repeated commendation of "inwardness." The greater the inwardness, the less attention to results is warranted. So one reads that the "absence of a result is precisely a determination of inwardness; for a result is something external, and a communication of results is an external relation between a knower and a non-knower."[16]

Inwardness is likewise characterized by intra-psychic struggle and temptation, the import of which cannot always be exhaustively or satisfactorily communicated to others. There are many occasions when "no one can know the facts except the individual himself, in his own consciousness of himself. . . ."[17] Abraham's trial is in Kierkegaard's eyes one such occasion, when concealment from Isaac, Sarah, and Eleazar appears justified. Abraham is unable to communicate "directly" with any of them. In the terminology of Hegel,

[16] Søren Kierkegaard, *Concluding Unscientific Postscript*, trans. David F. Swenson and Walter Lowrie (Princeton: Princeton Univ. Press, 1960), p. 257. Hereafter cited as CUP.
[17] Ibid., p. 352.

his duty cannot be "mediated," and this means, for Kierkegaard, that he cannot talk. Again, I shall not try to consider whether Kierkegaard does justice to Hegel. But at a minimum the contention is that the individual, in his particularity, cannot be contained by the social roles he fills or the community duties incumbent on all. His grounds for action exceed and sometimes go against the conditions for societal viability and may throw doubt upon the tasks a presumptuously inflated reason (note, for example, Hegel's account of *Vernunft*) assigns him according to his place in "world history." To assert oneself in one's particularity over against the "universal" is to have to do with one's own deepest self-identity, the "lofty dignity" assigned to every person, a sublime inner awareness of a status incommensurable with any single coherent structure of encompassing reality which the reason can grasp. One must attend to one's own lights even when why one does what one does is incommunicable to others.

Finally, Kierkegaard thinks Abraham is a knight of faith because he refers actively and directly to God. To guarantee that such referral will not become superfluous Kierkegaard proposes to speak of an "absolute *telos*" whose authority is always overriding. The absolute *telos* brings on the stage then a being to whom veneration is uniquely owed and to whose behests obedience is the fitting response. Abraham must be prepared to suspend anything, to obey God's behests whatever the cost. In the case of the trial, the ethical itself constitutes the temptation. If the "absolute duty toward God" is to have distinct and prevailing force, even the obligation to one's son (and Kierkegaard believes that the ethical had for Abraham "no higher expression than the family life") may have to give way with its authority "relativized." The device required for overridingness to be assured and the threat of superfluity avoided is the teleological suspension of the ethical. For the sake of the absolute *telos*, the ethical may have to be suspended insofar as it is part of the finite or is "the content of existence." Otherwise one remains within a sphere of duties to one's neighbor, religious obligation threatens to become tautological, and a direct relation to God is foreclosed. By going to Moriah Abraham attests that God remains for him the object of unique veneration. Assurance of overridingness, therefore, if seriously meant, requires the necessity of conflict in principle between religious and ethical obligation. Thus Kierkegaard plunges in:

> What ordinarily tempts a man is that which would keep him from doing his duty, but in this case the temptation is itself the ethical . . . which would keep him from doing God's will. But what then is duty? Duty is precisely the expression for God's will.[18]

II

It is time now to offer some assessments of his undertaking. I wish to ask first whether the contrasts he draws between ethical and religious obligation presuppose a characterization of the ethical which one may reasonably contest. One interpreter of the ethics of existentialism states the issue in this way:

> The familiar phrase Kierkegaard uses to describe Abraham's case—the "teleological suspension of the ethical"—can be somewhat misleading if it is not understood that the ethical that is transcended or suspended is the morality of general rules, and that the real effect of Kierkegaard's views is to expand the sphere of morality to include the requirement of obedience to God's particular commands.[19]

It is important in the interests of clarity to try to discover how far such a case for terminological expansion might go. How many of his contrasts might be accommodated if the account of the ethical in *Fear and Trembling* is critically scrutinized and other—particularly modern—characterizations introduced? Could some contrasts be modified, if not removed, without fatal compromise to Kierkegaard's religious program? If one seeks greater room for maneuver in one's characterization of the ethical, perhaps one may acquire a clearer sense of which disputes are verbal and which substantive.

It should be noticed then that the contrasts between religious and moral obligation on which Kierkegaard insists depend in a significant way on a quite distinctive characterization of the ethical.

[18] FT, p. 70.
[19] Frederick A. Olafson, *Principles and Persons* (Baltimore: Johns Hopkins Press, 1970), p. 28.

To recall the earlier description: 1) ethical judgments have to do with the results of actions, in accordance especially with the criteria of societal cohesion and the public welfare; 2) ethical reasons for action are universally communicable, and there seems a necessary connection between being able always to make oneself comprehensible to others and assuming a single coherent structure of reality which the reason can grasp; 3) the ethical is self-contained, and requires no necessary reference to God, or does not lead to a personal relation to him. Religious obligation, on the other hand, involves: 1) a personal undertaking, where the agent himself is tried and examined; the center of gravity remains the trial and its terror and not what is accomplished for society; 2) a status accorded the individual higher than and finally incommensurable with any rationally apprehended structure of reality surrounding him to which he must conform; 3) direct and active referral to God, to whom the agent has an absolute duty which, if it is to be genuinely absolute, may require at any moment resignation of all things "finite."

Concerning the first feature, one may well ask whether Kierkegaard is overly hasty in his assumption that a calculation of consequences must be an essential feature of "the ethical." Is this unwarranted stipulation on his part? Any number of persons have valued motive and character rather than results and success, and have supposed in so doing that they were engaged in moral commendation. Some have wished to ascribe "unqualified worth" to personal virtue and to it alone, without raising any question of a suspension of the ethical. Certainly many well-known disputes have occurred over such commendation. If nothing is unqualifiedly good except a "good will," must other objects (e.g., happiness) then be renounced, or are they at least compatible with it, even if not strictly part of it? Will concentration on the good will finish in smug, self-centered attention to inner purity? Or can one consistently be concerned with reasonably foreseen and actual consequences as well? Indeed, is there a practical equivalence between various traditional alternatives? To hold in any case that the value of a personal virtuous disposition is not altered or diminished in any way by its results (as Kierkegaard appears to do), or that an action itself derives its value not from its consequences but from the kind of intention the agent has, is to offer what many have regarded as a moral judgment, however unacceptable one may find it. The center of gravity may remain then on the agent's intentions and not on what is accomplished for society. So would it not be terminologically clearer to say that Kierkegaard espouses a certain anti-consequentialist morality? The issue is complicated by distinctive features of his account which encapsulate his own standards, whether one calls these religious or moral or both. He purports to see a dark purpose, however typically unconscious, in a preoccupation with results. The individual seeks to level "down the whole of existence to the idea of the state or the idea of society."[20] Such leveling may threaten individual dignity by wrongly according final priority to a social productiveness criterion of human worth.[21] One has finally to do with "a rebellion of the relative ends against the majesty of the absolute, an attempt to bring the absolute down to the level of everything else, an attack upon the dignity of human life, seeking to make man a mere servant of relative ends."[22]

Whether such a purpose actually motivates all those concerned with results is plainly questionable; the entire subject of consequentialism demands far more attention than Kierkegaard gives it. But it appears in any case that some of his attack on a calculation of consequences per se does not require a teleological suspension, if one thinks of the traditional options in ethical theory. More formidable contrasts remain.

III

The standard of socially beneficial results is closely linked, as we have seen, to the demand for universal communicability. Earlier I distinguished two possible senses in which the "universal" might be said to forbid concealment: the logical requirement of universalizability, which prevents one from acting on private, arbitrary stand-

[20] FT, p. 72.

[21] Kierkegaard's dislike of a certain sense of "utility" is pronounced, though he believes those in his own time should face what follows from their own anthropological premises. "It is odd that our age, which is so enthusiastic about utility, does not go so far, for example, that it abolishes all funerals and piety regarding the dead and recommends burning the bodies. Surely artificial fertilizer could be made in this way." *Søren Kierkegaard's Journals and Papers,* 1, p. 389.

[22] CUP, p. 382.

ards which one is unwilling to see applied to anyone else so circumstanced; and the metaphysical claim exemplified in Hegel's speculative philosophy that to understand one's own nature and what one ought to do, one must attend via reason to the entire intelligible structure of reality with which one is altogether commensurate. Let me take the second sense first, because the main lines of Kierkegaard's attack on Hegelian idealism are tolerably familiar.

Kierkegaard's case for justified concealment proceeds in part from his concept of the individual. He strives to rescue this concept from all absorptionist tendencies. In epistemology, the agent must be more than a particular expression of the universal; in metaphysics, more than an aspect of universal mind; in ethics, more than a member of society with its stations and duties. One encounters in Kierkegaard's treatment of Abraham such a distinctive concept of human nature, which bears obvious family resemblances to existentialist philosophy in general. The quest to specify rationally a single coherent structure in which everything has its place and to which all must adhere is held to be an illusory "myth of objectivity." The agent is not simply an observer of world history. This contention can be understood in moral terms: "Kierkegaard was passionately convinced that to treat the moral life of the individual as simply acting out of something that is already anticipated in the implicit logic of the world spirit was to make it too easy a thing."[23] Kierkegaard incorporates into his notion of the individual at least three elements. First, when the agent probes deeper than the transiency of the everyday, he apprehends the lofty dignity proper to each person, the inner awareness of a status which seems to belong outside space and time. He cannot or can no longer accept that he is simply a normal spatio-temporal object. A "sense of alienation," of being a stranger and sojourner upon earth, presses in on him. Perhaps some of this is akin to Kant's postulate of immortality; one's deepest commitments will not be "thrown back into a purposeless chaos of matter"; they possess an "eternal validity" in spite of physical decay. Kierkegaard believes therefore that one is driven toward a distinct set of concepts marking off the standpoint of the agent from the standpoint of the observer. So, secondly, the individual asserts himself in his particularity and fosters his inwardness when he abandons the pose of observer and

23 Olafson, *Principles and Persons,* p. 29.

ceases to find his identity or his vindication in the opinions of others. "It is only the lower natures which find in other people the law for their actions, which find the premises for their actions outside themselves."[24] Abraham's trial is, again, an event in which he himself is tested and no one else can make the movements for him. He cannot hope to pass on to others knowledge which will make their own movements easier than his own. No corpus on trials of this kind can be accumulated over the centuries which will accord to later generations a simpler task or superior vantage point. "Whatever the one generation may learn from the other, that which is genuinely human no generation learns from the foregoing. In this respect every generation begins primitively. . . ."[25] And third, a distinctively Protestant stress is added: the individual is immediately responsible before God. Every intermediary may be dispensed with, whether it be church, state, or tradition. Abraham differs from the tragic hero who does not enter into a private relation with the deity. It is a commonplace that such a stress often focuses on one absolute standard—God's will—even at the risk of indirect support for social and ecclesiastical anarchy. The agent is finally accountable to God alone and may stand in a direct, "unmediated" relation of obedience to him.

Naturally the question of the truth in each of these elements is disputable. A materialist might shrug off references to a status outside space and time as pious illusions; a sociologist might regard the contention that each generation begins primitively in any sense as wishful thinking; a Catholic might claim to see arrogance and eventual chaos in such radical subjectivity. Moreover, the elements seem not to be logically dependent on one another. While one finds their interlacing in Kierkegaard's case intelligible, the human autonomy implied in the second has for certain thinkers been severed completely from the divine autonomy implied in the third. I shall return later to certain troublesome issues about autonomy. At the moment the question is simply: does the case for justified concealment as presented thus far make sense only when the demand of universal communicability is tied to a Hegelian (à la Kierkegaard) account of reality? Suppose it is agreed that for someone who accepts Kierkegaard's account of individuality, the case for occasionally justified

24 FT, p. 55.
25 Ibid., p. 130.

concealment is cogent vis-à-vis the notion of reality contrasted with it. The agent needs to go beyond what is comprehensible in a society governed by established roles and the perpetuation of the status quo; he must make the decisive movements by himself; he is finally accountable to God alone. When, however, Kierkegaard claims that to say Abraham cannot be mediated is the *same* as to say that he cannot talk, is too much conceded to Hegel? Is Kierkegaard forced on his own terms to equate *Hegelian* mediation and meaningful human language of every possible sort? I think not. One may cite, for example, the influence of Kierkegaard on modern-day exponents of a distinctive religious "language game." Sometimes, however, Johannes *de silentio* indulges in crude equations which need interpretation in light of Kierkegaard's other writings. All I wish to observe now is that accounts of the ethical abound which do not embrace the speculative philosophy he attacks, which allow a central place to individual choice, for opposition to an ethic of "my station and its duties" and criticism of conventional moral opinions, for change in and conflict between substantive principles of action-guidance, and yet which rule out concealment in the sense of private arbitrary standards which one is unwilling to see applied to other persons in like circumstances. Such unwillingness is held to be appropriately subject to interpersonal challenge. When asked, the agent must offer reasons applicable to others whose situations resemble his own in the relevant ways, or be charged with logical inconsistency. The most interesting issue is, I think, whether explicitly or by implication the concealment Kierkegaard commends in opposition to speculative philosophy is also incompatible with the universalizability requirement as modern philosophers expound it. If so, then one cannot be satisfied to relegate his endorsement of silence to nineteenth-century philosophical warfare. If not, then here too one may perhaps modify a marked formal contrast between religion and morality.

Speaking roughly, universalizability is the logical thesis which prevents one from making different moral judgments about actions which one grants are exactly or relevantly similar.[26] While moral

---

[26] Here I shall assume the account of universalizability by its most influential modern exponent, R. M. Hare, in *The Language of Morals* (Oxford: Clarendon Press, 1961); *Freedom and Reason* (New York: Oxford Univ. Press, 1965); *Essays on the Moral Concepts* (London: Macmillan, 1972), esp. pp. 13–28.

judgments are not descriptive *simpliciter,* they do possess descriptive meaning. If one makes a moral judgment about something, it necessarily has to do with some feature of that thing. Any description of that feature depends upon the concept of similarity. One cannot consistently apply a descriptive term to the feature and decline to apply it in another case which is similar in the relevant respects. Insofar as moral judgments include descriptive meaning, they are universalizable. Moral judgments are thus repeatable in principle.

The principle to which one adheres in making a moral judgment need not, however, be thought of as existing *antecedently* to that judgment, as if all one has to do is consult the principle and apply it. Cases of extraordinary complexity arise, it may be allowed, when no appeal to an antecedently existent principle suffices. The agent may have to consider what ought to be done in the particular case without relevant precedents to guide him, or at least with unprecedented care. What the thesis requires is that the agent be prepared to grant that the judgment he makes has a bearing outside the particular case, that anyone so circumstanced ought to do so as well. The principle to which one adheres also need not be very general or simple, for one may distinguish universality from generality. A principle of action-guidance may be universalizable and still very precise and detailed, with qualifications written in and unusual features recognized. While all of the terms would be universal ones if the principle were specified, it may be so complex as to defy verbal formulation.

Now, it has been held that because moral judgments are universalizable we can regard moral thought as rational, just as the prescriptivity of such judgments links with our freedom to form our own opinions about moral issues. I shall consider the latter contention in the next section. The present question is this: can one make a cogent case that Kierkegaard's account of the trial passes the universalizability test, regardless of the terminological reasons the reader meets with initially for supposing not?

Any such case must first reckon with Kierkegaard's stress upon silence, which he sees as both unavoidable and justified. One finds, however, a confusing amalgam of points made on behalf of silence. Briefly, they seem to include:

1) The case in question is exceedingly complex, with so many unusual features which have to be recognized. One need think only

of the special religious perplexity, given Abraham's belief in the earlier promise. Any principle Abraham prescribes may not be verbally formulable, or at least may defy exhaustive specification. Moreover, God's command is sometimes represented as highly particular, for this person in this time and place. In short, to keep silence may attest to legitimate uncertainty that another case of unusual complexity is sufficiently like one's own to warrant anything approaching round table consideration of the licitness of the judgment made.

2) Kierkegaard appears to doubt whether a divine command is an appropriate subject for interpersonal argument. The hearer may not be called upon to deliberate, with God or with other persons, but simply to obey. Insistence on reasonable argument in the face of challenge where it is one's consistency which is on trial, seems somehow misplaced in the context.

3) Kierkegaard often evinces skepticism about the efficacy of reasonable argument in general when one must decide what to do. Moral and religious disagreements are in this life interminable. Unlike (say) Socrates in the Platonic dialogues, who is able to defeat his opponents partly because of the intrinsic dialectical superiority of his arguments, Kierkegaard is impressed by the fact that rational argument, whether spoken or written, does not seem to bring moral or religious unanimity. Indeed, he thinks cases roughly comparable in cogency and rigor can be marshaled for incompatible ideals of life. A decision is required: no direct transition appears to occur from the weighing of the pros and cons of various ideals to the personal espousal of any one of them.

4) Silence is also in place because one must make the movements by oneself. No knight of faith can finally render aid to another or make the movements easier or more assured. A partial secular analogy might be that one should not take one's opinions ready-made from others. To be a knight of faith is to suffer "the terrible responsibility of solitude."[27]

5) Finally, there are hints that a thesis about the nature and limits of human language as such stands behind the justification of silence. For one thing, Kierkegaard emphasizes the sheer significance of conscious activity and the inability of language to correspond

27 FT, p. 123.

adequately to it.[28] Words are no surrogate for actually making the movements. Then too, Abraham seems to run up against the boundaries of what is publicly intelligible, of what can ever be exhibited and argued about in human discourse. So "the relief of speech is that it translates me into the universal."[29] The knight of faith cannot find such relief, since "in the temporal world God and I cannot talk together, we have no language in common."[30] If Abraham hears a direct (non-sensory) command of God, nothing intelligible to all can be said about it, for he would have to speak another language altogether.

> He is unable to speak, he speaks no human language. Though he himself understood all the tongues of the world, though his loved ones also understood them, he nevertheless cannot speak —he speaks a divine language . . . he "speaks with tongues."[31]

The last point cannot feasibly be considered here. I have indicated previously that cryptic statements such as those cited would have to be interpreted in light of the entire Kierkegaardian literature; for example, his influence would have to be examined on modern thinkers who defend an autonomous religious language game intelligible at least to believers. What needs to be asked now is whether any of the remaining points necessarily contravene universalizability. The case for non-contravention might proceed as follows.

It has already been pointed out that universalizability as recently expounded allows for cases of extraordinary complexity. Abraham's trial is obviously such a case, where qualifications must be written in and unusual features recognized. Kierkegaard is not obliged, incidentally, to hold that every episode in the life of a knight of faith must possess such complexity. What he must grant is that a knight of faith is logically prevented from making a different judgment about another action of his own or someone else which he admits is exactly or relevantly similar. Kierkegaard seems in effect to concede this. While consistency is not his chief worry, he affirms that certain

---

[28] For elaboration on this point, see Adi Shmuëli, *Kierkegaard and Consciousness*, trans. Naomi Handelman (Princeton: Princeton Univ. Press, 1971), e.g., pp. 94–95.
[29] FT, p. 122.
[30] Ibid., p. 45–46.
[31] Ibid., p. 123.

salient features of the trial stand out and recur in other cases. These features are repeatable in principle and taken to have an important bearing outside the particular case. "The story of Abraham contains . . . *a* teleological suspension of the ethical."[32] Notice that he does not say *"the."* What Abraham does in going to Moriah is exemplary of his own past and possible future and of other knights of faith as well. Consider, for instance, Kierkegaard's treatment of Mary. She too experiences dread and distress, and cannot express herself to others in the moment; she like Abraham does not require worldly admiration; she is not a tragic heroine but by virtue of her faith attains something greater.[33] Kierkegaard observes elsewhere that everyone confronts the collision where the ethical becomes a temptation.[34] Every agent may presumably have his own Isaac in the form of some finite object of devotion which threatens to pass from human care, which of course Kierkegaard commends, to a worship he finds idolatrous. Such examples could be multiplied. Thus it is hard to see why a complexity which may defy exhaustive specification or a trial which tests primarily Abraham's obedience rather than his consistency is vulnerable to the charge that Abraham or Mary make arbitrary exceptions on their own behalf. They may agree that the reasons for their actions are applicable to anyone else so circumstanced.

The universalizability requirement also provides abundant logical room for criticism of conventional moral opinions, and for the importance of making one's own decisions. The agent is free to initiate rather than merely accept the judgments of his forebears or contemporaries, and assume the responsibility for guiding his own life. One may think that Kierkegaard mistakenly derides the role of reasonable argument in deciding what to do. His attack on speculative dogmatism threatens to rule out a courageous use of practical reason in acquiring as much clarity as possible, for oneself and with others, about what one does and why one does it. But for all his derision, universalizability does not forbid a stress on the significance of decision and personal espousal, and making the movements by oneself.

A final line of argument for saying that Kierkegaard's account

[32] Ibid., p. 77, italics mine.
[33] Ibid., pp. 75–76.
[34] CUP, p. 231.

of the trial passes the universalizability test is this. Tucked down in *Fear and Trembling* are a number of passages which suggest the explicit lengths to which Kierkegaard is prepared to go to specify conditions for any such trial and criteria for distinguishing a bona fide command from a temptation (*Anfechtung*). He appears then to think that certain salient features constitute part of the relevant circumstances of a trial which are repeatable in principle. Johannes qua observer does not remain silent about these salient features, even if only Abraham qua agent can determine whether in fact they obtain in his case. Let me try to identify them.

1) Abraham must be someone with seriously held moral and religious beliefs. Only upon such a person—"pious and God-fearing" —is such a test imposed.[35] And when he overrides the ethical even in the sense being queried here, he does not disregard or disparage it. Kierkegaard freely acknowledges that it is a glorious thing to be a tragic hero. 2) Abraham *cannot* hate Isaac in suspending the ethical. Abraham does not enjoy the prospect of inflicting pain. One gives up the *beloved;* apart from anguish and grief any question of a teleological suspension would seem trivial. That Abraham loves rather than hates Isaac costs Kierkegaard some tortured formulations. Consider one example, where two senses of "ethical" appear in the same sentence.

> . . . It does not follow that the ethical is to be abolished, but it acquires an entirely different expression, the paradoxical expression,—that, for example, love to God may cause the knight of faith to give his love to his neighbor the opposite expression to that which, ethically speaking, is required by duty.[36]

It seems one thing to say the ethical is "expressed," though irregularly or "paradoxically," another that it is "abolished," (and still another that it is "suspended"). However one construes this particular passage, it is clear throughout that "the absolute duty may cause one to do what ethics would forbid, but by no means can it cause the knight of faith to cease to love."[37] It may appear by conventional moral criteria that Abraham hates Isaac. "But if he really hates Isaac, he can be sure that God does not require this, for Cain and Abraham

35 FT, p. 42.
36 Ibid., p. 80.
37 Ibid., p. 84.

are not identical."[38] Loving Isaac "even more dearly" is a condition
for sacrificing him. It is terminologically odd to distinguish in this
way genuine love for one's son and the ethical, and Kierkegaard's
uneasiness strengthens the case perhaps for modifying his verbal
contrasts. I shall return to the sense Kierkegaard finally attaches to
Abraham's love for Isaac. 3) Abraham must rely on himself and not
on other persons. Apart from self-reliance, one can be certain he is
in temptation.

> Whether the individual is in temptation (*Anfechtung*) or is a
> knight of faith only the individual can decide. Nevertheless
> it is possible to construct from the paradox several criteria which
> he too can understand who is not within the paradox. The true
> knight of faith is always absolute isolation, the false knight is
> sectarian. . . . The knight of faith . . . is the individual, ab-
> solutely nothing but the individual, without connections or
> pretensions. This is the terrible thing which the sectarian mani-
> kin cannot endure. For instead of learning from this terror that
> he is not capable of performing the great deed and then plainly
> admitting it . . . the manikin thinks that by uniting with sev-
> eral other manikins he will be able to do it. But that is quite out
> of the question. In the world of spirit no swindling is toler-
> ated.[39]

Kierkegaard denounces as "the most terrible of all falsehoods—the
having an adherent."[40] One consequence of his individualism is
that there should never be, as a matter of religious principle, another human being to whom one surrenders totally one's reason
and will. No other person is morally or religiously invincible. Thus
no other human being can require of Abraham the obedience he
exemplifies in the trial.

These conditions will strike many as so general that the natural
question is, why does one bother? The question will be reinforced
for those who think the "morally relevant features" of a situation
have more to do with immediate actions and their discernible effects
in relation to societal criteria of right and wrong, than with certain
attitudes, dispositions, and intentions of the agent. Despite their
generality and their confinement largely to the solitary agent, the

[38] Ibid.
[39] Ibid., pp. 89–90.
[40] CUP, p. 233.

existence of such conditions is important to note. It buttresses the case for declining to accept Kierkegaard's verbal contrast between religion and morality without further ado. The justification of silence does not extend so far that Johannes qua observer is left with nothing to say. He is able to describe and assess to some extent an extraordinary case as well as more ordinary ones. He obviously assumes that the specification he offers does not necessarily lead to the sort of deliberation on the part of the agent which supplants obedience or prevents him from finally making the movements by himself.

Moreover, without the identification of these features, however vaguely, Kierkegaard's account of Abraham's trial is susceptible to sweeping comparisons with every sort of crime performed in the name of holy edict or under the impact of every variety of religious belief—comparisons Kierkegaard would doubtless find worse than misleading.

One modern example of a possible comparison is Charles Manson. He and certain of his followers were convicted of seven murders committed during July and August of 1969 in Los Angeles, with indications that this was by no means the total number.[41] The evidence amassed suggests that members of the "family" were influenced by a number of religious beliefs and communities, broadly defined. To Kierkegaard the influences would appear decidedly syncretistic; they seemed to include the figure of Jesus, the book of Revelation (especially Chapter 9), scientology, faith healing, telepathy, and satanism.

It would be open to Kierkegaard to contrast Abraham's trial with Manson's actions by bringing to bear salient features like those so far identified. Thus he might contend that Manson fails to exemplify the moral and religious seriousness which is a prerequisite for such a test being imposed. During the 1960s, Manson was a sometime forger, car thief, pimp, and armed robber; he taught male chauvinism and racism to members of the family; they performed what in Kierkegaard's eyes would be idolatrous practices such as the drinking of ritual dog blood in front of an altar, staging a mock crucifixion and resurrection with Manson in the role of Jesus, and so on. Manson appeared to wonder seriously for a time whether he was Christ

[41] The abhorrent details are found in Ed Sanders, *The Family: The Story of Charles Manson's Dune Buggy Attack Battalion* (New York: Dutton, 1971).

himself.[42] While Abraham is distinguished from Cain and is asked to give up the beloved, Manson is prepared to kill those who oppose him and whose existence therefore serves no purpose. He eventually determined that "now it's the pigs' turn to go up on the cross."[43] Manson also seemed to be the sort of sectarian who Kierkegaard thinks characterizes the false knight of faith. Manson strove to make his charisma irresistible and his authority unimpeachable. The process of greater fear and control went on to its melancholy end; participation in the group became increasingly forced; books were burned; individuality was suppressed. The family members who remained loyal all appeared to lack the strength of the solitary. And they were certainly willing to talk with one another about their deeds. They were prepared to surrender totally their reason and will to a human leader. The knight of faith, on the other hand, is to be a witness but never a teacher; "he feels the pain of not being able to make himself intelligible to others, but he feels no vain desire to guide others."[44]

The aptness of the comparison may be doubted. It is difficult to determine why the family murdered the persons they did—at least some of the reasons were evidently very "earthly" ones—and the issuance of a direct divine command was never, as far as I know, claimed. Nonetheless, certain religious beliefs were not without effect. My aim here is only to observe that Kierkegaard must try to prevent such sweeping comparisons by specification. And there is far more specification in *Fear and Trembling* than one may at first glance suppose. One may locate in fact an entire range of wider assumptions which stand behind Kierkegaard's treatment and provide a background of intelligibility for the peculiar agony Abraham endures. It would prove instructive to inquire further into the relation between background beliefs and moral judgments in the two cases. For example, Manson took killing less seriously perhaps because he described it as "discorporating" people. "Final" death was a metaphysical illusion; the essence of soul could not die because it had never been born. The body was dispensable. Such inquiry must, however, await another time and place.

[42] Cf., e.g., the treatment of Adler in Søren Kierkegaard, *On Authority and Revelation,* trans. Walter Lowrie (Princeton: Princeton Univ. Press, 1955).
[43] Sanders, *The Family,* p. 148.
[44] FT, p. 90.

I have attempted in this section and the previous one to suggest how a case might cogently go for saying that the final effect of Kierkegaard's views is expansion of the sphere of morality to encompass obedience to God's particular commands. There are good reasons for calling into question certain of Kierkegaard's contrasts between religious and moral duty. On several counts, however, which fall under the general heading of the "autonomy of morality," the expansion remains problematic. To these I now turn.

IV

One sense of autonomy has to do with the ultimate logical properties of whatever words one takes to be primary in moral discourse, e.g., "good," "right," and "duty." In the case of such words, their evaluative meaning is often said to be primary and to remain constant irrespective of the class of object to which they are applied.[45] To explain their meaning differs then from explaining the criteria for their application. They retain always a *commendatory* meaning which prevents their being derivable from or logically equivalent to any statement of fact. To call something good is to guide action or *prescribe*; it is not simply to state a fact about the world.

Prescriptivism as a metaethical theory has been widely discussed and sometimes energetically contested. I do not wish to try to pronounce on these controversies but only to ask whether Kierkegaard's account conflicts unavoidably with this first sense of the ultimate logical autonomy of primarily evaluative words. Suppose one assumes then that prescriptivity as well as universalizability are necessary conditions for moral rules and principles (leaving open the question whether they are also jointly sufficient). Must Kierkegaard be understood to be violating prescriptivity when he makes the following statement quoted earlier? "Duty is precisely the expression for God's will."[46]

This passage in particular has offended many moralists. W. G. Maclagan writes, for example:

Abraham's conduct is approved precisely because he was willing

---

[45] See Hare, *The Language of Morals*. He observes that the evaluative meaning of certain other moral words is secondary to the descriptive, e.g., "tidy" and "industrious" (p. 121).

[46] FT, p. 70.

to trample on his ethical convictions in order to obey the command of God. "Ordinarily speaking" (I quote from the translation by Robert Payne) "a temptation is something which tries
to stop a man from doing his duty, but in this case it is ethics
itself which tries to prevent him from doing God's will." It is
true that when Kierkegaard immediately goes on to say "But
what then is duty? Duty is quite simply the expression of the
will of God" his position may appear less unacceptable to the
moralist, inasmuch as Abraham is after all, it would seem, not
going against *duty*. But it would be a mistake to draw any
comfort from these words. All they indicate is that, with an
added increment of confusion, Kierkegaard has torn apart and
opposed "duty" and morality, so that "duty" itself is no longer
an ethical term. It is pointless to debate whether its absurdity
or its offensiveness is the more striking feature of such a view.[47]

Maclagan assumes too quickly that Kierkegaard must be literally
followed when he makes duty no longer an ethical term. We have
had occasion previously to query his characterization of the ethical
and it seems to me one may legitimately do so at this point too. Or
to put it more accurately: must we conclude that Kierkegaard is
proposing a definition in these sentences, so that duty *means* obedience to the will of God? Any such conclusion would be vulnerable
to the charge of violating the logical autonomy of duty as a primarily evaluative word. And if duty is offered as *logically* equivalent to
obedience to the will of God, the well-known objection arises that
Kierkegaard is then uttering an insignificant tautology. It is a mistake to think, the objection runs, that duty means obeying God,
because in ordinary usage, "Is obedience to God one's duty?" remains
an open question. Non-believers must not be and are not in fact
prevented by a definition from using duty to commend what they
want to commend.

When one considers the major distinctive features of Kierkegaard's work as a whole, it is hard to see why he should be concerned
to deny that right, good, or duty have a meaning which is independ-
dent of obeying God. If one asks what it is about the logic of good,
right, or duty which makes their meaning independent, the account
prescriptivism offers may do very nicely, especially since Kierkegaard

[47] W. G. Maclagan, *The Theological Frontier of Ethics* (London: G. Allen,
1961), p. 67.

has been interpreted in his ethical theory generally to be a kind of forerunner of the prescriptivists.[48] We noted earlier how Kierkegaard's work is directed against moral and religious unanimity. The agent must be free to form his own convictions about moral and religious questions. Ideals and ways of life differ, and no amount of argument will resolve them, because they are founded on choices. These are genuine disputes and not merely verbal misunderstandings. In saying that for Abraham, duty is obedience to God, Kierkegaard intends to utter more than an insignificant tautology. The believer has antecedently a meaning in using the word duty which he shares with non-believers, and which he continues to use for the purpose of commendation. His criterion of application differs in this instance. He is in agreement about the general public meaning of the word, and he uses it in the same way as non-believers. It is what he commends that is distinctive.

We may conclude that Kierkegaard's sentences can be plausibly understood in a fashion which does not violate the ultimate logical autonomy of duty as one primary word in moral discourse. Despite his own verbal contrast between duty and ethics, his use of the former word retains its commendatory meaning. If we say that commending is a different sort of linguistic activity from defining, his sentences may be construed to express this principle: one ought to obey God's will, even when it violates one's own antecedent judgments of those things which are right and wrong. The violation need not intrude, however, on what everyone logically means by right and wrong.

Kierkegaard's sensitivity to the reality of moral and religious disagreements does not lead him to conclude that no issue of truth or falsity is finally at stake between the bewildering variety of disputants. The truth values of rival commendations are definable from one cognitive point of view: God's. Yet human understanding can never achieve objective certainty about the truth values or objectively adjudicate the de facto moral and religious disagreements.[49] Our moral language properly allows for such disagreements through

---

[48] See, e.g., Paul L. Holmer, "Kierkegaard and Ethical Theory," *Ethics*, LXIII (April, 1953), pp. 157–70.

[49] On Kierkegaard's relation to noncognitive and eschatological verificationist accounts of religious language, see Merold Westphal, "Kierkegaard and the Logic of Insanity," *Religious Studies*, 7 (September, 1971), esp. pp. 205–07.

the application of primarily evaluative words to differing classes of objects.

V

In addition to the ultimate logical autonomy of meaning of primarily evaluative words such as good, right, and duty, there is what is often called the autonomy of the agent's response, including his own judgment. Does a divine command violate the agent's freedom to respond or preclude the free exercise of his judgment? To clarify what a view like Kierkegaard's allows and disallows, let me distinguish the following senses of agent-autonomy in relation to a putative divine command.[50]

1) ACCEPTANCE. Autonomy is positively insisted on in the sense that the agent must freely yield to God's sovereignty and assent to his command. In Kierkegaard's theological scheme, such freedom is extolled nearly as a matter of course, as when he comments, for instance, that God "communicates in creating, so as by creating to *give* independence over against Himself."[51] Kierkegaard might regard "acceptance" as too bloodless a word. Justice must be done to Abraham's struggle and suffering, the retention of his trust through calamity. Kierkegaard dwells on the religious significance and psychological richness embedded in the story, nuances which he thinks ethical analyses too often ignore. The knight of faith is concerned with a trial the dreadfulness of which he must endure alone; in the moment, as we have noticed, interpersonal arguments in the interests of consistency seem misplaced. Still, the command is binding only on the condition that he assents. One might risk extrapolation and say: Abraham must come to prescribe universally with God that X ought to be done. He must make the command his own; in this sense it is laid upon him through his own act and thus is reflexive in character.

Moreover, the joint prescription which God and Abraham make universally is never automatic or easy. If anything, Kierkegaard emphasizes more strongly than many defenders of moral autonomy

50 Cf. George Schrader, "Autonomy, Heteronomy, and Moral Imperatives," *The Journal of Philosophy*, LX (January 31, 1963), pp. 65–77.
51 CUP, p. 232.

the importance of independent acceptance as an implicate of faith. He differs from such defenders, to be sure, in commending an acceptance in submission. Nevertheless, his concept of faith requires him to stress independent acceptance. Since Kierkegaard takes sin and moral evil as real possibilities, to accept the will of God as one's own may involve a hard trial with a doubtful outcome, even for the ordinarily virtuous man. So, too, a believer who knows the will of God does not thereby spontaneously carry it out. More positively, the concept of faith itself must necessarily allow for the fact that the outcome is unconstrained. There is personal drama involved in whether divine sovereignty is acknowledged in general and the specific behest obeyed. A central feature of the concept of faith is undermined, then, unless allowance is made for an allegiance one might have forsaken.

2) RECOGNITION. May the agent employ his own antecedent moral criteria of judgment to evaluate whether a given command really has a divine origin? Can he avoid doing so? And should he bring his own criteria to bear to decide whether to follow a command, even supposing he knows it to be God's? Kant is one of those who maintains that the employment of one's antecedent moral criteria of judgment is unavoidable. Thus he contends that Abraham ought to have responded to the test as follows:

> "That I ought not to kill my good son is certain beyond a shadow of a doubt; that you, as you appear to be, are God, I am not convinced and will never be even if your voice would resound from the (visible) heavens."[52]

While Kant and Kierkegaard are allied on many matters, the way in which Kant treats the Abraham story exemplifies Kierkegaard's chief worry that God in certain characterizations of morality threatens to become an "invisible vanishing point." The worry is already anticipated in a journal entry Kierkegaard makes when he is only twenty-one, three years before he meets Regine Olsen, to whom he will be engaged for a time, and nine years before he writes *Fear and Trembling:*

> As a result of the development of the doctrine of the atonement which Clausen emphasises, the motive emphasised so

[52] Immanuel Kant, *Der Streit der Fakultäten* (Hamburg: Verlag von Felix Meiner, 1959), p. 62. Cf. Clive, "The Teleological Suspension . . . ," p. 76.

strongly in Holy Writ disappears, namely the love of God. By thus positing that there is no change in God in regard to us we are led back to an entirely Kantian standpoint: we ought to better ourselves because our reason tells us to do so, and God ends by playing a very subordinate role.[53]

We have seen how Kierkegaard wants to transform the subordinate role into an overriding one, where God remains from beginning to end the discriminable object of unique veneration. Kierkegaard proceeds by questioning whether the agent must bestow on his own antecedent criteria final adjudicating authority to judge either if a given command really has a divine origin or if he should follow it, even when he knows it to be God's. This procedure requires a distinction between Abraham's *knowledge* that it is God who commands Abraham to go to Moriah and his inability to *understand* the point of the journey. Kierkegaard appears to assume without question that Abraham hears with certainty, for it is God who permits him to recognize that it is a divinely imposed trial. Yet Abraham's own antecedent criteria of right and wrong are not overridingly authoritative. For in a fashion akin to Job, he must finally defer to a wisdom superior to his own. His obedience may presuppose a general confidence in the wisdom of God's commands, but it does not require in the situation a perfect understanding in accordance with his own autonomous moral lights. In this life at least, he must be prepared to change his mind. So he sets out, knowing that it is God who tries him, but not fully understanding the point of the command. Reasons for a distinction between knowledge and understanding will be considered in more detail presently.

[53] *The Journals of Kierkegaard*, trans. and ed. Alexander Dru (London: Oxford Univ. Press, 1959), p. 3. Kierkegaard has presumably in mind passages such as the following, where Kant, in discussing his definition of religion as "(subjectively regarded) the recognition of all duties as divine commands," observes: "This definition . . . obviates the erroneous representation of religion as an aggregate of *special* duties having reference directly to God; thus it prevents our taking on . . . *courtly obligations* over and above the ethico-civil duties of humanity (of man to man). . . . There are no special duties to God in a universal religion, for God can receive nothing from us; we cannot act for Him, nor yet upon Him." Immanuel Kant, *Religion Within the Limits of Reason Alone*, trans. Theodore M. Greene and Hoyt H. Hudson (New York: Harper, 1960), p. 142. Independent attention to (say) the first table of the Decalogue, the first love-commandment, or the ascetic part of moral theology appears thereby debarred.

3) ORIGINATION. A sense of autonomy which follows closely on (2) accords to the human agent the capacity to legislate duties for oneself. So far as the status of divine commands is concerned, the employment of one's antecedent moral criteria to evaluate whether a given command really has a divine origin is more than simply unavoidable. Such criteria appear to serve as the necessary and sufficient conditions for knowing any such command. Kant maintains, for example, that the command of God is unknowable except negatively as that which does not violate autonomous moral insight. Someone may think his encounter with God is majestic, but if it collides with one's own practical reason one should regard it as illusory. Kant disallows in principle any conflict between duties to God and duties to other rational creatures. He does so by making the latter duties autonomously ascertainable and the exhaustive criteria of the former.

The notion of "autonomously ascertainable" is a difficult one. I wish merely to note now that to say a command may be directed only to an agent whose will is independent is not necessarily to require origination in the agent himself. We have seen that Kierkegaard is prepared to press the first requirement as far as one consistently can. It has been argued, for instance, that reflexivity in itself does not entail a rejection of the view that a command derives from a source external to the agent, whether it be God or another person.[54] At least it seems an appropriate extrapolation from Kierkegaard to allow that the agent may impose the command on himself so that he comes to prescribe universally with God. And Kierkegaard's individualism prompts insistence that the agent must appropriate the command by himself. Yet Kierkegaard also thinks the point of origin must remain beyond the agent; something must be told to Abraham which he cannot tell to himself.

Kant on the other hand wishes to hold that all duties which men are to take as truly binding are knowable *in principle* through the "unassisted reason." *In fact,* he is prepared to acknowledge, men may be assisted by specific religious communities whose teachings serve to awaken them to duties they could and should have discovered solely through the use of their reason. But reason remains nonetheless the final arbiter and independently sufficient source of all

[54] Schrader, "Autonomy, Heteronomy . . . ," p. 67.

duties.[55] Indeed, it is the practical reason, and the "pure *moral* legislation" which it generates, which really constitutes the will of God
that "is primordially engraved in our hearts. . . ."[56] In this way it
seems that the need for a divine commander effectively disappears.
So one arrives at Kant's well-known case against the will of God as
the foundation of all or any part of morality. God's will, he claims,
cannot be known directly, but must be deduced from other ideas
logically distinct from it, and morality as conceived by Kant is the
chief of these.[57] If wholesale deduction is required, then an appeal
to God's will falls victim to the charge of circularity.

From such conclusions Kierkegaard draws back. On Kant's own
terms the worry that God becomes an invisible vanishing point may
need qualifying. If one were to do justice to Kant (as I cannot now),
one would have to consider the idea of God as the postulate of moral
seriousness, as the "moral ruler of the world," and so on. Enough
has been said, however, to indicate why Kierkegaard is wary. He
wants to save the God-givenness of certain commands from irrelevance and to question whether the practical reason is as competent
against error as Kant appears to suppose. Kierkegaard has in mind
something virtually like a religious critique of the powers of the
practical reason. His case requires that several of his wider beliefs
be identified more explicitly. I shall begin with those religious reasons for holding that complete understanding is out of place.

VI

We have observed at least two respects in which Abraham is unable
to understand what the point of the command can possibly be. The
command violates his ordinary *ethical* scruples in the senses already
discussed. In terms of any long-range "temporal" outcome, or wider
effects on the community now, it appears unjustified. The command
perplexes him *religiously*, in light of the foregoing promise. Kierkegaard's sensitivity to this aspect of the story is often overlooked. In
addition to the statements in *Fear and Trembling* such as the one
quoted earlier, references occur in the *Journals*, for example, to a

[55] Cf. Kant, *Religion Within the Limits of Reason Alone*, pp. 143–44.
[56] Ibid., p. 95.
[57] Immanuel Kant, *Foundation for a Metaphysics of Morals*, trans. Brendan
E. A. Liddell (Bloomington: Ind. Univ. Press, 1970), pp. 180–201.

"collision" between "God's promise about Isaac and God's demand that he sacrifice Isaac. . . ."[58]

Why is Kierkegaard disposed to stress moral and religious perplexity? The underlying reasons are several, and I shall identify three major ones. First, his concept of faith requires that Abraham must make the movements freely, without the constraint which, according to Kierkegaard, complete understanding may bring. If Abraham possesses more than a general confidence, if he is able to understand the full import of the command, then his faith seems inadmissibly forced. Room must be left for either "happy passion" or "offense"; the outcome is not assured in advance. Properly personal relations with God involve for Kierkegaard a decision on Abraham's part left undetermined by divine power or by moral reasoning which justifies incontrovertibly to others what he does.

Faith is also unconstrained in that it is not held lightly, and the desirability of holding it at all is a question on which persons notably disagree. The concept differs then from a tentative hypothesis that may be easily rejected in the face of conflicting evidence for reasons obvious and compelling to everyone.[59] To hold some proposition on faith is for Kierkegaard to hold on to it in the midst of suffering. Abraham endures through calamity; his faith is not measured, for example, in simple proportion to the number of personal blessings he receives. He retains his convictions about God even when he himself experiences pain and the prospect of shattering loss. What he accomplishes when he suffers, in the absence of reassurances from others, is a measure of how much faith he has. So Kierkegaard concentrates on the episode as a *trial.* Though it is a "transitional phase" after which one returns to a way of life in accordance with the ethical, one carries always the remembrance of its fearfulness. The trial is a direct test of Abraham's faith; he is to furnish this proof of his obedience. It turns out that God does not want the de facto sacrifice of Isaac. Is this the case in this instance only or in any conceivable instance? Kierkegaard refuses to assure us. To dwell on the happy ending might lead one to regard the episode as a sham test, with the outcome obviously desirable to everyone. What is clear is that God wants this demonstrable proof of

---

[58] *Søren Kierkegaard's Journals and Papers,* 1, p. 8; see also pp. 403–4.
[59] See Terence Penelhum, *Problems of Religious Knowledge* (London: Macmillan, 1971), pp. 132–43.

Abraham's faith apart from Isaac and the personal blessing promised through him. Kierkegaard contends that the notion of a trial is
one which ethics, as he characterizes it here, is ill prepared to incorporate. More generally, the concept of faith which includes persistence through calamity is one which believers and non-believers
are free to assess very differently. It seems not a matter which is readily understood and sympathized with by all. Believers may judge it
to be a special gift of grace and worthy of emulation, non-believers
as a noble illusion or a dishonest refusal to face the facts of cruel
chance in human affairs and an indifferent universe.

A second reason centers on the conditions for maintaining divine
elusiveness. These conditions include the following. 1) God is "incommensurable with the whole of reality."[60] 2) He retains the initiative in disclosures to men. 3) His governance exceeds human
understanding of it. Kierkegaard underscores a traditional conviction
that the absolute *telos* is not to be put on a level with other things. "It
is true that before God we human beings are all equal, but it is not
true either for me or for any particular individual, that God . . .
may be placed on a level with everything else."[61] God is not one
among a number of finite, limited entities; to speak of him as such
strikes Kierkegaard as blasphemous. He is utterly unique. The decisive objection to "mediation" stems from this belief. Mediation lets
the "absolute *telos* flow . . . exhaustively into the relative ends as its
concrete predicates."[62] The believer's relation to the absolute *telos*
cannot thus pour itself or else final veneration is threatened. So
one must posit an underived obligation or absolute duty to God.
"God it is who requires absolute love."[63] Kierkegaard adds that it
would be foolish to conclude from this that one should be lukewarm
to everything else. Still, the absolute relation may require that any
particular finite object be renounced. One must be willing to give
up anything for the sake of the absolute *telos*. The final worth of
creatures therefore may be appraised correctly only in relation to
God. They are to be valued, but never, absolutely, in themselves.
One may accordingly pass beyond the procedures by which men
customarily justify particular actions to one another, if such proce-

[60] FT, p. 45.
[61] CUP, p. 359.
[62] Ibid., p. 363.
[63] FT, p. 83.

dures contain no necessary reference to the absolute *telos*. God, moreover, may be known where and as he wills. Awareness of God is not subject to human control; he retains the initiative. And he may seem to withdraw, as it were, to maintain sovereignty and holiness. In relation to normal human thought and action Kierkegaard stresses the surd-like character of encounters with God. The religious paradigm is an irregularity "which is like God's omnipresence being evidenced by His invisibility, and a revelation through being a mystery"; it expresses the particular, the exceptional, "as for example by appealing to dreams, visions, and so forth."[64] Thus God remains in some ways incomprehensible and references to him opaque. There may be darkness and suffering—fear and trembling—even after his voice is heard. When reading Kierkegaard one thinks of Isaiah 55:8: "For my thoughts are not your thoughts, neither are your ways my ways, says the Lord." Human beings may properly challenge each other on the basis of prior criteria of moral evaluation. But the "infinite qualitative difference" between God and men prevents any straightforward transfer of this procedure. Men are not in a position to assess completely by virtue of autonomous moral insight the workings of divine providence. They may come to recognize a command insofar as God permits them to know that he issues it; this recognition need not extend to a full understanding of his governance.

Kierkegaard is impressed, thirdly, not only by a Kantian case for the limits of the theoretical reason laboring under the blight of finitude, but also by the theological case for the corrupting effects of sin which extend to the practical reason striving to establish right answers to given dilemmas. Vice as well as finitude makes unavailable to men the absolute point of view, from which things and events are good or evil as God evaluates them. Certain dour strains in Kierkegaard's thought make him skeptical of the competence of the practical reason. He is impressed by what he takes to be "the constant rebellion, the permanent revolt against God,"[65] and the distortions and derangements this produces in the way men in fact reflect.

All three reasons encounter formidable difficulties and deserve lengthy elucidation. I shall, however, only identify one modest (to

[64] CUP, p. 231.
[65] Søren Kierkegaard, *Training in Christianity*, trans. Walter Lowrie (Princeton: Princeton Univ. Press, 1960), p. 89.

Kierkegaard) consequence for the issues before us. Taken cumulatively, the three reasons provide a background of intelligibility for the following sort of statement, which suggests the different attitudes appropriate to other persons and to God.

> If your beloved or friend asked something of you which out of honest love and in concern you had decided was harmful to him, then you must take the responsibility if you express love by complying instead of expressing love by denying the fullfillment of the desire. But God you are to love in unconditional obedience, even if what he demands of you may seem to you to be to your own harm—yes, harmful to his cause. For the wisdom of God is not to be compared with yours, and God's governance is not, in duty bound, answerable to your prudence. All you have to do is to obey in love.[66]

The reasons above likewise make possible a theological twist to something that universalizability appears formally to allow. I noted earlier that the principle to which one adheres in making a moral judgment need not be thought of as existing antecedently to that judgment. The agent may have to consider what ought to be done in the particular case without relevant precedents to guide him. Kierkegaard wants to say that one reason for the possible lack of relevant precedents has to do with the openness the believer must sustain toward God. One may hold for the best of human reasons (e.g., what conduces to societal viability) that a certain action toward another person is wrong. The judgment is antecedent, at least in the sense of temporally before. And it may well be virtually exceptionless in that no human being can justifiably commend otherwise to another. Yet if God commanded the action, one would have to change one's mind. One could grant, indeed the believer would insist, that anyone else similarly circumstanced ought to change his mind as well. If God commands X, Abraham should obey; anyone so situated should obey. One may stipulate in advance that anyone, or at least any believer, ought to continue dispositionally to be open to a divine command. In this sense, one might say counterfactually, one is always open. What Kierkegaard denies is that men are in a position to furnish *themselves* with complete guarantees against the bare possibility of being wrong. The believer has no absolute veto of this sort. He must remain open not only because complex cases arise

[66] Søren Kierkegaard, *Works of Love,* trans. Howard and Edna Hong (New York: Harper, 1962), p. 36.

where no appeal to an antecedently existent principle will do, but because over against God, he may always be in the wrong.[67]

VII

Though Abraham, for the reasons mentioned, does not fully understand, it seems not quite right to say that his obedience is represented as a blind, moment-to-moment submission to a choice-offering, where he just bows slavishly before capricious superior power. There appear to be limits of a sort to what God can command. Abraham combines general trust with specific perplexity and in-principled openness. Kierkegaard seems to hold that while God must not be expected to justify his ways to man's own satisfaction, Abraham may still possess a general confidence that such ways are more than mere inscrutable fiat. Let us compare a well-known part of Lincoln's Second Inaugural:

> Both read the same Bible, and pray to the same God; and each invokes His aid against the other. . . . The prayers of both could not be answered; that of neither has been answered fully. The Almighty has His own purposes. "Woe unto the world because of offences: for it must needs be that offences come; but woe to that man by whom the offence cometh!" If we shall suppose that American Slavery is one of those offences which, in the providence of God, must needs come, but which, having continued through His appointed time, He now wills to remove, and that He gives to both North and South, this terrible war, as the woe due to those by whom the offence came, shall we discern therein any departure from those divine attributes which the believers in a Living God always ascribe to Him? Fondly do we hope—fervently do we pray—that this mighty scourge of war may speedily pass away. Yet, if God wills that it continue, until all the wealth piled by the bond-man's two hundred and fifty years of unrequited toil shall be sunk, and until every drop of blood drawn with the lash, shall be paid by another drawn with the sword, as was said three thousand years ago, so still it must be said "the judgments of the Lord, are true and righteous altogether."[68]

---

[67] See the concluding sermon in Søren Kierkegaard, *Either/Or,* II, trans. Walter Lowrie (Garden City, N.Y.: Doubleday, 1959).

[68] *The Collected Works of Abraham Lincoln,* VIII, ed. Roy P. Basler (New Brunswick, N.J.: Rutgers Univ. Press, 1953), p. 333.

Lincoln emphasizes more than Kierkegaard that men may discern, at least approximately, the justice of providential action, in this instance in the congruency between the blood of unrequited toil and of military slaughter. Still, "the Almighty has His own purposes" in which one may be confident, though neither side perceives them with full clarity. Kierkegaard stresses in particular the attribute of love. He declines to speculate here on whether "God is loving" is a contingent truth about him. So far as men are concerned, it is a truth nevertheless. However God is committed, he is committed. Is it better to suppose, if anything speculative is ventured, that God's will and his intellect are ultimately one? Kierkegaard prefers to concentrate on the situation of the subordinate human agent who may trust in the attribute of love, even though any total rationale remains hidden. What Abraham must not demand is that the divine governance be invariably answerable to his puzzlement. To be a knight of faith is to remain confident that the command is loving. But to close the gap in any given instance between a general trust in the attribute of love and the conditions for its full demonstration could necessitate seeing the situation from God's point of view. To this Abraham does not aspire. He is not a world-creator. His belief includes acceptance of his inability to see how this love may apply in a given case.

Still it makes sense to ask, does Abraham not need *some* basis for his confidence if his obedience is to be more than slavish submission? Lincoln can point at least to our own sense of the congruency between toil and slaughter, tragic though it is. What can Abraham appeal to? Kierkegaard's answer is difficult to get clear, but I think it is roughly as follows. Abraham has a basis not in antecedent moral insight which requires satisfaction, but in his own prior cumulative experience of God. Kierkegaard speaks of the individual joining experience to experience and in so doing, becoming God's intimate acquaintance.[69] The religious point tirelessly stressed is that there is no further *telos* beyond God as an end in himself. What Abraham appears confident about on the basis of his experience is that God's commands have always to do with fostering a relation with him. That is their end, the criterion which overrides every other possible consideration, including the "ethical" and even the special promise to Abraham. He trusts that the command which leads him to Moriah

    [69] Søren Kierkegaard, *Edifying Discourses*, II, trans. David F. Swenson and Lillian Marvin Swenson (Minneapolis, Minn.: Augsburg, 1945), p. 154.

is no exception. So Kierkegaard proceeds to build into the meaning of the love in question the feature of God-relatedness. Note the points implied. 1) God cannot command (say) "cruelty for its own sake," if this involves turning men finally from himself, i.e., violating the attribute of love. 2) The "highest life" for any person is "a life in communion with God";[70] any action which enhances this life is almost analytically defined as loving. 3) Given what God is believed to seek incessantly in all his actions with men, one cannot do anything to Isaac which is "finally" unloving if one obeys God. Abraham is confident that unless he obeys God, he cannot "love" Isaac. For God will not, *eo ipso*, command what is unloving. And God has nothing higher than himself to give, to Abraham, Isaac, or anyone else.

These last observations are reminiscent of Thomas Aquinas. And so a comparison of Kierkegaard's account with that of Aquinas will also prove instructive, especially since Aquinas elaborates his position more clearly at certain points.[71] Aquinas justifies what Abraham does by reference to what he thinks are intelligible reasons for God to command certain things which it would not be right for persons to commend to one another. These reasons have to do with the difference between creator and creature: "when Abraham consented to slay his son (Gen. 22), he did not consent to murder, because his son was due to be slain by the command of God, Who is Lord of life and death. . . ."[72] The order which persons are obliged to observe between themselves need not in every respect bind God. Since he is the author of life and death it makes sense for him to exercise his governance in accordance with his wisdom. And "if a man be the executor . . . by divine authority, he will be no murderer any more than God would be."[73] The inviolability of moral prohibitions is relative then to the authority of the one who prescribes them.

[70] *The Journals of Kierkegaard,* trans. Dru, p. 244.

[71] Aquinas discusses the Abraham case as one among a number requiring special attention. The standard "solutions" preferred for this class of cases during the Middle Ages and the Reformation are distinguished in Roland H. Bainton, "The Immoralities of the Patriarchs According to the Exegesis of the Late Middle Ages and of the Reformation," *Harvard Theological Review,* 23 (January, 1930), pp. 39–49.

[72] Thomas Aquinas, *Summa Theologica,* I-II, q. 100, a. 8, ad 3; from *Basic Writings of Saint Thomas Aquinas,* II, ed. Anton C. Pegis (New York: Random House, 1945), pp. 843–44.

[73] Ibid., p. 844.

One commentator queries whether Thomas always adheres consistently to this justification, with its stress on the differences between God and men and God's freedom to dispose of any created good as he wills.[74] However one decides that question, it is clear that Aquinas always places one limit on what God may fittingly do. He cannot turn men away from himself. Of this men may be confident in advance. "God can do what he wants with men and human relations as long as he is still relating them positively to himself as their final end."[75] The mundane welfare of the neighbor is a subordinate good to this end. Abraham's and Isaac's relation to God takes priority over the life and death of either of them.

Kierkegaard certainly agrees, as we have seen, that distinctive reasons obtain which make it appropriate for God to require things which we should not ask of one another. For Kierkegaard too, the mundane welfare of the neighbor is a subordinate good to the end of communion with God.[76] Yet Aquinas stresses these reasons more explicitly in connection with the Abraham episode. Kierkegaard seems to assume them but goes on to emphasize Abraham's special agony because of God's prior promise to him.[77]

Aquinas and Kierkegaard will be compared at certain other points in the last two sections. At present I want to underscore the pivotal beliefs they appear to share. The limits to what God can command have to do with relating persons positively to himself as their final

[74] John G. Milhaven, "Moral Absolutes and Thomas Aquinas," *Absolutes in Moral Theology?* ed. Charles Curran (Washington, D.C.: Corpus, 1968), pp. 154–85. As with Kant, I cannot hope to do justice to Aquinas' general views. The comparisons with Kierkegaard offered here have only to do with certain passages.

[75] Ibid., p. 163.

[76] In *Agape: An Ethical Analysis* (New Haven: Yale Univ. Press, 1972), esp. pp. 263–67, I identified three generic characteristics which, in religious ethics, often serve to specify the meaning of a person's "well-being": 1) the "God-relation," and a concern to foster conscious awareness of it; 2) "welfare" as a blanket heading for interests in physical survival, acquirement of skill and knowledge, and so on; 3) "freedom" as the capacity to exercise individual preference, make an effort, and the like, in relation to a wide range of ideals, material objects, etc. There I observed that more attention should be given to the interrelations between these three characteristics and whether and in what ways they may conflict in practice. The examples of possible conflict were confined, however, largely to considerations falling under either welfare or freedom. For a religious thinker like Kierkegaard, overriding priority is assigned to communion with God. What is noted above may serve therefore to expand slightly on the very cryptic remarks in the earlier volume.

[77] See, e.g., FT, p. 36.

end. In furtherance of that end he is free to alter the normal moral obligations which persons justifiably commend to one another. In the case of Abraham, God may fittingly impose such a trial because he is the author of life and death and in order to enhance communion with him.

VIII

Some further reference needs to be made, however tentatively, to the first half of the distinction between knowledge and understanding. How much is claimed for the degree of certainty Abraham has that it is really God who commands him to sacrifice his son?

Some interpreters of Kierkegaard deny the need for any such distinction. They take Abraham's fear and trembling to include uncertainty that it is God who commands.[78] As they see it, Kierkegaard allows that Abraham may himself acknowledge the possibility that he is deceived in what he hears and mistaken in what he does. The episode does not escape the normal limitations of the human situation; any revelation is subject to historical and social relativities in the same way that other sorts of knowledge may be. The waters here are both deep and murky, and several interpretations have some claim to plausibility. Yet the following passage suggests the need for a distinction such as the one I am urging.

> And there he stood, the old man, with his only hope! But he did not doubt, he did not look anxiously to the right or to the left, he did not challenge heaven with his prayers. He *knew* that it was God the Almighty who was trying him, he knew it was the hardest sacrifice that could be required of him; but he knew also that no sacrifice was too hard when God required it—and he drew the knife.[79]

Kierkegaard also refers to the knight of faith as someone "who is aware of a direct command of God."[80] And again, the knight of faith is in continuous personal communion; "he becomes God's intimate acquaintance, the Lord's friend, and (to speak quite humanly)

[78] See, e.g., Libuse Lukas Miller, *In Search of the Self* (Philadelphia: Muhlenberg, 1962), pp. 187–88.
[79] FT, p. 36. My italics.
[80] Ibid., p. 80.

that he says 'Thou' to God in heaven, whereas even the tragic hero only addresses Him in the third person."[81]

Many of those who would agree that a distinction between knowledge and understanding is required and that Kierkegaard clearly does assume Abraham knows with certainty, criticize him for assuming too easily what is surely the most contestable of claims. How many knights of faith—confirmed as such, let us suppose, in accordance with the conditions identified in the last section—are seriously prepared to say they know God's command so specifically and unambiguously that no possibility of significant error on their part obtains? Does Kierkegaard's own stress on the corrosive effects of sin not cut both ways? If the competence of the practical reason is thereby called into question, why is any epistemic certainty not also? Many think that at a minimum Kierkegaard neglects to consider such questions sufficiently, especially when Abraham is offered as a paradigm for every succeeding generation.[82]

Kant seizes on the possibility of significant error as an admission one cannot honestly avoid. The basis for asserting an injunction as terrible as the one to Abraham is a historical document and "never apodictically certain." Kant takes it as obvious that the possibility of error remains in all cases of "historical and visionary faith." Hence "it is unconscientious to follow such a faith" when it violates "a human duty which is certain in and of itself."[83] Few negative duties are as certain as the prohibition against murder.

It is notable that both Aquinas and Kierkegaard decline to speculate in detail on how God issues direct commands. For Aquinas, the dispensations the patriarchs receive simply come via "an inward inspiration."[84] Direct intervention in human moral affairs by God or the Holy Spirit is affirmed to be possible, but no explanation is at-

---

[81] Ibid., p. 88.

[82] See, e.g., Martin Buber, "On the Suspension of the Ethical," *Eclipse of God*, trans. Maurice S. Friedman (New York: Harper, 1957), pp. 115–20.

[83] Kant, *Religion Within the Limits of Reason Alone*, p. 175.

[84] Thomas Aquinas, *Summa Theologica*, III (Supplement), q. 65, a. 2; from *The "Summa Theologica" of St. Thomas Aquinas*, Fifth Number, trans. Fathers of the English Dominican Province (New York: Benziger, 1922), p. 336. See the reference to "per inspirationem internam" in Aquinas' *Commentarium in Sent.*, IV, d. 33, q. 1, a. 2. See also Aquinas, *Summa Theologica*, II-II, q. 89, a. 1, ad 3; from *The Summa Theologica of St. Thomas Aquinas*, II, trans. Fathers of the English Dominican Province (New York: Benziger, 1947), p. 1579. Cf. as well John Mahoney, S.J., "The Spirit and Moral Discernment in Aquinas," *The Heythrop Journal*, XIII (July, 1972), pp. 282–97.

tempted of precisely how it occurs. Kierkegaard's assumption seems not unlike Aquinas' "inward inspiration." It is plain that Kierkegaard wants the relation between the individual and God to be direct and immediate—this is one of the things the teleological suspension is designed to guarantee. The immediacy connotes an actual, privileged awareness not reducible to empirical descriptions.

If one asks why there is such paucity of speculation, the answer for both men is, I think, that it is better so. The conditions for divine elusiveness adduced earlier preclude for Kierkegaard an explanation by the ordinary canons of public intelligibility of how God issues direct commands. What he insists on is that the focus must remain on human obedience. The command must do more than set the agent free to ponder, interpret, and apply. It must be sufficiently unambiguous to leave room pre-eminently for obedience or disobedience; one's perplexities and scruples must not occupy the center of the stage. Kierkegaard is confident that God permits Abraham to know with the requisite certainty, despite the corrosive effects of sin, so as to make the trial a test of fidelity.

It would be ludicrous to attempt to say very much in addition here about the intricate topics of religious epistemology which are beginning to loom before us. One must stop an essay of this kind at some point, and console oneself with contemplations of future undertakings. So I must be satisfied now to identify a belief Kierkegaard shares with many orthodox thinkers and which stands crucially behind his confidence that God may permit someone to know that he issues a command. Despite Kierkegaard's affirmation of divine sovereignty and holiness, he denies that transcendence must be construed in such a way that it makes no difference as to what is the case or what persons ought to do. I shall not consider whether his denial can be maintained without contradiction; that is an issue on which many have differed significantly, and it too deserves separate attention. Behind Kierkegaard's confidence is a belief that God's relation to the world is such that he may intervene actively and at any time, and in such a way as to bear directly on what men ought to do. Among the numerous concepts of God and of his relation to the world which appear to be logically possible, Kierkegaard does not have, for example, an Aristotelian view of God's transcendence. He summarizes his own view in a discourse published in 1855 entitled "The Unchangeableness of God." To cite it will serve to fill in further the background beliefs in the context of which *Fear and Trembling* should be understood.

> God is unchangeable. In His omnipresence He created this visible world—and made Himself invisible. He clothed Himself in the visible world as in a garment; He changes it as one who shifts a garment—Himself unchanged. Thus in the world of sensible things. In the world of events He is present everywhere in every moment; in a truer sense than we can say of the most watchful human justice that it is present everywhere, God is omnipresent, though never seen by any mortal; present everywhere in the least even as well as in the greatest. . . . In each moment every actuality is a possibility in His almighty hand; He holds all in readiness, in every instance prepared to change everything; the opinions of men, their judgements, human greatness and human abasement; He changes all, Himself unchanged. When everything seems stable (for it is only in appearance that the external world is for a time unchanged, in reality it is always in flux) and in the overturn of all things, He remains equally unchanged. . . .[85]

IX

Before concluding, it seems important to summarize briefly a possible formulation of the teleological suspension which remains congruent with much of Kierkegaard's program but is perhaps more modest. Here religious duty *can* but *need not* conflict with our ordinary antecedent judgments of right and wrong. The formulation I have in mind can be extracted from certain passages in Aquinas. We have already noted some basic affinities between Aquinas and Kierkegaard. Yet Aquinas appears more modest at two junctures in particular.

1) Even in those passages where Aquinas is most concerned to stress the differences between creator and creature, he declines to relish any irrational quality in divine commands. For God to enjoin one to take a life does not finally contradict "right reason" and this in a fashion analogous to Aquinas' understanding of miracle.

[85] Translated from the Danish in Shmueli, *Kierkegaard and Consciousness*, p. 53.

Fornication is said to be a sin, because it is contrary to right reason. Now man's reason is right, in so far as it is ruled by the Divine Will, the first and supreme rule. Wherefore that which a man does by God's will and in obedience to His command, is not contrary to right reason, though it may seem contrary to the general order of reason: even so, that which is done miraculously by the Divine power is not contrary to nature, though it be contrary to the usual course of nature. Therefore just as Abraham did not sin in being willing to slay his innocent son, because he obeyed God, although considered in itself it was contrary to right human reason in general, so, too, Osee sinned not in committing fornication by God's command. Nor should such a copulation be strictly called fornication, though it be so called in reference to the general course of things. Hence Augustine says (Conf. iii. 8): *When God commands a thing to be done against the customs or agreement of any people, though it were never done by them heretofore, it is to be done;* and afterwards he adds: *For as among the powers of human society, the greater authority is obeyed in preference to the lesser, so must God in preference to all.*[86]

Here as elsewhere Aquinas strives to retain continuities between grace and nature. Just as a miracle does not contradict nature, but is only contrary to the common course of nature, so no divine command to kill should be called murder since God is the author of life and death. Aquinas is concerned in general to construe a divine command as changing "natural morality" either by addition or by redefinition, so that "murder," "fornication," and so on, are not in question after all.

Kierkegaard, on the other hand, is prepared to live with discontinuities, to question more radically societal judgments of right and wrong and yet to allow a "secular ethic" to stand on its own feet without requiring any referral to God, whether "implicitly" or from some "fully comprehensive" vantage point. For such an ethic, what Abraham sets out to do is bound to seem culpable. A direct collision of assessments between it and religious faith cannot be avoided. If Abraham carries out his intention the consequence in the eyes of society must lead to a verdict of murder; if he remains obedient to his personal lights he himself sees it as a sacrifice. Herein lies the pain

[86] Thomas Aquinas, *Summa Theologica*, II-II, q. 154, a. 3, ad 2; from *The Summa Theologica of St. Thomas Aquinas*, II, p. 1817.

which can well make a person sleepless. Two irreducibly different descriptions of the same episode are at issue. Though Kierkegaard is careful to say that "it is only by faith one attains likeness to Abraham, not by murder,"[87] one wonders if there is something nearly frivolous and rhetorical in Kierkegaard's repeated references to faith making it "a holy act to be willing to murder one's son. . . ."[88] We noted earlier Kierkegaard's seeming uneasiness in contrasting love for Isaac and the ethical. At least if one thinks of a standard definition of murder, such as "the unauthorized killing of innocent life," the effort of Aquinas to redescribe what Abraham sets out to do makes persuasive sense. Whatever the courtroom verdict, the believer thinks he has the highest and perhaps the only conceivable authorization for taking innocent life, and it seems inappropriate for *him* to be content to define it as murder.

2) Aquinas also treats the possibility of a command such as the one issued to Abraham as remote and exceptional. The believer need not dwell on it, since in practical terms it does not constitute a real possibility to be taken actively into account. It is not applicable typically or to everyone. More than enough is enjoined or forbidden by the primary and secondary precepts of the natural law to occupy one's moral energies. Aquinas might also argue that to treat the possibility of such a command as remote or exceptional is not to derogate divine sovereignty, unless one thinks that God is able to act only as an immediate cause, which in itself seems a limiting notion.

Kierkegaard is less disposed to stress the rarity of the sort of command issued to Abraham. Personal consultations between the knight of faith and God are in place at every point. The image, he might say, is never of a bureaucracy with impersonal orders issued from on high. So the general possibility of direct divine interventions in human moral affairs is one with which the knight of faith must continuously reckon. He may face another trial at the very next moment. When it is observed that Abraham returns with Isaac and is never tested similarly again, one can only presume this to be for Kierkegaard a *post eventum* description. Kierkegaard is more preoccupied than Aquinas with the senses in which a rational ethic—while praiseworthy—is corruptible. One may grow content with routine and settle for what is familiar and stabilizing. Kierkegaard wants an

87 FT, p. 42.
88 Ibid., p. 41.

existence close to the edge, where eruptions are expected, and one makes one's way in the midst of crags and lightning flashes.

It is arguable nonetheless that Aquinas' account stressing rarity reflects more accurately the experience of most believers. Yet finally one must point out that this more modest formulation does not simply remove the sting from a teleological suspension or an ethics expanded to include obedience to direct commands. It is open to Kierkegaard to ask whether Aquinas' effort to regard direct divine commands as exceptional constitutes in the end a decisive difference between them. For Thomas grants the possibility in principle. Kierkegaard might well go on to argue that, ironically, the most arresting feature in the last statement cited from Aquinas is not Thomas' insistence that God's will is not finally contrary to right reason, but that he quotes Augustine approvingly. For Augustine offers what Kierkegaard could take as a version of the teleological suspension of the ethical: "When God commands a thing to be done against the customs or agreement of any people, though it were never done by them heretofore, it is to be done. . . ." A religious duty still *can* conflict with our ordinary sense of moral duty. The believer ought then to continue dispositionally to be open. He is not in a position to furnish himself with an absolute veto.

Whether one should call such dispositional openness a teleological suspension of the ethical, or characterize the ethical in such a way that one allows in principle for new universal prescriptions in obedience to divine commands, might seem to Kierkegaard, when pressed, to be after all a subsidiary terminological question. I have tried nonetheless to suggest how a case for the latter alternative might intelligibly go. The substantive issues remaining include in either case the final authority and existential possibility of any such command. Let me conclude then by citing another episode which seems relevantly similar. While Kierkegaard would not approve of everything in the following account, it catches with remarkable accuracy, I think, much of what one finds in *Fear and Trembling*.

Jung recalls that when he was twelve years old he was overwhelmed by a thought which he did not want to think, something he feared even to approach. For three days he desperately resisted it. Finally he asked himself whether God "wishes to test my obedience by imposing on me the unusual task of doing something against my own moral judgment and against the teachings of my religion, and even against His own commandment. . . ."[89] He concluded that God desired him to show courage and go through with it.

I gathered all my courage, as though I were about to leap forthwith into hell-fire, and let the thought come. I saw before me the cathedral, the blue sky. God sits on His golden throne, high above the world—and from under the throne an enormous turd falls upon the sparkling new roof, shatters it, and breaks the walls of the cathedral asunder.

So that was it! I felt an enormous, an indescribable relief. Instead of the expected damnation, grace had come upon me, and with it an unutterable bliss such as I had never known. I wept for happiness and gratitude. The wisdom and goodness of God had been revealed to me now that I had yielded to His inexorable command. It was as though I had experienced an illumination. A great many things I had not previously understood became clear to me. That was what my father had not understood, I thought; he had failed to experience the will of God, had opposed it for the best reasons and out of the deepest faith. And that was why he had never experienced the miracle of grace which heals all and makes all comprehensible. He had taken the Bible's commandments as his guide; he believed in God as the Bible prescribed and as his forefathers had taught him. But he did not know the immediate living God who stands, omnipotent and free, above His Bible and His Church, who calls upon man to partake of His freedom, and can force him to renounce his own views and convictions in order to fulfil without reserve the command of God. In His trial of human courage God refuses to abide by traditions, no matter how sacred. In His omnipotence He will see to it that nothing really evil comes out of such tests of courage. If one fulfils the will of God one can be sure of going the right way.[90]

[89] C. G. Jung, *Memories, Dreams, Reflections,* ed. Aniela Jaffé, trans. Richard and Clara Winston (London: Collins, 1967), p. 56.

[90] Ibid., pp. 56–57.

THE RELATION OF THE MORAL AND THE NUMINOUS IN OTTO'S NOTION OF THE HOLY

John P. Reeder, Jr.

1. Rudolf Otto, in the ninth edition of *Das Heilige*, says that theology, in its effort to capture the element of the "Irrationale," the nonrational nonmoral "numinous" aspect of the holy, often propounds the mistaken idea

> . . . that God is *exlex*, that good is good because God wills it, not that God wills the good, because it is good; the doctrine of an absolutely fortuitous will [*Zufallswille*] in God, which in fact would make him a "capricious despot."[1]

Otto found this picture of God and his relation to morality in Luther and identified it as especially characteristic of Islam. In another passage, he noted:

> . . . Islam is accused of giving the ethical demand a fortuitous character [*Character des 'Zufälligen'*] which only has validity through the fortuitous will of the divine. . . .[2]

Actually, Otto combines two motifs in this image of God. First, there is "good is good because God wills it" or, as he puts it in the Islam passage, "only valid through the will of the divine."[3] I take

[1] *Das Heilige* (Breslau: Trewendt und Grenier, 1922), p. 127. Translation mine. See *The Idea of the Holy*, trans. John W. Harvey (New York: Oxford Univ. Press, 1958), pp. 101–2 (hereafter, IOH). This translation was made from the ninth edition, plus certain additions from the fourteenth.

[2] *Das Heilige* (1922), p. 113. Translation mine. Cf. IOH, pp. 90–91.

[3] In later editions Otto omitted the "good is good . . ." section of the first passage above and retained only the "fortuitous will . . . capricious despot" part. See *Das Heilige* (Munich: Biederstein Verlag, 1947), p. 120; and *Das Heilige* (Munich: Verlag C. H. Beck, 1963), pp. 125–26 (hereafter, German

it that "will" in this context means desire or decision and hence command. "Good" signifies what is morally right. That good is good "because" God wills it, or that the ethical demand only has validity through his will, can be construed as the claim that "right" or "rightness" means and only means "willed by God." On the other hand, one could understand it as the assertion that God wills the meaning of rightness, whatever that is taken to be, in our conceptual system. That is, God's creative will establishes the logical form and content of rightness in our experience. This second interpretation by no means implies, although it permits, the claim that in our conceptual system "right" means and only means "willed by God." However, it, like the first, makes the establishment of the meaning of rightness a matter of the will of God. Either rightness itself simply means willed by God or, whatever it means, it is a product of God's will. Neither view in itself is equivalent, as Otto seems to assume, to the notion of God as "exlex." God as *exlex* puts the deity "outside" any notion of a moral "law"; to define "right" by "willed by God" or to make the meaning of rightness a product of God's will makes his will the sole determinant *of* that law. Either interpretation of "good is good . . ." or "only valid through . . ." puts God "outside" the moral law only in the sense that its meaning is his creation.

Second, in the passage which begins with "good is good because God wills it," Otto adds the notion of a fortuitous divine will or *Zufallswille*, as if the two themes were equivalent. Furthermore, he adjoins the thought that if God's will is fortuitous, he would be a "'capricious despot.'" In the Islam passage, Otto simply blends the idea of validity through the will of the deity and the characterization of that will as fortuitous. I gather that Otto means by a fortuitous will one that is not governed by an intention or purpose but one which is simply *moved* by an arbitrary whim or caprice.[4]

However, on neither interpretation of "good is good . . ." or "only valid through . . ." does it necessarily follow that God's will is for-

---

editions referred to as DH, with year of publication). However, he retained the "ethical demand having validity through the will of the divine" in the passage on Islam. See DH (1947), p. 107; and DH (1963), p. 112. Hence it still seems legitimate to discuss the basic motif which "valid through the will of the divine" and "good is good because God wills it" both express.

[4] "Capricious" could be taken to mean having changeable or fickle intentions; however, I think Otto wanted to convey the idea of a non-intentional whim or impulse.

tuitous and capricious. That right simply means and only means willed by God or that the meaning of rightness is a product of God's will does leave open the possibility that his will could be fortuitous and capricious. Rightness would be rightness even if it were, but these characterizations of the divine will do not necessarily follow. One could hold, on the contrary, that God's will is expressive of purposes or intentions which reflect his essence.

Nonetheless, the fortuitous-capricious element is just as essential in the mistaken picture of God as the "good is good because God wills it" theme. Indeed, one can consider the fortuitous-capricious will image alone, as Otto evidently intended one to do in his revision of the first passage. Theology, in its zeal to depict the numinous, often emphasizes it to such an extent that the rational-moral disappears altogether.[5] If one's "psychology" is poor, that is, if one's awareness of the numinous feeling through which one experiences the divine is dim and uncertain, then one might confuse the sense in which the deity has a nonrational nonmoral numinous dimension with the idea of a fortuitous-capricious will. Even if one's psychology is clear, one might choose a poor way to articulate one's awareness of the numinous and hence commit a fault of expression.[6] In any case, to picture God as a fortuitous-capricious will *would* make him *exlex*; it would remove the moral aspect of his nature altogether. It would oppose God and morality, instead of calling attention to the moral *and* the numinous aspects of the holy.

Furthermore, the notion that God's will determines the meaning of rightness, in either of the senses we discussed above, is retained in the Islam passage. Combined with the fortuitous-capricious will image, it evidently had significance for Otto as an element in the "caricature" produced by an overemphasis on the numinous. Thinking of God as fortuitous-capricious will puts him entirely beyond morality. Such a will is not moved by moral intentions or purposes; God would not be *capable* of moral goodness. However, if one goes on to claim that *such* a will determines the very meaning of moral rightness, then one destroys what Otto calls the "absoluteness" of morality.[7] By "absoluteness," I believe he means that the meaning

[5] IOH, p. 91.

[6] IOH, p. 102. One may choose a poor "ideogram." See Section 2.

[7] DH (1922), p. 127; DH (1963), p. 126. By *Ethos* here I take Otto to mean morality, or more specifically moral rightness. Harvey has "moral values." IOH, p. 102.

of moral rightness is logically autonomous; its logical "validity" does not rest ultimately on an external fortuitous will.[8] For Otto, one would simply not be talking about "morality" if it were not absolute. Thus if morality's meaning were a function of divine caprice, then in Otto's eyes it would be pointless to attribute moral goodness to God. To make God's will fortuitous and capricious is to put him outside morality; to make morality a product of that will is to destroy the very conception of morality on the basis of which Otto conceived of God as good.

2. Otto denies then that one can picture God's numinous aspect as a fortuitous will which establishes the meaning of rightness; as we will see, such a picture is a poor "ideogram" of the numinous. What does Otto mean, however, by the nonrational or "numinous"? He begins his book by acknowledging that Christian theology, and every "theistic" religion, characterizes the divine being by certain "attributes" or predicates such as "spirit, reason, purpose, good will, supreme power, unity, selfhood" which are "analogous" to those used to depict human beings with "reason and personality." In men these attributes are "qualified by restriction and limitation," but in God they are "absolute" or "completed [*'vollendete'*]."[9] Otto means, I believe, that God can be characterized as a rational and moral being. He is not only capable of moral goodness, he possesses it to a supreme degree.[10] Moreover, since rational and moral attributes are *"concepts,"* God is also *"rational"* in the same sense as any object is which can be "thought conceptually":

> The nature of the deity described in the attributes above mentioned is, then, a rational nature.[11]

Otto goes on to claim, nevertheless, that it is a mistake to think that these concepts or predicates "exhaust [*erschöpfen*]" the "essence [*Wesen*]" of deity.[12] There is, as Otto puts it in Chapter II, a "moment" or element in deity which "eludes comprehension in terms of

---

[8] See Section 7, where I briefly discuss Otto's metaethical theory. His operative notion of morality includes certain normative principles such as justice and the motive of doing one's duty for its own sake. Cf. IOH, p. 5.

[9] IOH, p. 1. DH (1922), p. 1; DH (1963), p. 1.

[10] IOH, p. 5.

[11] Ibid., p. 1. DH (1922), p. 1; DH (1963), p. 1.

[12] IOH, pp. 1–2. DH (1922), p. 2; DH (1963), p. 2.

concepts" and to it he gives the name "numinous."[13] The numinous aspect of deity is not just beyond our knowledge.[14] Nor does it simply transcend our *powers* of comprehension (*Fassungskraft*).[15] For instance, the *"absoluteness"* of the rational attributes cannot be *"thought home, thought out."* We can "conceive," or, shall we say, entertain (*es unterliegt unserem Begriffsvermögen*) the idea of the completion or perfection of the attributes but we cannot fully bring it to mind, we cannot realize what it would be like (*es überschreitet die Grenzen unserer Fassungskraft*).[16] However, the numinous

> is that which lies altogether outside what can be thought, and is, alike in form, quality, and essence, the utterly and "wholly other."[17]

Otto seems to refer here to "concepts" in two different ways. He begins by saying that the numinous eludes concepts in the specific sense of those notions used to depict men as rational-moral agents. Then he seems to use "concept" in a much broader way, to designate the instruments by which we comprehend experience in general.[18] In this sense concepts are what rational-moral agents *employ*.[19] Keeping a Kantian background in mind, men have theoretical and practical (moral) reason, and men use it in the world of their experience. The numinous, however, not only eludes the notions which

[13] IOH, pp. 5–7.
[14] Ibid., p. 28.
[15] Ibid., p. 141. DH (1922), p. 173; DH (1963), p. 170.
[16] IOH, p. 141. DH (1922), p. 173; DH (1963), p. 170.
[17] Ibid. Here Otto is specifically talking about the numinous as "mysterium" but his remarks are generic. Another way he puts the distinction is to say that the absoluteness of the attributes is "unerfasslich," the mysterium "unfasslich."
[18] Thomas McPherson makes a similar distinction in "Religion as the Inexpressible," *New Essays in Philosophical Theology*, eds. Anthony Flew and Alasdair MacIntyre (London: SCM Press, 1963), p. 135. McPherson, however, puts the contrast as one between "hard" or "abstract" terms and any notion "put into words."
[19] Concepts in this sense seem to include, as H. J. Paton points out, both Kantian "categories" and "Ideas of Reason," ideas of the absolute or unconditioned. *The Modern Predicament* (London: G. Allen, 1955), pp. 137–38. As Paton notes, Otto seems to use these indifferently. I think Otto means that the numinous eludes the rational, both in the sense of categories which constitute the a priori structure of our awareness of empirical experience and also in the sense of "Ideas" by which our reason reaches toward the absolute, ideas which have no empirical objects. Thus one conceptualizes God when one thinks of him, for example, as *cause* and as *absolute* goodness. Cf. IOH, pp. 20–21, 140.

in particular mark off the nature of men as rational and moral beings, it also eludes the powers *of* that nature.

But what does it signify that the numinous eludes conceptualization in moral terms? At one point, Otto seems to claim that the numinous is

> in itself indifferent towards morality [*an sich selber gegen das Ethische auch gleichgültig sein*] and can be considered for itself.[20]

On the other hand, at another point Otto clearly indicates that the notion "indifferent to morality" as it appears in certain theological writings is not a conceptual affirmation:

> With Böhme, as with Luther, the non-rational energy and majesty of God and his "awefulness" appear conceptualized and symbolized [*erfasst und versinnlicht*] as "Will." And with Böhme, as with Luther, this is conceived as fundamentally independent of *moral* elevation or righteousness, and as indifferent toward good or evil action.[21]

This will, says Otto, is a "Wrath" which

> would be quite meaningless if taken literally in the sense of a real conceivable and apprehensible anger.[22]

A will or wrath indifferent to morality is a human conception but not a conception *of* the numinous. It is a "symbol" or "ideogram" which names or indicates the numinous, but does not grasp it in the frame of human concepts.[23] Thus if one takes Otto's thesis in the broad sense, one simply cannot think or say precisely how the numinous stands in relation to morality. One may indeed experience what from one's own perspective is unjust suffering at the hands of the "eternal creative power," as Job did.[24] From its effects, the numinous

[20] DH (1922), p. 7; DH (1963), p. 6. Trans. mine. Harvey has, ". . . can be in itself ethically neutral" (IOH, p. 6).

[21] IOH, p. 107. DH (1922), p. 134; DH (1963), p. 132.

[22] IOH, p. 107.

[23] Ibid. Cf. IOH, pp. 18–19, 24, and 77.

[24] IOH, p. 80. Otto seems to assume that Job attributes his suffering to the numinous. Elsewhere, however, Otto argues that the idea of divine causality belongs to the rational side of God. Cf. IOH, pp. 20–21, on "createdness" and "creaturehood" and pp. 88–91 on predestination. Job may lose himself in "creature-consciousness" and experience the numinous as a transcendent "value," but the note of divine determination seems to be presupposd, here at least.

may seem indifferent to good or evil and hence capable of both.[25] But one is not entitled to characterize conceptually the numinous or its relation to anything, including morality.

Thus Otto wanted to account *historically* for those examples of religious interpretation where the divine is taken to be indifferent to the canons of human morality. *Logically,* however, his thesis that the numinous eludes our conceptual framework altogether precludes him from ascribing to this side of the divine indifference or any other relation to morality. Therefore only the passage where he treats "indifferent to morality" as an ideogram is congruent with his basic theme. Indeed Otto might well have said that to take "indifferent to morality" as a conceptual affirmation is to make the classic mistake of taking ideograms for more than they are.[26] The idea of *God* as a fortuitous will which establishes the meaning of rightness is a "perplexed endeavor to find a name" for the numinous, that is, it is a poor ideogram because it gives the numinous so much weight in the idea of the holy that the moral is reduced to the product of a capricious will.[27] The side of the holy characterized by a goodness which has its own "autonomous" meaning disappears. "Indifferent to morality," however, is permissible if taken only as an ideogram for the *numinous,* over against the moral side of the holy.

3. One cannot conceptualize the relation of the numinous to morality but Otto believes that one can "know," in a sense we will explore later, that the numinous is intimately intertwined with rational and moral attributes in the idea of the holy. However, he seems to put his point in two different ways. When he says that the concepts depicting God as a rational and moral being do not "exhaust" the idea of deity, one gets the impression that they do at least

[25] IOH, p. 106. Cf. the story of the new bridge which is destroyed, along with its builder, by a cyclone, where "Utter meaninglessness seems to triumph over richest significance, blind 'destiny' seems to stride on its way over prostrate virtue and merit" (IOH, p. 81).

[26] IOH, pp. 91, 77, 107.

[27] Ibid., p. 101. Cf. pp. 90–91. Otto seems to say that an ideogram of the numinous cannot remove the possibility of ascribing moral goodness to the other side of the holy. The image of a fortuitous will which establishes the meaning of rightness "outweighs" the rational-moral in the idea of the holy since it would be incompatible with the concept of an autonomous meaning of moral rightness. The question is, however, how a non-conceptual ideogram can conflict with a *concept* of the meaning of moral rightness.

properly characterize part of its "essence" or fundamental nature. One gets the same impression when Otto uses the metaphor of the "sides" of the divine, or speaks of "moments." However, he also says that these concepts are applied to the numinous itself, namely to that to which they precisely do not apply. They "are about and are valid of an Irrational [*sie geradezu nur von und an einem Irrationalen gelten und sind*]."[28] Otto says that these concepts are "essential" attributes of deity but nonetheless *"synthetic"* essential attributes.[29] Synthetic but essential means that the concepts are legitimately "attributed [*beigelegt*] to . . . an object which is not and cannot be known through them, but only in another characteristic way."[30] At another point he says that when the numen becomes the "guardian, ordainer and author" of "meanings derived from social and individual ideals of obligation, justice and goodness," these meanings "enter into the very essence of the numen and charge the term with ethical content."[31]

In the former way of speaking, Otto seems to assert that the deity has a dual nature, so that the concepts properly characterize one of its aspects but not the other. In the latter, his image is that of an object with one nature, the numinous, which is in itself not susceptible of predication by concepts but to which we nonetheless apply "essential predicates," that is, predicates which in some way grasp the very nature of their "bearer." Otto probably assumes, in the latter way of speaking, that there is also that about the numinous which makes it susceptible of such predication. The difficulty is that the numinous then is not strictly numinous, that is, by definition something *not* susceptible of conceptual comprehension. The numinous becomes like the "holy" itself, both susceptible and not. Thus the former mode of expression—the divine with a rational-moral side and a numinous side—probably represents Otto's thought more clearly. At one place Otto himself says that it is "impossible to rationalize the Irrational."[32]

---

[28] DH (1922), p. 2; DH (1963), p. 2. Trans. mine. Harvey, IOH, p. 2, has, "they in fact imply a non-rational or supra-rational Subject of which they are predicates."

[29] IOH, p. 2.

[30] DH (1963), p. 2. Trans. mine. DH (1922), p. 2, has "zukommen" for "beigelegt."

[31] IOH, p. 110.

[32] DH (1963), p. 77. This statement occurs in "Was Heisst Irrational?", which does not appear in DH (1922). The new section does appear in DH

Even so, however, it is not simply a matter for Otto of two elements of equal weight in the "complex" idea of the holy. There is a process in the history of religions in which the numinous is "'rationalized' and 'moralized.'"[33] The rationalization and moralization take place *"am* Numinosen," that is, upon or on the numinous.[34] The process is a "filling up [*Erfüllung*] with new content."[35] Otto does not only mean, it seems to me, that the numinous precedes the rational-moral in a historical or even a psychological sense. Rather he seems to have in mind that the numinous is the foundation of the holy in a metaphysical and a logical sense. The rationalization takes place *"am* Numinosen," upon the numinous and is *enclosed* by it (*wird von ihm umfasst*).[36] Another metaphor of Otto's is that of depth—the numinous represents the "depths" of the divine. It is the concern of the Church, says Otto, "to nurture the rational in the idea of God on the subsoil [*auf dem Untergrunde*] of its irrational element and thus to protect its depths."[37] The numinous is the "innermost core" of every religion and "without it no religion would be worthy of the name."[38]

Once the process is complete one can speak of the "interpenetration" or "indissoluble synthesis" in which the two elements exist,[39] but the numinous has a special role in the combination. I believe that Otto has in mind in the category of the holy something roughly analogous to the concept of a "father." If we assume that the idea of a father includes both biological parenthood and a social-moral role, we could say that both elements are "essential" for the full "complex" concept. However, we could also assert that biological fatherhood is the factual context and hence the logical presupposition or foundation for the additional element of the social role. Accord-

---

(1947). Harvey includes part of the material, but not the statement above, at the end of chap. VIII of IOH.

[33] IOH, p. 109. Cf. pp. 6 ff.

[34] IOH, p. 110; DH (1922), p. 138, DH (1963), p. 135. Trans. mine. Harvey has *"on the basis of* the numinous consciousness . . ."* Cf. IOH, p. 75.

[35] DH (1922), p. 139; DH (1963), p. 136. Harvey has "the completion and charging" (IOH, p. 111).

[36] DH (1922), p. 94; DH (1963), p. 95. Harvey has ". . . the setting within which the ethical and rational meaning is consummated" (IOH, p. 75).

[37] DH (1963), p. 133. This is a slightly revised version of DH (1922), p. 136. Cf. IOH, p. 108.

[38] IOH, p. 6.

[39] IOH, pp. 75, 110.

ingly, both rational-moral and nonrational–nonmoral are essential
elements in the idea of the holy, but the latter is the logical basis for
the yoking of the two. It is wrong, therefore, to argue that Otto
equated the divine with the numinous; it is also wrong to claim that
he gave each equal weight.

4. For Otto, then, the rational-moral and the numinous together
comprise the category of the holy. He does not leave the matter here,
however, but introduces the notion of "schematization" both as a
clarification of the type of relation between the two elements and as
an explanation of their union. The rational and moral predicates
do not simply serve to fill out the nature of the divine beyond the
numinous. In addition they serve to "schematize" it.

What does Otto mean by "schematization"? He introduces the
idea in the context of a discussion of the "law of the association of
feelings." According to Otto, just as ideas can resemble and excite
one another, so with feelings.[40] However, sometimes such an association is not just a "chance connection [*Zufallsverbindung*]" but
is a "necessary connection [*notwendige Verbindung*]" "according to
principles of essential correlation [*nach Prinzipien wesensmässiger
Zusammengehörigkeit*]."[41] When a feeling or idea resembles
another only by "external analogy," then their connection is acci-
dental or a matter of chance and is not lasting. On the other hand,
"we see religious feeling in permanent connection with other feelings," a connection which is not a matter of chance association but
is necessary, since it rests not on external analogy but on an
"essential correlation." Schematization, then, or rather the "Grunde
der Verbindung," the ground of the connection *between* category
and schema, is an example of such an "essential correlation."[42] On
this basis, for Kant succession in time schematizes the category of
causality, and, Otto concludes,

> . . . the relation of the rational to the non-rational element
> in the idea of the holy or sacred is just such a one of "schema-

[40] IOH, p. 42.
[41] DH (1922), p. 59; DH (1963), pp. 60–61. Trans. mine. Cf. IOH, p. 45.
For "wesensmässiger Zusammengehörigkeit," Harvey has "true inward affinity
and connection." Later, however, he has "essential correspondence" for
"wesentliche Zusammengehörigkeit."
[42] Ibid. Trans. mine.

tization," and the non-rational numinous fact, schematized by the rational concepts we have suggested above, yields us the complex category of "holy" itself. . . .[43]

Otto is saying, I believe, that certain concepts characterize, in completed form, one side of God and also stand in relation to the numinous side in some sort of fundamental structural correlation.[44] This group of notions not only directly qualify one aspect of the divine but stand in a special type of relation to the numinous.

I believe that this is Otto's view, but one could argue that in the course of the book schematization replaces direct attribution. That is, one could say that earlier Otto intended to claim that the rational-moral attributes are predicated directly of the numinous and not of another "side" of the holy. Later, the argument would run, Otto simply exchanges the language of predication or attribution for that of schematization. One would be left with a simple contrast between ideograms and the schematizing group of concepts, instead of the more complicated picture of ideograms of the numinous, attributes which qualify the other side, and the notion of schematization as a link between the attributes and the numinous.

Otto's presentation *is* confusing, for just as he sometimes speaks as if one directly predicated the numinous, so at points he sounds as if he meant that attributes were to be applied to the numinous only as schemata. For instance, in one passage he discusses the notions which schematize the *fascinans* aspect of the numinous:

> The ideas and concepts [*Vorstellungen und Begriffe*] which are the parallels or "schemata" on the rational side of this non-rational element of "fascination" are love, mercy, pity, comfort [*Liebe Erbarmen Mitleid Hilfswilligkeit*]; these are all "nat-

---

[43] IOH, p. 45. Harvey reproduces Otto's own quotation marks around "Schematisierung" applied to the relation of rational and nonrational in the idea of the holy.

[44] Bernhard Häring contrasts schematization, as part of Otto's notion of the development of the numinous into the complex category of the holy, with his presentation of the "essence" of the holy, apart from the developmental context. *Das Heilige und das Gute: Religion und Sittlichkeit in ihrem Gegenseitigen Bezug* (Krailling vor München: Erich Wewel Verlag, 1950), p. 170. Only the latter, says Häring, gives the ethical an essential, inseparable, and intrinsic connection to the numinous. However, as we have seen, schematization is precisely Otto's attempt to bring out the necessary and essential relation of the numinous and the moral. The issue is how an evolutionary perspective is compatible with the connection envisaged in schematization.

ural" elements of the common psychical [*seelischer*] life, only they are here thought of as absolute and in completeness. But important as they are for the experience of religious bliss or felicity, they do not by any means exhaust [*erschöpfen*] it.[45]

Here certain psychological notions which serve as schemata are presented in language which reminds one of the way he talked about predication: the schemata are "natural" elements in "absolute" form and they stand on the "rational side" of the holy. Moreover, when he is talking about the evolution of the "complex" idea of the holy, he often refers to the "filling up" of its content as schematization, rather than as attribution or attribution-*cum*-schematization. Nevertheless I do not believe Otto intended to take back with his left hand what he has given with his right, namely, that the rational, moral, and psychical group of attributes do qualify one side of the divine nature. He does not intend to *substitute* the notion of schematization through these attributes for predication. Schematization does not have to do with another way, in addition to ideograms, to speak of the numinous, but it refers to the relation of the numinous to the attributes which qualify the other side of the holy.[46]

5. Schematization, then, has to do with the relation of the attributes of one side of the holy to the other, numinous, side. But what exactly does it mean for Otto? One could get the impression that Otto's interest, at least in his initial presentation, is not in schematization per se. He begins by identifying a type of relation between feelings or ideas, a "necessary connection according to principles of inner essential correlation," which he finds illustrated in the connection between Kantian category and schema, or more precisely,

---

[45] IOH, p. 31; DH (1922), p. 40; DH (1963), p. 43. Cf. IOH, p. 140, where Otto identifies "Justice, moral will, and the exclusion of what is opposed to morality" as the ideas which schematize the *tremendum* and "goodness, mercy, love" as those which schematize the *fascinans*.

[46] Also confusing is another set of issues related to Otto's use of "analogy." On the opening page, he says that the attributes are "thought of by analogy [*in Entsprechung*] with our human nature" (IOH, p. 1; DH [1922], p. 1; DH [1963], p. 1). An ideogram is also an analogy ("*Entsprache*") (IOH, pp. 18–19; DH [1922], p. 21; DH [1963], p. 21). Are ideograms external analogies, as distinguished from schemata? Both ideograms and schemata are presented as different in kind from that to which they refer, namely the numinous. Yet how can there be analogy or essential correlation where the elements are different in kind?

such a correlation is the "Grunde" of the connection between them. He then declares, however, not simply that this type of relation also exists between rational-moral and numinous in the idea of the holy, but that schematization does.[47] Although he puts quotation marks around schematization, he seems to argue that the Kantian notion applies, *mutatis mutandis,* to the relation of the rational-moral and the numinous in the idea of the holy. Let us look briefly then at Kant's own presentation of the idea.

For Kant, the "schematism of the pure concepts of the understanding" is proposed as the answer to the question, "How, then, is the *subsumption* of intuitions under pure concepts, the *application* of a category to appearances, possible?"[48] As we recall, in the first *Critique,* Kant distinguishes "Sinnlichkeit" and "Verstand," sensibility and understanding, the former being the capacity of the mind to receive the data of empirical experience and the latter the source of pure or a priori concepts, i.e., "categories." To "subsume" an "object," given in sense experience, under an a priori category, Kant says that there must be something in the category "which is represented in the object" to be subsumed.[49] However, "pure concepts of understanding" are "quite heterogeneous from empirical intuitions. . . ."[50]

Kant's solution is to posit a "third thing," the "schema" of a concept, which is a "formal and pure condition of sensibility to which the . . . concept of understanding is restricted."[51] A schema for an a priori concept or category of the understanding seems to be a partic-

[47] For the sake of convenience I will not always add "psychical" or "psychological" to the list of attributes which qualify one side of the divine and also stand in the schematization relation to the numinous. Otto often simply uses "rational," by which I think he means "conceptual," thus indicating the entire range of characteristics attributable to one side of the holy, not simply the attribute of rationality per se.

[48] *Immanuel Kant's Critique of Pure Reason,* trans. Norman Kemp Smith (London: Macmillan, 1956), p. 180.

[49] Ibid.

[50] Ibid.

[51] Ibid., p. 182. For mathematical or a posteriori concepts, a schema can be defined as the "representation of a universal procedure of imagination in providing an image for a concept" (*Critique,* p. 182). However, with pure or a priori concepts, a schema is a "transcendental product of imagination," which links the pure categories with any object in time (*Critique,* p. 183). For the latter, there is no question of a specific *image,* as S. Körner points out in *Kant,* (Penguin, 1960), p. 72.

ular setting in time.[52] Time is (with space) the a priori formal condition of sensibility but at the same time "is contained in every empirical representation of the manifold."[53] Thus the schemata of pure
concepts are "determinations" which bring them into the arena of
time and thus link them with objects given in "sensible intuitions."

For example, the schema of the category of substance is the "per-
manence of the real in time, that is, the representation of the real as
a substrate of empirical determination of time in general, and so as
abiding while all else changes."[54] To take another example, the
schema or "temporal determination" of causality is "succession" in
time. As S. Körner notes, although causality is not equivalent to
succession in time, the former could not refer to anything in experience without the latter.[55] Thus without schemata "the pure concepts can find no object."[56]

That Otto introduces schematism in the context of his discussion
of the "association of ideas" is at first surprising, since we would have
expected it later, if he were following the Kantian parallel, along
with his treatment of the numinous as a priori. Just as the "rational
ideas of absoluteness, completion, necessity and substantiality, and no
less so those of the good as an objective value" are not derived from
sense experience but originate in an "original and underivable capacity of the mind implanted in the 'pure reason' independent of
all perception," so the elements of the numinous and the "feelings"
which go with them are a priori.[57] Like Kant's categories, the numinous does not arise "out of" but only "by means of" or "through"
sense experience.[58] The numinous as a priori goes back to the
"'ground of the soul,'" which is deeper than pure reason but is the

---

[52] *Critique*, p. 183. Time is the a priori condition of every experience, in-
cluding inner experience of the empirical self. Cf. Körner, *Kant*, p. 72.
H. J. Paton thinks that schematism should include space as well. *Kant's
Metaphysic of Experience* (London: G. Allen, 1951), Vol. II, n. 4, pp. 28–29.
W. H. Walsh notes another passage where Kant seems to suggest substituting
space for time: "Schematism," in *Kant: A Collection of Critical Essays*, ed.
R. P. Wolff (Garden City, N.Y.: Doubleday, 1967), p. 81.

[53] *Critique*, p. 181.
[54] Ibid., p. 184.
[55] *Kant*, p. 74.
[56] *Critique*, p. 186.
[57] IOH, p. 112.
[58] Ibid., pp. 112–13.

"deepest foundation of cognitive apprehension [*Erkenntnis-grunde*]."[59]

We would expect therefore that schematization might be developed for Otto, parallel with Kant, as a link between the numinous a priori category and its own proper object, the numinous aspect of the deity, just as schematism is the link between a priori categories and their objects given in empirical intuitions. However, for Otto, to "know [*kennen*]" is not limited to conceptual understanding [*"begriffliches Verstehen"*].[60] One can "know" the numinous as it is given directly in numinous feeling.[61] Otto does not seem to locate any hiatus between the numinous a priori category and the object of numinous experience such that a schema of some sort would be required.

Alternatively, Robert Davidson takes Otto to be presenting through the notion of schematism a way in which the *rational* a priori categories can be directly applied to the numinous, just as schematism for Kant links them to the objects of empirical experience.[62] Davidson argues that Otto, however, in order to "preserve the autonomy of religion," links the numinous as an a priori category with the rational a priori instead of following a Kantian parallel in which the numinous would have to be presented as "concrete qualities of . . . feeling," that is, as *non*-a priori intuition. Thus, says Davidson, Otto "discards the essential feature of this aspect of Kant's thought and renders it unintelligible in attempting to adapt it to his own needs."[63]

In the first place, since schemata are not empirical concepts for Kant, but a priori conditions of sensibility, the fact that Otto links the numinous a priori to the rational-moral a priori is not disconcerting. Furthermore, Otto's aim is not, as Davidson seems to take it to be, to provide for the "intelligible comprehension of numinous feeling and intuition" through rational-moral categories. Schematization does not pretend to offer "intelligible comprehension" of the numinous. Davidson is right to think that should Otto have understood schematization as a way of grasping the numinous conceptually he would have violated his basic thesis. But this was not Otto's aim. Even

[59] Ibid., pp. 112–13. DH (1922), p. 141; DH (1963), p. 138.
[60] IOH, p. 135; DH (1922), p. 166; DH (1963), p. 163.
[61] Cf. IOH, pp. 10–11.
[62] *Rudolf Otto's Interpretation of Religion.* (Princeton: Princeton Univ. Press, 1947), pp. 187–88.
[63] Ibid., p. 188.

if one held that Otto substitutes schematization through rational-moral predicates for direct attribution to one side of the divine, one would not have to presume that the former was supposed to provide "intelligible comprehension" in a rational-moral sense. All Otto claims for schematization is the knowledge of a "necessary connection" between rational-moral and numinous, not comprehension.

The crucial point against Davidson, however, is that for Otto, the rational-moral a priori categories are said to schematize the numinous, rather than being schematized in order to apply to it. Davidson assumes that Otto's situation parallels Kant's, where the problem is how to apply the rational categories to empirical objects. Otto puts the question differently, however, and has the rational-moral categories doing the schematizing rather than being schematized.

Thus schematization does not seem to function to link the numinous a priori with its own object. Nor, as Davidson thought, does it allow the numinous to be comprehended in rational-moral terms. For Otto, as I said, the idea of schematization provides a way of affirming a "necessary connection according to principles of essential correlation" between the rational-moral and the numinous. The sides of the holy are not left utterly discontinuous. For Kant, schematism produces categories capable of application to the objects of experience; for Otto schematization produces a category adequate to the elements of the divine. But what can we say about this use of schematization by Otto? Is even the rough parallel with the Kantian model justified?

a. In the first place, the sort of problem which schematization overcomes for Otto is entirely different from Kant's. There are, of course, various views of what Kant's problem was and was not. However, one line of interpretation seems sound to me. The pure categories, based on the "forms of judgment" specified in formal logic, represent logical "forms" or "functions" which do not contain in themselves the means by which they can be applied or can refer to the objects of empirical intuition.[64] Schematization is the doctrine of how this disability is removed. Kant's terminology is confusing, however, for he continually calls the pure categories and the schematized ones by

---

[64] See Norman Kemp Smith, *A Commentary to Kant's 'Critique of Pure Reason'* (London: Macmillan, 1918), pp. 340, 334; Paton, *Kant's Metaphysic*, Vol. II, pp. 26–27, 18–19.

the same names.[65] For example, the pure category "ground and consequent," based on the "hypothetical" if-then form of judgment, is referred to as "cause and effect," which is actually the schematized category of a ground which produces a consequent in time. The pure category of "subject and predicate" is referred to as "substance and accident," the schematized category of a permanent "substratum" of all changing predicates or accidents.[66]

G. J. Warnock suggests another view of the problem Kant was getting at. A notion like "causality" is not a "sensible characteristic" of things.[67] Thus there is a different sort of relation between causality and events than there is between roundness, for instance, and round things. According to Jonathan Bennett, however, this "truth" is merely a "vague one about the generality, and the distance from raw intuitions, of the concept of cause."[68] "Canineness," for example, is also not a sensible characteristic, but for a different reason, namely that "its meaning has a family-resemblance pattern."[69] If this was Kant's problem, says Bennett, it was not a very significant one.[70]

Thus Bennett and Warnock disagree about the importance of the distinction between sensible characteristics and concepts like causality. But the crucial point is that they are talking about the schematized, not the pure category. They both agree that causality or cause and effect is not a sensible characteristic. It is indeed the case that a schematized category *applies* to sensible objects as they appear in time but is not an empirical abstraction like roundness. The issue for Kant in the doctrine of schematization, however, does not have to do with the relation of causality to sensible events but with the

---

[65] For instance, Paton notes that Kant continually speaks of ground and consequent as cause and effect (*Kant's Metaphysic,* Vol. II, p. 53). He refers, however, to other remarks of Kant (ibid., pp. 53–54). Both Paton and Smith argue that what Kant often refers to as categories are actually schematized categories. Cf. Smith, *A Commentary,* p. 340.

[66] See *Kant's Metaphysic,* Vol. II, pp. 52–54. According to Paton, in the "categorical" form of judgement, subject and predicate are interchangeable. In the pure category, however, the "subject is regarded as a subject which can never be a predicate" (ibid., pp. 52–53). Paton thinks Kant could have argued simply that "thought demands something to think about by means of its concepts" (ibid., p. 53, n. 1).

[67] "Concepts and Schematism," *Analysis,* 9, 5 (1948–49), pp. 80–81.

[68] *Kant's Analytic* (Cambridge: Cambridge Univ. Press, 1966), p. 150.

[69] Ibid.

[70] Ibid.

relation of the pure category of ground and consequence to causality. Thus Bennett's depreciation of Warnock's rendition of the
Kantian problematic misses the point. A pure category no less than
a schematized one is not a sensible characteristic, but this is not the
difficulty to which schematization is addressed.[71]

Bennett himself, however, catches the sense of the Kantian issue
elsewhere when he distinguishes between "conditionality" and
"conditionality-in-time."[72] Similarly, W. H. Walsh, who states the
problem at one point as Warnock did,[73] also notes Kant's distinction
between the "logical significance" of the pure categories and the
"real significance" of the schematized ones, and uses the phrase
"ground and consequent" to refer to the unschematized category
behind cause and effect.[74] The difference then between these two
interpreters is that for Bennett the only point Kant isolated is this:

> . . . the categories are extremely general concepts whose ap-
> plication to the empirical world is of no interest unless accom-
> panied by . . . other concepts as well; and . . . these will al-
> ways include temporal ones as well. . . .[75]

For Bennett such a pure category as "conditionality" would be of
"no interest" or would say "uselessly little" about the empirical world
unless temporality and other concepts are adjoined. For Walsh, following Kant, it would be of no use whatsoever, for it would not
apply *of itself*. If Bennett really is talking here about the pure categories, then it is difficult to see what use or application they could
have unless conceived in a temporal setting.

In any case, the type of difficulty, which Kant's doctrine was designed to overcome, is quite different from Otto's.[76] Kant's problem
has to do with the relation of formal or abstract a priori categories

[71] Bennett makes the same sort of error when he argues that if the issue is
how a "general concept" is "homogeneous with a more specific one which falls
under it," then there is no more problem about how an orange falls under "substance" than there is about how a particular dog falls under "dog" (*Kant's
Analytic*, pp. 148–49). The issue, however, is not how substance is related to
substances, but how "subject" is related to "substance."

[72] *Kant's Analytic*, p. 151.

[73] "Schematism," p. 76.

[74] Ibid., p. 75, 81.

[75] *Kant's Analytic*, p. 151.

[76] I do not pretend to offer a definitive interpretation of the Kantian problem
or solution, but simply to indicate the sorts of uses to which Kant and Otto put
the concept of schematization.

to the empirical world. Otto's problem does not have to do with the reference of the numinous, but with the fact that it is inadequate by itself to designate the holy. In this sense, following for the moment Walsh's appropriation of a distinction between "meaning" and "reference," Otto's problem falls under the former, Kant's under the latter.[77] Otto's problem is to relate the aspects of the *idea* of the holy, not to show how the composite a priori category can relate to its object.

b. Furthermore, although there is debate about the interpretation and the adequacy of the Kantian solution, the type of solution Kant offers is different from Otto's since the problem is so different.

According to Paton, the schemata are "universal characteristics . . . which must belong to all objects *as objects in time.*"[78] All objects given to sensibility, for instance, exhibit "necessary succession" and therefore we are able to apply the category of ground and consequent to them. The pure category ground and consequent becomes the "concept of a ground which always precedes its consequent in time," that is, the "schematized category of cause and effect."[79] The "transcendental time-determinations," or characteristics of objects insofar as they are temporal allow "us to subsume appearances (or objects) under the category."[80] Paton rejects Smith's thesis that the transcendental schemata *are* the schematized categories: ". . . *ground and consequent* as applied and restricted to the transcendental schema of *necessary succession* becomes the schematized category of *cause and effect.*"[81]

[77] "Schematism", p. 75. Walsh is echoing here Körner's interpretation of schematization. According to Körner, "non-referential rules" govern the "logical grammar" of concepts, their relation to other concepts. "Referential rules" govern the application of concepts or "link concepts to perception" (Körner, *Kant*, p. 71). Kant's problem then was to develop referential rules which determine the "specific conditions" under which a category "is applied to objects of experience in general" (ibid., p. 72).

[78] *Kant's Metaphysic*, Vol. II, p. 19.

[79] Ibid., pp. 18–19. Cf. pp. 22–23. Paton says on p. 54, n. 3 that by "necessary succession" he means "regular" succession. See n. 98, p. 418.

[80] Ibid., pp. 29–30. See R. P. Wolff's criticism of Kant's use of the notion of subsumption. *Kant's Theory of Mental Activity* (Cambridge: Harvard Univ. Press, 1963), pp. 207–8.

[81] Ibid., pp. 40–41. As Paton points out, however, Kant himself never uses the expression "schematized category." Cf. pp. 66–69. I find Paton convincing here but Wolff favors Smith. *Kant's Theory*, pp. 217, 223. Walsh also says that the schema is a kind of second category. "Schematism," p. 81. Bennett, on the basis

Bennett, however, offers another interpretation of Kant's doctrine:

> Calling something a feline carnivore is just calling it a carnivore and a cat; and saying of something that the concept of conditionality-in-time applies to it is just saying that the concept of conditionality applies to it and that it is temporal.[82]

Thus for Bennett Kant's "solution" boils down simply to using the category in conjunction with temporality or, in other words, in a temporal context.

However, Kant's solution is not simply to apply, e.g., conditionality *independently* to objects which are *also* temporal. His argument is that ground and consequent, i.e., conditionality, cannot be applied in a temporal context unless the objects of temporal experience exhibited *certain* characteristics. Unless the objects of experience exhibited a particular kind of temporal characteristic, e.g., regular succession, one could not think of temporal objects in terms of ground and consequent. One must have the notion of *successive* events in order to think of one event as ground and the other as consequent, of one as cause and the other as effect. Bennett's way of stating the point seems to imply that one can independently apply, e.g., conditionality, to something to which temporality also independently applies. For Kant, however, one cannot apply conditionality were it not for a certain characteristic of temporal objects. The pure category cannot be independently applied.

In any case, for Kant, schematism is a matter of linking the pure concept to a temporal setting. For Otto, it is not really a matter of conceiving the numinous in the sort of setting which would make it applicable to an object in that setting, but of adding the rational-moral on top, as it were, of the numinous so that *together* they form the complex category of the holy which can grasp the holy as object. The addition in question in Otto is not simply that of another con-

---

of an admittedly ambiguous remark later in the *Critique*, says that the schema is the category itself with the condition of temporality added. *Kant's Analytic*, p. 151. Bennett, however, does not quote the complete passage: "In the principle itself [synthetic a priori] we do indeed make use of the category, but in applying it to appearances we substitute for it its schema as the key to its employment, or rather set it alongside the category, as its restricting condition, and as being what may be called its formula" (*Critique*, p. 212 [A 181; B 224]). Bennett quotes only through "schema," whereas the "set it alongside" corresponds to the interpretation I am supporting.

82 *Kant's Analytic*, p. 151.

cept as the condition of the necessary or useful *applicability* of another, but of the addition of another concept fully co-ordinated with the first. Temporality is an a priori condition of sensibility itself, so that in this general sense Otto keeps the parallel with Kant when he adds the rational to the numinous a priori. However, temporality is added for Kant as a condition of the exercise or, following Bennett, of the useful exercise, of the pure concept—ground and consequent becomes cause and effect. The temporal characteristic or schema is *present* of course, but only as a condition for the application of the one concept. For Otto, on the other hand, the two categories *jointly apply*; he does not raise the issue whether separately or together they are in need of some other "mediating" concept, parallel with temporality, in order to apply to their object. Otto characterizes his sense of schematization as a blending (*sich einschmelzen*)[83], an interpenetration (*Durchdringung, Ineinandertreten*)[84] with a warp (*Aufzug*) and a woof (*Einschlag*).[85] These images depict a kind of joining or merging, rather than the provision of a concept which provides the setting or condition for *another* in order to secure its application.

The rational-moral attributes, therefore, do not schematize the numinous in anything like the sense in which temporal schemata schematize pure categories. The rational-moral categories, conceived parallel to time as an a priori determination of sensibility, would have to put the numinous a priori into such a form that it could apply to a rational-moral object, corresponding to *empirical* objects, were the Kantian parallel complete. On the contrary, for Otto adding the rational-moral to the numinous is the completion of the meaning of a category both of whose aspects reflect the nature of the object to which they are to apply—the object is the holy not the rational-moral side of God.

What is the significance of the sense in which schematization in Kant and in Otto are different? If Otto does assume that the type of merger he has in mind is similar to Kant's, then his account seems intended to have explanatory force. As schematization for Kant is an explanation of a basic aspect of our conceptual framework, so for

[83] DH (1922), p. 62; DH (1963), p. 64; IOH, p. 48.
[84] DH (1922), p. 60; DH (1963), p. 61; IOH, p. 46. DH (1922), p. 167; DH (1963), p. 165; IOH, p. 136.
[85] DH (1922), pp. 63–64; DH (1963), pp. 64–65; IOH, pp. 48–49.

Otto it explains the process by which the numinous and the rational-moral are linked in the idea of the holy. However, the force of Kant's explanation rests on the *necessity* of temporal "determinations" for the application or reference of a pure concept. If Otto's problem is not one of reference but of the basic meaning of the category, then his schematization cannot borrow, even *mutatis mutandis*, the explanatory force of Kant's doctrine. In the absence of a more complete parallel with Kant's sense of schematization, or some alternative theory, Otto's use of the concept simply amounts to the delineation of the merger of the elements in the idea of the holy and the *assertion* that their relation consists of a necessary connection based on an essential correlation.

6. Even if the types of operation in the two senses of schematization were similar, Otto would face another question: how can there be an analogy between a connection of elements in a basic aspect of our conceptual framework and a relation involving the non-conceptualizable numinous? Otto goes on to say that we have a "synthetic a priori" knowledge of the relation of the elements in the idea of the holy. Indeed, the connection of the elements in a Kantian synthetic a priori does bear a closer resemblance to what Otto wants to assert about the idea of the holy than the relation of schema and category did. But what is at issue is precisely the analogy between this basic part of our conceptual structure and any connection which involves the non-conceptual.

Otto identified the necessary connection between category and schema as a priori in the section on schematization in Chapter VII. Later, in the second chapter on the holy as an a priori category (Chapter XVII) he says that the "inner necessity" of the correlation of the rational-moral and the numinous is felt to be self-evident, but that to account for its self-evidence, we have to assume a " 'synthetic a priori knowledge.' "[86] According to Otto, the connection is not logically necessary, by which I take it he means "analytic"; it does not "logically follow" that any particular god is moral in nature.[87] We have a synthetic a priori knowledge of the essential correlation

---

[86] DH (1963), p. 165. Trans. mine. Cf. DH (1922), p. 167. Harvey has: "an obscure a priori knowledge of the necessity of this synthesis" (IOH, p. 136).
[87] DH (1963), p. 165; DH (1922), pp. 167–68; IOH, p. 136.

and hence the necessary connection of the rational-moral and the numinous in the idea of the holy.

What shall we say about Otto's recourse to "synthetic a priori"? The difficulty involves first of all Otto's fundamental attempt to posit a numinous a priori *category*.

Søren Holm argues that for Otto in IOH the numinous a priori is independent of ordinary sense experience but is not a "transcendental" precondition of the experience of the numinous object.[88] On the contrary, argues Holm, the numinous a priori refers to a unique *type* of experience. Holm's thesis, however, requires us to disregard all of Otto's references to the numinous a priori as a special cognitive capacity. It may be that Otto extends the idea of a priori category to include a kind of numinous "sensibility" but he certainly retained some parallel to the Kantian notion of the contribution which "understanding" brings to experience.

If one brings to Otto a distinction P. F. Strawson makes about Kant, one could argue a less radical thesis, namely that Otto retains a parallel only to half of Kant's notion. Strawson argues that Kant confused two senses of a priori. In the first or "austere" sense, a concept is a priori "if it was an essential structural element in any conception of experience we could make intelligible to ourselves." In the second, which expresses Kant's "transcendental idealism," a concept is a priori if "its presence as a feature of experience was attributable entirely to the nature of our cognitive constitution and not at all to the nature of those things, as they are in themselves, which affect that constitution to yield experience."[89] One could argue, then, that Otto in effect retains a parallel with one sense of the Kantian a priori and drops another, namely, that he keeps the notion of an element of our cognitive psychology independent of sense experi-

---

[88] "Apriori and Urphänomen bei Rudolf Otto," *Rudolf Otto's Bedeutung für die Religionswissenschaft und die Theologie Heute: Beihefte der Zeitschrift für Religions- und Geistesgeschichte,* ed. Ernst Benz (Leiden: Brill, 1971), p. 81.

[89] *The Bounds of Sense* (London: Methuen, 1966), p. 68. Strawson feels that Kant's attempt to explain the "necessary general features of experience" by reference to "their source . . . in our cognitive constitution" is "incoherent" (pp. 15–16). He has two chief arguments: first, that since experience presupposes the "necessary features," one could not gain knowledge of them by examining one's own cognitive psychology; second, that if space and time are just capacities to be affected by objects not themselves in space and time, then the notion of "being affected" is unintelligible (pp. 32, 41).

278 Religion and Morality

ence but discards any parallel to the notion of a *logical* constituent in any possible awareness of an object of experience.

Otto certainly seems to stress the idea of the numinous a priori as an element in our "cognitive constitution." Early in *The Idea of the Holy* Otto says that the numinous is a *"sui generis . . .* mental state."[90] It is a "primary and elementary datum in our psychical life."[91] When he comes later to discuss the holy as an a priori category, his discussion of Kant reflects Strawson's psychological sense of a priori. Kant, ". . . referring to empirical knowledge . . . distinguishes that part which we receive through impressions and that which our own faculty of cognition supplies from itself."[92] Just so the numinous a priori (as part of the holy as a priori) "issues from the deepest foundation of cognitive apprehension that the soul possesses," a "hidden substantive source from which the religious ideas and feelings are formed, which lies in the mind independent of sense experience."[93]

If Otto had spoken solely of a "feeling," one might be tempted to think that what he says about a special cognitive capacity refers only to it. However, what he refers to as a unique part of our cognitive constitution involves not only "feeling" but also "ideas": there is a hidden substantive source from which religious *ideas* and feelings are formed. Elsewhere he speaks of a numinous "category of interpretation [*eine Deutungs-* . . . *kategorie*]."[94] Thus he does seem to retain a parallel with the logical sense of the Kantian a priori.

What Otto does not explain, however, is how his numinous a

[90] IOH, p. 7.

[91] IOH, p. 9. These two quotations seem to support Holm's thesis but I think they should be interpreted in the light of other passages.

[92] IOH, p. 113. In his notion of the numinous a priori as part of our cognitive constitution, Otto could not be said to duplicate Kant's "transcendental idealism." He does not seem to suggest that the awareness gained through the numinous capacity is to be sharply distinguished from the nature of the numinous object as it is in itself.

[93] IOH, pp. 113–14. Cf. DH (1922), p. 142: ". . . Quell von Vorstellungs-und Gefühls-bildung. . . ." Also cf. IOH, p. 112; and DH (1922), p. 141, where he speaks of "Ideen" and "Gefühle."

[94] IOH, pp. 5, 7; DH (1922), pp. 5, 7; DH (1963), pp. 5, 7. (DH [1922] has "category of interpretation and valuation [*Bewertung*]" on pp. 5 and 7; IOH does not include interpretation on p. 7; DH [1963] omits "Deutung" on p. 5 but has it on p. 7. I will discuss valuation in Section 7.) Otto begins here by talking of the category of the holy, but shifts immediately to a discussion of the holy without its rational-moral half.

priori capacity can yield a "Deutungs-kategorie" which has a sub-stantial analogy to a Kantian category. By definition the numinous must be non-conceptual. One can express numinous feeling in ideo-grams, but how can numinous feeling issue in a "Kategorie" which retains any analogy with a category in the conceptual sphere?[95]

Moreoever, if there is a basic difficulty in Otto's designation of the numinous as a category, insofar as it embodies an analogy with the logical sense of a Kantian a priori, then the problem is com-pounded when he speaks of the idea of the holy as a category and takes its elements to be related in a way analogous to the connection of elements in a synthetic a priori, a notion fundamentally related in Kant to the idea of an a priori concept.

As Strawson puts it, the notion of the synthetic a priori can be taken to correspond to Kant's basic "programme . . . of determining the fundamental general structure of any conception of experience such as we can make intelligible to ourselves."[96] The synthetic a priori for Kant is a principle or rule for the "objective employment" of the schematized category.[97] Schematization is the condition for the application of the pure categories to sensible intuition; synthetic a priori principles are the rules of their application.

Thus a synthetic a priori judgment is a principle or rule which puts a *category* (schematized, of course) into operation. Whatever "connection" is posited in the principle reflects the meaning of the category itself. For instance, the connection of ground and conse-quent which when schematized becomes cause and effect is expressed in a corresponding synthetic a priori principle.[98] Furthermore, in a note added to the second edition of the *Critique*, Kant distinguished

[95] Cf. IOH, p. 6; DH (1922), pp. 6–7: the numinous is a "feeling-response," a "Gefühlsreflex." (DH [1963], p. 6, has "Moment" here instead of "Gefühls-reflex" but this does not indicate any theoretical change in light of the many other references to "feeling" throughout IOH.)

[96] Strawson thinks that Kant really develops no clear idea of the synthetic a priori since he links it to the, for Strawson, "incoherent" model of the faculties of our "cognitive constitution" (*The Bounds of Sense*, pp. 43–44; cf. pp. 15–16).

[97] *Critique*, p. 196.

[98] Strawson argues that Kant illegitimately moves from the idea of a necessary order of successive perceptions to the idea of succession as causally necessary (*The Bounds of Sense*, pp. 137 ff.). He allows, however, that "our concepts of objects are linked with sets of conditional expectations. . . ." What he denies is there must always be an "explanatory condition" of every change or that every such condition must be "strictly sufficient" (pp. 144–46). See his parallel critique of Kant's notion of substance (pp. 125 ff.).

between two types of "combination," "composition" and "connection."[99] In the first, the "constituents do not necessarily belong to one another."[100] In the second, "its constituents *necessarily belong to one another*, as, for example, the accident to some substance, or the effect to the cause."[101] The second is the "synthesis of that which, though *heterogeneous,* is yet represented as combined *a priori.*"[102] It can refer either to the "*physical* connection of the appearances . . ." or to their "*metaphysical* connection in the *a priori* faculty of knowledge."[103]

Otto has an a priori connection of the "metaphysical" sort in mind. What he is saying, I believe, is that the elements of the holy as a "category" are related in a way analogous to the connection of the elements in one of the Kantian a priori categories. As Kantian categories are expressed in synthetic a priori principles in relation to objects of possible experience, so the category of the holy with its elements can be thought of as taking a form analogous to that of a synthetic a priori. Hence, our knowledge of the necessary connection between the elements of the idea of the holy is analogous to our knowledge of the relation of the elements in a synthetic a priori principle.

Otto's problem is to show how there can be a "necessary connection" based on an "essential correlation" between the numinous and the rational-moral, but his use of the notion of a synthetic a priori to signify such a connection and our knowledge of it raises the fundamental issue of the appropriateness of the analogy. He wants to claim that the connection of the numinous and the rational-moral is like the synthetic a priori relation of cause and effect; that is, a connection which is neither empirical nor a matter of logical or "analytic" necessity, but one which reflects, as Strawson puts it, "the structure of any conception of experience such as we can make intelligible to ourselves." However, just as he has not explained how there can be an analogy between a non-conceptual numinous a priori and a Kantian a priori concept, so he has not explained how the relation of the elements of the holy can be analogous to the con-

99 *Critique*, p. 197.
100 Ibid.
101 Ibid., p. 198.
102 Ibid.
103 Ibid.

nection found in a synthetic a priori principle. It is one thing to argue that there is a "heterogeneity" between cause and effect which is overcome, as it were, in the logical structure of any intelligible conception of experience. It is another to argue that there is an analogy between this conceptual synthesis and the synthesis of the conceptual and the non-conceptual in the "idea" of the holy.[104] The analogy with the synthetic a priori founders on Otto's basic thesis itself, the non-conceptualizability of the numinous. Otto does not explain how one can use an analogy with the fundamental tool of our conceptual apparatus to interpret a relationship in which the non-conceivable numinous is an element. Nor does he explain how there can be an analogy to the "knowledge" which is proper to the basic constituents of our *conceptual* framework. Interestingly enough, as we will shortly see, later in his life Otto did not attempt to use an analogy with the analysis of the structure and knowledge of our conceptual framework to "account" for the "self-evidence" of the necessary connection, but was content to rely on a "certainty" given in "feeling."

7. Otto also suggests another sort of relation between the numinous and the moral which goes significantly beyond the "essential correlation" claim. At one point in *The Idea of the Holy*, he said that the numinous possesses in itself "supreme worth" or *"objective value"* which "claims our homage," in contrast to its subjective value or potential for the "beatitude of man." The latter is the numinous as *fascinans*, the former the numinous as *augustum*. Our response to the numinous as *augustum* is not

> . . . simply "fear" in face of what is absolutely overpowering, before which there is no alternative to blind, awe-struck obedience. *"Tu solus sanctus"* is rather a paean of *praise*, which . . . recognizes and extols a value, precious beyond all conceiving. The object of such praise is not simply absolute might . . . but a might that has at the same time the supremest *right* to make the highest claim to service. . . .[105]

[104] Note also the dissimilarity between the "heterogeneity" of a priori categories and objects of empirical intuition, overcome by schemata, and the gap between the conceptual and the non-conceptual. Otto first locates his necessary connection, as we remember, in the linkage of a schema and then roots it in a synthetic a priori relation.

[105] IOH, p. 51–52.

Moreover, says Otto, the value of the numinous as *augustum* is the "nonrational ground (*Urgrund*) and source (*Ursprung*) of all possible objective values."[106]

The idea of numinous value as the ground and origin of all objective values is not developed here but is taken up again in *Freiheit und Notwendigkeit*, his posthumously published "conversation with Nicolai Hartmann about the autonomy and theonomy of values."[107] Earlier Otto had published a series of essays in which he proposed "to determine more exactly the content and relation" of " 'Sittengesetz' " and " 'Gotteswille.' "[108] Actually in these essays he develops his own ethical theory. His central claim is that "value," not only of the will but of things and experiences, is, along with "justice" or "rights," the basis of moral obligation. Thus "moral" or "ethical" value refers to the value which yields moral obligation. In *Freedom and Necessity*, Otto finally grapples with the relation of ethical value to the divine.

Otto identifies Hartmann's third "antinomy" between religion and

[106] DH (1963), p. 67; DH (1947), p. 63. Otto evidently added this in some later edition. It does not appear in DH (1922), p. 67. Cf. IOH, p. 51.

[107] *Freiheit und Notwendigkeit*, with "Nachwort" by Th. Siegfried (Tübingen: Verlag von J. C. B. Mohr [Paul Siebeck], 1940) (hereafter, FN). Nicolai Hartmann, *Ethics*, trans. Stanton Coit (New York: Macmillan, 1932), Vol. III, pp. 260–74. I have limited my essay to IOH and *Freedom and Necessity* since Otto makes his basic claims in these works. See also the "Introduction," "What is Sin?" and "The Prophets' Experience of God," in *Religious Essays*, trans. Brian Lunn (Oxford: Oxford University Press, 1931). In *India's Religion of Grace and Christianity Compared and Contrasted* (New York: Macmillan, 1930) and *Mysticism East and West* (New York: Macmillan, 1932), he illustrates the relation of the numinous and the moral through contrasts between Western and Eastern traditions.

[108] "Wert, Würde und Recht," *Zeitschrift für Theologie und Kirche*, Vol. 12.1 (1931), pp. 1–67; "Wertgesetz und Autonomie," ZTK, Vol. 12.2 (1931), pp. 85–110; "Das Gefühl der Verantwortlichkeit," *Zeitschrift für Religionspsychologie*, Vol. 3 (1930), pp. 49–57 and 109–36; "Das Schuldgefühl und seine Implikationen," ZRP, Vol. 4 (1931), pp. 1–19; "Pflicht und Neigung," *Kant-Studien*, Vol. 37 (1932), pp. 49–90. For an examination of Otto's unpublished lectures on ethics see Georg Wünsch, "Grundriss und Grundfragen der Theologischen Ethik Rudolf Otto," ZTK, Vol. 19 (1938), pp. 46–70. I have had the benefit of a paper by Jack Boozer, "The Boundary Between the Ethical and the Religious in Rudolf Otto's Thought," given at the 1971 meeting of the American Academy of Religion and reproduced in the papers of the "Philosophy of Religion and Theology" section (*Philosophy of Religion and Theology: 1971*). According to Professor Boozer, unpublished essays with the titles "Sittengesetz und Gotteswille" and "Der Gotteswille" are in the possession of the University Library at Marburg.

morality as the "really genuine" one. This is the antinomy, as Otto summarizes it, between the "autonomy of good in and through itself and theonomy, the establishment of all 'laws' by God."[109] According to Otto, echoing Hartmann, the "demands of conscience" have a "validity [*Gültigkeit*]" which cannot be established by a "Will" but which is "given necessarily, lawlike, and irreducibly in the nature of things."[110] Does this mean then that God is superfluous for morality, the conclusion Hartmann drew? On the contrary, says Otto, we experience the "feeling of the Holy" as a value feeling [*Wertgefühl*]. In consequence the field of value is broadened and deepened beyond the merely ethical. Furthermore, all ethical values are subordinated to this one.[111] (Otto is evidently using "holy" here in its numinous sense alone, hence the contrast between the holy as value and ethical value.) Negatively, "sin" or the violation of the respect due the holy is extended to cover all ethical wrongdoing. Positively, the "holy" is "the ground, the basis of possibility, and the source (*fundus, Möglichkeitsgrund, Urquell*) of all actual or possible values in the world and the world beyond." We are both aware that what God commands is right in terms of "autonomous" value, and that this same divine reality as value is the "ground" of all values.[112]

Otto goes on to explain that God's will is not "contingent."[113] Even if *we* apprehend moral values as "valid" in themselves, could God have determined, through his creative will, that what we take to be right, e.g., love, is wrong, and what we take to be wrong, e.g., hate, is right?[114] Is what seems to us unchangeable the "contingent" product of God's "free" will which is not "bound" or "determined" by anything? Otto says that in so far as the holy is nonrational in the depths of its essence, concepts like "contingency or necessity" do not apply.[115] However, as a preliminary way of thinking, one can

[109] FN, p. 8. Hartmann, *Ethics*, Vol. III, pp. 264–66.
[110] FN, p. 9. This passage reflects Otto's theory of "objective" value. Cf. n. 127 below.
[111] Ibid., pp. 9–10.
[112] Ibid., p. 11.
[113] Ibid., pp. 12–13 ff.
[114] Ibid., p. 13.
[115] Ibid., p. 14.

say that since a holy will is a "value will," it in no sense acts in a "wholly undetermined and arbitrary way."[116]

Furthermore, it is by no means the case that God is somehow bound by a law which is outside and above him; there are no gods beside God.[117] On the contrary, we should think of God not as a capricious despot, but as an "inconceivable self-founded value depth [*in sich ruhender Werttiefe*]"[118] such a god is the creator of a world of values, which are rays or beams from his eternal "Urwert." The creator allows the "Urautonomie" of value which he bears in himself to shine in creation.[119] Thus the "will of God" is only the human expression for the "demanding element" which belongs to eternal value and its "reflection" in the creature.[120] "Value demand" and "will demand" are bound into one.[121]

Otto's strategy in facing Hartmann is to deny the terms of the antinomy as Hartmann states them. In the first place, the situation is not such that there is an "ideal mode of Being peculiar to values" set over against the reality of God.[122] Creaturely being and its value are both due to the creative power of God. The values men apprehend are metaphysically dependent on God:

> As the ideal essence of things is from God and in infinite refractions and shadings imitates the divine essence in the narrow realm of the creaturely world, so the reflection of divine value adheres to this image of God. . . .[123]

> All worldly essences are analogies to one of the elements of the being of God and the value which rests on each of them is an emitted spark of the value-glory of God himself. . . .[124]

In the second place, Otto argues that it is not a question of either

116 Ibid., pp. 14–15. Otto seems to use "contingent" and "arbitrary" indifferently. He evidently equates absolute "freedom" with an arbitrary or "undetermined" will. However, one should not confuse this sense of contingent with the idea of a "contingent" creation. To argue that creation need not exist or could exist in some different way does not necessarily imply that its present shape is arbitrary.

117 Ibid., p. 12–13.
118 Ibid., p. 15.
119 Ibid., p. 15.
120 Ibid., p. 18.
121 Ibid.
122 Hartmann, *Ethics,* Vol. III, p. 265.
123 FN, p. 15.
124 Ibid., p. 18.

being able to have knowledge of moral values independently of God or of having them delivered by the divine as a lawgiver. Otto fully subscribes to Hartmann's claim that men are independently capable of recognizing moral values. The moral knowledge men have is part of the creator's arrangement of things. Men possess the power of "objective valuation," which is conscience. God's commands do not require blind obedience but are "intelligible in respect to their validity."[125]

Thirdly, Otto also agrees with Hartmann that moral values have a validity which is logically autonomous. Values exist, logically speaking now, "aus sich heraus." "To offend the honor of another, to neglect oneself through lack of discipline, to choose lies instead of truth, is bad or evil and what is evil should not exist."[126] As we know, Otto denies that what seems valid on its own ground, that is, on the basis of its own logical content, is really *"a parte Dei"* contingent or arbitrary. In contrast to Hartmann, who says that "It is inherent in the nature of God . . . [that] nothing can be of value on any other ground, except that he wills it," Otto says that such an idea is not demanded by the nature of God and that indeed such a being would not be God but a "capricious despot." (Here again we find Otto identifying "capricious" will and "good is good because God wills it.") Moral values and norms have an independent content which is not a product of the fortuitous-capricious will of a divine legislator (this was also his point, I believe, in IOH).[127]

---

[125] Ibid., p. 11. The epistemological autonomy Otto recognizes here parallels the second sense of *"Autonomie"* which he identifies in "Wertgesetz und Autonomie," pp. 108–9. The first corresponds to the theme of logical autonomy which I discuss next. The third, the autonomy of affirmation or appropriation by the self-legislating will, is paralleled here by a passing reference to an inner "Ja-sagen zur Gültigkeit" (FN, p. 11). At another point Otto makes the puzzling remark that through an "insight" of "feeling," not of "understanding [*Verstand*]," one can affirm that what God commands is "incontrovertibly right" (FN, p. 12). He means, I believe, that through religious feeling one knows as an article of *religious* faith that whatever God commands is going to be right. This is knowledge about *God*. One can also know through rational ethical judgment ("Vernunft als sittliche Urteilskraft") that what God actually commands is right ("Wertgesetz und Autonomie," p. 108). Presumably one knows in religious feeling that the numinous is the metaphysical and logical "ground" of moral values, but see my remarks just ahead.

[126] FN, p. 12.

[127] CF. "Wertgesetz und Autonomie," p. 108. "The autonomous is . . . that which through itself is a law and that which out of itself a prescription [*Gebot*] results. . . . It is the inner value of an object with regard to the prescription,

However, Otto does try to preserve, I believe, some sense in which moral value is logically dependent on the divine, although he is not at all specific about it. The passages in which he employs the imagery of streaming rays of moral value emitted or reflected from numinous value signify not only a metaphysical source of value in God, but carry the connotation of some sort of logical dependence:

> Values, then, which confront us in the world as demanding or attracting, do not stand to the eternal meaning and value of God as a separate and rival entity but are, as it were, their own extensions [*Verlängerungen*] in the world.[128]

He seems—one must be tentative but the impression is strong—to be arguing that while good is good because a capricious God wills it would compromise the logical autonomy of moral value the notion of moral value as the "reflection" of numinous value does not. Thus he tries to protect himself against the idea of a fortuitous, arbitrary, or contingent morality while keeping a sense of the logical dependence of moral value on its divine source.

But if Otto claims that moral value reflects or imitates numinous value, then its meaning is not *perfectly* autonomous. What exactly is at stake for Otto in his effort to keep both autonomy and dependence through the notion of "reflection"?

As we have seen, Otto contrasts the idea that moral value is established by a capricious will and the notion that it has its own autonomous "irreducible" meaning. If the meaning of moral value which men apprehend as sufficient to carry its own "demand" actually rested on such a will, then its sufficiency would be penultimate and derivative. One would not only refer to the will or command as the causal source of the meaning of moral value, one would understand that its logical justification or "validity" no longer rests in

---

and the object itself, through its meaning, with regard to its value." Ethical "laws" are not established by a will but "with a definite meaning of an object its value is necessarily 'given' . . . out of the 'nature' or the essential meaning of the object itself." Moreover, says Otto, "moral value [*Wertgesetz*] is not established, made, given, devised by us or our reason; it is not invented, but is simply to be found, come upon, discovered, perceived. Law and prescription stand starkly objective over against us with their validity, as objective as the range of things to be recognized stand over against our perception. They are absolutely *given*." An examination of Otto's ethical theory would be another task altogether. Suffice it to say that his theory is cognitivist and that it is objectivist, in the sense that the validity of valuation is independent of the valuer.

128 FN, p. 18.

itself alone. One gets the impression that what exercised Otto was the issue of autonomous sufficiency versus a derivative "validity."

On the other hand, Otto does not seem to insist on the absolute autonomy of moral value since he argues that it is patterned after numinous value. Indeed, he takes the notion that a *non-arbitrary* will of God establishes the meaning of value as a way to express his own "reflection" thesis. He does not consider the idea of establishment by a non-arbitrary will in its own right, but the very fact that Otto takes it as a way of expressing his own "reflection" thesis would argue that for him it does not threaten what he wanted to maintain. Establishment by a capricious will not only makes the sufficiency of moral value derivative, it roots it ultimately in an arbitrary source. There is no continuity of meaning between the arbitrary will and moral value. Thus the notion of establishment by an arbitrary will saps the significance of the meaning of moral value. Its validity not only does not rest in itself alone, but its basis is ultimately arbitrary. However, if moral value is dependent on a non-arbitrary will which reflects God's essence, then although its meaning is still derivative, it corresponds through God's will to the meaning of divine value. Although its sufficiency is not absolutely autonomous, it partakes of the sufficiency of divine value.

It may be, then, that Otto was more troubled by the idea that the meaning of moral value is established by an arbitrary will than he was about autonomy or sufficiency per se. He is satisfied with the imperfect autonomy of moral value which the reflection model retains. Moral value does not have absolute autonomy but it corresponds to the meaning of numinous value. To be sure, by virtue of this conformity, moral value can be said to share derivatively in the autonomy of numinous value. The reflection model gives Otto a type of autonomy, although it is not absolute. But what seems crucial is not the autonomy in itself but the fact that the meaning of moral value is fashioned on divine meaning, rather than resting on an arbitrary basis.

The difficulty with Otto's view, then, is not so much in his effort to combine logical autonomy with some form of logical dependence, but with the substance of his suggestion. First, one would have to question the notion of an imitation of a divine essence which he incorporates into his basic idea that creaturely being and value are metaphysically dependent on God. But bypassing the classic logical and metaphysical issues here, there are questions more directly relevant to the inquiry of this essay. If Otto had in mind that moral value is logically dependent on numinous value in the sense that one idea reflects or is modeled on another, then either numinous value is moral, at least in part, or moral value must simply be defined in terms of numinous value. The first alternative, however, threatens the distinction between the moral and the numinous, for by definition numinous value cannot be moral. On the other hand, if there were a definition of moral value in terms of numinous value—moral value means and only means the creaturely "reflection" of numinous value—"good is good because God wills it" would have been avoided only to fall into another mode of defining away the logical autonomy of moral value. Moral value would not possess its autonomous validity as *moral* but only as the creaturely extension of numinous value. Moreover, this way of gaining logical dependence would clearly destroy the distinction between the moral and the numinous.

Thus in one sense Otto has raised the stakes considerably in *Freiheit und Notwendigkeit*. The relation between the moral and the numinous is now pictured not merely as a "necessary connection according to an essential correlation," but the latter is pictured as the "Ground and Source" of the former in a metaphysical and, as I argued, logical sense. We might have expected Otto to argue that moral values were "reflections" of the moral aspect of the divine but he goes further and claims that their source lies in numinous value. He does of course present the case now in terms of the relation between numinous value and humanly perceived moral value but it is no distortion of his argument to take him to assume that the numinous is the "ground" of the moral in the holy itself. Thus Otto not only develops the "ground and origin" sentence in *The Idea of the Holy* but his argument itself extends the general point I made, that the numinous is the foundational element in the idea of the holy.

However, I have withheld the point which is most significant for our purposes until now. Unlike *The Idea of the Holy*, where Otto did attempt to explicate the nature of the relation between numinous and moral through an analogous application of the Kantian analysis of our conceptual apparatus, here he explicitly denies that his use of the language of exemplary "essences" should be taken as a straightforward theoretical affirmation. We cannot assert [*auszusagen*] anything about the relation between the creator and the world.[129] But in "pious feeling" we attribute the world to God and "hear" in our apprehension of moral "value" the claim of divine value.[130] The idea that moral value is a "radiation" of numinous value is only an image, a *"Bild,"* but one which is not empty for our "feeling of truth."[131] Such images (and, he adds, doctrines) do not fully illumine the issue but let us glimpse an eventual solution.[132] We cannot go beyond images but they strike something which is "certain enough in our dark feelings."[133]

Otto did not explain in IOH how a substantive analogy with Kant's analysis of the basic logical structure of our experience could be used to explicate and justify his claims about the unique non-conceptualizable numinous and its relation to morality.[134] In *Freiheit und Notwendigkeit,* however, while he raises the stakes in terms of what he suggests about the relation of the numinous and the moral, he lowers them in another. While he does continue to designate the numinous as a "category of value," he makes no pretense of bringing any explication or justification derived from an analysis of human reason or morality to bear on the "ground and source" relation, but anchors his certainty in "feeling." He admits the imagistic character of the ground and source relation, even if he does not explicitly raise the question of the logical status of the concept of "value" as applied to the numinous.

But how can "images," on the basis of which we can only say that moral values are, "as it were," "extensions" of the numinous, really "bring something to the surface" which is "certain" in feeling? If images function like ideograms, then they bear no conceptual freight. If they are more than ideograms, how do they bring to the surface what they do without conceptualization? As with "necessary connection according to an essential correlation," the issue is

[129] Ibid., p. 16.
[130] Ibid.
[131] Ibid., p. 17.
[132] Ibid.
[133] Ibid., p. 18.
[134] Even if one detached the notion of a necessary or essential connection from the Kantian analytic, the difficulty would remain: how can one apply a connection from the conceptual sphere, however interpreted, to the relation of the numinous and the moral.

how the relation of the non-conceptual to the conceptual can be presented even as analogous to the *concept* of a ground and source relation. Otto wants to deny any conceptual carry-over from the "image"; yet what he claims one knows in feeling seems to rely on such a transfer. If he does in fact rely on a substantive conceptual analogy, then he violates his own insistence that the numinous cannot be brought within our conceptual frame.[135] Moreover, whether he can even maintain his distinction between numinous and moral value and still claim a "ground and source" relation is in doubt, as I argued above.

8. We cannot, then, for Otto, conceptualize the relation of the numinous to morality but we can apprehend it as "value" and "know" in some sense that it stands to moral value as ground and source. Otto is attempting to avoid, on the one hand, the theological position which makes the nature of the divine congruent with the norms of human morality, and, on the other hand, the position which allows the nature of the divine to be essentially discontinuous with human norms. In *Freedom and Necessity* he argues that God's will is not arbitrary, for God wills according to his essence. This view is equivalent for him to the notion of moral value as the metaphysical and logical "reflection" of numinous value. Otto's claim is that God's essence is in part characterized by "completed" moral attributes, but that in another part it is not. The latter, however, is the ground and source of the former so that the unity of the holy is preserved.

Nonetheless, with Job, we can experience the "subordination" of all moral value to numinous value:

> The *mysterium*, simply as such, would merely . . . be part of the "absolute inconceivability" of the numen, and that, though it might strike Job utterly dumb, could not convict him inwardly. That of which we are conscious is rather an *intrinsic value* in the incomprehensible—a value inexpressible, positive,

135 My remarks here merely raise a basic issue for Otto's religious epistemology. For a recent study, see Ansgar Paus, *Religiöser Erkenntnisgrund: Herkunft und Wesen der Apriori Theorie Rudolf Ottos* (Leiden: E. J. Brill, 1966). Cf. John Morrison Moore, *Theories of Religious Experience with Special Reference to James, Otto, and Bergson* (New York: Round Table Press, 1938); Davidson, *Rudolf Otto's Interpretation of Religion;* and Malcolm Diamond, *Contemporary Philosophy and Religious Thought: An Introduction to Philosophy of Religion* (New York: McGraw-Hill, 1974), Chap. V.

and "fascinating." This is incommensurable with thoughts of rational human teleology and is not assimilated to them: it remains in all its mystery. But it is as it becomes felt in consciousness that Elohim is justified and at the same time Job's soul brought to peace.[136]

Otto does not explicitly discuss the possibility of a conflict between numinous and moral value in *Freedom and Necessity*. However, in light of his treatment of Job in IOH, it is licit to infer that the ground and source relation allows for such a conflict. Otto would have to go on to argue, it seems, that while men usually recognize the *moral* rightness of what God commands, a command could be given which would conflict with moral value but which should be obeyed out of respect for numinous value.[137]

William of Ockham believed that creation, including morality, was radically "contingent," that is, whether it existed and how it existed depended on the will of God. Yet for Ockham, as for Otto, at least according to some interpreters, God's will is not arbitrary, for it reflects his essence.[138] Ockham, however, may also have held—how he should be interpreted here is far from clear—that God could replace the Decalogue with its opposite.[139] Otto and Ockham would diverge then, not on the question whether God's will is arbitrary or not, but in their *theological* convictions about the essence of God.

[136] IOH, p. 80. In FN, p. 10, Otto speaks of a "displacement [*Hinordnung*]," "subordination [*sich Unterordnen*]," or "putting into the service [*in Dienst Treten*]" of all moral values in relation to the numinous. He does not explicitly here allow for a conflict but his terminology seems to permit an extension back to the example of Job in IOH.

[137] In a passage which appears in DH (1963) but not in DH (1922) Otto discusses stages or elements in the "Mysterium." As the "Wholly Other," the *mysterium* or *mirum* can transcend our categories ("above reason"), set itself in opposition to our categories ("against reason"), or elicit irreconcilable, antithetical affirmations about itself ("the antinomical"), pp. 35–36. Otto finds the last two elements not only in mysticism but also in Job and Luther. The "against reason" motif suggests the possibility of a conflict between numinous and moral value.

[138] See Helmar Junghans, *Ockham in Lichte der Neueren Forschung: Arbeiten zur Geschichte und Theologie des Luthertums*, Vol. XXI (Berlin und Hamburg: Lutherisches Verlagshaus, 1968), for a review of work on Ockham.

[139] Philotheus Boehner, O.F.M., argued that when Ockham claims that God can command anything which is not self-contradictory, he is engaged in a "mental experiment" in which we "set aside all other attributes of God and view only God's power in itself." William of Ockham, *Philosophical Writings* (New York: Bobbs-Merrill, 1964), xlix. Also see Boehner, *Collected Articles on Ockham* (St. Bonaventure, N.Y.: The Franciscan Institute, 1958), pp. 151–54.

In the end, for all he says about the numinous, Otto inclines more to the position which makes the divine congruent with human norms than to its opposite. Numinous value can conflict with human "teleology," but it is the ground and source of moral value. Moral value can be overridden but it could never be overturned.[140]

[140] Profs. William Christian, Malcolm Diamond, and Gene Outka kindly offered helpful criticisms of earlier drafts of this essay.

PART III

Modern Philosophical Discussions

IS MORALITY LOGICALLY DEPENDENT ON RELIGION?

William K. Frankena

I

One of the central issues in our cultural crisis, on any view, is that of the relation of morality to religion. That morality is dependent on religion is widely maintained by theologians arguing for the need of a return to religion, by moralists seeking to promote virtue, civic or personal, by educators advocating the teaching of religion in the public schools, and, of course, by many laymen and parents, not to mention politicians trying to impose an oath on teachers and other state employees, and political theorists trying to re-establish democracy and Western culture on their "true basis." And, indeed, if morality (and hence politics) is dependent on religion, then we must look to religion as a basis for any answer to any personal or social problem of any importance; but, if not, we may answer at least some of these problems on an "independent bottom," as people used to say; for example, on the basis of history, science, and practical experience. If morality is dependent on religion, then we cannot hope to solve our problems, or resolve our differences of opinion about them, unless and in so far as we can achieve agreement and certainty in religion (not a lively hope); but, if it is not entirely dependent on religion, then we can expect to solve at least some of them by the use of empirical and historical inquiries of a publicly available and testable kind (inquiries that are improving in quality and scope).

Nevertheless, although the thesis that morality is dependent on religion is of such crucial importance, and is so often asserted, as-

sumed, or clung to, it is rarely, if ever, very carefully formulated or
argued for by those who believe it.[1] The thesis itself is both vague
and ambiguous, and the arguments for it are often such as might
inspire a modern Celsus to complain again of the lack of intellectual
seriousness of the Christians. In this paper, therefore, I shall try
to make a contribution to contemporary philosophical thinking by
discussing with some care the claim that morality is dependent on
religion. But I cannot try to deal with this claim in all of its forms,
and so will concentrate on just one of them—the claim that morality
is *logically* dependent on religion—and on some of the arguments
that are or might be used to support it. My discussion will be almost
entirely critical and negative, but this is not due to any desire to disparage religion. It is due rather to a conviction that even religious
thinkers should think clearly and rigorously when they speak or
write about the relations of morality to religion.

Those who think that morality is dependent on religion need not
and do not always mean that it is logically dependent on religion.
They may mean only that it is *causally* or *historically* dependent on
religion, or that it is *motivationally* or *psychologically* dependent
on religion. However, they generally do not make clear in just what
sense they hold morality to be dependent on religion (or, for that
matter, just what they mean by morality, and how much of it or
what form of it is dependent on religion, or what they mean by religion); and they do often seem to say or at least suggest that morality is logically dependent on religion or theology. Thus, Reinhold
Niebuhr writes that the ethic of Jesus "proceeds logically from the
presuppositions of prophetic religion," and that "The justification
for these demands [of the ethic of Jesus] is put in purely religious
and not in socio-moral terms. We are to forgive because God forgives; we are to love our enemies because God is impartial in his

[1] There have been some good discussions of it by philosophers. See especially
Hywel D. Lewis, *Morals and the New Theology* (New York: Harper, 1947);
and *Morals and Revelation* (London: G. Allen, 1951); Arthur C. Garnett,
Religion and the Moral Life (New York: Ronald, 1955); and *Can Ideals and
Norms be Justified?* (Stockton, Calif.: College of the Pacific, 1955); W. G. Maclagan, *The Theological Frontier of Ethics* (London: G. Allen, 1961); Richard
B. Brandt, *Ethical Theory* (Englewood Cliffs, N.J.: Prentice-Hall, 1959),
chap. 4. Also papers by Kai Nielsen and others in *Christian Ethics and Contemporary Philosophy,* ed. Ian Ramsey (London: SCM Press, 1966).

love."[2] Hence he seems to be thinking that these demands depend on prophetic religion, not just causally or motivationally, but also logically. This is the question I wish to discuss, though not merely with respect to Niebuhr or to the ethics of Jesus.[3]

II

The claim that morality is logically dependent on religion is still not very clear, however. Let us distinguish between terms or concepts on the one hand and judgments or propositions on the other, and then let us distinguish two groups under each heading:

- A. Ethical terms or concepts like "good," "bad," "right," "wrong," "ought," "obligation," "virtue," etc.
- B. Religious or theological terms or concepts like "God," "immortal," "the Atonement," "the will of God," "divine forgiveness," etc.
- C. Ethical judgments like
  "We ought to love and worship God"
  "We ought to love our neighbor as ourselves"
  "The good is communion with God"
  "Suffering is evil"
  "It is wrong to kill"
  "It is right to keep promises"
  Etc.
- D. Religious or theological beliefs or propositions like
  "There is a God"
  "Jesus of Nazareth is the Son of God"
  "Jesus of Nazareth atoned for our sins"
  "God loves and forgives us"
  "Our souls are immortal"
  "God commands us not to kill"
  Etc.

Here some may interpose and say that the terms and judgments I

2 Reinhold Niebuhr, *An Interpretation of Christian Ethics* (New York and London: Harper, 1935), pp. 37, 46. See also Joseph Fletcher, *Situation Ethics* (Philadelphia: Westminster Press, 1966; London: SCM Press, 1966), p. 49; and Karl Barth, *Community, State and Church* (Garden City, N.Y.: Doubleday, 1960), p. 78.

3 I discuss it and other forms of the thesis that morality is dependent on religion, though rather briefly, in William K. Frankena, "Public Education and the Good Life," *Harvard Educational Review*, 31 (1961), pp. 413–26.

call "ethical" seem to them to be just as "religious" as the others. In a sense they are, for we do ordinarily conceive of a religion as including a moral code. If we speak in this way, then of course we must regard ethics as inseparable from religion, for it will be a part of religion. But it does not follow that we *must* conceive of ethics as a part of religion. Nor does it follow that the terms and judgments listed under A and C depend in any way on the terms and judgments listed under B and D. And these are the interesting questions for our purposes.

To continue, then, we may take the thesis that morality is logically dependent on religion as including one or more of the following four claims:

1. The terms and concepts of ethics (A) are to be defined by reference to (derived from or analyzed into) those of religion (B); i.e., the judgments of ethics can be translated into theological ones.
2. The judgments of ethics (C) can be logically inferred, deduced, or derived from those of theology (D).
3. Ethical judgments can be justified by being derived logically from theological ones.
4. Ethical judgments can be justified only by being logically inferred from theological ones, that is, they depend logically on religious beliefs for their justification.

Here (3) entails (2). Taken together, they say that religious or theological premises are *sufficient* to justify logically some or all ethical principles. On the other hand, (4) says that they are *necessary* for the justification of all ethical judgments. Again, if (1) is true, then (2) and (4) are true, and (3) will be true *if* theological propositions can themselves be justified. However, for our purposes, (2), (3), and (4) are the really interesting claims, and (1) is of interest only in so far as it is used to support (2), (3), or (4). It is hard to see how (2), (3), or (4) can be maintained without at least implying (1) or something like it, but some theologians, like Niebuhr, do seem to maintain them without explicitly asserting (1) and without thinking they presuppose (1). Hence we shall discuss (2), (3), and (4), and deal with (1), not for its own sake, but only as a support for (2), (3), or (4). In any case, of them all, (4) is the most crucial claim.

III

Let us now take up claim (2). It asserts that certain religious beliefs logically entail certain ethical beliefs, and that the latter can be logically inferred from the former. The view that ethics depends logically on religion does include making this claim. But it should be noted that, when a theologian says "C, because D" or "D, therefore C," where D is a theological proposition and C is an ethical one, he may not mean strictly to assert that C follows logically from D by itself. He may not be making his whole argument explicit. There are such things as enthymemes, and he may be presenting an enthymematic argument, as we often do. Thus, when he says, following I John 4:11, "God loves us, therefore we ought to love one another," what he may be thinking is this:

(a) God loves us.
(b) We ought to love those whom God loves.
(c) Therefore we ought to love one another.

But then he is thinking that (c) follows logically, not from (a) alone but from (a) together with (b). And (b), it should be observed, is an ethical premise, not a theological one; it is assumed in the argument, and may not itself rest on any theological premise. Now, it may be that when a theologian presents arguments of the form "(a), therefore (c)," in which he appears to reason from a theological premise to an ethical conclusion, he *always* means to be understood as giving an enthymematic argument in this fashion. However, if this is so, then he is always assuming some ethical premise or other, and he cannot claim that any ethical conclusion can be derived from theological premises alone. In short, since he presupposes certain ethical premises like (b), he is not really holding that ethics rests logically on religion. To hold this he must believe that his "(a), therefore (c)" is, sometimes at least, the whole story—that certain theological propositions by themselves logically entail certain ethical conclusions.

That this can be so has, however, often been categorically denied, even by some theologians. "No Ought from an Is," "No ethical conclusion from non-ethical premises"—from Hume on this has been a familiar dictum, its neglect being generally castigated nowadays as "the naturalistic fallacy." And, properly construed, it is a perfectly correct dictum. By the ordinary canons of logic a conclusion containing the term "ought" or "right" cannot be logically derived from premises which do not contain this term, except in such cases as "It is raining, therefore either it is raining or we ought to be kind to animals," which can hardly afford aid and comfort to theologians who make claim (2) or even to those who advocate kindness to animals. In this sense any theologian who offers us an argument of the form

(a) God loves us,
(c) Therefore we ought to love one another,

thinking that (c) follows logically from (a) alone without the help of any (b) which introduces the term "ought," is making a logical mistake. So far, then, it does look as if claim (2) cannot possibly be correct.[4]

It might be argued in reply that the canons just appealed to are those of deductive logic, and that in inductive reasoning one may, at least sometimes, affirm a conclusion containing a word, W, on the basis of premises which do not contain it, without violating any of the appropriate logical rules. This line of thought is worth exploring in connection with the "No Ought from an Is" dictum, since this dictum is usually pronounced with deductive reasoning in mind, but to explore it now would carry us too far afield. But whatever might come of it, it does not seem likely to give much solace to our theologians, since the inferences they are interested in making can hardly be classified as inductive ones.[5]

It has also been suggested that there is a "third logic," in addition to those of induction and deduction, whose canons warrant such inferences from factual premises to ethical conclusions as "I have promised to do X, therefore I ought to do X," or "Doing Y will injure someone, therefore it is wrong to do Y." But this suggestion has not been very convincingly worked out, and it is hard to see how

[4] With this paragraph cf. remarks by M. Black, "The Gap Between 'Is' and 'Should,'" *Philosophical Review*, LXXIII (1964), pp. 167 ff.; G. I. Mavrodes, "On Deriving the Normative from the Nonnormative," *Papers of the Michigan Academy of Science, Arts and Letters*, LIII (1968), pp. 353–65.

[5] Julius Kovesi has interesting things to say in this connection. See his *Moral Notions* (New York: Humanities Press, 1967; London: Routledge, 1967), chap. 1.

the canons of this third logic would differ from what are usually regarded as the moral principles that we ought to keep promises and not to injure anyone. In any case, the suggestion has not been taken up by theologians in support of claim (2), and, even if there is something in it, it is by no means clear that it will help them to justify the inferences they are concerned to make.[6]

There is another move that would be more likely to appeal to them. This is to question the sharpness of the distinction between factual judgments and ethical ones, and particularly the distinction between judgments of the sort listed under D above and those listed under C. Thus it might be contended that the so-called religious or theological beliefs included in D are not really so purely factual as we have been assuming, and that if we dig into them we in fact find that they themselves include an ethical commitment or "ought" in such a way that ethical conclusions *can* be *logically* inferred from them (without any special canons). There is a good bit to be said for this line of thought. Still, it seems to me that, if it is correct, then it simply turns out that the beliefs listed under D are complex, each consisting of an ethical belief conjoined with a non-ethical one (which could theoretically be expressed in value-neutral terms). And then the interesting question is whether any ethical conclusions follow logically from these more carefully stated non-ethical propositions alone. The answer to this question still may, and it looks as if it must, be negative. In any case, however, it is hard to see what is gained by saying that ethical beliefs rest on religious ones if these religious ones themselves turn out to be in some sense or in part ethical. Hence I do not see that this move does anything to support claim (2), except in a verbal way, even if it is otherwise well taken.[7]

[6] See Brandt, *Ethical Theory*, pp. 71–76.

[7] This move is made by Dorothy Emmet, *Facts and Obligations* (London: Dr. Williams Trust, 1958); and Patterson Brown, "Religious Morality," *Mind*, NS LXXII (1963), pp. 235–44. It is discussed by Kai Nielsen, D. Z. Phillips, and Ian Ramsey in Ramsey, ed., *Christian Ethics and Contemporary Philosophy*, pp. 134 ff., 157 ff., 143. See also R. M. Hare, "Descriptivism," reprinted in W. D. Hudson, ed., *The Is-Ought Question* (New York: St. Martins, 1969; London: Macmillan).

IV

So far, it appears that the "No Ought from an Is" dictum is substantially correct and that claim (2), if understood in any interesting sense, is mistaken. However, the theologians who assert claim (2) are not yet vanquished. It is not usual for them to offer explicit definitions of ethical terms like "good," "right," "ought," etc., but they sometimes do. At any rate, at the present point in the discussion, a theologian might contend that ethical conclusions can be logically inferred from religious or theological propositions (even if these are purely "factual" in some sense), because ethical terms can be defined by reference to religious or theological ones, i.e., because claim (1) is true. For example, he might say that "We ought to love one another" follows logically from "God commands us to love one another," because "ought" *means* "commanded by God." One might reply that he is then using the definitional statement " 'Ought' means 'commanded by God' " as a kind of premise of his argument; but he might rejoin that, while this is true, the additional premise is a definition and so is not an ethical statement proper but rather a logical or semantical one, and that therefore he is still deriving an ethical conclusion logically from premises that are not ethical. And yet, he might add, since my premises contain a definition of "ought," I am not sinning against the rule that the term "ought" cannot appear in the conclusion of an argument if it is not present in its premises.

The point is that one can go logically from Is to Ought, from "non-ethical" premises to "ethical" conclusions, as claim (2) requires, *if* "ought" and other ethical concepts can be satisfactorily defined in terms of theological or metaphysical ones. The question, then, is whether any such theological definitions are satisfactory. One cannot answer it, as is sometimes done, by arguing that such definitions cannot be satisfactory, since one cannot get an Ought out of an Is, for to argue thus is to beg the question. Now, theological definitions have been rebutted ever since Plato wrote the *Euthyphro* by a variety of arguments, the chief of which was expressed as follows by Richard Price in the eighteenth century:

> Right and wrong when applied to actions . . . do not signify merely that such actions are commanded or forbidden [by

God] . . . [If they did] it would be palpably absurd in any case to ask whether it is *right* to obey a command [of God], or *wrong* to disobey it, and the proposition, *obeying a command* [of God] *is right* . . . would be most trifling, as expressing no more than that obeying a command [of God] is obeying a command [of God]. . . .[8]

Such criticisms of theological definitions do not seem to me to be as immediately fatal as they are usually thought to be, but I cannot discuss them here. In fact, I shall not now examine the various theological definitions of "right" and other ethical terms that may be offered.[9] Whatever they are, if they are not merely arbitrary, they must be offered either as reportive elucidations of what we *do* mean by these terms or as recommendations about what we *should* mean by them. I am inclined to think that the criticisms just referred to do show that theological definitions will not do simply as reports of what we do mean. But, even if they did correctly report what we do mean, one could still ask if we should go on using them in this sense. *A fortiori*, if they are proposals about our future use of ethical terms, we may ask for reasons why we should adopt them. Either way, it seems to me that accepting the definition offered as a basis for our future speech, thought, and action is tantamount to accepting a moral principle. I do not mean that a definition is a moral principle. What I mean is that, when one accepts a definition of any term that can be called ethical, one has already in effect accepted an ethical standard. For example, when one agrees to take "right" to mean "commanded by God," and at the same time to use it as a key term in one's speech, thought, and action, this is tantamount to accepting the moral principle "We ought to do what God commands" as a guide in life.[10]

If this is so, then, when a theological definition is offered us, we may always ask why we should adopt this definition, and to answer

---

[8] Richard Price, *A Review of the Principal Questions in Morals,* ed. David Raphael (Oxford: Clarendon Press, 1948), p. 16; see also p. 41.

[9] For such an examination, see Brandt, *Ethical Theory,* pp. 71–76. L. Bergstrom has attacked the view that one can go logically from Ises to Oughts *if* ethical concepts are defined in terms of non-ethical ones, in "Meaning and Morals," in a volume on *Contemporary Philosophy in Scandinavia.* Even if he is right, his point will not rescue claim (2).

[10] My point may not hold for definitions of the kind that have been proposed by F. C. Sharp or R. Firth (see Brandt, *Ethical Theory,* pp. 173 ff.), but these are not theological definitions.

us the theologian in question must provide us with a justification of the corresponding moral principle. And the point is that he cannot claim that either it or the definition follows logically from any religious or theological belief (which is not itself a disguised ethical judgment). He may, of course, still offer such beliefs as part of the justification of his definition and principle but he cannot argue that they *suffice* to establish them *logically*. And if he asserts that they are *necessary* to establish them he is shifting to claim (4).

A persistent theologian may reply that his proposed definition is not tantamount to a normative principle in disguise—that it is not itself a moral judgment assigning the predicates "good," "right," or "ought" to a certain object or kind of object but rather a semantical rule for assigning them. This may be. But even then the definition needs justification, and one cannot claim to justify it by arguing that it follows *logically* from certain theological beliefs. What J. S. Mill calls "considerations capable of determining the intellect to give its assent" must be provided, but they must not be regarded as establishing the definition in a strict logical sense. However, as I have indicated, it seems to me that they will have to be the same considerations that would determine the intellect to give its assent to the corresponding moral principle, no more and no less—in other words that, in the case of an ethical term, a "definition" is an expression of an accepted or proposed moral principle.

If all this is so, then ethical judgments and principles cannot be said in any very important sense to follow logically from religious or theological beliefs. That they do is only really plausible if the inference is said to be warranted by a definition, but then we may ask about the status of the definition. Whether it is simply the expression of an assumed ethical principle or a semantical rule for the use of ethical terms, it can hardly be thought to be logically deducible from religious or theological premises. I conclude therefore that the theologian must give up or not make claim (2). If he wishes to maintain that an ethics does follow from his theology, he must hold that this is so, not in a strict logical sense, but in some other. About the possibility of such a view I shall say a little at the end of this paper.

V

So much for claim (2). Putting aside claim (3) for the moment, let us now take up claim (4), which alleges that religious or theological premises are *logically necessary* for the justification or vindication of ethical judgments and principles. It may take at least two forms: (a) the claim that certain religious or theological premises are logically required for the justification of a certain ethics, e.g., that of the Judeo-Christian tradition or that of Western democratic culture, and (b) the claim that some religious or theological premises or other are logically required for the justification of any and every ethical judgment or principle whatsoever. Of these two, the second is for our purposes the more important.

That theistic premises are logically necessary for the justification of certain ethical principles seems unquestionable. To justify the duty of keeping the sacraments some such argument as the following is necessary, if the justification is to be logically cogent:

(a) We ought to obey and worship God.
(b) He commands us to worship him by keeping the sacraments.
(c) Therefore, we ought to keep the sacraments.

Here (b) is a theological belief, and something of the kind is needed to yield the conclusion. Again, the justification of any duties toward God or toward Jesus does seem logically to require premises to the effect that there is a God, that Jesus is his Son, etc. This is hardly surprising—the justification of ethical principles that involve religious or theological terms seems bound to presuppose religious or theological premises. The important question is whether the justification of ethical principles that do not contain such terms, e.g., "We ought to love one another" or "It is wrong to kill," logically requires an appeal to such premises.

Here the theologian may bring in claim (1) again and reply that the justification of all such principles must involve an appeal to theistic premises of some kind since "ought," "wrong," etc., are to be defined in theistic terms. For example, he may say, the justification of "It is wrong to kill" logically depends on the premise "God commands us not to kill" because "X is wrong" *means* "X is forbidden by God." But, of course, if this is the line taken in defense

of claim (4), then again everything depends on the status and justifiability of the definitions offered. We may ask why we should accept them at this crucial point in our thinking, and again it seems
clear that the answer to this question does not *logically* require an
appeal to any religious or theological beliefs. If what was said before
is correct, then justifying a definition at this point is equivalent to
justifying the corresponding ethical standard, and one cannot claim
that this justification logically depends on certain theistic premises
without in effect begging the question. Even if the definition is just
a semantical rule and not an expression of an ethical principle, accepted or proposed, it still cannot be said logically to presuppose any
religious beliefs.

It appears, therefore, that if one wishes to maintain that the justification of any and every ethical principle depends on an appeal to
premises of a theistic kind, then one must hold that this is so, not in
a strict logical sense, but in some other.

VI

So far, however, we have been considering only definitions of ethical terms like "right" and "ought" as steps in making out the logical
dependence of ethics on religion. But for the theologian who has
been following recent developments in moral philosophy two rather
more sophisticated ways of defending claim (4) are open. (a) When
it is asked if the methods of inductive reasoning are justified, the
answer is sometimes given, "Of course they are! What we *mean* (in
certain kinds of cases) by saying that a conclusion is 'justified' is precisely that it is reached by the methods of inductive reasoning." A
theologian might, then, say in a similar vein that religious or theological beliefs are logically required for the justification of ethical
ones because what we mean by saying that a belief is "justified" is
that it is shown to be based on a set of religious or theological presuppositions about man and the universe. However, to say that this
is what we do mean by "justified" as applied to beliefs seems clearly
mistaken; we do not regard theistic premises as required for the
justification of scientific or historical beliefs, and I doubt we would
regard a belief as justified merely by the fact that it is based on theistic presuppositions unless we regarded these presuppositions as themselves justified by considerations other than their being theistic.

But, if it is replied that at any rate this is what we ought to mean by "justified," then we may ask for reasons—that is, for a justification of this proposal—and it is not obvious that such a justification could be given or that it would have to include an appeal to religious presuppositions. To assume that it would have to include such an appeal, moreover, would simply beg the question.

It would be more plausible to contend that we do or should regard a belief as justified if and only if we can show that it is logically entailed by some basic view of man and the universe, whether this is theistic or not.[11] To such a contention some of the remarks just made would also apply, but in any event it would not help to support claim (4) unless it is unfairly assumed that all ultimate views about the universe are *ipso facto* religious even when they are non-theistic —an assumption we shall deal with shortly.

(b) S. E. Toulmin has suggested that the justification of *moral* or *ethical* rules logically entails an appeal to considerations of the general welfare because what we mean by calling a rule "moral" or "ethical" is precisely that its justification rests on such an appeal.[12] Similarly our sophisticated theologian might hold that what makes it necessary (logically) to bring religious or theological considerations into the justification of actions or rules of action is not the meaning of "right," "ought," or even the meaning of "justified," but the meaning of "moral" itself—that we mean or should mean by a *moral* justification of an action or principle of action only one which relates it to a set of religious views about the world, perhaps by showing that it is commanded by God, perhaps in some other way. He would then be arguing that claim (4) is true because of the very meaning of "morality." Now, if he offers his definition of "moral" and "morality" as an elucidation of what we ordinarily mean, he is not only not imitating Toulmin, he is contradicting him. And I am inclined to think that many people do so closely associate morality and religion that he may be right as far as their usage is concerned. In the first paragraph of his preface to *The Scope and Nature of University Education,* for example, Cardinal Newman is clearly

[11] William Lillie seems to hold this, in *An Introduction to Ethics* (London: Methuen, 1961), p. 10. Cf. Sir Sarvepalli Radhakrishnan, *Eastern Religions and Western Thought,* 2d ed. (London: Oxford Univ. Press, 1940), p. 80.

[12] Stephen Toulmin, *An Examination of the Place of Reason in Ethics* (Cambridge: Cambridge Univ. Press, 1950), Pt. III. Here, too, one can find the notion of a "third logic" referred to earlier.

using "moral" and "religious" as synonyms. To this extent Toulmin
may be wrong. But the fact that Toulmin's view is as plausible as it
is shows that our theologian is probably also wrong; many people
certainly do not use the term "moral" as he holds they do. Atheists
and secularists do not so use it, and neither does Niebuhr when, in
the passage quoted earlier, he contrasts "socio-moral terms" with "religious" ones. Here Niebuhr is, in fact, speaking good Toulminese,
if not good English.[13]

If, on the other hand, our theologian offers his definition of
"moral" and "morality" as a recommendation about what we should
mean—and I see no reason why he should not—then again we may
ask him to provide reasons why our intellects should give their assent. Perhaps he can, but until he does, it must suffice to point out
that he cannot make use here of the claim that morality *is* logically
dependent on religion, and that he has in effect changed claim (4)
into a proposal that we *ought* so to conceive morality as to make it
dependent on religion, which is by no means obvious.

Thus the two moves envisaged here do not serve effectively to
rescue claim (4), and we may hold to the conclusion stated at the
end of the previous section.

VII

Before we take up claim (3), it will be well for us to consider a few
arguments and contentions put forward by writers who hold that
morality is dependent on religion and to see what they come to in
the present context. One is the familiar contention that a "natural"
ethics based on reason and experience cannot suffice, and that therefore a special divine revelation is necessary for an adequate morality.
This I have no wish to deny; the question is what it proves. It does
not prove that all moral principles depend on revelation, for it allows that some may be based on reason and experience. In fact, it
does not prove that revelation provides us with any basic *ethical*
principles not otherwise known to us. It may be that revelation only
provides new sources of motivation, a point not relevant to our problem. Or it may be that revelation also provides us with additional
theological insights about the universe and our place in it, which

[13] In connection with this paragraph see Brandt, *Ethical Theory*, pp. 71 f.,
355 ff.

enable us to infer new derivative duties from basic ones already known to us. For instance, if we learn from revelation that Jesus has atoned for our sins, we can then deduce the new obligation to show gratitude to him from the already known principle that we ought to be grateful to benefactors. But this fact would only show that these particular derivative ethical judgments depend on revealed theological premises for their justification, not that any of our basic ethical principles do. But suppose we allow that by revelation we learn new *basic* principles we could not know otherwise. It does not follow that these new ethical principles logically require any theological premises for their justification. Though revealed, they may still be logically independent of all non-ethical propositions, even theological ones. They may even be incapable of being justified at all.[14] Being known only by divine revelation does not entail being logically dependent on theology, paradoxical as this may seem. Even the dialectical theologians, so fond of paradoxes, have missed this point.

A second contention, insisted on by Catholic writers in particular, is put by Dietrich von Hildebrand in these words, "morality as such essentially presupposes God's existence."[15] His point is that nothing can exist if there is no God—no world, no human society, no morality, no moral truth. This again I have no wish to deny, though I do not believe it can be proved by rational argument, as St. Thomas and his followers do. But to say that something depends on God for its existence is not to say that it rests logically on any theological propositions. To put it poetically, "Only God can make a tree," but it does not follow that a tree is somehow rooted in theology. Its "hungry mouth" may still need to be pressed "against the earth's sweet-flowing breast." Similarly, even if morality objectively presupposes God's existence in the sense indicated, its basic principles may still be self-evident, or they may even depend logically on "the earth's sweet-flowing breast" of experience, as the conclusions of physics do. Von Hildebrand sees this, and even insists on it, when he immediately adds that his contention does not mean "that we must have a knowledge of God's existence . . . in order to grasp [moral values]

---

[14] E.g., they may be self-evident to God, though not to us, and so not dependent in his sight on any non-ethical premises, not even on theological ones.

[15] Dietrich von Hildebrand, *Christian Ethics* (New York: McKay, 1953), p. 455. See also p. 457.

together with their call and obligation." But this means that it does not entail claim (4), as one might be tempted to think.

Some writers who hold that ethics depends on theology appear to reason as follows. To say that we ought to live in a certain way is to say that it is required for the completion or fulfillment of our being or nature. But love of and communion with God and this alone will complete or fulfill our being or nature. Therefore God is our good and we ought to love him and do what will bring us into communion with him. Thus we arrive at an ethics, and hence our ethics depends on theology. Tillich and the two Niebuhrs, for example, seem to reason in this way, at least at times.[16] Tillich does so in arguing that ethics is, or should be, neither "autonomous" nor "heteronomous," but rather "theonomous." This sounds grand, but let us look closer. The ethical conclusion does seem to presuppose certain theological premises, e.g., that God exists and that we stand in certain relations to him. But the first and basic step in the argument is not a theological proposition in any proper sense. It is simply a basic definition or principle of obligation and it does not seem to depend on theology for its justification. Moreover, if it is taken as basic, it will yield an ethics even without the help of theological premises. For all that it says, biology, psychology, and sociology might suffice to tell us how to live in order to complete our natures or fulfill our beings, and, if this were so, nothing more would be needed to give us an ethics. A theonomous ethics follows only if theological premises are required for us to know how to realize the tendencies of our nature, but this is not obvious and must be shown. However, even if it is true, there is still the question whether or not the basic presupposition that we ought to do what will fulfill our natural tendencies is itself acceptable. As I say, *it* does not seem to depend logically on any religious or theological beliefs. What is more, it would be disputed by all those who refuse to take "nature" as a norm.

A fourth line of thought, which one hears over and over in recent discussions, and which has already been referred to, goes like this: Every ethical system or moral code depends on some set of ultimate beliefs about man, the meaning of the universe, and his place in it;

[16] Here, see Paul Tillich, *Love, Power and Justice* (New York: Oxford Univ. Press, 1960), pp. 76 ff.; Reinhold Niebuhr, *The Nature and Destiny of Man* (New York: Scribner, 1941), I, chap. X; H. Richard Niebuhr, "The Center of Value," in *Moral Principles of Action*, ed. Ruth Anshen (New York: Harper, 1952), pp. 162–75.

therefore every ethical code or system depends on a religion of some kind. Thus Reinhold Niebuhr writes,

> In any case both the foundation and the pinnacle of any cultural structure are religious; for any scheme of values is finally determined by the ultimate answer which is given to the ultimate question about the meaning of life.[17]

It is easy to be taken in by this kind of argument. The trouble with it is not so much in its assertion that every ethics rests on a set of ultimate metaphysical beliefs, though some would quarrel with this too, as in its use of the term "religion." It uses this term so widely that all ultimate views about the world, and not only theistic ones, are religions, even atheism and naturalism. One can do this, of course, and if one does, then claim (4) becomes true by virtue of the definition of "religion." But it does not follow—though the unwary reader of such an argument, and even its unwary author, may well draw this conclusion—that an ethics always must depend on a *theistic* view of the world. But this is the interesting question, the question we are concerned with here. The argument being discussed may win a victory but it is a hollow and verbal one.

There is a similar ploy—I do not know a better word for it—which one sometimes encounters. This consists in admitting or insisting that our basic ethical principles and value judgments are simply fundamental commitments or postulates which we make or adopt for the guidance of our lives, and then claiming that any such basic commitment or postulate is *ipso facto* an act of religious faith, concluding that therefore every ethics rests on religion.[18] Again, this ploy makes claim (4) verbally true by defining "religion" in a very wide sense—in such a wide sense that any basic ethical or value commitment is by definition an act of religious faith. Then, of course, every ethics rests on an act of "religious" faith, but this does not mean that ethics necessarily rests on a *theistic* faith. For in this wide sense even the ethics of an atheist or of a naturalist would be religious, as John Dewey makes clear in *A Common Faith*. It seems to me to be simply misleading to use the term "religion" in this way. In any event, however, the ploy in question does nothing to show that basic

[17] Reinhold Niebuhr, *The Children of Light and the Children of Darkness* (New York: Scribner, 1960), p. 125.
[18] See, e.g., John A. Hutchison, *The Two Cities* (Garden City, N.Y.: Doubleday, 1957).

ethical principles and value judgments depend logically on beliefs of a theological nature. For all it shows, they may rest on nothing at all. In fact, in taking them to be essentially postulates of faith, its employers seem to be regarding them as logically antonomous and as *not* logically deducible even from theology.[19]

The sixth and last contention I want to say something about here is very similar, only it depends on the meaning of "morality" as well as that of "religion." A. C. Garnett comes very close to stating it in his *Religion and the Moral Life,* otherwise a careful and sensible book.[20] It runs as follows: morality by its very nature involves an attitude of supreme devotion to some cause or object, a state of what Tillich calls "ultimate concern"; but this is precisely what is meant by "religion" or by "religious faith"; hence morality is necessarily religious. That morality calls for ultimate commitment in quite this way might be disputed; the theologians who contrast "mere morality" with religious ethos apparently would deny it. But let us grant this point; any moralist is bound to call for a very high devotion to his ideal. The criticisms just expressed in dealing with the fourth and fifth lines of thought apply here again. In any case, however, this sixth line would only show that morality requires an agent to be ultimately devoted to an ideal, it would not show that this ideal depends for its justification on any religious beliefs of a theistic sort.[21] It may be that no man can be or remain ultimately concerned unless he has such beliefs, or that he is hopelessly deluded if he is ultimately concerned without having such beliefs, but these are further points and do not bear on our question.

VIII

It has appeared that most, if not all, of the actual and possible methods of supporting claims (2) and (4), or, in other words, of showing that morality is logically dependent on religion, involve explicit or implicit definitions either of ethical terms like "right" or "ought," or of more epistemic terms like "justified," or of the terms

---

[19] Cf. Fletcher, *Situation Ethics,* pp. 47–49.

[20] Garnett, *Religion and the Moral Life,* pp. 5 ff.

[21] Garnett sees this, and does not believe ethics is logically dependent on theistic beliefs. See ibid., pp. 13 ff. For him the dependence of morality on theism is psychological, not logical.

"morality" and "religion" themselves. It has also appeared, I think, that all of them fall short on one count or another. I conclude that neither claim (2) nor claim (4) has been or can be established. This brings us at long last to claim (3), which says that ethical judgments can be justified by being derived logically from theological ones, and which can now be dealt with rather briefly. In part, claim (3) simply repeats claim (2), viz., that ethical judgments are logically deducible from religious ones, and so has already been covered. But claim (3) also says that ethical judgments would in fact be justified if they were shown to be based on certain theological beliefs. Now, this part of claim (3) could be held to be true by virtue of the meaning of "justified," but we have already seen that this view is not plausible. In fact, I believe, we would not and should not think that our ethical beliefs were justified by being shown to rest on and follow from certain religious or theological beliefs unless we thought that these were themselves in some way rationally justifiable. Hence claim (3) can only be true, it seems to me, if religious beliefs of a theistic kind can be justified.

I have no wish to deny that the essential beliefs of theism are in some sense justifiable, though I doubt that they can be proved by argument in any rationally conclusive way. But this raises a large and age-old issue that cannot be discussed here. It does seem to me, however, that the outcome of this debate is by no means clear and that, to this extent, the truth of claim (3) is uncertain. In fact, the conviction that this is so is part of what motivates me in writing this paper. However deep and sincere one's own religious beliefs may be, if one reviews the religious scene, contemporary and historical, one cannot help but wonder if there is any rational and objective method of establishing any religious belief against the proponents of other religions or of irreligion. But then one is impelled to wonder also if there is anything to be gained by insisting that all ethical principles are or must be logically grounded on religious beliefs. For to insist on this is to introduce into the foundations of any morality whatsoever all of the difficulties involved in the adjudication of religious controversies, and to do so is hardly to encourage hope that mankind can reach, by peaceful and rational means, some desirable kind of agreement on moral and political principles. It also encourages ethical and political skepticism in those who do not or cannot accept the required religious beliefs. That is why it strikes me as important to reject the view that all morality is logically dependent on religion and to leave open the possibility that at least some important ethical judgments can be justified independently of religion and theology—a possibility which, fortunately, many theologians already accept. Of course, one cannot simply reject the view that morality is dependent on religion for this reason; if it rests on good grounds, we must still espouse it. But, as we have seen, it does not rest on good grounds.

Motives for rejecting a view may be countered by motives for accepting it. No doubt one motive for arguing that morality is dependent on religion is a desire to establish the importance of religious faith. One must, however, be careful here. For one can hardly at the same time contend that morality has no sound basis unless it rests on religion and admit that there is no good argument for religion except that it is necessary as a basis for morality. This is neither good logic nor good religion. If one is honestly to hold that morality can be established if and only if it is grounded in religion, then one must also believe that religion has adequate grounds of its own to stand on.

IX

Thus none of the claims involved in the thesis that morality is logically dependent on religion can be regarded as established, and the thesis itself, in particular claim (4), which is its really crucial part, is only doubtfully salutary either to morality or to religion. In thus attacking *that* thesis, however, I have said nothing about other claims that have been made about the relation of morality to religion. I have not contended that morality is in no way dependent on religion for dynamics, motivation, inspiration, or vision. Nor have I contended that religion adds nothing to morality—it may add motivation, an additional obligation to do what is right, new duties, a new spirit in which to do them, a new dimension to already existing duties, or a sense of sin. All this may be true for anything that has been said here. But none of it entails the thesis that morality is *logically* dependent on religion of a theistic kind, and I am here concerned only to dispute *this*. I am not even arguing that "natural law," "natural morality," and "moral philosophy" are sufficient, certainly not that they are omnicompetent. For all that I have said, it may still be that no adequate ethics can be developed without the help of religious beliefs as premises in addition to certain basic ethical ones, and, if this is so, ethics does still rest on religion in a sense—not for its basic principles but for the development of its working rules and conclusions, or at least some of them. This too I have not been concerned to deny (or to affirm).

I cannot end, however, without pointing out a direction for further inquiry. To what has been said the following reply is apt to be made. "If or in so far as morality does not depend on religion for its justification, how is it to be justified? Must we not choose between saying that ethical principles rest on religion and saying that they have no justification whatever?" This may be the real conviction behind the thesis we have been discussing. But from our conclusion that ethical principles are not all logically dependent on theology, it does not follow that they cannot be justified in any objective and rational sense. Some of them may still be provable on non-theological grounds, or they may be self-evident and hence self-justifying. Many theologians have, in fact, admitted one or another of these alternatives. I doubt both that basic ethical judgments are self-evident and that they can be proved logically by derivation from other propositions, whether these are religious ones or not. But, even if this is so, it does not follow that they cannot be justified in any objective and rational way. It seems to me that Mill was right when, having said that a basic ethical principle is neither intuited nor amenable to strict proof, he added (in a passage already borrowed from):

> We are not, however, to infer that its acceptance or rejection must depend on blind impulse, or arbitrary choice. There is a larger meaning of the word "proof" [I would rather say "justification"], in which this question is as amenable to it as any other of the disputed questions of philosophy. The subject is within the cognizance of the rational faculty. . . . Considerations may be presented capable of determining the intellect either to give or withhold its assent. . . .[22]

I think that it is in this "larger meaning" of justification that Mill thought he could justify the doctrine that pleasure is the good by showing that pleasure is the ultimate object of all desire. At any rate,

[22] John Stuart Mill, *Utilitarianism*, from *Mill's Ethical Writings*, ed. J. B. Schneewind (New York: Collier, 1965), p. 279.

suppose that it could be conclusively shown that pleasure is the basic object of desire. This would not prove logically that pleasure alone is desirable or good, but would it not be in some sense "reasonable" to draw this conclusion and "absurd" to offer something other than pleasure as the *summum bonum?*[23] If so, then there is after all a sense, though not a strictly logical one, in which factual considerations may serve to justify ethical conclusions. Moreover, if this example is at all a fair one, it also shows that theological premises are not necessarily required in justifications of this sort.

Of course, it may be replied that religious considerations are among those capable of thus determining the intellect to give its assent to a certain ethical principle. In fact, I am inclined to think that they are. Suppose again that one has a sincere belief in or convincing experience of God as love and vividly realizes what this means, as Bergson's mystics do. Must he not take the "law of love" as his guiding principle in life, and regard it as entirely reasonable that he should do so? It seems to me plausible to claim that religious beliefs and experiences do *suffice* to justify this, and perhaps other, ethical principles in this wider sense of the word "justify," at least for those who have them.[24] It does not follow, however, that they are *necessary* to justify those ethical principles even in this larger sense, for it may be that certain non-religious considerations are also capable of determining the intellect to give them its assent. *A fortiori*, it does not follow that religious considerations are necessary to determine it to give its assent to *any* ethical principle *whatsoever*.

There are also other lines along which philosophers, including analytical philosophers, have sought or are seeking to develop the possibility suggested by Mills' sentences. I mention the one just described because it involves a kind of justification theologians are bound to take seriously. In any case, however, until they show that no objective and rational kind of justification of ethical judgments can be given if we reject the claim that morality is logically dependent on religion, we may relinquish this claim without fear. If they admit that such a larger kind of objective and rational justification of ethics is possible, but insist that it requires religious premises, though not in a logical sense of "requires," they may be right for all

23 Cf. Aristotle, *Nicomachean Ethics*, bk. X, chap. 2: "Those who object that that at which all things aim is not necessarily good are talking nonsense."
24 See Lillie, *An Introduction to Ethics*, p. 328.

that I have shown here.[25] Indeed, I believe that this is the line to be taken by theologians who wish to hold that religion is required to justify the principles of morality (and not merely to motivate people to act according to them). I myself think that even this weaker claim about the dependence of morality on religion is at best true only if it is carefully qualified. But that is another story.

[25] My point about Mill does, however, throw doubt on such a view.

A MODIFIED DIVINE COMMAND
THEORY OF ETHICAL WRONGNESS

Robert Merrihew Adams

I

It is widely held that all those theories are indefensible which attempt to explain in terms of the will or commands of God what it is for an act to be ethically right or wrong. In this paper I shall state such a theory, which I believe to be defensible; and I shall try to defend it against what seem to me to be the most important and interesting objections to it. I call my theory a *modified* divine command theory because in it I renounce certain claims that are commonly made in divine command analyses of ethical terms. (I should add that it is *my* theory only in that I shall state it, and that I believe it is defensible—not that I am sure it is correct.) I present it as a theory of ethical *wrongness* partly for convenience. It could also be presented as a theory of the nature of ethical obligatoriness or of ethical permittedness. Indeed, I will have occasion to make some remarks about the concept of ethical permittedness. But as we shall see (in Section IV) I am not prepared to claim that the theory can be extended to all ethical terms; and it is therefore important that it not be presented as a theory about ethical terms in general.

It will be helpful to begin with the statement of a simple, *un*-modified divine command theory of ethical wrongness. This is the theory that ethical wrongness *consists in* being contrary to God's commands, or that the word "wrong" in ethical contexts *means* "contrary to God's commands." It implies that the following two statement forms are logically equivalent.

(1) It is wrong (for A) to do X.
(2) It is contrary to God's commands (for A) to do X.

Of course that is not all that the theory implies. It also implies that (2) is conceptually prior to (1), so that the meaning of (1) is to be explained in terms of (2), and not the other way round. It might prove fairly difficult to state or explain in what that conceptual priority consists, but I shall not go into that here. I do not wish ultimately to defend the theory in its unmodified form, and I think I have stated it fully enough for my present purposes.

I have stated it as a theory about the meaning of the word "wrong" in ethical contexts. The most obvious objection to the theory is that the word "wrong" is used in ethical contexts by many people who cannot mean by it what the theory says they must mean, since they do not believe that there exists a God. This objection seems to me sufficient to refute the theory if it is presented as an analysis of what *everybody* means by "wrong" in ethical contexts. The theory cannot reasonably be offered except as a theory about what the word "wrong" means as used by *some but not all* people in ethical contexts. Let us say that the theory offers an analysis of the meaning of "wrong" in Judeo-Christian religious ethical discourse. This restriction of scope will apply to my modified divine command theory too. This restriction obviously gives rise to a possible objection. Isn't it more plausible to suppose that Judeo-Christian believers use "wrong" with the same meaning as other people do? This problem will be discussed in Section VI.

In Section II, I will discuss what seems to me the most important objection to the unmodified divine command theory, and suggest how the theory can be modified to meet it. Section III will be devoted to a brief but fairly comprehensive account of the use of "wrong" in Judeo-Christian ethical discourse, from the point of view of the modified divine command theory. The theory will be further elaborated in dealing with objections in Sections IV to VI. In a seventh and final section, I will note some problems arising from unresolved issues in the general theory of analysis and meaning, and briefly discuss their bearing on the modified divine command theory.

II

The following seems to me to be the gravest objection to the divine command theory of ethical wrongness, in the form in which I have stated it. Suppose God should command me to make it my chief end in life to inflict suffering on other human beings, for no other reason than that He commanded it. (For convenience I shall abbreviate this hypothesis to "Suppose God should command cruelty for its own sake.") Will it seriously be claimed that in that case it would be wrong for me not to practice cruelty for its own sake? I see three possible answers to this question.

(1) It might be claimed that it is logically impossible for God to command cruelty for its own sake. In that case, of course, we need not worry about whether it would be wrong to disobey if He did command it. It is senseless to agonize about what one should do in a logically impossible situation. This solution to the problem seems unlikely to be available to the divine command theorist, however. For why would he hold that it is logically impossible for God to command cruelty for its own sake? Some theologians (for instance, Thomas Aquinas) have believed (a) that what is right and wrong is independent of God's will, *and* (b) that God always does right by the necessity of His nature. Such theologians, if they believe that it would be wrong for God to command cruelty for its own sake, have reason to believe that it is logically impossible for Him to do so. But the divine command theorist, who does not agree that what is right and wrong is independent of God's will, does not seem to have such a reason to deny that it is logically possible for God to command cruelty for its own sake.

(2) Let us assume that it is logically possible for God to command cruelty for its own sake. In that case the divine command theory seems to imply that it would be wrong not to practice cruelty for its own sake. There have been at least a few adherents of divine command ethics who have been prepared to accept this consequence. William Ockham held that those acts which we call "theft," "adultery," and "hatred of God" would be meritorious if God had commanded them.[1] He would surely have said the same about what I

---

[1] Guillelmus de Occam, *Super 4 libros sententiarum*, bk. II, qu. 19, O, in Vol. IV of his *Opera plurima* (Lyon, 1494–96; réimpression en fac-similé,

have been calling the practice of "cruelty for its own sake."

This position is one which I suspect most of us are likely to find somewhat shocking, even repulsive. We should therefore be particularly careful not to misunderstand it. We need not imagine that Ockham disciplined himself to be ready to practice cruelty for its own sake if God should command it. It was doubtless an article of faith for him that God is unalterably opposed to any such practice. The mere logical possibility that theft, adultery, and cruelty might have been commanded by God (and therefore meritorious) doubtless did not represent in Ockham's view any real possibility.

(3) Nonetheless, the view that if God commanded cruelty for its own sake it would be wrong not to practice it seems unacceptable to me; and I think many, perhaps most, other Jewish and Christian believers would find it unacceptable too. I must make clear the sense in which I find it unsatisfactory. It is not that I find an internal inconsistency in it. And I would not deny that it may reflect, accurately enough, the way in which some believers use the word "wrong." I might as well frankly avow that I am looking for a divine command theory which at least might possibly be a correct account of how *I* use the word "wrong." I do not use the word "wrong" in such a way that I would say that it would be wrong not to practice cruelty if God commanded it, and I am sure that many other believers agree with me on this point.

But now have I not rejected the divine command theory? I have assumed that it would be logically possible for God to command cruelty for its own sake. And I have rejected the view that if God commanded cruelty for its own sake, it would be wrong not to obey. It seems to follow that I am committed to the view that in certain logically possible circumstances it would not be wrong to disobey God. This position seems to be inconsistent with the theory that "wrong" means "contrary to God's commands."

I want to argue, however, that it is still open to me to accept a modified form of the divine command theory of ethical wrongness. According to the modified divine command theory, when I say, "It is wrong to do X," (at least part of) what I *mean* is that it is contrary to God's commands to do X. "It is wrong to do X" *implies* "It

---

Farnborough, Hants., England: Gregg Press, 1962). I am not claiming that Ockham held a divine command theory of exactly the same sort that I have been discussing.

is contrary to God's commands to do X." But "It is contrary to God's commands to do X" implies "It is wrong to do X" only if certain conditions are assumed—namely, only if it is assumed that God has the character which I believe Him to have, of loving His human creatures. If God were really to command us to make cruelty our goal, then He would not have that character of loving us, and I would not say it would be wrong to disobey Him.

But do I say that it would be wrong to obey Him in such a case? This is the point at which I am in danger of abandoning the divine command theory completely. I do abandon it completely if I say both of the following things.

(A) It would be wrong to obey God if He commanded cruelty for its own sake.

(B) In (A), "wrong" is used in what is for me its normal ethical sense.

If I assert both (A) and (B), it is clear that I cannot consistently maintain that "wrong" in its normal ethical sense for me means or implies "contrary to God's commands."

But from the fact that I deny that it would be wrong to disobey God if He commanded cruelty for its own sake, it does not follow that I must accept (A) and (B). Of course someone might claim that obedience and disobedience would both be ethically permitted in such a case; but that is not the view that I am suggesting. If I adopt the modified divine command theory as an analysis of my present concept of ethical wrongness (and if I adopt a similar analysis of my concept of ethical permittedness), I will not hold either that it would be wrong to disobey, or that it would be ethically permitted to disobey, or that it would be wrong to obey, or that it would be ethically permitted to obey, if God commanded cruelty for its own sake. For I will say that my concept of ethical wrongness (and my concept of ethical permittedness) would "break down" if I really believed that God commanded cruelty for its own sake. Or to put the matter somewhat more prosaically, I will say that my concepts of ethical wrongness and permittedness could not serve the functions they now serve, because using those concepts I could not call any action ethically wrong or ethically permitted, if I believed that God's will was so unloving. This position can be explained or developed in either of two ways, each of which has its advantages.

I could say that by "X is ethically wrong" I mean "X is contrary to the commands of a *loving* God" (i.e., "There is a *loving* God and X is contrary to His commands") and by "X is ethically permitted" I mean "X is in accord with the commands of a *loving* God" (i.e., "There is a *loving* God and X is not contrary to His commands"). On this analysis we can reason as follows. If there is only one God and He commands cruelty for its own sake, then presumably there is not a *loving* God. If there is not a loving God then neither "X is ethically wrong" nor "X is ethically permitted" is true of any X. Using my present concepts of ethical wrongness and permittedness, therefore, I could not (consistently) call any action ethically wrong or permitted if I believed that God commanded cruelty for its own sake. This way of developing the modified divine command theory is the simpler and neater of the two, and that might reasonably lead one to choose it for the construction of a theological ethical theory. On the other hand, I think it is also simpler and neater than ordinary religious ethical discourse, in which (for example) it may be felt that the statement that a certain act is wrong is *about* the will or commands of God in a way in which it is not about His love.

In this essay I shall prefer a second, rather similar, but somewhat untidier, understanding of the modified divine command theory, because I think it may lead us into some insights about the complexities of actual religious ethical discourse. According to this second version of the theory, the statement that something is ethically wrong (or permitted) says something about the will or commands of God, but not about His love. Every such statement, however, *presupposes* that certain conditions for the applicability of the believer's concepts of ethical right and wrong are satisfied. Among these conditions is that God does not command cruelty for its own sake—or, more generally, that God loves His human creatures. It need not be assumed that God's love is the only such condition.

The modified divine command theorist can say that the possibility of God commanding cruelty for its own sake is not provided for in the Judeo-Christian religious ethical system as he understands it. The possibility is not provided for, in the sense that the concepts of right and wrong have not been developed in such a way that actions could be correctly said to be right or wrong if God were believed to command cruelty for its own sake. The modified divine command theorist agrees that it is logically possible[2] that God should command cruelty for its own sake; but he holds that it is unthinkable that God should do so. To have *faith* in God is not just to believe that He exists, but also to trust in His love for mankind. The believer's concepts of ethical wrongness and permittedness are developed within the framework of his (or the religious community's) religious life, and therefore within the framework of the assumption that God loves us. The concept of the will or commands of God has a certain function in the believer's life, and the use of the words "right" (in the sense of "ethically permitted") and "wrong" is tied to that function of that concept. But one of the reasons why the concept of the will of God can function as it does is that the love which God is believed to have toward men arouses in the believer certain attitudes of love toward God and devotion to His will. If the believer thinks about the unthinkable but logically possible situation in which God commands cruelty for its own sake, he finds that in relation to that kind of command of God he cannot take up the same attitude, and that the concept of the will or commands of God could not then have the same function in his life. For this reason he will not say that it would be wrong to disobey God, or right to obey Him, in that situation. At the same time he will not say that it would be wrong to obey God in that situation, because he is accustomed to use the word "wrong" to say that something is contrary to the will of God, and it does not seem to him to be the right word to use to express his own personal revulsion toward an act against which there would be no divine authority. Similarly, he will not say that it would be "right," in the sense of "ethically permitted," to disobey God's command of cruelty; for that does not seem to him to be the right way to express his own personal attitude toward an act which would not be in accord with a divine authority. In this way the believer's concepts of ethical rightness and wrongness would break down in the situation in which he believed that God commanded cruelty for its own sake—that is, they would not function as they now do, because he would not be prepared to use them to say that any action was right or wrong.

[2] Perhaps he will even think it is causally possible, but I do not regard any view on that issue as an integral part of the theory. The question whether it is causally possible for God to act "out of character" is a difficult one which we need not go into here.

III

It is clear that according to this modified divine command theory, the meaning of the word "wrong" in Judeo-Christian ethical discourse must be understood in terms of a complex of relations which believers' use of the word has, not only to their beliefs about God's commands, but also to their attitudes toward certain types of action. I think it will help us to understand the theory better if we can give a brief but fairly comprehensive description of the most important features of the Judeo-Christian ethical use of "wrong," from the point of view of the modified divine command theory. That is what I shall try to do in this section.

(1) "Wrong" and "contrary to God's commands" at least contextually imply each other in Judeo-Christian ethical discourse. "It is wrong to do X" will be assented to by the sincere Jewish or Christian believer if and only if he assents to "It is contrary to God's commands to do X." This is a fact sufficiently well known that the known believer who says the one commits himself publicly to the other.

Indeed "wrong" and such expressions as "against the will of God" seem to be used interchangeably in religious ethical discourse. If a believer asks his pastor, "Do you think it's always against the will of God to use contraceptives?" and the pastor replies, "I don't see anything wrong with the use of contraceptives in many cases," the pastor has answered the same question the inquirer asked.

(2) In ethical contexts, the statement that a certain action is wrong normally expresses certain volitional and emotional attitudes toward that action. In particular it normally expresses an intention, or at least an inclination, not to perform the action, and/or dispositions to feel guilty if one has performed it, to discourage others from performing it, and to react with anger, sorrow, or diminished respect toward others if they have performed it. I think this is true of Judeo-Christian ethical discourse as well as of other ethical discourse.

The interchangeability of "wrong" and "against the will of God" applies in full force here. It seems to make no difference to the expressive function of an ethical statement in a Judeo-Christian context which of these expressions is used. So far as I can see, the feelings and dispositions normally expressed by "It is wrong to commit suicide" in a Judeo-Christian context are exactly the same as those normally expressed by "It is against God's will to commit suicide," or by "Suicide is a violation of the commandments of God."

I am speaking of attitudes *normally* expressed by statements that it is wrong to do a certain thing, or that it would be against God's will or commands to do that thing. I am not claiming that such attitudes are *always* expressed by statements of those sorts. Neither am I now suggesting any analysis of the *meaning* of the statements in terms of the attitudes they normally express. The relation between the meaning of the statements and the attitudes expressed is a matter about which I shall have somewhat more to say, later in this section and in Section VI. At this point I am simply observing that in fact statements of the forms "It is wrong to do X," "It is against God's will to do X," "X is a violation of the commandments of God," normally do express certain attitudes, and that in Judeo-Christian ethical discourse they all typically express the same attitudes.

Of course these attitudes can be specified only within certain very wide limits of normality. The experience of guilt, for instance, or the feelings that one has about conduct of others of which one disapproves, vary greatly from one individual to another, and in the same individual from one occasion to another.

(3) In a Judeo-Christian context, moreover, the attitudes expressed by a statement that something is wrong are normally quite strongly affected and colored by specifically religious feelings and interests. They are apt to be motivated in various degrees by, and mixed in various proportions with, love, devotion, and loyalty toward God, and/or fear of God. Ethical wrongdoing is seen and experienced as *sin*, as rupture of personal or communal relationship with God. The normal feelings and experience of guilt for Judeo-Christian believers surely cannot be separated from beliefs, and ritual and devotional practices, having to do with God's judgment and forgiveness.

In all sin there is offense against a person (God), even when there is no offense against any other human person—for instance, if I have a vice which harms me but does not importantly harm any other human being. Therefore in the Judeo-Christian tradition reactions which are appropriate when one has offended another person are felt to be appropriate reactions to any ethical fault, regardless of whether another human being has been offended. I think this affects rather importantly the emotional connections of the word "wrong" in Judeo-Christian discourse.

(4) When a Judeo-Christian believer is trying to decide, in an ethical way, whether it would be wrong for him to do a certain thing, he typically thinks of himself as trying to determine whether it would be against God's will for him to do it. His deliberations may turn on the interpretation of certain religiously authoritative texts. They may be partly carried out in the form of prayer. It is quite possible, however, that his deliberations will take forms more familiar to the nonbeliever. Possibly his theology will encourage him to give some weight to his own intuitions and feelings about the matter, and those of other people. Such encouragement might be provided, for instance, by a doctrine of the leading of the Holy Spirit. Probably the believer will accept certain very general ethical principles as expressing commandments of God, and most of these may be principles which many nonbelievers would also accept (for instance, that it is always, or with very few exceptions, wrong to kill another human being). The believer's deliberation might consist entirely of reasoning from such general principles. But he would still regard it as an attempt to discover God's will on the matter.

(5) Typically, the Judeo-Christian believer is a nonnaturalist objectivist about ethical wrongness. When he says that something is (ethically) wrong, he means to be stating what he believes to be a fact of a certain sort—what I shall call a "nonnatural objective fact." Such a fact is objective in the sense that whether it obtains or not does not depend on whether any human being thinks it does. It is harder to give a satisfactory explanation of what I mean by "nonnatural" here. Let us say that a nonnatural fact is one which does not consist simply in any fact or complex of facts which can be stated entirely in the languages of physics, chemistry, biology, and human psychology. That way of putting it obviously raises questions which it leaves unanswered, but I hope it may be clear enough for present purposes.

That ethical facts are objective and nonnatural has been believed by many people, including some famous philosophers—for instance, Plato and G. E. Moore. The term "nonnaturalism" is sometimes used rather narrowly, to refer to a position held by Moore, and positions closely resembling it. Clearly, I am using "nonnaturalist" in a broader sense here.

Given that the facts of wrongness asserted in Judeo-Christian ethics are nonnatural in the sense explained above, and that they accordingly do not consist entirely in facts of physics, chemistry, biology, and human psychology, the question arises, in what they do consist. According to the divine command theory (even the modified divine command theory), in so far as they are nonnatural and objective, they consist in facts about the will or commands of God. I think this is really the central point in a divine command theory of ethical wrongness. This is the point at which the divine command theory is distinguished from alternative theological theories of ethical wrongness, such as the theory that facts of ethical rightness and wrongness are objective, nonnatural facts about ideas or essences subsisting eternally in God's understanding, not subject to His will but guiding it.

The divine command account of the nonnatural fact-stating function of Judeo-Christian ethical discourse has at least one advantage over its competitors. It is clear, I think, that in stating that X is wrong a believer normally commits himself to the view that X is contrary to the will or commands of God. And the fact (if it is a fact) that X is contrary to the will or commands of God is surely a nonnatural objective fact. But it is not nearly so clear that in saying that X is wrong, the believer normally commits himself to belief in any *other* nonnatural objective fact. (The preceding sentence presupposes the rejection of the Moorean view that the fact that X is wrong[3] is an objective nonnatural fact which cannot and should not be analyzed in terms of other facts, natural or nonnatural.)

(6) The modified divine command theorist cannot consistently claim that "wrong" and "contrary to God's commands" have exactly the same meaning for him. For he admits that there is a logically possible situation which he would describe by saying, "God commands cruelty for its own sake," but not by saying, "It would be wrong not to practice cruelty for its own sake." If there were not at least some little difference between the meanings with which he actually, normally uses the expressions "wrong" and "contrary to God's commands," there would be no reason for them to differ in

---

[3] Moore took goodness and badness as primitive, rather than rightness and wrongness; but that need not concern us here.

their applicability or inapplicability to the far-out unthinkable case. We may now be in a position to improve somewhat our understanding of what the modified divine command theorist can suppose that difference in meaning to be, and of why he supposes that the believer is unwilling to say that disobedience to a divine command of cruelty for its own sake would be wrong.

We have seen that the expressions "It is wrong" and "It is contrary to God's commands" or "It is against the will of God" have virtually the same uses in religious ethical discourse, and the same functions in the religious ethical life. No doubt they differ slightly in the situations in which they are most likely to be used and the emotional overtones they are most apt to carry. But in all situations experienced or expected by the believer as a believer they at least contextually imply each other, and normally express the same or extremely similar emotional and volitional attitudes.

There is also a difference in meaning, however, a difference which is normally of no practical importance. All three of the following are aspects of the normal use of "it is wrong" in the life and conversation of believers. (a) It is used to state what are believed to be facts about the will or commands of God. (b) It is used in formulating decisions and arguments about what to do (i.e., not just in deciding what one *ought* to do, but in deciding *what to do*). (c) It expresses certain emotional and volitional attitudes toward the action under discussion. "It is wrong" is commonly used to do all three of those things at once.

The same is true of "It is contrary to God's commands" and "It is against the will of God." They are commonly used by believers to do the same three things, and to do them at once. But because of their grammatical form and their formal relationships with other straightforwardly descriptive expressions about God, they are taken to be, first and last, descriptive expressions about God and His relation to whatever actions are under discussion. They can therefore be used to state what are supposed to be facts about God, even when one's emotional and decision-making attitude toward those supposed facts is quite contrary to the attitudes normally expressed by the words "against the will of God."

In the case of "It is wrong," however, it is not clear that one of its functions, or one of the aspects of its normal use, is to be preferred in case of conflict with the others. I am not willing to say, "It would be wrong not to do X," when both my own attitude and the attitude of most other people toward the doing of X under the indicated circumstances is one of unqualified revulsion. On the other hand, neither am I willing to say, "It would be wrong to do X," when I would merely be expressing my own personal revulsion (and perhaps that of other people as well) but nothing that I could regard as clothed in the majesty of a divine authority. The believer's concept of ethical wrongness therefore breaks down if one tries to apply it to the unthinkable case in which God commands cruelty for its own sake.

None of this seems to me inconsistent with the claim that part of what the believer normally means in saying "X is wrong" is that X is contrary to God's will or commands.

IV

The modified divine command theory clearly conceives of believers as valuing some things independently of their relation to God's commands. If the believer will not say that it would be wrong not to practice cruelty for its own sake if God commanded it, that is because he values kindness, and has a revulsion for cruelty, in a way that is at least to some extent independent of his belief that God commands kindness and forbids cruelty. This point may be made the basis of both philosophical and theological objections to the modified divine command theory, but I think the objections can be answered.

The philosophical objection is, roughly, that if there are some things I value independently of their relation to God's commands, then my value concepts cannot rightly be analyzed in terms of God's commands. According to the modified divine command theory, the acceptability of divine command ethics depends in part on the believer's independent positive valuation of the sorts of things that God is believed to command. But then, the philosophical critic objects, the believer must have a prior, nontheological conception of ethical right and wrong, in terms of which he judges God's commandments to be acceptable—and to admit that the believer has a prior, nontheological conception of ethical right and wrong is to abandon the divine command theory.

The weakness of this philosophical objection is that it fails to note the distinctions that can be drawn among various value concepts. From the fact that the believer values some things independently of his beliefs about God's commands, the objector concludes, illegitimately, that the believer must have a conception of ethical right and wrong that is independent of his beliefs about God's commands. This inference is illegitimate because there can be valuations which do not imply or presuppose a judgment of ethical right or wrong. For instance, I may simply like something, or want something, or feel a revulsion at something.

What the modified divine command theorist will hold, then, is that the believer values some things independently of their relation to God's commands, but that these valuations are not judgments of ethical right and wrong and do not of themselves imply judgments of ethical right and wrong. He will maintain, on the other hand, that such independent valuations are involved in, or even necessary for, judgments of ethical right and wrong which also involve beliefs about God's will or commands. The adherent of a divine command ethics will normally be able to give reasons for his adherence. Such reasons might include: "Because I am grateful to God for His love"; "Because I find it the most satisfying form of ethical life"; "Because there's got to be an objective moral law if life isn't to fall to pieces, and I can't understand what it would be if not the will of God."[4] As we have already noted, the modified divine command theorist also has reasons why he would not accept a divine command ethics in certain logically possible situations which he believes not to be actual. All of these reasons seem to me to involve valuations that are independent of divine command ethics. The person who has such reasons wants certain things—happiness, certain satisfactions—for himself and others; he hates cruelty and loves kindness; he has perhaps a certain unique and "numinous" awe of God. And these are not attitudes which he has simply because of his beliefs about God's commands.[5] They are not attitudes, however, which presuppose judgments of moral right and wrong.

[4] The mention of moral law in the last of these reasons may presuppose the ability to *mention* concepts of moral right and wrong, which may or may not be theological and which may or may not be concepts one uses oneself to make judgments of right and wrong. So far as I can see, it does not *presuppose* the *use* of such concepts to make judgments of right and wrong, or one's adoption of them for such use, which is the crucial point here.

[5] The independence ascribed to these attitudes is not a *genetic* independence. It may be that the person would not have come to have some of them had it not been for his religious beliefs. The point is that he has come to hold them in such a way that his holding them does not now depend entirely on his beliefs about God's commands.

It is sometimes objected to divine command theories of moral obligation, or of ethical rightness and wrongness, that one must have some reason for obeying God's commands or for adopting a divine command ethics, and that therefore a nontheological concept of moral obligation or of ethical rightness and wrongness must be presupposed, in order that one may judge that one ought to obey God's commands.[6] This objection is groundless. For one can certainly have reasons for doing something which do not involve believing one morally ought to do it or believing it would be ethically wrong not to do it.

I grant that in giving reasons for his attitudes toward God's commands the believer will probably use or presuppose concepts which, in the context, it is reasonable to count as nontheological value concepts (e.g., concepts of satisfactoriness and repulsiveness). Perhaps some of them might count as moral concepts. But all that the defender of a divine command theory of ethical wrongness has to maintain is that the concept of ethical wrongness which occurs in the ethical thought and discourse of believers is not one of the concepts which are used or presupposed in this way. Divine command theorists, including the modified divine command theorist, need not maintain that *all* value concepts, or even all moral concepts, must be understood in terms of God's commands.

In fact some well-known philosophers have held forms of divine command theory which quite explicitly presuppose some nontheological value concepts. Locke, for instance, says in his *Essay*,

> Good and evil . . . are nothing but pleasure or pain, or that which occasions or procures pleasure or pain to us. *Morally good and evil*, then, is only the conformity or disagreement of our voluntary actions to some law, whereby good or evil is drawn on us from the will and power of the law-maker. . . . [*Essay*, II.xxviii.5][7]

Locke goes on to distinguish three laws, or types of law, by reference to which actions are commonly judged as to moral good and evil: "(1) The *divine* law. (2) The *civil* law. (3) The law of *opinion* or *reputation*, if I may so call it" (*Essay*, II.xxviii.7). Of these three

[6] I take A. C. Ewing to be offering an objection of this type on p. 112 of his book *Ethics* (London: English Univs. Press, 1953).

[7] I quote from John Yolton's edition of *An Essay Concerning Human Understanding*, 2 vols. (London and New York: Everyman's Library, 1967).

Locke says that the third is "the common *measure of virtue and vice*" (*Essay*, II.xxviii.11). In Locke's opinion the terms "virtue" and "vice" are particularly closely attached to the praise and blame of society. But the terms "duty" and "sin" are connected with the commandments of God. About the divine law Locke says,

> This is the only true touchstone of *moral rectitude;* and by comparing them to this law, it is that men judge of the most considerable *moral good* or *evil* of their actions: that is, whether, as *duties or sins,* they are like to procure them happiness or misery from the hands of the ALMIGHTY. [*Essay*, II.xxviii.8]

The structure of Locke's analysis is clear enough. By "good" and "evil" we *mean* (nontheologically enough) pleasurable and painful. By "morally good" and "morally evil" we *mean* that the actions so described agree or disagree with some law under which the agent stands to be rewarded or punished. By "duty" and "sin," which denote the most important sort of moral good and evil, we *mean* (theologically now) actions which are apt to cause the agent good or evil (in the nontheological sense) because they agree or disagree with the law of God. I take it that the divine command theory advocated by Peter Geach,[8] and hinted at by Miss Anscombe,[9] is similar in structure, though not in all details, to Locke's.

The modified divine command theory that I have in mind does not rely as heavily as Locke's theory does on God's power to reward and punish, nor do I wish to assume Locke's analysis of "good" and "evil." The point I want to make by discussing Locke here is just that there are many different value concepts and it is clearly possible to give one or more of them a theological analysis while giving others a nontheological analysis. And I do assume that the modified divine command theorist will give a nontheological analysis of some value concepts although he gives a theological analysis of the concept of ethical wrongness. For instance, he may give a nontheological analysis, perhaps a naturalistic one or a noncognitivist one, of the meaning of "satisfactory" and "repulsive," as he uses them in some contexts. He may even regard as *moral* concepts some value concepts of which he gives a nontheological analysis.

[8] In *God and the Soul* (London: Routledge, 1969), chap. 9.
[9] G. E. M. Anscombe, "Modern Moral Philosophy," *Philosophy*, XXXIII (1958), pp. 1–19.

For it is not essential to a divine command theory of ethical wrongness to maintain that all valuing, or all value concepts, or even all moral concepts, depend on beliefs about God's commands. What is essential to such a theory is to maintain that when a believer says something is (ethically) *wrong*, at least part of what he means is that the action in question is contrary to God's will or commands. Another way of putting the matter is this. What depends on beliefs about God and His will is: not all of the religious person's value concepts, nor in general his ability to value things, but only his ability to appraise actions (and possible actions) in terms of their relation to a superhuman, nonnaturally objective, law. Indeed, it is obvious that Judeo-Christian ethics presupposes concepts that have at least ethical overtones and that are not essentially theological but have their background in human social relations and political institutions—such as the concepts of promise, kindness, law, and command. What the specifically theological doctrines introduce into Judeo-Christian ethics, according to the divine command theory, is the belief in a law that is superior to all human laws.

This version of the divine command theory may seem *theologically* objectionable to some believers. One of the reasons, surely, why divine command theories of ethics have appealed to some theologians is that such theories seem especially congruous with the religious demand that God be the object of our highest allegiance. If our supreme commitment in life is to doing what is right just because it is right, and if what is right is right just because God wills or commands it, then surely our highest allegiance is to God. But the modified divine command theory seems not to have this advantage. For the modified divine command theorist is forced to admit, as we have seen, that he has reasons for his adherence to a divine command ethics, and that his having these reasons implies that there are some things which he values independently of his beliefs about God's commands. It is therefore not correct to say of him that he is committed to doing the will of God *just* because it is the will of God; he is committed to doing it partly because of other things which he values independently. Indeed it appears that there are certain logically possible situations in which his present attitudes would not commit him to obey God's commands (for instance, if God commanded cruelty for its own sake). This may even suggest that he values some things, not just independently of God's commands, but more than God's commands.

We have here a real problem in religious ethical motivation. The Judeo-Christian believer is supposed to make God the supreme focus of his loyalties; that is clear. One possible interpretation of this fact is the following. Obedience to whatever God may command is (or at least ought to be) the one thing that the believer values for its own sake and more than anything and everything else. Anything else that he values, he values (or ought to) only to a lesser degree and as a means to obedience to God. This conception of religious ethical motivation is obviously favorable to an *un*modified divine command theory of ethical wrongness.

But I think it is not a realistic conception. Loyalty to God, for instance, is very often explained, by believers themselves, as motivated by gratitude for benefits conferred. And I think it is clear in most cases that the gratitude presupposes that the benefits are valued, at least to some extent, independently of loyalty to God. Similarly, I do not think that most devout Judeo-Christian believers would say that it would be wrong to disobey God if He commanded cruelty for its own sake. And if I am right about that I think it shows that their positive valuation of (emotional/volitional pro-attitude toward) doing *whatever* God may command is not clearly greater than their independent negative valuation of cruelty.

In analyzing ethical motivation in general, as well as Judeo-Christian ethical motivation in particular, it is probably a mistake to suppose that there is (or can be expected to be) one only thing that is valued supremely and for its own sake, with nothing else being valued independently of it. The motivation for a person's ethical orientation in life is normally much more complex than that, and involves a plurality of emotional and volitional attitudes of different sorts which are at least partly independent of each other. At any rate, I think the modified divine command theorist is bound to say that that is true of his ethical motivation.

In what sense, then, can the modified divine command theorist maintain that God is the supreme focus of his loyalties? I suggest the following interpretation of the single-hearted loyalty to God which is demanded in Judeo-Christian religion. In this interpretation the crucial idea is *not* that some one thing is valued for its own sake and more than anything else, and nothing else valued independently of it. It is freely admitted that the religious person will have a plurality of motives for his ethical position, and that these will be at least partly independent of each other. It is admitted further that a desire to obey the commands of God (*whatever* they may be) may not be the strongest of these motives. What will be claimed is that certain beliefs about God enable the believer to integrate or focus his motives in a loyalty to God and His commands. Some of these beliefs are about what God commands or wills (contingently—that is, although He could logically have commanded or willed something else instead).

Some of the motives in question might be called egoistic; they include desires for satisfactions for oneself—which God is believed to have given or to be going to give. Other motives may be desires for satisfaction for other people; these may be called altruistic. Still other motives might not be desires for anyone's satisfaction, but might be valuations of certain kinds of action for their own sakes; these might be called idealistic. I do not think my argument depends heavily on this particular classification, but it seems plausible that all of these types, and perhaps others as well, might be distinguished among the motives for a religious person's ethical position. Obviously such motives might pull one in different directions, conflicting with one another. But in Judeo-Christian ethics beliefs about what God does in fact will (although He could have willed otherwise) are supposed to enable one to *fuse* these motives, so to speak, into one's devotion to God and His will, so that they all pull together. Doubtless the believer will still have some motives which conflict with his loyalty to God. But the religious ideal is that these should all be merely momentary desires and impulses, and kept under control. They ought not to be allowed to influence voluntary action. The deeper, more stable, and controlling desires, intentions, and psychic energies are supposed to be fused in devotion to God. As I interpret it, however, it need not be inconsistent with the Judeo-Christian ethical and religious ideal that this fusion of motives, this integration of moral energies, depends on belief in certain propositions which are taken to be contingent truths about God.

Lest it be thought that I am proposing unprecedented theological positions, or simply altering Judeo-Christian religious beliefs to suit my theories, I will call to my aid on this point a theologian known for his insistence on the sovereignty of God. Karl Barth seems to me to hold a divine command theory of ethics. But when he raises the question of why we should obey God, he rejects with scorn the suggestion that God's *power* provides the basis for His claim on us. "By deciding for God [man] has definitely decided not to be obedient to power as power."[10] God's claim on us is based rather on His grace. "God calls us and orders us and claims us by being gracious to us in Jesus Christ."[11] I do not mean to suggest that Barth would agree with everything I have said about motivation, or that he offers a lucid account of a divine command theory. But he does agree with the position I have proposed on this point, that the believer's loyalty is not to be construed as a loyalty to God *as* all-powerful, nor to God *whatever* He might conceivably have willed. It is a loyalty to God *as* having a certain attitude toward us, a certain will for us, which God was free not to have, but to which, in Barth's view, He has committed Himself irrevocably in Jesus Christ. The believer's devotion is not to merely possible commands of God as such, but to God's actual (and gracious) will.

V

The ascription of moral qualities to God is commonly thought to cause problems for divine command theories of ethics. It is doubted that God, as an agent, can properly be called "good" in the moral sense if He is not subject to a moral law that is not of His own making. For if He is morally good, mustn't He do what is right *because* it is right? And how can He do that, if what's right is right because He wills it? Or it may be charged that divine command theories trivialize the claim that God is good. If "X is (morally) good" means roughly "X does what God wills," then "God is (morally) good" means only that God does what He wills—which is surely much less than people are normally taken to mean when they say that God is (morally) good. In this section I will suggest an answer to these objections.

Surely no analysis of Judeo-Christian ethical discourse can be regarded as adequate which does not provide for a sense in which the believer can seriously assert that God is good. Indeed an adequate

---

[10] Karl Barth, *Church Dogmatics*, Vol. II, Pt. 2, trans. G. W. Bromiley and others (Edinburgh: T. & T. Clark, 1957), p. 553.

[11] Ibid., p. 560.

analysis should provide a plausible account of what believers do in fact mean when they say, "God is good." I believe that a divine command theory of ethical (rightness and) wrongness can include such an account. I will try to indicate its chief features.

(1) In saying "God is good" one is normally expressing a favorable emotional attitude toward God. I shall not try to determine whether or not this is part of the meaning of "God is good"; but it is normally, perhaps almost always, at least one of the things one is doing if one says that God is good. If we were to try to be more precise about the type of favorable emotional attitude normally expressed by "God is good," I suspect we would find that the attitude expressed is most commonly one of *gratitude*.

(2) This leads to a second point, which is that when God is called "good" it is very often meant that He is *good to us*, or *good to* the speaker. "Good" is sometimes virtually a synonym for "kind." And for the modified divine command theorist it is not a trivial truth that God is kind. In saying that God is good in the sense of "kind," one presupposes, of course, that there are some things which the beneficiaries of God's goodness value. We need not discuss here whether the beneficiaries must value them independently of their beliefs about God's will. For the modified divine command theorist does admit that there are some things which believers value independently of their beliefs about God's commands. Nothing that the modified divine command theorist says about the meaning of ("right" and) "wrong" implies that it is a trivial truth that God bestows on His creatures things that they value.

(3) I would not suggest that the descriptive force of "good" as applied to God is exhausted by the notion of kindness. "God is good" must be taken in many contexts as ascribing to God, rather generally, qualities of character which the believing speaker regards as virtues in human beings. Among such qualities might be faithfulness, ethical consistency, a forgiving disposition, and, in general, various aspects of love, as well as kindness. Not that there is some definite list of qualities, the ascription of which to God is clearly implied by the claim that God is good. But saying that God is good normally commits one to the position that God has some important set of qualities which one regards as virtues in human beings.

(4) It will not be thought that God has *all* the qualities which are virtues in human beings. Some such qualities are logically inapplica-

ble to a being such as God is supposed to be. For example, aside from certain complications arising from the doctrine of the incarnation, it would be logically inappropriate to speak of God as controlling His sexual desires. (He doesn't have any.) And given some widely held conceptions of God and His relation to the world, it would hardly make sense to speak of Him as *courageous*. For if He is impassible and has predetermined absolutely everything that happens, He has no risks to face and cannot endure (because He cannot suffer) pain or displeasure.[12]

Believers in God's goodness also typically think He lacks some human virtues which would *not* be logically inapplicable to a being like Him. A virtuous man, for instance, does not intentionally cause the death of other human beings, except under exceptional circumstances. But God has intentionally brought it about that all men die. There are agonizing forms of the problem of evil; but I think that for most Judeo-Christian believers (especially those who believe in life after death), this is not one of them. They believe that God's making men mortal and His commanding them not to kill each other, fit together in a larger pattern of harmonious purposes. How then can one distinguish between human virtues which God must have if He is good and human virtues which God may lack and still be good? This is an interesting and important question, but I will not attempt here to formulate a precise or adequate criterion for making the distinction. I fear it would require a lengthy digression from the issues with which we are principally concerned.

(5) If we accept a divine command theory of ethical rightness and wrongness, I think we shall have to say that *dutifulness* is a human virtue which, like sexual chastity, is logically inapplicable to God. God cannot either do or fail to do His duty, since He does not have a duty—at least not in the most important sense in which human beings have a duty. For He is not subject to a moral law not of His own making. Dutifulness is one virtuous disposition which men can have that God cannot have. But there are other virtuous dispositions which God can have as well as men. Love, for instance.

---

[12] The argument here is similar to one which is used for another purpose by Ninian Smart in "Omnipotence, Evil, and Superman," *Philosophy*, XXXVI (1961), reprinted in Nelson Pike, ed., *God and Evil* (Englewood Cliffs, N.J.: Prentice-Hall, 1964), pp. 103–12.

I do not mean to endorse the doctrines of divine impassibility and theological determinism.

It hardly makes sense to say that God does what He does *because* it is right. But it does not follow that God cannot have any reason for doing what He does. It does not even follow that He cannot have reasons of a type on which it would be morally virtuous for a man to act. For example, He might do something because He knew it would make His creatures happier.

(6) The modified divine command theorist must deny that in calling God "good" one presupposes a standard of moral rightness and wrongness superior to the will of God, by reference to which it is determined whether God's character is virtuous or not. And I think he can consistently deny that. He can say that morally virtuous and vicious qualities of character are those which agree and conflict, respectively, with God's commands, and that it is their agreement or disagreement with God's commands that makes them virtuous or vicious. But the believer normally thinks he has at least a general idea of what qualities of character are in fact virtuous and vicious (approved and disapproved by God). Having such an idea, he can apply the word "good" descriptively to God, meaning that (with some exceptions, as I have noted) God has the qualities which the believer regards as virtues, such as faithfulness and kindness.

I will sum up by contrasting what the believer can mean when he says, "Moses is good," with what he can mean when he says, "God is good," according to the modified divine command theory. When the believer says, "Moses is good," (a) he normally is expressing a favorable emotional attitude toward Moses—normally, though perhaps not always. (Sometimes a person's moral goodness displeases us.) (b) He normally implies that Moses possesses a large proportion of those qualities of character which are recognized in the religious-ethical community as virtues, and few if any of those which are regarded as vices. (c) He normally implies that the qualities of Moses' character on the basis of which he describes Moses as good are qualities approved by God.

When the believer says, "God is good," (a) he normally is expressing a favorable emotional attitude toward God—and I think exceptions on this point would be rarer than in the case of statements that a man is good. (b) He normally is ascribing to God certain qualities of character. He may mean primarily that God is kind or benevolent, that He is *good to* human beings or certain ones of them. Or he may mean that God possesses (with some exceptions) those qualities of character which are regarded as virtues in the religious-ethical community. (c) Whereas in saying, "Moses is good," the believer was stating or implying that the qualities of character which he was ascribing to Moses conform to a standard of ethical rightness which is independent of the will of Moses, he is not stating or implying that the qualities of character which he ascribes to God conform to a standard of ethical rightness which is independent of the will of God.

VI

As I noted at the outset, the divine command theory of ethical wrongness, even in its modified form, has the consequence that believers and nonbelievers use the word "wrong" with different meanings in ethical contexts, since it will hardly be thought that nonbelievers mean by "wrong" what the theory says believers mean by it. This consequence gives rise to an objection. For the phenomena of common moral discourse between believers and nonbelievers suggest that they mean the same thing by "wrong" in ethical contexts. In the present section I shall try to explain how the modified divine command theorist can account for the facts of common ethical discourse.

I will first indicate what I think the troublesome facts are. Judeo-Christian believers enter into ethical discussions with people whose religious or anti-religious beliefs they do not know. It seems to be possible to conduct quite a lot of ethical discourse, with apparent understanding, without knowing one's partner's views on religious issues. Believers also discuss ethical questions with persons who are known to them to be nonbelievers. They agree with such persons, disagree with them, and try to persuade them, about what acts are morally wrong. (Or at least it is normally *said*, by the participants and others, that they agree and disagree about such issues.) Believers ascribe, to people who are known not to believe in God, beliefs that certain acts are morally wrong. Yet surely believers do not suppose that nonbelievers, in calling acts wrong, mean that they are contrary to the will or commandments of God. Under these circumstances how can the believer really mean "contrary to the will or commandments of God" when he says "wrong"? If he agrees and disagrees with nonbelievers about what is wrong, if he ascribes to them beliefs that certain acts are wrong, must he not be using "wrong" in a nontheological sense?

What I shall argue is that in some ordinary (and I fear imprecise) sense of "mean," what believers and nonbelievers mean by "wrong" in ethical contexts may well be partly the same and partly different. There are agreements between believers and nonbelievers which make common moral discourse between them possible. But these agreements do not show that the two groups mean exactly the same thing by "wrong." They do not show that "contrary to God's will or commands" is not part of what believers mean by "wrong."

Let us consider first the agreements which make possible common moral discourse between believers and nonbelievers. (1) One important agreement, which is so obvious as to be easily overlooked, is that they use many of the same ethical terms—"wrong," "right," "ought," "duty," and others. And they may utter many of the same ethical sentences, such as "Racial discrimination is morally wrong." In determining what people believe we rely very heavily on what they say (when they seem to be speaking sincerely)—and that means in large part, on the words that they use and the sentences they utter. If I know that somebody says, with apparent sincerity, "Racial discrimination is morally wrong," I will normally ascribe to him the belief that racial discrimination is morally wrong, even if I also know that he does not mean *exactly* the same thing as I do by "racial discrimination" or "morally wrong." Of course if I know he means something *completely* different, I would not ascribe the belief to him without explicit qualification.

I would not claim that believers and nonbelievers use *all* the same ethical terms. "Sin," "law of God," and "Christian," for instance, occur as ethical terms in the discourse of many believers, but would be much less likely to occur in the same way in nonbelievers' discourse.

(2) The shared ethical terms have the same basic grammatical status for believers as for nonbelievers, and at least many of the same logical connections with other expressions. Everyone agrees, for instance, in treating "wrong" as an adjective and "Racial discrimination is morally wrong" as a declarative sentence. "(All) racial discrimination is morally wrong" would be treated by all parties as expressing an A-type (universal affirmative) proposition, from which consequences can be drawn by syllogistic reasoning or the predicate

calculus. All agree that if X is morally wrong, then it isn't morally right and refraining from X is morally obligatory. Such grammatical and formal agreements are important to common moral discourse.

(3) There is a great deal of agreement, among believers and nonbelievers, as to what types of action they call "wrong" in an ethical sense and I think that that agreement is one of the things that make common moral discourse possible.[13] It is certainly not complete agreement. Obviously there is a lot of ethical disagreement in the world. Much of it cuts right across religious lines, but not all of it does. There are things which are typically called "wrong" by members of some religious groups, and not by others. Nonetheless there are types of action which everyone or almost everyone would call morally wrong—such as torturing someone to death because he accidentally broke a small window in your house. Moreover any two people (including any one believer and one nonbeliever) are likely to find some actions they both call wrong that not everyone does. I imagine that most ethical discussion takes place among people whose area of agreement in what they call wrong is relatively large.

There is probably much less agreement about the most basic issues in moral theory than there is about many ethical issues of less generality. There is much more unanimity in what people (sincerely) say in answer to such questions as "Was what Hitler did to the Jews wrong?" or "Is it normally wrong to disobey the laws of one's country?" than in what they (sincerely) say in answer to such questions as "Is it always right to do the act which will have the best results?" or "Is pleasure the only thing that is good for its own sake?" The issue between adherents and nonadherents of divine command ethics is typical of basic issues in ethical and metaethical theory in this respect.

(4) The emotional and volitional attitudes normally expressed by the statement that something is "wrong" are similar in believers and nonbelievers. They are not exactly the same; the attitudes typi-

---

[13] Cf. Ludwig Wittgenstein, *Philosophical Investigations*, 2d ed. (Oxford: Blackwell, 1958), Pt. I, sec. 242: "If language is to be a means of communication there must be agreement not only in definitions but also (queer as this may sound) in judgments." In contemporary society I think it may well be the case that because there is not agreement in ethical definitions, common ethical discourse requires a measure of agreement in ethical judgments. (I do not mean to comment here more broadly on the truth or falsity of Wittgenstein's statement as a statement about the conditions of linguistic communication in general.)

cally expressed by the believer's statement that something is "wrong" are importantly related to his religious practice and beliefs about God, and this doubtless makes them different in some ways from the attitudes expressed by nonbelievers uttering the same sentence. But the attitudes are certainly similar, and that is important for the possibility of common moral discourse.

(5) Perhaps even more important is the related fact that the social functions of a statement that something is (morally) "wrong" are similar for believers and nonbelievers. To say that something someone else is known to have done is "wrong" is commonly to attack him. If you say that something you are known to have done is "wrong," you abandon certain types of defense. To say that a public policy is "wrong" is normally to register oneself as opposed to it, and is sometimes a signal that one is willing to be supportive of common action to change it. These social functions of moral discourse are extremely important. It is perhaps not surprising that we are inclined to say that two people agree with each other when they both utter the same sentence and thereby indicate their readiness to take the same side in a conflict.

Let us sum up these observations about the conditions which make common moral discourse between believers and nonbelievers possible. (1) They use many of the same ethical terms, such as "wrong." (2) They treat those terms as having the same basic grammatical and logical status, and many of the same logical connections with other expressions. (3) They agree to a large extent about what types of action are to be called "wrong." To call an action "wrong" is, among other things, to classify it with certain other actions, and there is considerable agreement between believers and nonbelievers as to what actions those are. (4) The emotional and volitional attitudes which believers and nonbelievers normally express in saying that something is "wrong" are similar, and (5) saying that something is "wrong" has much the same social functions for believers and nonbelievers.

So far as I can see, none of this is inconsistent with the modified divine command theory of ethical wrongness. According to that theory there are several things which are true of the believer's use of "wrong" which cannot plausibly be supposed to be true of the nonbeliever's. In saying, "X is wrong," the believer commits himself (subjectively, at least, and publicly if he is known to be a believer) to the claim that X is contrary to God's will or commandments. The believer will not say that anything would be wrong, under any possible circumstances, if it were not contrary to God's will or commandments. In many contexts he uses the term "wrong" interchangeably with "against the will of God" or "against the commandments of God." The heart of the modified divine command theory, I have suggested, is the claim that when the believer says, "X is wrong," one thing he means to be doing is stating a nonnatural objective fact about X, and the nonnatural objective fact he means to be stating is that X is contrary to the will or commandments of God. This claim may be true even though the uses of "wrong" by believers and nonbelievers are similar in all five of the ways pointed out above.

Suppose these contentions of the modified divine command theory are correct. (I think they are very plausible as claims about the ethical discourse of at least some religious believers.) In that case believers and nonbelievers surely do not mean exactly the same thing by "X is wrong" in ethical contexts. But neither is it plausible to suppose that they mean entirely different things, given the phenomena of common moral discourse. We must suppose, then, that their meaning is partly the same and partly different. "Contrary to God's will or commands" must be taken as expressing only part of the meaning with which the believer uses "wrong." Some of the similarities between believers' and nonbelievers' use of "wrong" must also be taken as expressing parts of the meaning with which the believer uses "wrong." This view of the matter agrees with the account of the modified divine command theory in Section III above, where I pointed out that the modified divine command theorist cannot mean exactly the same thing by "wrong" that he means by "contrary to God's commands."

We have here a situation which commonly arises when some people hold, and others do not hold, a given theory about the nature of something which everyone talks about. The chemist, who believes that water is a compound of hydrogen and oxygen, and the man who knows nothing of chemistry, surely do not use the word "water" in entirely different senses; but neither is it very plausible to suppose that they use it with exactly the same meaning. I am inclined to say that in some fairly ordinary sense of "mean," a phenomenalist, and a philosopher who holds some conflicting theory about what it is for a physical object to exist, do not mean exactly the same thing by

"There is a bottle of milk in the refrigerator." But they certainly do not mean entirely different things, and they can agree that there is a bottle of milk in the refrigerator.

VII

These remarks bring us face to face with some important issues in the general theory of analysis and meaning. What are the criteria for determining whether two utterers of the same expression mean exactly the same thing by it, or something partly different, or something entirely different? What is the relation between philosophical analyses, and philosophical theories about the natures of things, on the one hand, and the meanings of terms in ordinary discourse on the other hand? I have permitted myself the liberty of speaking as if these issues did not exist. But their existence is notorious, and I certainly cannot resolve them in this essay. Indeed, I do not have resolutions to offer.

In view of these uncertainties in the theory of meaning, it is worth noting that much of what the modified divine command theorist wants to say can be said without making claims about the *meaning* of ethical terms. He wants to say, for instance, that believers' claims that certain acts are wrong normally express certain attitudes toward those acts, whether or not that is part of their meaning; that an act is wrong if and only if it is contrary to God's will or commands (assuming God loves us); that nonetheless, if God commanded cruelty for its own sake, neither obedience nor disobedience would be ethically wrong or ethically permitted; that if an act is contrary to God's will or commands that is a nonnatural objective fact about it; and that that is the only nonnatural objective fact which obtains if and only if the act is wrong. These are among the most important claims of the modified divine command theory—perhaps they include the very most important. But in the form in which I have just stated them, they are not claims about the *meaning* of ethical terms.

I do not mean to reject the claims about the meanings of terms in religious ethical discourse which I have included in the modified divine command theory. In the absence of general solutions to general problems in the theory of meaning, we may perhaps say what seems to us intuitively plausible in particular cases. That is presumably what the modified divine command theorist is doing when he claims that "contrary to the will or commands of God" is part of the meaning of "(ethically) wrong" for many Judeo-Christian believers. And I think it is fair to say that if we have found unresolved problems about meaning in the modified divine command theory, they are problems much more about what we mean in general by "meaning" than about what Judeo-Christian believers mean by "wrong."[14]

[14] I am indebted to many who have read, or heard, and discussed versions of this essay, and particularly to Richard Brandt, William Frankena, John Reeder, and Stephen Stich, for helpful criticisms.

DOES RELIGIOUS FAITH CONFLICT WITH MORAL FREEDOM?

Donald Evans

I was assigned to the public information office so I had a good look at army propaganda. The training films, for example, were grotesque—persuading people to accept chemical and biological warfare; there was one in particular about some scientists in West Virginia who'd perfected the bubonic plague. . . . Breaking with the church was good, because it taught me that one can doubt a huge, powerful organization's rightness. When some hillbilly sergeant would tell me, "You've got to have faith in your government," I'd find myself thinking, "If I can question the Big Bopper up there, I can certainly question you, you dingaling." [An American deserter, quoted in the Toronto *Star*, June 14, 1969]

If religion is understood in an authoritarian way, a break away from it is necessary for moral freedom. Instead of submitting without question to "Big Bopper" and to other authorities such as government or church, a man begins to make up his own mind on many matters. For some people the change of consciousness called "the death of God" is a liberating event, for God has seemed to be a threat to human dignity, maturity, and freedom. Indeed, many people would agree with the philosopher Patrick Nowell-Smith when he rejects religious morality as "infantile" and finds maturity and freedom only in a secular morality.[1]

Does religious faith conflict with freedom in making moral decisions? Sociological evidence indicates that, in general, it does. Wil-

---

[1] "Morality: Religious and Secular," in *Christian Ethics and Contemporary Philosophy*, ed. Ian T. Ramsey (London: SCM Press, 1966).

liam Eckhardt, summarizing the results of many sociological studies, says this:

> Instead of teaching people the "truth" which is supposed to make them "free" (and therefore responsible), it would seem that religion generally teaches people to escape from freedom into the autocratic arms of whatever rules and regulations may be currently prevalent, making them into authoritarian, bureaucratic, compulsive, conformist, conservative, militarist (at least in the West), nationalist, and racialist personalities, fit to serve well the rules and regulations designed to keep them in their personal places and to maintain the social status quo.[2]

Eckhardt's conclusions need not be accepted unreservedly. He himself notes that the generalizations do not apply to all religious individuals and groups. Also, we may question his move from statistical correlations to claims concerning the influence of religion. Perhaps religion is less the cause of the various attitudes than it is the effect of some of them. Or perhaps religiosity and the other attitudes have as their main cause some unmentioned psychological factor, not easily accessible in sociological studies. Nevertheless the main tenor of Eckhardt's findings seems indisputable. Much religion, perhaps most religion, is associated with attitudes which are in conflict with moral freedom. People who simply do what they're told are not free. They say, "He knows what is best," or "His word is law." Sometimes "he" is human (father, sergeant, president, or pope), sometimes divine. In either case submission is a form of willing slavery.

But not all religion is authoritarian; nor is an anti-authoritarian independence and autonomy the only alternative. In this essay I shall argue that some religious convictions, namely those expressed in a contemporary Christian creed, are compatible with moral freedom, where this freedom is understood to be "responsive" rather than "willful." My focus will be on the creed and on "responsive" freedom. The creed deserves serious philosophical scrutiny, for it expresses a broad consensus within a main-line denomination and within a wide range of contemporary theology, and it differs radically from authoritarian versions of Christianity against which philosophers and others have protested in the name of freedom. The "responsive" view of freedom which is presupposed in the creed will

[2] *Peace Research,* 2, 9 (Oakville, Ontario: Canadian Peace Research Institute, September, 1970).

gradually emerge in the course of the essay. On such a view, freedom increases rather than decreases when an agent is receptive to the (non-authoritarian) influence of another agent and to the depths within himself which are beyond his direct control. I shall be contrasting this with a "willful" notion of freedom, in which freedom is a power to do what one wills, a power exercised over others so as to reduce their power over oneself, which reduces one's own power; or it is a power over oneself, an ability to use at will various physical and intellectual skills which one has acquired.

Although this is primarily a philosophical essay, it includes a great deal of theology and psychology. The theology is included because it seems obvious to me that the best way for a philosopher to consider issues of faith and freedom is to explore religious convictions in detail and depth within their theological framework; otherwise he risks religious irrelevance. An exposition of a creed in the context of contemporary theology provides an undeniably religious focus for philosophical analysis, criticism, and reflection. The psychology is included because my thesis is that the religious convictions expressed in the creed, if properly understood, are compatible with moral freedom, and because I shall be assuming that the meaning of the statements expressing these convictions is intrinsically connected with *psychological* states or events in the speaker who properly understands the statements. Indeed, I shall argue that an inner receptivity is the psychological condition for the basic attitudes which are rendered explicit in the religious convictions, and for the moral impulse which is expressed in the moral convictions. Logical issues concerning connections of meaning between "We believe in God" and "Love and serve others" are thus inseparable from psychological issues concerning connections between psychological states or events. In some studies of relations between religion and morality, logical issues and psychological issues are considered separately. This can be a useful procedure, for it is sometimes useful to consider logical relations between statements in abstraction from the experiential depth of understanding and the strength of conviction of particular persons who make the statements. In this essay, however, we will consider statements as they are profoundly understood and authentically affirmed, statements whose meaning is intrinsically connected with psychological states and events in speakers who are neither superficial nor inauthentic.

A NEW CREED

In 1968 the General Council of the United Church of Canada approved a new creed for use in congregational worship. This creed is not a doctrinal test, setting forth a minimum of belief necessary for church membership; nor is it a denominational statement of faith or "confession," elaborating what most United Churchmen believe; nor is it an ecumenical creed, though it may eventually be used in many other denominations. Nevertheless it does express an important religious consensus. It is a liturgical summary of some central convictions which have a claim to be representative within the largest Protestant church in Canada, for the creed has been approved by its highest court and is actually in use in congregations. And it has a special advantage in view of the focus of this essay. Unlike an ecumenical creed such as the Apostles' Creed, it includes explicit moral convictions, and it links these with the convictions concerning God. Here it is, with the lines numbered for easy reference:

(1) Man is not alone; he lives in God's world.
(2) We believe in God:
(3)   who has created and is creating,
(4)   who has come in the true Man, Jesus, to reconcile and
           make new,
(5)   who works in us and others by his Spirit.
(6) We trust him.
(7) He calls us to be his church:
(8)   to celebrate his presence,
(9)   to love and serve others,
(10)   to seek justice and resist evil,
(11)   to proclaim Jesus, crucified and risen, our judge and
           our hope.
(12) In life, in death, in life beyond death, God is with us.
(13) We are not alone.
(14) Thanks be to God.

Obviously this creed is relevant to our problem concerning the relation between religious and moral convictions. I have an additional, personal reason for considering it: I was on the committee which drafted it, so I can interpret it with a fair degree of confidence. I know how a group of theologians (academics, pastors, and laymen) labored on it for several years, working through many different versions. It was designed so as to be open to a variety of interpretations, and there were differences of interpretation within the committee itself; but I am sure that my own interpretation is not idiosyncratic. And I know many of the varied reasons and varied meanings which were pondered as the present wording gradually emerged. I should note, however, that my interpretation of the creed is influenced not only by committee discussions but also by a wide range of contemporary writings in theology and philosophy of religion. Readers who wish to probe some of the problems at greater depth should make use of my references and the bibliographies at the end of the essay.

The simple beauty and brevity of the creed were achieved at a price. Some ideas which the committee thought to be very important theologically had to be omitted. These omissions should be noted, since the ideas are part of the theological consensus which underlies the creed, and that consensus is what matters most. For example, there were two omissions from line 5. The first was the idea of liberation. Many committee members held that the main work of the Spirit is the liberation of man. Indeed, some saw in liberation a central unifying idea for the whole creed, uniting together all the various activities of God.[3] But no satisfactory wording concerning liberation could be found. The second omission in line 5 occurred when an earlier wording was changed. The line had read, "He works within us and *among* us by his Spirit." This suggested that God not only acts directly within each individual, deep in the psyche, but also in relations between individuals, in society. (We shall consider some of the actions "among" men later in the essay.) The line was changed because it seemed even more important to make explicit the conviction that God is at work in non-Christians as well as Christians; so now it reads, "He works in us *and others* by his Spirit." We shall see that the words "and others" are of immense significance in interpreting the whole creed: the divine activity which is somehow linked with human moral activity is an activity in non-

[3] The word "liberation" includes much of the meaning of two other traditional words which have previously been more popular: "salvation" and "redemption." Liberation is not only a central theme in contemporary Christian theology; it is also proposed as a central concept for comparative religion. See William Nicholls, "Understanding Religion after the 'Death of God,'" *Theoria to Theory*, Vol. 2, no. 3 (1968); and "Liberation as a Religious Theme," *Canadian Journal of Theology*, 16, 3–4 (1970).

Christians as well as Christians, in atheists and agnostics as well as religious believers. But the words "among us" in the earlier version will also be borne in mind.

Line 9 involved an omission. There was general agreement that a Christian is called to love not only his neighbor but also *himself*. God helps a man to accept and to confirm himself; this is a psychologically necessary precondition for accepting and confirming others. But if line 9 had read "to love our neighbor as ourselves," the word "serve" would have had to be deleted. It was thought that "serve" was important, since "love" by itself might connote only an attitude, whereas "serve" clearly connotes practical activity. It also connotes an absence of concern about acquiring or maintaining social status and authoritarian power.

Another important omission is the word "mystery." Early drafts of the creed referred explicitly to the mystery of God, suggesting that God's activities and presence transcend man's intellectual and practical grasp and evoke in man a response of awe and wonder. Unfortunately the word "mystery" had to be left out because of necessary rearrangements in the wording and the structure of the creed. But I know from my own experience that when the creed is used in congregational worship, it does express wonder in response to mystery; the liturgical context reinforces what many of the words of the creed already indicate.

Line 1 was vigorously debated in the committee. The present version stresses a contrast between the feeling that man is alone in a starkly impersonal cosmos (Sartrian "forlornness") and the feeling that a trustworthy spiritual power is present everywhere in the world. There is also a suggestion that since man lives in God's world, he is responsible to God; that is, man should regard himself neither as an isolated impotent infant nor as an isolated omnipotent deity but as a passive and active responder to divine activity. The line also hints at other themes which some members of the committee proposed: meaningless versus meaningful life, alienation versus at-homeness, separation versus togetherness, anxiety versus inner peace. Note that all these various themes mention alternatives to faith. Indeed, to say "man is not alone" is to mention an alternative conviction, namely that man *is* alone. In the committee there was some uneasiness, especially during the early discussions, about beginning a creed with a negative statement, even when it is immediately followed by

"He lives in God's world." The uneasiness arose, I think, not so much from the grammatical form of the opening, but from the haunting allusion to the possibility of unfaith. But this realism is a merit of the creed. The Christian maintains his faith that man lives in God's world and is thus not alone *in spite of* much that goes on in the world, and *in spite of* his own tendencies to unfaith—to self-isolation, alienation, and anxiety. When he says the creed, he reaffirms his conviction and his commitment: "Though sometimes I seem to be alone, and though sometimes I live as if I were, I am not alone. Though I sometimes live in resigned despair or strident self-assertion, responding to a world which seems indifferent or hostile, I reaffirm my trust in God." This real tension within the typical Christian believer is implied in line 1. Indeed, for some theologians the line may suggest an aloneness which is not an alternative to Christian faith but a necessary ingredient in that faith. Some theologians, influenced by mystical, existentialist, or psychoanalytic experience and thought, hold that a man must experience the absence of God if he is to become genuinely aware of the divine presence. He must experience an utter aloneness, a nothingness within and a nothingness without, as the context in which he then comes to understand what it means to believe that God is with him. He must experience darkness, captivity, and insecurity if he is to become aware of divine light, liberation, and peace. To me it seems that there is a great deal of truth in this approach, but I do not know whether it is a universal spiritual law for all men rather than the path for some. Certainly it is at most a subordinate theme in the theology which lies behind the creed, which views aloneness mainly as an alternative to faith, not an ingredient in it. Indeed, by the time we reach line 13, aloneness has disappeared even as an alternative. "We are not alone" is a ringing declaration, a confident way of summing up the many ways in which the creed has proclaimed the intimate relation of man to God. As we shall see, the creed sets forth divine activities and human responses. It involves an internally connected set of concepts which link the activities and the responses, a coherent overall pattern of meaning for the believer. In my interpretation of the creed I shall assume that the pattern is unreservedly held and applied by the believer, whose faith is thus an ideal faith. This assumption is, of course, unrealistic. I make it so as to reduce the obscurity and complexity of the topic. Nevertheless it is important to remember that a man who affirms the creed has a faith which falls short—often far short—of the ideal. There is a serious danger that if he is not genuinely aware of this, he will use the creed to support the self-deceptive fantasy that he has already achieved or received a final self-unifying certainty. Such a fantasy petrifies a man in his present stage of personal and spiritual development and reinforces his resistance to being changed by God. In this essay, however, we will not be considering the very real risk of bad faith in affirming a creed —using it to prevent the very receptivity to God which the creed expresses.

The essay thus far has all been introductory. In the rest of the essay there are two parts, each of which has five sections. The first five sections are reflections concerning the creed, considered under the following headings: basic attitudes of trust, hope, wonder, etc., as responses to divine activities; basic attitudes, explicit faith, and implicit faith; receptivity to divine activity which comes *via* other men and *via* one's own inner depths; the divine call which enables and directs men to love; love, justice, and particular moral decisions. At the end of this first part one broad conclusion is that the creed does not dictate particular moral decisions, but does set them in a distinctive Christian context. In the final five sections of the essay, five aspects of this context are discussed: responsive freedom as a directed and dependent freedom to love; the influence of the basic attitudes on particular decisions; the role of a world view in which fact and value are inseparable; the importance of a community's common moral vocabulary; the commitment to Jesus as moral paradigm.

DIVINE ACTIVITY AND HUMAN RESPONSE

The creed begins and ends with man in relation to God. In between, it sets forth this relation, a relation of human responses to divine activities. The creed refers to a number of different divine activities: God creates, comes, reconciles, makes new, liberates ("works"), and calls. Two further activities are implied by the words "with us" (line 12): God accompanies men in their journey through life and beyond, and God confirms men, providing his strength, support, and backing. All these activities go on in the present, in which man responds, although they have gone on in the past and will continue into the future. God *has come* in Jesus, here and now, though of course God *came* in Jesus many years ago and *will come* in Jesus, our hope, as we move into the future. Note also that all the activities of God are activities to which the Christian believer responds. Most of the activities have men as their object; God does something directly *to* men. In the case of the activity of creation, the creed omits any explicit object-word. The believer does not say, "who has created and is creating *the world*," for this might suggest a cosmological theory which can be understood and accepted without any basic attitudinal responses. Instead, the creed places the creative activity of God alongside other divine activities on behalf of man ("has come," "reconcile," "make new," "works") as the focus for a basic human trust (line 6). The believer expresses his conviction that God acts creatively on behalf of man in the world and in his own personal existence. Some men may believe that the fundamental power or powers which dominate man's natural and social environment and which bring about human existence are impersonal, or, if personal, neutral; they are not related either positively or negatively to human fulfillment. Other men may believe that these powers are hostile to human fulfillment. The Christian believer, however, is convinced that the source of his own personal existence is also a creative, trustworthy power, everywhere active in his environment as a reliable friend of man. The Christian's pervasive, generalized attitude in life, as expressed in the creed, is thus trustful, responsive, and relaxed, rather than wary, willful, and anxious. For a non-Christian, the expression "God the Creator" may mean an impersonal power, or a neutral personal power, or a malevolent personal power. But for the Christian believer, God's creative activity, like any divine activity, is trustworthy by definition. No activity counter to human fulfillment counts as divine activity.[4] Since Christians include human *freedom* as an element in human fulfillment, divine activity by definition cannot be contrary to human freedom. This definitional assumption of Christian theology is not, of course, in itself an answer to the critic who claims that Christian convictions conflict with moral freedom. Some religious authoritarians have an idea of freedom which is close to what everyone else, including many Christians, would call non-freedom. What matters is the content given to the idea of freedom.

[4] Cf. H. Richard Niebuhr, *The Responsible Self* (New York: Harper, 1963), p. 119.

In general, we shall see that there is a mutual interconnection of meaning[5] between divine activity and human attitudinal response. We cannot understand what is meant by talk about divine activity in a Christian creedal context if we try to think of it in abstraction from attitudinal responses. And the extent of our understanding depends on the extent of our responses.

Let us now consider more carefully some of the responses which are indicated in the creed. I propose that they be divided into three kinds: attitudinal, receptive, and practical. We shall consider attitudinal responses first. These include trust (line 6), joy (line 8), hope and courage (lines 11 and 12), gratitude (line 14), and wonder or awe (throughout). These are attitudes towards God, who is active wherever there is a mysterious process of creation, reconciliation, renewal, liberation, or confirmation in human life. Each attitude is of such a kind as to be connected in meaning with one or more of the activities: trust in divine creativity, joy in divine reconciliation, hope based on divine confirmation, gratitude for divine renewal, wonder at divine liberation, etc. To be convinced of divine activity involves having the specific attitude and other attitudes; having the specific attitude, if explicit, involves being convinced of the divine activity and other divine activities. The attitude is "fitting" or "appropriate" as a response to divine activity because of an internal connection of meaning between response and activity. Usually there is no simple one-to-one correlation between a kind of divine activity and a kind of attitudinal response. For example, divine creativity is connected with trust, gratitude, and other attitudes; trust is connected with divine creativity, divine liberation, and other activities.

The various attitudinal responses are expressed in *worship*, which the creed describes as a celebration of the divine presence (line 8). Although the main attitude indicated by the word "celebrate" is joy, the other worshipful attitudes were meant to be included: trust, hope, gratitude, and wonder. (In each case, as we shall see later, the attitude is a "basic" one, unrestricted and pervasive in its scope; it is a stance of the whole being in relation to the whole environ-

---

[5] For a more technical discussion of this interconnection see Donald Evans, *The Logic of Self-Involvement* (London: SCM Press, 1963; New York: Herder & Herder, 1969), esp. pp. 74–78, 106–14, 145–60, 174–88. See also H. Richard Niebuhr, *The Responsible Self*, pp. 57, 65.

ment.) One reason for the choice of the word "celebrate" was that the note of joy should be clearly evident somewhere in the creed; but there were other reasons, of course, such as the associations with both "celebrations" of sacraments and "celebrations" in secular life. The word "presence" emphasizes the fact that divine activities are activities to which men respond here and now, personally and directly. God is actively present to man. The word "presence" thus fits in well with the rest of the creed. We should note, however, the absence of an expression which is important in Christian theology: the divine "word." Worship is often depicted as a response to the divine "word." This is compatible with the creed. All the divine activities are understood by means of human language, so the activities communicate meaning to man, and are responded to in terms of their meaning. Worship, then, may be defined as the expression of such-and-such basic attitudes to God in response to the active, meaningful presence of God. And God may be defined as the active, meaningful presence to whom men fittingly respond in worship (expressions of basic attitudes).

Both definitions, however, are incomplete, for we have only been considering the first kind of response to God, the attitudinal. There are two others, the receptive and the practical. Later we shall consider practical responses, especially the moral responses as sketched in lines 9 and 10: "to love and serve others, to seek justice and resist evil." The receptive response, however, is the central focus of faith, the human starting point for both Christian worship and Christian morality. Receptivity towards God is, of course, an attitude, and might therefore seem to belong among the other "attitudinal" responses to God. It differs, however, in being the *sine qua non*, the precondition, of the other attitudes. For whereas for Christians the attitudinal responses to God presuppose that God is acting in a man, receptivity is what *allows* God to act in a man. God cannot act in a man unless the man permits it. Instead of being receptive to divine activity a man can block, impede, and resist it. Instead of allowing God to liberate him, a man can reinforce his own self-imprisoning defenses. God does not help those who help themselves; he helps those who realize their own need of help. God creates new life in those who acknowledge the destructive elements in their lives and let go of them. God speaks to those who are willing to listen to him. God is present to those who are open to receive him. The activities of God, to which men respond attitudinally, are activities within men which do not occur unless there is a receptive response. This is true even in the case of divine *creativity*, which has to be received, allowed, welcomed by the believer if it is to be recognized for what it is, and responded to with trust and gratitude. At an unconscious level, a man may reject divine creativity, not allowing it to sustain him against physical or psychical suicide.

The notion of "unconscious resistance" is very important in any reflections concerning receptivity. For example, a man may be resisting divine liberation, not allowing God to free him from bondage to the rigidities of his present character-structure, without being conscious of anything except some anxiety and some inhibitions in his responses to other people. The notion of the unconscious here has affinities with that in modern psychoanalysis, but it is also linked with a traditional theological conception of sin as an "ignoring" of God, a culpable "not-knowing" of what one in some way already knows, a form of paradoxical self-deception.[6] Thus I am bringing together psychoanalysis and theology when I speak of an "unconscious resistance" to divine activity within oneself.

IMPLICIT FAITH AND BASIC ATTITUDES

In so far as a man is conscious of a liberating process going on within himself, he is *not* resisting divine activity, whether consciously or unconsciously; as resistance decreases, liberation increases; as receptivity increases, liberation increases. Indeed, a reference to unconscious receptivity is involved in a theological interpretation of the phrase "in others" (line 5). God works in non-Christians, including many who do not understand what is going on in terms of inner receptivity to divine activity. They *are* inwardly receptive to divine activity and they are conscious of much that a genuinely receptive Christian experiences: an inner freedom, basic attitudes of trust, hope, gratitude, joy, and wonder, and a relatively unhibited love for themselves and their fellowmen. They also may express their

---

[6] Cf. Reinhold Niebuhr, *The Nature and Destiny of Man*, Vol. I, (London: Nisbet, 1941), chaps. 7–9. Cf. Evans, *Logic of Self-Involvement*, pp. 197–204. I realize that my essay here presupposes that there is some truth in psychoanalytic and theological ideas concerning unconscious states (or, at least, degrees of awareness receding from that which is fully explicit and acknowledged). If a critic rejects this presupposition he will also be rejecting much of the essay.

basic attitudes in art, as they create and celebrate beauty in the world —though without explicitly worshiping God. But they do not interpret any of this in terms of their own inner receptivity to divine activity. In the eyes of a Christian, such men have faith, but it is implicit rather than explicit.

The creed expresses an explicit faith. For Christians, the creed renders explicit the convictions which are implicit in the basic attitudes, whether these be in Christians or in non-Christians. Before we examine the notion of "implicit" faith, I should say more about the basic attitudes.[7] The word "basic" is commonly used for what I want to designate, but it may be misleading. By a "basic" attitude I do *not* mean an attitude which is, in the psychological history of an individual, the main *origin* of other attitudes; a child's trust in his parents would be "basic" in this genetic sense of the word, but not in mine. Rather, an attitude is "basic" when it is an attitude of the whole human being to the whole universe, when it is pervasive in scope, both temporal scope in the life of the man and spatial scope of application in the world. Consider, for example, basic trust. Temporally, it provides continuity and inner harmony for a life as a whole; it is like a musical ground bass[8] pervading the polyphony of man's transitory trusts and distrusts. Spatially, basic trust extends all-inclusively to whatever it is that pervades the whole cosmos, giving it some unity; often a man regards the trustworthiness of a particular person or persons as being somehow representative of the whole, in spite of the frequent untrustworthiness of this or that item in his natural and social environment. A basic attitude differs from other attitudes not only in its unrestricted, pervasive scope (internal and external) but also in its apparent lack of determinate content. Basic trust and basic hope, for example, may continue even when it seems that there is nothing in which to trust or for which to hope. Actually there *is* a content, but it can only be understood in relation to whatever goes on within a man when he is inwardly receptive. In the next section I shall try to describe this elusive and mysterious happening. Meanwhile, however, I shall add some reflections concerning basic trust and then turn to the notion of "implicit" faith.

[7] Concerning basic attitudes and religious convictions see Bibliography B.

[8] Cf. Dietrich Bonhoeffer, *Letters and Papers from Prison* (London: Fontana, 1959), pp. 99–100. For Bonhoeffer the "ground bass" is not an attitude, but God.

Concerning basic trust I spoke of the trustworthiness of a particular person being regarded as somehow representative of the whole. I seemed to be opting for the second of two alternatives considered by H. Richard Niebuhr:

> It remains questionable whether the self is led more to trust in the ultimate because it finds all the finite beings about it unreliable, or more because it is led by stages from trust in the near-at-hand to trust in the ultimate. Is it because all finite powers on which we have relied for value have failed us that we turn to the ultimate? or because we have seen traces of the structure of faith in the whole realm of being that we are led to confidence in Being simply considered?[9]

But as I went on, talking about "nothing in which to trust," I was closer to the first alternative, which finds finite things unreliable and therefore trusts only in the ultimate. Any adequate account of faith needs to include both alternatives, just as it needs to consider "aloneness" both as a rival to faith and as an ingredient in faith. My own reflections concerning the dialectic of trust begin with the conviction that the trustworthy God acts primarily through men. Hence he who cannot trust men cannot trust God, though he who trusts solely in men is evading human frailty and mortality. A trust in God which is not supported by a trust in men (oneself and others) is likely to be a flight from both, a self-deceptive clinging to a fantasy; but to focus an unlimited trust on limited men is both unwise and idolatrous. All this, however, is only the rudiments of a dialectic of trust; the subtleties and complexities are beyond the scope of this essay.

Concerning the notion of "implicit faith" the first thing to recognize is that expressions of attitude usually *imply* beliefs. To put it more strictly, the speaker who expresses an attitude usually, in saying what he does, implies that he has such-and-such beliefs. Such implication,[10] though not the same as an entailment between propositions, is a logical relation. Expressions of attitude are not the only speech-acts which carry implications. In saying, "The cat is on the mat," I *imply* that I believe that the cat is on the mat. In saying, "I

[9] H. Richard Niebuhr, *The Responsible Self,* p. 120.
[10] Concerning this kind of implication, see Evans, *Logic of Self-Involvement,* chap. 1. See also J. Cook Wilson (Bibliography B) concerning "presuppositions" of attitudes, which are similar to implications.

promise to come tomorrow," I *imply* that I intend to come tomorrow. Consider some expressions of attitude. In saying, "I trust John," I imply that I believe that John is trustworthy. In saying, "I am grateful to Mary," I imply that I believe Mary did something beneficial for me. In saying, "I trust whoever it is that is sending us the information," I imply that I believe that some person is sending us the information. In saying, "I am grateful to whoever it is that turned over my wallet to the police," I imply that I believe that someone turned over my wallet to the police. In all such cases the implication is clear and rigorous, since the words used to express the attitude make evident to us the belief that is implied. But if the attitude is a *basic* attitude, the implication need not be clear and rigorous. A basic attitude need not be already articulated so that the implied beliefs are obvious, or even explicitly indicated. Consider basic trust. Since it has unrestricted scope and no specific, exclusive focus, people can intelligibly and reasonably differ as to *whether* any corresponding belief is implied and, if one is implied, *what* that belief is. Earlier I used the expression "whatever it is that pervades the whole cosmos, giving it unity," for it is difficult to indicate what basic trust is without explicit reference to some positive belief, however vague, that is implied. It is difficult, but it is not impossible. A minimal believer can deny that any *positive* belief is implied, and a skeptical agnostic can deny that any belief at all is implied. The minimal believer holds that although his attitude implies a belief that there is a reality towards which he focuses his trust, this reality can only be described in a strictly negative way, as *not* being any describable particular, and *not* being restricted temporally or spatially. The skeptical agnostic holds that having such an indeterminate belief is indistinguishable from having no belief at all. The differences between minimal believer and skeptical agnostic, where both have basic trust, may or may not be clear and important. What I want to note here is that the Christian believer goes beyond both, though he concedes that there is much truth in their *via negativa.* He understands his own basic trust and that of others as implying a belief in God, "a trustworthy spiritual power present everywhere in the world," active within a man when he is inwardly receptive. (This religious conviction, when it renders explicit a basic trust, promotes and sustains that trust, though it cannot by itself create that trust.)

Thus if a Christian says to an agnostic who has basic trust, hope, gratitude, etc., "You have an implicit faith in God," he is offering an interpretation which the agnostic is logically free to reject.[11] The interpretation is not a wily maneuver in a Christian apologetic specially devised for outsiders; for the Christian his own explicit faith in God is logically implied by his own basic attitudes, which resemble those of the agnostic. Indeed, he is sometimes as agnostic as the agnostic, not interpreting his own experience in terms of his explicit faith. Sometimes, however, he does so interpret it. To be a Christian is, in part, to accept a way of talking and thinking such that basic attitudes are understood in a distinctive way. It is to accept and to bear witness to an interpretative framework concerning some "depth-experiences"[12] or "peak-experiences"[13] common to many men, including non-Christians. The most fundamental experience is understood in terms of receptivity to divine activity. To this we now turn. (Later we shall consider basic attitudes again, in relation to moral freedom.)

RECEPTIVITY TO DIVINE ACTIVITY

Christians believe that there is a kind of creative or providential activity in society, as in nature, which does not depend on human receptivity, whether conscious or unconscious. But a conviction concerning this activity presupposes, both for understanding and for acceptance, a receptivity to divine activity within oneself.

The creed indicates the pattern of receptivity in lines 11 and 12:

to proclaim Jesus, crucified and risen, our judge and our hope.
In life, in death, in life beyond death, God is with us.

11 We have seen that the agnostic need not express his basic attitude in words such that his speech-act implies that he has Christian theistic beliefs. There is another position open to him, which I should mention here. Even when a man expresses a particular trust, saying, "I trust John," his implication that he believes John is trustworthy is *"prima facie"* rather than "indefeasible" (see Evans, *Logic of Self-Involvement*, p. 47). That is, he can disclaim *what* he implies, though he cannot deny *that* he implies it: "I acknowledge that in saying, 'I trust John,' I imply that I believe John is trustworthy; but (and the word "but" is needed), I do not so believe—I'm irrational here, trusting the non-trustworthy." Similarly an agnostic might concede that in his expression of basic trust he implies that he believes in God, while denying that he does actually so believe, and acknowledging his irrationality: "I have a basic trust, and this implies that I believe in a trustworthy supreme being, but I don't."

12 Cf. Donald Evans, "Differences between Scientific and Religious Assertions," *Science and Religion*, ed. Ian Barbour (New York: Harper, 1967); Gregory Baum, *Faith and Doctrine* (New York: Newman Press, 1969), chap. 2.

13 Cf. Abraham H. Maslow, *Religions, Values and Peak-Experiences* (New York: Viking, 1970).

The believer is receptive to crucifixion-death and judgment, and to risen life and hope. First, he has to expose himself to judgment, to critical scrutiny, which shows him that part of himself which is destructive and enslaving, a part which has to be abandoned, to be left to die. In this shattering crisis of judgment, the Christian is enabled to acknowledge the truth about himself which has been exposed, and to let go of his old, defensive sources of security; for he allows the creative, liberating power of God to give him new life and hope. As old patterns of life are exposed and abandoned, it seems as if he were dying; he is "giving himself away." But the Christian finds that God confirms his sense of his own identity and reality, and gives him new creative energies. God liberates men from domination by destructive and enslaving elements within themselves so that men can become creative and free. God liberates men from despair and drabness, granting hope and wonder. In a world where death had seemed to represent an ultimate cosmic untrustworthiness, God frees men from anxiety, or enables them to bear it; whatever happens, even in death, God is with us, giving new life. The condition of divine activity within a man, however, is receptivity. This is not a matter of "earning" a divine reward, or "doing" something by oneself to which God then responds. It is a matter of letting go, permitting, allowing, yielding, not resisting, welcoming. It is not a willful exercise of one's existing powers or abilities. It is allowing oneself to be empowered, enabled to live creatively in basic trust, hope, gratitude, joy, and wonder.

Except for creative or providential activity in nature and in social processes and structures, divine activity is always in one sense "within" a man, for that is where the receptive man provides an "opening" for God. But the "route" or "medium" of the divine activity may be either within the man or outside him. God may inspire him, touching the unconscious depths of his personality directly; but God may also act via other people; God works "in others" (line 5) in a sense which we have not yet considered: he acts in others *for us and towards us.* He acts via the words and deeds which others, both Christian and non-Christian, address to us. Indeed, the way in which another man influences me when I am receptive to him is a basic analogy for the divine-human relation.

The underlying structure of the creed can now be summarized, as follows: Where the believer or any man is receptive, God is active within him, bringing about change. The change gives rise to attitudinal responses and practical responses. On the one hand, there are new attitudes which may be expressed in worship towards God. On the other hand, there are new activities towards men. This practical, man-ward aspect has two elements: witness and morality. The Christian bears witness to the divine activity in men—in Jesus, in fellow-Christians, in other men, and in himself. The idea of witnessing is suggested in line 11: "to proclaim Jesus . . ." Later we will examine the distinctive Christian witness to *Jesus,* but here we should note that the creed as a whole is meant not only as a prayerful communication to God but also as a proclamation to men, bearing witness to divine activity and human response. As we have seen, a Christian explicitly accepts and proclaims a theological interpretation of what is already going on in human beings. In this essay, I shall restrict the word "witness" to this explicit interpretative act, although Christians sometimes extend its meaning so as to refer to that to which the interpretation is applied, for example, exemplary moral activity. In this extended sense, a Christian "bears witness" to God when his own inner receptivity to divine activity is expressed in loving actions; but so also does a non-Christian. In the interests of clarity let us maintain a distinction between "witness" and "morality." And let us see how the creed introduces morality.

MORALITY AND THE CALL TO LOVE

Lines 9 and 10 are obviously moral in content:

> to love and serve others [and ourselves],
> to seek justice and resist evil

My reason for adding "and ourselves" was given earlier. The immediate question here is "How is moral activity related to the divine activities and human responses, both attitudinal and receptive?" In the creed, the link is provided by the word "calls." God calls us to be his church, and being his church involves not only worship (line 8) and witness (line 11) but also moral activity (lines 9 and 10). Note that the creed does not say, "He commands (orders, decrees, etc.) . . ." or "He designs (purposes, manufactures, etc.) . . ." The primary image of God in the creed is neither an absolute monarch, exercising unquestionable political or legal authority, nor a master craftsman, designing and making artifacts (including man) to fulfill his own purposes rather than theirs. Morality is here understood in a context of calling (*klesis*) rather than of law (*nomos*) or of purpose (*telos*).[14]

In its Christian theological setting, the word "call" has three distinguishable elements:

(a) call *together* (out of godless life into a community, an assembly, a church or "*ekklesia*," which means "the called ones");

(b) call *forth* (evoke, create, liberate, enable, empower);

(c) call *upon* (urge, exhort, appeal, challenge, ask to volunteer, direct).

Element (a), which stresses the communal nature of Christian faith and life, will be considered later, but I note two things here. One is that there is a tautology: "He calls us to be his church [i.e., his called ones]." The other is that the called ones are those who are receptive to divine activity, whether consciously (the "visible" church) or unconsciously (the "invisible" church). Elements (b) and (c) are more important here. God both enables and exhorts. For example, God's calling to love others is related both to a man's ability and to a man's obligation to love others, both to "can" and to "ought." But the "ought" comes not as an order but as an exhortation, a challenge, an appeal in relation to what a man now can do, empowered by God.

Let us consider (b) first, the element of enabling, empowering by God. We have already looked at the fundamental Christian convictions concerning this. Divine activity liberates the receptive man from that which impedes his growth towards whole-hearted, creative living. And divine activity is itself creative, not only confirming the man in his present existence but also providing new creative energies and powers. We saw how the attitudinal responses of trust, gratitude, hope, joy, and wonder are expressed in worship. Here, however, we should notice the relation between these attitudinal responses and moral activity. This has two aspects: self and others. We will consider them in turn.

[14] The notion of "*telos*" here, with its stress on the artisan-artifact analogy, is rather narrow—likewise in H. Richard Niebuhr, who has influenced me. Such a narrow notion is useful in typologies of moral views. But as I proceed, the reader will observe that *klesis* can be interpreted as a species of *telos*, in a less narrow sense of "*telos*": men are called to a mode of existence which *optimally fulfills* them, a life of responsive freedom, being liberated to love.

In some philosophies and theologies, a man's way of dealing with himself is not a moral matter. Instead, it is dealt with under "prudence" or "self-interest" in contrast with "moral duty" or "moral altruism." In the Christian theology which we are considering, however, the kind of love which a man should have for himself is similar to the kind of love which he should have for others. "Love your neighbor as yourself." What kind of love should he have for himself? In one way, he should *not* love himself. Receptivity to divine activity involves abandoning a false defensive self, giving it up. But receptivity also brings a new self-regard and self-acceptance, a new wholeheartedness in wanting and willing. Trust and hope and gratitude and wonder as basic attitudes toward God at work in one's natural and social environment are also basic attitudes toward God at work within *oneself*, liberating one's own energies and desires, creating abilities, confirming one in one's humanity. If a man is receptive to divine activity and has these basic attitudes toward God, he is given a new freedom to want or desire or "wish" wholeheartedly, without inhibition or internal division, for himself. "Doing the will of God" does not mean that every action must conform to what God commands or plans or wants. It does not even mean that every action must be a response to some specific activity of God in a particular situation. In much of life, what is called "God's will" is simply that *as receptive men we do what we want to do,* that we become fully aware of our deepest needs and impulses and act accordingly.[15] At the risk of being misleading, we can parody Sartre and say, "*Since* God exists, everything is permitted." That is, since God is active within the receptive man, enabling and encouraging him to be wholehearted, the man can want anything and act accordingly, except where this would impair his own receptivity, or contradict his love for others. There are various alternatives to such a wholehearted self-affirmation. A man may want and act in an alternating conformity and defiance towards other men, rarely wanting or acting on his own. He may do this toward an imaginary authoritarian god as well. Or he may try to repress and inhibit his wanting, trying to isolate himself from others and the world, trying to ignore such deep desires as the passion to give and receive affection. ("It is better *not*

[15] This is a central theme in William Lynch, *Images of Hope* (Baltimore: Helicon Press, 1965), esp. pp. 155–57; cf. Robert Johann, *Building the Human* (New York: Herder & Herder, 1968), pp. 145–47.

to have loved and lost. . . .") Or he may turn some one thing into
an absolute, an obsessive, compulsive cause to which he devotes
himself, ascribing unconditional value to it, making it his (idolatrous) ultimate concern. Or he may view himself "objectively," from
outside, as if he were a complex machine, to be manipulated and
controlled in a detached "value-free" way. These are all alternatives
to being receptive to God and thereby being able to want wholeheartedly for oneself. We must remember that being receptive to
God is not necessarily a conscious state. In so far as an avowed atheist or agnostic is able to love himself, to want wholeheartedly, accepting and respecting himself, this is for the Christian an indication
that he is unconsciously receptive to divine activity, which comes to
him via other men and via his own psychic depths without his recognizing it as such. On the other hand, a man may be consciously,
in his own eyes, a Christian, yet unconsciously resisting divine
activity. He may recite the creed, agreeing with what he takes to be
its meaning, while being unconsciously unreceptive, having only
superficial attitudinal responses of trust, hope, gratitude and wonder, and not allowing himself to be liberated to love himself.

God also enables a man to love *others*. We have seen that in
coming to love himself a man drops a variety of defenses against
self-knowledge and self-acceptance: the competitive/conforming pattern, repression and self-isolation, compulsive fanaticism, and "value-
free" detachment. These are all ways by which one also keeps *others*
at a distance, not being open to them as they really are. When the
defenses are dropped, in the new security provided by the divine
activity and the attitudinal responses, a man accepts and respects
not only his own fundamental needs and wants, but also those of
others. He becomes aware of these, forming a common humanity.
And since divine activity comes to him not only from within his own
psychic depths but also via love from others, and since divine activity
also comes to others via his own love as well as from within themselves, there is a mutuality of human love in all this, a giving and
receiving in which God acts. A man can not only be liberated by
God, acting through others; he can also be the medium through
which God liberates others. To love others is, in part, to desire and
foster their liberation to a life of wholehearted wanting and self-
affirmation. It is also, of course, to desire the satisfaction of their

ordinary needs, like one's own—whether these be for food or health or recognition.

We have been considering the divine call as an *enabling* call, a calling-*forth* by which a man is empowered to love himself and others. But it has not been possible to keep the element of enablement distinct from the element of calling-*upon*, of exhortation or challenge. What a man now *can* do is what he *ought* to do. Sometimes the divine challenge may be to love oneself better ("Stop letting yourself down, wallowing in your despair and self-hatred") and sometimes to love others better ("Give him some of the affection which he needs as much as you do"). In each case the divine challenge is to do what the divine activity enables him to do. The new freedom is a power which includes within itself a spur in a given direction; it combines ability and obligation, "can" and "ought"; it comes as both a gift and a directive, an enabling and an impelling. A man can resist the divine activity, rejecting the new freedom, but in so far as he accepts it, he does not receive an independent ability, which is henceforth at his own disposal to use at will in any way he chooses; he does not then have a willful freedom to love or not to love. The new freedom is a *responsive* freedom, which depends on continuous receptivity to God, and which is an ability with a built-in direction—to love oneself and others. Responsive freedom is dependent and directed freedom. A man who accepts the divine call allows himself to be changed, dependent on God's liberating activity within as he becomes a different person, loving people more deeply and spontaneously. A man is freed to love. This leaves many alternative options open for action, for he can love himself and others in many different ways. But some particular options—unloving ones—are ruled out. He is enabled and directed to love, but he is also disabled and diverted from non-love. The extent to which a man allows himself to be changed determines the extent to which he understands what the divine call is, and what love of self and others is. Love of self and others is not only an indication of (conscious or unconscious) love-receptivity towards God. As viewed by Christian theology, the three loves grow and are understood together.

LOVE AND JUSTICE

How does a man best express his love toward others? It is not only a "spiritual" matter of encouraging in others a receptivity towards

God by allowing himself to be a medium of divine activity towards
them. There is also, as we saw, a desire that their ordinary "material"
human needs be satisfied. One of the reasons for including the word
"serve" in the creed was to stress this less elusive but very important
expression of love for the whole person, who may be hungry or
thirsty or sick or lonely. But even this addition is not enough. People exist in society, with its impersonal institutions and power structures, where corporate injustice and corporate evil are major sources
of spiritual and material destructiveness in human life. Love is rationally expressed in *political* activity as well as in the intimacy of
personal or small-group activity. Obviously a change in the power
structure of society may be more effective than private charity in re-
ducing hunger. But the elusive "spiritual" realm is also affected by
the institutional framework of society. The extent to which a man is
able to "let go" of himself and be receptive to divine activity depends
in part on what the political and economic power structure has done
to him. Receptivity is deadened by the resignation and despair and
self-contempt which tend to be fostered among the oppressed in an
unjust society; it is also deadened in the oppressors by their arrogance
and callousness.

Seeking justice is thus one way of actively expressing love for
others, a love which the creed understands as arising from a gift and
directive received by individual men as God acts within them. Seeking justice also has another context in the creed. I noted a conviction
that God is somehow active among men in ways which do not depend on human receptivity, whether conscious or unconscious. This
activity in human society, like that in nature, is believed to be creative or providential, and the response to it is basic trust. But the
activity is also believed to be God's promotion of *justice* in the institutional relations which exist among men, a justice which stresses
the *liberation* of the oppressed. There is not only a divine liberation
in individuals but also a divine liberation in society, in politics.
When a man seeks to promote justice he is thus participating in a
divine activity which is already going on in society. This is a different
way of conceiving the promotion of justice. The idea of participation
in God's political activity is different from the idea of expressing in
society a capacity and a challenge to love which one has received
interiorly and individually from God. The two ideas are compatible,
but the idea of participation is secondary in the theology which forms

the background of the creed. A serious difficulty for the participation idea is that it assumes we can somehow *identify* what God is doing politically and then join in. Such an approach can reinforce political fanaticism. On the alternative approach, the decision as to how to express one's love politically is a matter to be decided alongside non-Christians by using one's political reason, which is admittedly fallible.

More generally, the theology of the creed leaves largely open the ways in which love is to be expressed, whether in personal or political contexts. This openness is encouraged, not because love is thought to be somehow by itself a way of knowing what one ought to do in each particular situation, but because love by itself is not enough. Other elements are needed, for example, moral reasoning. Indeed, whether a man has a loving or a defensive life-stance, whether he is receptive or unreceptive to divine activity within him, whatever his conscious religious or anti-religious ideas, he still has to *think* about what he ought to do in particular situations. He may make moral decisions with great deference to moral rules or with great concern to be "situational." The creed leaves open the issue as to the relative importance of rules and situations, an issue which faces men whether they accept the creed or reject it.

Love is an inner motivating state and stance, in which and from which a man affirms and accepts himself and others. Love by itself is not a self-sufficient faculty by which a man rightly perceives what he ought to do, or a sufficient criterion in accordance with which he rightly decides what he ought to do. Love may seem to be such a faculty because a man whom God has enabled and directed to love realizes in some situations that he has been rendered unable and unwilling to do such-and-such a wrong action; and because such a man knows that he recognizes and responds to human needs which without love he would not perceive. And love may seem to be such a moral criterion because a loving man may summarily refer to his own right actions as being "loving" and his own wrong actions as being "unloving." Since love has been a factor in many or all of his moral decisions, talk about love as a faculty or a criterion is not entirely misleading; but love is *a* faculty among others, *a* criterion among others. Other things have been involved: a man's basic attitudes, his world view, his moral framework, his empirical knowledge, and his rational deliberations.

We have seen that the creed does not dictate particular moral decisions, but it does set moral decision making in a distinctive context for Christians. Five aspects of this context can be distinguished, each one being important in our consideration of faith and moral freedom: responsive freedom to love, basic attitudes, world view, moral vocabulary, and Jesus as paradigm. We shall consider each briefly in turn.

RESPONSIVE FREEDOM TO LOVE

Earlier I noted the Christian conviction that the activity of God comes via the influence of other men and via a man's own unconscious depths. Receptivity to God involves a receptive stance towards other men and towards one's inmost self.

Toward other men, a man abandons the effort to control, to wield power and authority. The "willful" freedom which is appropriately exercised over his own skills, whether physical or intellectual, is not imposed on another man. Yet receptivity does not mean submissively accepting control imposed by another man. Instead one man allows another man to help him to change within, to become what he can not willfully *make* himself become.

Receptivity towards one's own unconscious depths also involves a "letting go" of willful control. A man allows himself to be changed by an upsurge of vital energies which impel him in unforeseen directions. When a man is open to the inner dynamism of the psyche he loses the security of the order which he has already imposed on his life. If he empties his mind of the orderly structures which he has concocted as his defense against inner chaos, and waits expectantly for something to happen, he somehow overcomes his anxiety, somehow trusts the forces within him in spite of the risk. The new freedom which then may come is a spontaneous, creative freedom. It is not like a skill which a man can methodically develop and then exercise at will. Such skills are important in human life, though I have classified them under "willful" freedom, which is a derogatory term; willful freedom is not intrinsically evil. What is evil is the extension of a willful-freedom approach to all aspects of life, instead of being receptive to other men and to one's unconscious drives.

Many kinds of receptivity to others and to one's own depths have been advocated by Christian theologians,[16] but there are three main points of agreement. The first is that the activity of God comes to the receptive man via the others and via a man's own depths. The second point is that the activity of God evokes in the receptive man some basic attitudes of trust, hope, joy, gratitude, and wonder which may be expressed in worship. In the next section we will consider the relation between these basic attitudes and moral decisions. The third point is that the activity of God is a call which enables and directs a man to love, that is, to affirm and accept himself and others. This theological conviction thus includes a built-in criterion concerning what is to be acknowledged as divine activity. Whatever enables and directs a man to love comes from God, whatever disables and diverts him from love does not.

But this is an oversimplification, which may even misleadingly suggest that receptivity is redundant in religion and morality. A man does not already know what love is, and hence what divine activity is, prior to being receptive; he understands only to the degree that he is receptive. Nor is love the only criterion. If a man has the basic attitudes which we have considered, this is also a sign that he has been receptive to activity which is divine. Nor is love a *clear* criterion, for it is an elusive inner state and stance which may be expressed in a variety of ways, and is only one factor in the moral decision making and behavior of the agent, as we have seen. In spite of all this, however, it is important to note that, for the Christian, love is a criterion for what counts as divine. Thus religious convictions partly depend on moral convictions (though in a dialectical and dynamic way which is remote from Kant's account of religion and morality).

In this essay, however, our main interest is in the dependence of morality on religion. Concerning this issue, the notions of receptivity and of responsive freedom are crucial. Receptivity to divine activity is understood by Christians mainly in terms of an analogy with receptivity to the activity of another agent. Even divine activity within the depths of the psyche is partly understood in this way. Traditional language concerning the "will of God" reflects this personalistic

[16] See Bibliographies C and D. Buber, May, and Farber are not, of course, Christian theologians. Buber, a Jew, has greatly influenced Christian theology. May shows the influence of Tillich's theology at crucial points. Farber's two realms of freedom are directly relevant to theology.

analogy. The language is easily misunderstood if the only notion of "will" that a man has is one which is linked with willful freedom rather than responsive freedom, for then the will of God is construed as an absolute instance of a power to use others for one's own purposes. To do the will of someone else, be he human or divine, is then to submit in what would otherwise be a power struggle. It is to evade responsibility for making up one's own mind concerning what one ought to do. Even if one believes that the other's will is wise and benevolent, one's own freedom of decision is lost. In contrast with this, if "will of God" is understood in the context of responsive freedom, no such implications follow when a man prays, "Thy will be done." The divine will is *like*, and acts *through*, the other person and the unconscious depths. These gratuitously free a man to love if he responds. The Christian believes that these liberating influences are the gifts of God. To respond to a man who says, "Thou," to me, and to respond to the creative *"eros"* within myself, is to respond to God. In each case there is a "letting go" of oneself, a self-abandonment, a kind of inaction. But it is not a resigned submission to the willful will of another. It is a discovery and a liberation and an expression of one's own true self. This occurs not when a man exercises his own willful freedom, but when he responds to divine activity.

I have indicated how the idea of responsive freedom which is presupposed in the creed is in conflict with authoritarian interpretations of the "will of God." But the idea is also in conflict with some secular views, in which each man tries to become for himself an authoritarian "god" over his own life. On these views the ideal is a maximal self-sufficiency and independence, a minimal dependence on other men for help or influence in becoming what one has decided to become. There is also an attempt to become independent of one's own unconscious urges by willfully imposing law and order on oneself—a law which one may discover by the use of reason (Kant),[17] or invent (Sartre). The ideal is *autonomy* and the enemy is *heteronomy*. Since these are the exhaustive alternatives on this view, there is no place for responsive freedom—or it is misinterpreted

[17] In general, it seems to me that Kant's conception of moral freedom in *Religion Within the Limits of Reason Alone* is in fundamental conflict with Christian faith and life. His conception renders the core of Christian theology either unintelligible or repugnant—i.e., convictions concerning a divine grace which enables and inspires and directs a man if he is responsive.

and classified as a form of heteronomy. As for theology, God is either identified with one's own self-imposed law (and thus with one's own will) or rejected as a heteronomous "Big Bopper," a threat to freedom and dignity, a deity whose "death" seems to provide a liberation. For the theology of the creed, this is a mistake. Nevertheless God *is* a threat to human autonomy. This is not because God is a heteronomous authority, demanding submission to his controlling will, but because he calls each man to "let go" of his attempt at autonomy and, instead, to become receptive to his call. The call comes in ways beyond a man's control, via other men and via his own hidden depths. Responsive freedom is a dependent and directed freedom, as we have seen. A man depends on the activity of God as he is enabled and directed to love.

As a postscript to this section I should note that although responsive freedom abandons the willful will, it fosters a *responsive will*, or, in psychoanalytic terms, an *ego-in-relation*. Although a man is *directed* to love, he also *directs* his love. Although he *receives* vital energy from others and from his own depths, this enables him to *affirm* himself. Although he is *dependent* on what is beyond his control, he is thereby strengthened to think and live *decisively*. Although he "gives himself *away*" to others, he discovers and nourishes a new *self* which deeply influences others. Other features of the responsive will might be mentioned, but here my purpose is merely to see that my contrast between willful freedom and responsive freedom does not give rise to the mistaken impression that responsive freedom eliminates or minimizes the will and the *ego*, granting reality only to what is received from others or from the unconscious forces of the *id*. Obviously the idea of a responsive will deserves a study which is far beyond the scope of this essay. In the next section we turn to a different topic, the relevance of basic attitudes to moral decisions.

BASIC ATTITUDES AND MORAL DECISIONS

In my exposition of the creed I tried to show how convictions concerning divine activity involve, as part of their meaning, various basic attitudes: trust, hope, joy, gratitude, and wonder. How are these attitudes related to the making of particular moral decisions? The relation is very complex and subtle, but I will sketch a few of its more prominent features:

(1) From a basic attitude no particular action follows in a particular situation. A basic attitude can be instantiated or expressed in a variety of ways in any one situation. "I have basic attitude A" and "The situation is such-and-such" do not entail "I ought to do X." Nor from "*He* has basic attitude A" plus "The situation is such-and-such" can I deduce "He will decide he ought to do X" or "He will do X."

(2) A basic attitude nevertheless contributes to the distinctive "style" or "timbre" or "spirit" of a particular action.

(3) A basic attitude is sometimes a necessary condition psychologically for seeing what ought to be done and/or for being able to do it. For example, a man who lacks basic hope may be unable to discern and utilize a way out of a difficult human predicament.

(4) The basic attitudes expressed in the creed are contrary to a variety of alternative attitudes, each of which is appropriately expressed in a *world view* which in turn is linked with a characteristic moral stance. I shall give three oversimplified examples of this. First, some attitudes are expressed in *conflictual* world views, in which humanity (and sometimes also the cosmos) is divided into two roughly equal and warring camps, one side being absolutely right and the other absolutely wrong. Such world views promote a *crusading* morality, in which the Bad Guys have no value or rights over against the fanatical, self-righteous zeal of the Good Guys. Second, some attitudes are expressed in *technological* world views, in which whatever is real can only be known objectively, with a scientific detachment which enables men to control and manipulate reality; there is no reality known responsively. Such world views are today often linked with a *quantitative utilitarianism,* a "social engineering" approach to political morality and a "behavior therapy" approach to private morality. Third, there are *alienated* world views, in which an individual or a small, closely related group feels strange in an alien environment; no meaning or value or vital activity can be discerned in nature or in the institutions and historical processes of society—only within oneself or one's group does one feel at home, if at all. Such world views encourage a *privatized,* opting-out morality, with no ecological or political dimensions.

(5) Basic Christian attitudes are expressed in a world view which has its own link with a characteristic moral stance. The world view is neither thoroughly conflictual nor technological nor alienated, though radically revised elements of each of these can be included.

First, there is a conflict between forces of good and forces of evil, but evil is always present to some extent on *both* sides of any human conflict. (When the committee included "resist evil" in the creed, the evil envisaged was both inside and outside the individual, inside and outside his group.) The goal is not total victory for one human side, but reconciliation (cf. line 4: "to reconcile and make new").

Second, a scientific, technological world view is subordinated to the awareness of realities which can only be known responsively; and a calculative form of utilitarianism, though appropriate as part of one's approach to many moral problems, is subordinated to the requirements of responsive freedom. As for an alienated world view, it has some measure of truth, for the supreme clue to reality is to be found within intimate personal relations or within the depths of the psyche, but God is also active in nature and in society; ecology and politics have great religious and moral significance; one ought not to "opt out."

None of the elements in a Christian world view dictate any particular answer to particular questions of moral decision: "What precisely is the loving thing to do in this situation?" But they do affect such decisions, in two distinguishable ways. On the one hand, the world view expresses basic attitudes, which themselves affect moral decisions, as I have noted. On the other hand, the dominant imagery in the world view provides an important element in the way the situation of moral choice is understood. To this we now turn.

"ONLOOKS" AND CHOICES

In *The Logic of Self-Involvement*[18] I introduced the term "onlook" to refer to the way of understanding situations which is typically expressed by "I look on x as y." For example:

I look on nature as a vindictive enemy.
I look on the state as my father.
I look on human history as a drama whose crisis is imminent.
I look on men as clever apes.
I look on the body as the prison of the spirit.

In this essay I will not repeat my analysis of onlooks, but I should note again their most significant features. If I look on x as y, I assume

18 Evans, *The Logic of Self-Involvement*; see entries under "onlook" in Index of Subjects.

that there is some obviously appropriate way of treating *y*, and I judge that *x* is sufficiently like *y* to be treated in similar ways. I am judging that *x* really is sufficiently like *y*, yet the judgment of sufficient likeness is inseparable from a decision concerning how to be or behave towards *x*. Deciding-that and deciding-to, "is" and "ought," come together.

A world view usually includes onlooks such as those cited above. These are obviously important in making moral decisions, though they do not by themselves determine what precisely ought to be done in a particular situation. An onlook applied to the situation will affect the selection of relevant facts and will provide within itself the move from "is" to "ought," though the precise specification of the "ought" will also be linked with the particular facts of the situation, and require further judgment and decision by the agent.

Christian Scripture and tradition include an abundance of onlooks. A few of these are mentioned or suggested in the creed. A Christian may look on his daily life as death-and-resurrection ("crucified and risen"), or as a journey ("in life, in death, in life beyond death") or as an active battle against evil ("resist evil") or as a courtroom drama culminating in a verdict ("our judge") or as a grateful offering of oneself as a gift in response to manifold gifts from God ("thanks be to God"). Many of these onlooks are also applied to the large-scale events of human history. There are also onlooks concerning nature (God's property, for which man is steward) and all other men (God's children, all in the same family with me).

Do onlooks reduce moral freedom? As Iris Murdoch has pointed out,[19] the answer to such a question depends on one's conception of moral freedom. Some philosophers hold what I shall label the "is-then-ought" conception: for maximal moral freedom the agent should first describe the facts of his situation in neutral and literal language which does not commit him morally in any way; then he makes his moral decision, "I ought to do X," applying or creating a (universalized) moral rule whose only value-word is "ought." No value-laden, non-literal description of the situation should bias the moral decision in any particular direction, though once the decision is made an onlook (parable, image, symbol, myth) may legitimately have a role in inspiring a man to act on his decision. Moral freedom

[19] "Vision and Choice in Morality," *Aristotelian Soc. Sup. Vol.* (1956); also in Ian Ramsey, ed., *Christian Ethics and Contemporary Philosophy.*

is a freedom to make up one's own mind as to what one ought to do, not being logically compelled to a moral conclusion because of an onlook which one has brought to the situation. For such philosophers, if any onlooks are to have a role, they should be selected and appraised in a purely moral judgment based on neutral literal facts. In contrast with this "is-then-ought" approach, some philosophers propose what I call "onlooks" and maintain that these are necessary in order to come to know what situations *really* are, and what I as an agent *really* am. They maintain that moral behavior should arise as an awareness of these realities, which are apprehended in value-laden imagery. Moral freedom is then not a matter of making up one's own connections between what is and what ought to be, but of having an imaginative moral insight which combines "is" and "ought": "*x* is sufficiently like *y* to be treated like *y*." To decide freely is to decide *knowingly*, aware of what one's situation really is, because one has viewed it correctly. To call for "moral" appraisal of all onlooks is a mistake, for the "is-then-ought" philosopher is wrongly assuming that a non-moral stance towards the world provides superior awareness of reality and wrongly assuming that moral rules accepted without onlooks are morally superior.

I have sketched two extreme and oversimplified positions in this controversy concerning onlooks and freedom. It seems to me that neither position in its pure form, excluding the other, is tenable; rather, a complex combination and revision of both is needed for both secular and religious morality. But it seems to me that Christian theology has a special stake in rejecting the first position as it stands and in claiming some truth for some version of the second. Christians differ concerning which onlooks in Scripture and tradition concerning God, world, and man are central and which are peripheral or discardable, but there is a general agreement that some of the onlooks provide a reliable way of coming to know what *really* is the case, while also involving broad commitments to *be* and to *behave*, thus bringing "is" and "ought" together. A Christian may think that a neutral, non-literal description of a situation is very helpful, and that sometimes it is all that is needed prior to moral decision; but as an all-inclusive stance in epistemology and morality it must be rejected as inadequate and misleading. It is part of Christian faith to look on situations, at least sometimes, in terms of Christian onlooks.

Is a man's freedom reduced by looking at a situation in terms of a Christian onlook? The answer to this question depends on one's conception of moral freedom, as we have seen. But there is an additional problem which should be mentioned. The reason for accepting a Christian onlook is partly that it has the *authority* of Scripture or tradition behind it. One does not simply make a private individual judgment, though many modern theologians would allow for a "testing" of the onlooks in one's own experience.[20] To be a Christian is to respond to a call to identify oneself with a community of the called, the church, in which one acknowledges some *authority* in ways which are relevant to morality—not only in the matter of onlooks, but also in one's basic moral vocabulary. There is no sharp line between onlooks and moral vocabulary, but the former differ in being more clearly non-literal and imaginative. To this moral vocabulary we now turn.

MORAL VOCABULARY AND AUTHORITY

A number of contemporary philosophers,[21] influenced by the later Wittgenstein or by one strand in natural-law ethics, have stressed the importance of the vocabulary of moral terms which a man brings to situations of choice. Moral reflection is not what the "is-then-ought" philosophers depict. It is not primarily a matter of first describing the facts of a situation and the probable consequences of alternative actions in a neutral, nonmoral way, and then deciding what one ought to do. Rather, it is primarily a matter of probing the *meaning* of a moral term in relation to a proposed course of action. One asks, for example, whether the action would or would not be an instance of "adultery." Concerning other actions one might ask whether they would or would not be instances of "slander," "torture," "breach of confidence," "stealing," "loving action," "temperance," "justice," "restitution," "direct killing of the innocent," "rudeness," "cowardice," "disloyalty to a friend," or "lying." Among contemporary moral agents we hear such questions as these: "Would this be 'personally authentic' or 'counter-revolutionary,' or 'racist' or 'authoritarian' or 'sexually repressive'?" Opponents of this form of

---

[20] See John Baillie, *The Idea of Revelation in Recent Thought* (New York: Columbia Univ. Press, 1956), pp. 36–40, criticizing Austin Farrer, *The Glass of Vision* (London: Westminster, 1948).

[21] See Bibliography E.

moral reflection do not deny that it occurs, but they prefer a form in which such value-laden terms are quickly replaced by neutral ones, or avoided entirely. Suppose a man takes a loaf of bread from a bakery, without permission or payment, for his starving family. Instead of asking whether this counts as "stealing" one asks, directly, whether it is morally right, whether he ought to have done it. If a woman becomes pregnant by a concentration camp guard as the way of being discharged to return to her husband and children, don't ask "Was this adultery?" but ask, directly, "Ought she to have done it?"

In this controversy between moral-vocabulary theorists and "is-then-ought" theorists, as in the controversy between onlook theorists and "is-then-ought" theorists, I find it impossible to adopt one position to the total exclusion of the other. But the moral-vocabulary approach does have special relevance and importance for Christian morality, so we shall consider it carefully. The first step is to note that philosophers who emphasize moral vocabulary differ among themselves concerning three crucial issues: stringency, universality, and specificity. Concerning *stringency*, three positions can be distinguished concerning what follows from, say, "X is an instance of *lying*": (i) X is morally wrong (there is an exceptionless moral rule prohibiting lying); (ii) X is morally wrong unless there is a strong moral reason for overriding the fact that X is lying (there is a moral rule prohibiting lying, but it is not exceptionless); (iii) one morally relevant consideration concerning X, a consideration which cannot, morally, be omitted, is that X is lying. Concerning *universality*, one position is that for all men (or alternatively, for all genuinely moral agents), there is a basic common moral vocabulary. The other position is that there is a variety of moral vocabularies, each moral framework being held and practiced by a different group, even within the same society; a man can decide to identify himself with one group and its moral framework rather than with another, but once he has done so he does not then decide whether or not it matters that a term within that framework applies to what he plans to do; by identifying himself with the group he has at the very least committed himself to position (iii) concerning stringency. Concerning *specificity*, there are differences as to whether only such broad terms as "loving," "unjust," or "authentic" belong in the moral vocabulary or whether more specific terms such as "lying," "stealing," or "adultery" belong as well. Also, if the latter do belong, there are differences as to whether an exceptionless-rule position applies only to the broad terms or also to the specific terms.

I have sketched some of the issues in recent discussions of moral-vocabulary ethics since they are very relevant to the issue of religious faith and moral freedom. Some conservative forms of Christian theology have suppressed moral freedom, claiming (a) *unquestionable* divine *authority* for (b) a *traditional* set of moral terms (c) applied in rules which are *exceptionless* even though fairly specific and (d) applied in rules which are allegedly mandatory for *all* human agents, both inside and outside the Christian community. This eliminates the possibility of individual human decision concerning the following: (a) whether the moral framework should be tested, questioned, or even scrutinized in relation to human experience and moral insight; (b) whether new moral terms should be permitted alongside or replacing the ancient ones; (c) whether the terms, including the specific ones, should all be applied with exceptionless stringency; and (d) whether or not to identify oneself with this or that moral community. Such an inherently conservative and authoritarian morality is obviously contrary to moral freedom. That such a morality has existed and still exists is obvious. Alasdair MacIntyre[22] has even argued that theism requires some such morality for its very existence. The decline of theistic faith is as much the effect as the cause of the decline of such a morality: "If everything is permitted, God does not exist." It seems to me that MacIntyre is correct in so far as he is showing a logical and sociological connection between authoritarian morality and an authoritarian form of theism. Each reinforces and complements the other.

But what about the religious and moral convictions expressed in the United Church creed? To say this creed is to identify oneself with a Christian community which has a moral vocabulary: "love," "serve," "justice," "evil," "reconcile," "make new." Two other terms are suggested by the creed: "sacrifice" and "courage." The phrase "crucified and risen," which I have interpreted in relation to the dynamics of inner receptivity, also has a moral connotation; it suggests a willingness to sacrifice, to give up what one wants, even life itself, for the sake of others. Earlier I noted that courage (a tradi-

[22] See Bibliography E; cf. Peter Winch, "Authority," in *Aristotelian Soc. Sup. Vol.* (1958).

tional moral virtue) is implied in line 12. We could also add two terms which the committee reluctantly failed to include: "forgive" and "peace." Some influential modern theologians would want to add "humanize" or "responsible" or "revolutionary." If we include all these terms we have a basic moral vocabulary which some non-Christians may share[23] with Christians, even if some of the Christian connotations for terms are included, for example, "justice" as a partiality for the poor and the powerless, and "evil" as a real power operative in institutional structures and within individuals. Is this a freedom-suppressing moral framework? Let us consider it in relation to the points considered above: (a) The moral framework is not placed beyond testing or scrutiny. (b) There is no prohibition of new moral terms to modify or replace traditional ones. (c) The terms are very broad, so that even if they are interpreted for use in exceptionless moral rules, plenty of scope for decision in application remains—what counts as "love," "service," "justice," "evil," etc. (d) A man is free to reject the moral framework of the creed and to accept instead that of some other community; a common moral vocabulary for all men has yet to be created.

If a man accepts the broad moral framework he thereby accepts a structure which will enter his moral reflections and affect his moral decisions. As we have seen, to accept the moral framework of a group is to relinquish decision making as to whether or not it matters morally that a term within that framework applies to what one plans to do.[24] This is a restriction on freedom if a man's ideal of freedom in moral deliberation and decision is as follows: first, he describes his situation in non-evaluative terms, deciding for himself what facts count as morally relevant; then he decides what he ought to do. If he is to follow this procedure he cannot bring to the situation a moral vocabulary which, by virtue of the public meaning of the words within a group, *determines* that some of the facts are morally relevant. He himself must decide everything except the facts if he is to be free. Some critics of this position have argued that it is un-

[23] Elsewhere I have explored one possibility of working towards a common moral vocabulary—a common set of very general moral principles for decisions in international relations; see Donald Evans, ed., *Peace, Power and Protest* (Toronto: Ryerson Press, 1967), chaps. 1, 2.

[24] If changes of moral vocabulary are allowed by the group, a man's thought and action may gradually contribute to gradual changes in the moral framework; I am ignoring this complication here.

intelligible: a man can only decide some moral matters if others are for him *not* open to his own decision.[25] Whether or not this criticism is correct, my own claim here is clearly warranted: an "is-then-ought" conception of freedom in moral reflection is not the only possible position. A man may be free in that he has freely accepted a moral framework which then limits his freedom of decision as to what counts as morally relevant.

But the creed involves a further complication. Although a man who rejects all the explicit religious convictions in the creed is free to decide for or against the creed's moral framework, a man who accepts the explicit religious convictions does not regard himself as being free in this respect. The appropriate practical response to the divine activity is action in accordance with the broad moral framework. Divine activity does not direct a man to act against that framework; whatever influence seems to be so directing a man is not divine. Thus morality becomes a criterion in theology. Yet theology is not thereby made redundant to morality, for a man does not *adequately* understand by his own unaided powers what the terms mean ("love," "service," etc.). He grows in understanding as he responds to the divine activity and as he interprets that activity in accord with the religious convictions of the creed. In accepting the creed he is identifying himself with a community in which the moral convictions are connected with religious convictions. Both sets of conviction have an authority for him within the Christian community, in which he says both, *"We believe . . ."* and, *"He calls us to be his church . . . to love and serve others. . . ."* This is different from the situation of a man who adopts roughly the same moral framework but without the religious convictions to reinforce its authority. Nevertheless the Christian's religious convictions need not be regarded as providing additional restrictions on his moral freedom. Rather, the conscious response to divine activity within, the basic attitudes, and the onlooks of a Christian world view all enhance his freedom—as he understands freedom.

To summarize: the relation between religious convictions and moral convictions in the creed enhances moral freedom if freedom is primarily responsive rather than willful and if freedom is promoted more by understanding a situation in terms of onlooks and

[25] Phillips and Mounce, Bibliography E, pp. 12, 17, 18.

an accepted moral vocabulary than by understanding it in the strictly literal and non-evaluative terms of "is-then-ought" philosophy. The creed's religious convictions are a threat to moral freedom only if maximal freedom means being minimally influenced by other agents—their actions towards oneself, their onlooks and their moral vocabulary—in making moral decisions; and if it means being minimally dependent on other agents for help in becoming what one ought to become.

There remains one more element in the creed to consider: Christian convictions concerning *Jesus*.

JESUS, FAITH, AND MORALITY

Although the creed stresses the importance of Jesus and is very rich in its allusions to him, there is little that raises issues concerning moral freedom in addition to those we have already considered. So I shall only note very briefly some of the main convictions.[26]

Jesus, "the true Man," is the paradigm of human faith and morality. His life and teaching provide the norm for the faith and morality expressed in the creed and outlined in my exposition: inner receptivity to divine activity; basic attitudes of trust, hope, joy, wonder, and gratitude; God enabling and directing man to love. Jesus is the perfect man, the ideal of responsiveness both to God and to other men.

Jesus is also divine. The creed indicates two ways in which this is so. First, Jesus is the unique locus of divine activity, unique in that there is an identity between his activities and God's. "God . . . has come in the true Man, Jesus, to reconcile and make new." This echoes II Corinthians 5:19, "God was in Christ, reconciling the world to himself." The identity continues in the present, for the Christian understands the divine activity within himself, to which he is receptive, as being identical with that of the risen Christ. Second, worshipful attitudes which are appropriate towards God are also appropriate towards the risen Jesus, "our judge and our hope." Jesus, like God, is the focus of basic hope, and also of basic trust, joy, wonder, and gratitude.

The Christian's faith is directed at Jesus in several different ways. First, the faith of Jesus as norm and example of faith is a guide and an encouragement to the Christian, whose own faith is defective and weak; Jesus not only exemplifies faith, he also evokes it. Second,

[26] See Bibliography F for the theological background of my exposition.

the divine activity in Jesus is believed to be representative of all divine activity, and so the warrant for a Christian's basic trust, hope, etc., in spite of all that tends to challenge and undermine them. Since God is not only like Jesus but was and is uniquely active in Jesus, faith is not a blind step into total darkness, and faith is not based solely on one's own inner states, though these are necessary. Third, the Christian attributes implicit faith, whether in himself or in non-Christians, to the activity of the risen Christ, which is identical with God's activity. Fourth, the Christian finds in Jesus a focal interpretative symbol for understanding divine activity in nature, history, and society. For example, a Christian world view takes the original event of death-and-resurrection as a symbol or onlook which is in principle applicable to everything. Some theologies speak of the "cosmic Christ."

How is Jesus more directly related to the making of moral decisions? There are four ways, which we have already considered without explicit reference to Jesus, in the previous four sections of the essay. First, Jesus' love provides the test for what is to count as love. Second, Jesus' basic attitudes provide the paradigm for basic trust, hope, etc. Third, Jesus' parables, whether taught or enacted (e.g., washing the disciples' feet) provide onlooks for situations of moral choice. Fourth, Jesus' moral teaching provides much of the moral vocabulary for the Christian community. Of these four points it seems to me that only the first raises a further issue concerning moral freedom. In accepting Jesus as moral paradigm, accepting Jesus' love as the criterion for love, Jesus' life as the ideal life, the Christian is not merely allowing responsive freedom in relation to another man and he is not merely identifying himself with a group, its onlooks, and moral vocabulary. He is modeling himself on another man. Does this reduce moral freedom? If when Smith models himself on Jones, this means trying to turn himself into a duplicate of Jones, Smith's moral freedom *is* reduced; he is no longer free to be and to become himself. But there are other ways in which Smith can model himself on Jones, ways of "identifying" with Jones, which can be *liberating*. Instead of slavish literal imitation, Smith adapts Jones's style of life to his own needs and capacities and situation. Indeed, identification with another person is an important and perhaps necessary step in the process of human maturation. When a Christian accepts Jesus as moral paradigm, some such liberating process occurs, or ought to occur. I am sure that is what the creed means when it expresses commitment to "the true Man, Jesus." Many theological and psychological subtleties would need to be explored in a thorough study of the idea of Jesus as moral paradigm. I refer the reader to J. M. Gustafson and R. S. Lee concerning this matter.[27]

Before I conclude this essay, I shall set forth the over-all structure of my presentation in schematic form:

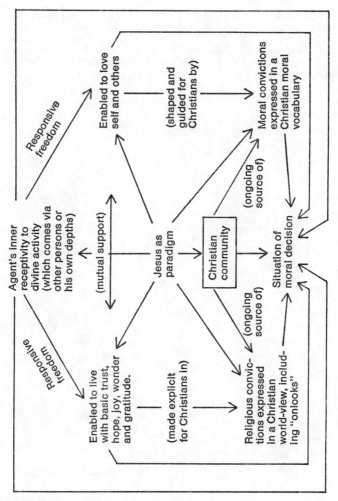

[27] See Bibliography F.

CONCLUSION

The main conclusion of this essay can be stated quite simply: the religious convictions of the creed are connected with the moral convictions and with the making of moral decisions in a variety of ways which enhance rather than restrict moral freedom—unless freedom is understood in "willful" or "is-then-ought" ways.[28]

[28] Earlier drafts of this essay were revised in response to illuminating criticisms by Howard Adelman, James Beckman, David Burrell, James Gustafson, Stan Hauerwas, Phillip McKenna, Graeme Nicholson, Millard Schumaker, and Wilfred Cantwell Smith. Where the essay has a psychoanalytic dimension, it depends largely on my experience of "communication therapy" in Therafields, a Toronto community.

BIBLIOGRAPHIES

A: GENERAL THEOLOGICAL BACKGROUND

H. Richard Niebuhr, *The Responsible Self* (New York: Harper, 1963).

Gregory Baum, *Man Becoming* (New York: Herder & Herder, 1970); and *Faith and Doctrine* (New York: Newman Press, 1969), chap. 2; cf. Donald Evans "Gregory Baum's Theology of Liberation", *Studies in Religion*, I, 1 (Univ. of Toronto Press, 1971); cf. James Burtchaell, "The Purpose of the Church", *Commonweal* (September 4, 1970).

Sam Keen, *Apology for Wonder* (New York: Harper, 1969), chaps. 5–7; and *To a Dancing God* (New York: Harper, 1970).

William Lynch, *Images of Hope* (Baltimore: Helicon Press, 1965).

Paul Tillich, *The Courage to Be* (London: Nisbet, 1952); *Dynamics of Faith* (New York: Harper, 1957); *Morality and Beyond* (London: Routledge, 1964).

James M. Gustafson, *Christ and the Moral Life* (New York: Harper, 1968), esp. chaps. 1, 2, 7.

Martin Buber, *I and Thou* (New York: Scribner, 1958); cf. Maurice Friedman, *Martin Buber and the Life of Dialogue* (New York: Harper, 1955), chaps. 11, 22.

B: BASIC ATTITUDES

J. Cook Wilson, *Statement and Inference*, I (Oxford: Clarendon Press, 1926), sections 565–81; also in Ninian Smart, ed., *His-*

torical Selections in the Philosophy of Religion (London: SCM Press, 1962); cf. John Baillie, *Our Knowledge of God* (London: Oxford, 1939), sections 5, 6, 20.

Gabriel Marcel, *Homo Viator* (New York: Harper, 1962), pp. 7–67.

Peter Berger, *A Rumor of Angels* (New York: Doubleday, 1969), pp. 61–71.

Sam Keen, *Apology for Wonder* (New York: Harper, 1969), chap. 7.

James M. Gustafson, "The conditions for hope: reflections on human experience," *Continuum*, 7, 4 (Winter 1970).

L. Wittgenstein, "A Lecture on Ethics," *Philosophical Review*, 74 (1965).

Donald Evans, "Ian Ramsey on Talk about God," *Religious Studies* (June and October 1971).

Schubert Ogden, *The Reality of God and Other Essays* (New York: Harper, 1964), pp. 27–43; "The Task of Philosophical Theology," *Future of Philosophical Theology*, ed. Robert A. Evans (Philadelphia: Westminster Press, 1971).

Paul Tillich, *The Courage to Be* (London: Nisbet, 1952), chaps. 2, 6.

Gregory Baum, "The Baptism of Desire," *The Ecumenist* (May–June 1964).

Friedrich Schleiermacher, *The Christian Faith* (Edinburgh: Clark, 1928), sections 3–5, 15–17, 29–30 (similar theological method, different basic attitude).

C: RECEPTIVITY TO DEPTHS WITHIN SELF

Rollo May, *Love and Will* (New York: Norton, 1969), chaps. 5–8.

Leslie H. Farber, *The Ways of the Will* (New York: Harper, 1968), chaps. 1, 2, 5.

James N. Lapsley, ed., *The Concept of Willing* (New York: Abingdon, 1967), pp. 195–206, which are by Lapsley.

Dorothy Emmet "On 'doing what is right' and 'doing the will of God,'" *Religious Studies*, Vol. 3, no. 1 (October 1967); and "Religion and the Social Anthropology of Religion," *Theoria to Theory*, Vol. 3, no. 1 (October 1968).

Evelyn Underhill, *Mysticism*, rev. ed. (London: Methuen, 1930), chap. 7.

See also Bibliography A: Keen, Lynch, Tillich.

D: RECEPTIVITY TO OTHER PERSONS

H. Richard Niebuhr, *The Responsible Self*, chap. 1.
H. H. Farmer, *The World and God* (London: Nisbet, 1935), chap. 1.
Gabriel Marcel, *Homo Viator* (New York: Harper, 1962), pp. 7–67.
See also Bibliography A: Baum, Lynch, Buber.

E: PHILOSOPHERS ON MORAL VOCABULARY

Eric D'Arcy, *Human Acts* (Oxford: Clarendon Press, 1963), chap. 1.
Julius Kovesi, *Moral Notions* (London: Routledge, 1967).
Herbert McCabe, *What Is Ethics All About?* (Washington: Corpus, 1969), chap. 3.
D. Z. Phillips and H. O. Mounce, *Moral Practices* (London: Routledge, 1969).
Alasdair MacIntyre, "Atheism and Morals," in Alasdair MacIntyre and Paul Ricoeur, *The Religious Significance of Atheism* (New York: Columbia Univ. Press, 1969); also *Secularization and Moral Change* (London: Oxford Univ. Press, 1967), pp. 50–53.
Philippa Foot, "Moral Beliefs," *Proc. Aristotelian Soc.*, LIX (1958); also "Goodness and Choice," *Aristotelian Soc. Sup.*, Vol. XXXV (1961).
Donald Evans, "Love, Situations and Rules," *Norm and Context in Christian Ethics*, eds. Gene H. Outka and Paul Ramsey (New York: Scribner, 1968), esp. pp. 383–92.
Paul Ramsey, "The Case of the Curious Exception," *Norm and Context in Christian Ethics.*
Donald Evans, "Paul Ramsey on Exceptionless Moral Rules," *American Journal of Jursiprudence* (Notre Dame Law School, 1971).

F: JESUS, FAITH, AND MORALITY

Donald M. Baillie, *God Was in Christ* (New York: Scribner, 1948), chaps. 1, 2, 3, 5.

Van A. Harvey, *The Historian and the Believer* (New York: Macmillan, 1966), chaps. 6, 7, 8.

Norman Perrin, *Rediscovering the Teaching of Jesus* (New York: Harper, 1967), chap. 3.

James M. Gustafson, previous works cited and "The Relation of the Gospels to the Moral Life," *Jesus and Man's Hope II*, Donald Miller and D. Y. Hadidiau, eds. (A Perspective Book, Pittsburgh Theological Seminary, Pittsburgh, Pa.).

H. Richard Niebuhr, *The Responsible Self*, pp. 149–78.

R. S. Lee, *Freud and Christianity* (London: J. Clarke, 1948), chaps. 11, 12.

Keith Ward, *Ethics and Christianity* (London: G. Allen, 1970), chaps. 5–6, 9–13.

THE SIMPLE BELIEVER[1]

R. M. Hare

I

I must start with an apology. The philosophy of religion, to which these lectures will be devoted, is not a speciality of mine. It is, indeed, a subject which fastidious philosophers do not like to touch. This is not merely because it is a confused subject—that could be said of other branches of philosophy—but because the whole atmosphere of the subject is such as to put a premium on unclarity of thought. The confusion is not of philosophical origin; nor do the problems with which I shall be dealing belong to the class sometimes confidently called "pseudo-problems." They have been generated, rather, by the quite genuine perplexities of those who want to call themselves Christians, and yet cannot bring themselves to believe what Christians are supposed to have to believe. These people have been appealing for help to the theologians for a long time; they have received a great deal of comfort but not much clarification—because the issues have not been faced in the clear light which only a thorough understanding of the concepts involved could give. The philosophers, for their part—those few of us who have cared to soil our fingers—have contributed, perhaps, a little towards their understanding; but our failure to make any decisive progress has prompted in some the

Copyright © 1973 by R. M. Hare.
[1] The first and third of the three Nathaniel Taylor lectures delivered at the Yale Divinity School in December 1968. The kindness and encouragement I received there are largely responsible for my abandoning my resolution not to publish these thoughts. I am still, however, too dissatisfied with the second lecture to print it.

thought that the concepts are inherently confused and can never be clarified. For the rest—the non-philosophers—hardly anybody has any interest in achieving clarity; it would be too harsh and unpleasant. And such philosophical work as has been done on these questions has not (or so it would appear) made much impact on those who are most troubled by them.

There thus remains a cleavage between philosophically sophisticated people who have (or think they have) some understanding of the issues, but do not care very much about them, and the unsophisticated, who care (or think they care) very much, but are in a complete muddle. This may explain what usually happens—at any rate in England—on the rare occasions on which these matters are discussed at professional meetings of philosophers. There are three main parties to these discussions—if we exclude those who either because of lack of interest, or because of lack of confidence that they know their own mind, stay silent. The first party consists of the orthodox Christians; the second of the downright no-nonsense atheists. The third party is made up of those courageous people who, like Professors Braithwaite and van Buren, want to be Christians and yet to hold a faith which is defensible against the attacks of the philosophically well-armed atheist. A member of this third party produces some version of the Christian faith which he thinks is both defensible and genuinely Christian; the other two parties then at once form a holy-unholy alliance and have no difficulty at all in making him look silly. "How could you possibly pretend," they say in chorus, "that you are a Christian, when all you believe is *that?*"

When I refer to these three parties, I do not mean to imply that there are no other voices which are or ought to be heard, but only that these are the loudest. The predominant impression that one receives from any gathering in which the orthodox and the atheists are present and speak their minds is that they are united in ridiculing my third party, whom I shall call the Christian empiricists. As I shall be saying again later, the reason why the atheists ally themselves with the orthodox in this way is that they have an obvious interest in making the Christian religion as absurd a faith as possible, in order the easier to justify their rejection of it. The reason why the orthodox ally themselves with the atheists is harder to see. It would be merely mischievous to suggest that they have taken the old Greek proverb "Everything noble is difficult" and, by a familiar logical fallacy, converted it into the proposition that everything difficult is noble, and think that because it is so very difficult to believe the things which they say that Christians have to believe, peculiar merit is acquired by those few elect who manage to do it. Though some do seem to believe *quia absurdum*, a more likely explanation in most cases is that they do not believe *quia* anything at all. This is not to say that they lack arguments to defend their beliefs once acquired.

It is to be hoped that the orthodox Christians, who have, with the help of the atheists, thus easily made fools of their supposedly Christian brethren, are not so pleased with their victory as to ignore its consequences. It can safely be predicted that, if the third party were finally and decisively eliminated, and the orthodox and atheists were left to fight out the clear issue remaining between them, the orthodox would find themselves in a tactically much less defensible position than that in which they now are. For, once the issues are seen clearly—once, that is, the condition is firmly laid down that in order to be called a Christian one has to believe all the things that the orthodox say they believe, and believe them literally—then nobody with any claim to rationality is going to say that he is a Christian.

The orthodox appear so strong a party only because they have the support of a very large number of Christians—probably the huge majority of educated ones—who have so far been able to avoid the issue just because it has not been put to them clearly. Theologians have produced a succession of devices for concealing from Christians the starkness of the choice which, if the orthodox and the atheists are right, they have to make. Even the orthodox will often make use of these evasions if hard pressed. The reason why the vast majority of educated Christians are people who have evaded the issue is that those educated people who have not evaded it have ceased to be Christians. If there is no third alternative besides orthodoxy, strictly and clearly interpreted, and atheism, it is likely that most thinking people will choose the latter.

I now come back to the apology which I said I had to make. I must ask your indulgence if I say something that I have said before on many occasions. The position has been as I have just described it for at least twenty years. At the beginning of this period I wrote a little piece on the subject which has become so notorious that I have many times wished that I had never published it. I wrote it within the compass of twenty-four hours because I liked the face of the man who wanted it for his new magazine, and was too good-natured to refuse. This was the article in which the word "blik" first got into the literature. Very shortly after that I wrote a longer article which I never published, but, after reading it to one or two societies, put it away in a file and forgot about it. Then, much later (in fact only a few years ago) all the fuss started about God being dead. Thinking that my old paper might be of interest, I took it out of its box and was astonished to find that it had suddenly become topical. Indeed, I thought that if the issues in that old controversy had been properly understood, much that has since been written would either not have been written at all, or would have been written more clearly. Since I myself have never been able to state the issues any more clearly than I did in that paper, I made it the basis of a lecture I gave in Oxford as part of one of my courses as Wilde Lecturer, and added two more on related subjects. It is a revised version of these three lectures that I shall be giving you here at Yale; the other five lectures in the first Wilde series, which was called "The Relations between Religion and Morality" have been diverted into other channels.

I am going to introduce you to the situation, as I see it, by telling you a story. There was once a Simple Believer. If you asked him, "Is there a God?" he would reply, "Of course." And if you then asked him, "What is he like?" he would say "He is something like a man (for it says in the Bible that God made man in his own image); and he lives in Heaven, which is a place far up in the sky; and he made both Heaven and Earth in six days in the year 4004 B.C., as you can find by doing some calculations based on the information given in the Bible. He made it in the manner described in Genesis; and he continues to rule the world by causing things to happen in it according to his will; and especially he causes things to happen which are for the good of those that believe in him; for God is loving, etc."

This sort of belief satisfied the Simple Believer until, at an impressionable age, he met another person, whom I will call the Simple Unbeliever. The Simple Unbeliever said, "Surely you don't believe *that* any more? We know now, for it has been established by science, that a being like a man couldn't possibly live up in the sky." (The conversation took place before the days of space travel.) "If you know any science at all, you know that he couldn't survive for a moment;

and in any case, if he did exist on some star, how could he intervene from that distance in our affairs? And as for him making the world in 4004 B.C., we know that the world is much older than that. And he couldn't intervene in the world, since we know—for science tells us—that the world proceeds on its way by immutable scientific laws; so how could he make any difference to what happens in the world?"

The Simple Believer's faith was considerably shaken by all this; for he found on reflection and inquiry that most people believe that what science says, is true, and in his heart of hearts he believed so too. The picture that the Simple Unbeliever gave of the findings of science was, indeed, crude and oversimplified; but that could be remedied without altering its impact upon his former simple beliefs. Fortunately, while he was in this state of incipient doubt, he met a third person, whom I will call the Sophisticated Believer. The Sophisticated Believer set the Simple Believer's doubts at rest by saying, "You have been taking the Bible too literally. Of course, if you have these 'literal and low conceptions of sacred beings,'[2] your beliefs won't stand up against the latest scientific discoveries. If you want to survive the advance of empirical science, you must at all costs *keep out of the way* of the scientists; and this isn't at all difficult. Of course God (God the Father, that is) isn't like a man to look at—the Thirty-nine Articles say that he has neither body, parts, nor passions. And of course Genesis is only legend, although it is of deep symbolical significance. The Creation certainly wasn't like it says in Genesis, and there's no need to believe that it happened in 4004 B.C. You have been taking much too literally the statement that God made the world in six days—'day' here is to be interpreted as meaning an epoch of very great but unspecified length, so that the Genesis story (so far as chronology goes, at any rate) can be reconciled with whatever science discovers about the age of the universe. This is an example of what I mean by 'keeping out of the scientists' way'; you must be careful to say nothing that they can ever disprove. And in the same way to say that God rules the world is not to say anything that science would contradict. Aren't the laws of science the very best evidence that the world is ordered by a mastermind? For everywhere we turn we see things happening, not just by chance and haphazard, but according to the most precise laws. In believ-

---

[2] The phrase is taken from Hogarth's inscription beneath his print "Enthusiasm Delineated."

ing in God, you aren't asked to believe anything about the world except what common sense and science (which is organized common sense) would allow. Religion is not about material things but about the things of the spirit."

This sort of comfort satisfied the Simple Believer, until he met the Simple Unbeliever again. This time the Simple Unbeliever had been reading Freud, and all about Pavlov's dogs. When he heard what the Sophisticated Believer had said about the things of the spirit, he exclaimed, "But that won't do either now, you know. The distinction between the spiritual and the material is nothing but what Ryle calls a 'Cartesian myth.'[3] Scientists don't only find out the laws that govern what you call the material world, but also those that govern what you call the things of the spirit. We can often give very good explanations of people's religious beliefs, for example, in terms of their early upbringing. No doubt if I knew more about *your* early upbringing I could account for your religious beliefs. The phenomena which you call spiritual and those which you call material are all just phenomena; science will explain them all in the end by the methods which have been so successful hitherto. Of course not everything has been explained yet; but that is a stimulus to us to go on looking for the true scientific explanations of things. Your talk about the things of the spirit is just an impediment to our researches, because it makes people think that there is something in the way people behave which is out of the reach of scientific inquiry. The Sophisticated Believer was quite right to tell you to keep out of the way of the scientists—I only wish you would; but to succeed in doing so you will have to move faster and farther than he thinks."

The Simple Believer was of course troubled by this; so he went hurrying back to the Sophisticated Believer, who had been of such assistance to him before, in the hope that he would provide an answer. And he did provide an answer; for if a believer is sophisticated enough, he can provide an answer to anything. He said, "You mustn't be upset by this kind of thing. When I said, the last time we met, that religion did not contradict science, I didn't mean to confine myself to what are called the physical sciences. I included the biological sciences; and, now that psychology has become respectable, I have no hesitation in including that too. Of course the religious

[3] Gilbert Ryle, *The Concept of Mind* (London: Hutchinson, 1949), chap. 1.

believer doesn't want to contradict the psychologist, any more than he wants to contradict the physiologist. Come to that, he doesn't want to contradict *anybody*. Even when the religious person and the psychologist are talking about the same sort of phenomena, they are talking about them in a quite different way. When St. Francis gets swellings on his hands, the psychologist calls it 'hysterical stigmatization'; but the Christian will call it a miracle. And both will be perfectly right. In general, science is concerned with counting, measuring, observing, and predicting; religion is concerned with worship. Therefore it is quite impossible for the statements of the two to contradict one another. Statements about God creating and loving the world are statements of a different logical category from those about nebulae or atoms or bacteria or neurones; and so a person can go on making both kinds of statement without being in any way inconsistent. That is to say, it is perfectly possible to be a scientist and a religious believer at the same time—why, look at all the people who do it!"

While the Sophisticated Believer was offering this comfort, and the Simple Believer was on the way to being comforted, they did not notice that a friend of theirs was standing nearby and listening to what they were saying. He was there quite by accident, and had not meant to join in the conversation at all. But what he heard was too much for him, and he burst in, "But I don't see what the devil is left of your religion after you have said this. Your religious utterances used to consist of plain assertions about the existence of a Being about whose character, though exalted and mysterious, you had at any rate some idea. But now, in your determination to say nothing that anybody could disagree with, you have been surreptitiously whittling down your religion until there's nothing left of it but words, and a warm and womblike feeling that still sometimes comes over you when you utter them. Surely you must have heard of the invisible gardener!"

The two Believers both said that they hadn't heard of the invisible gardener; so the Sophisticated Unbeliever (as I will call him) went to the library and got out *New Essays in Philosophical Theology*,[4]

[4] Anthony Flew, "Theology and Falsification," *New Essays in Philosophical Theology*, eds. Anthony Flew and Alasdair MacIntyre (London: SCM Press, 1955), p. 96; also reprinted in *The Existence of God*, ed. John Hick (New York: Macmillan, 1964), p. 225.

and started to read from Flew's article (from which, by the way, I stole the example about St. Francis which I have just used). He chose Flew's version of the parable, not Wisdom's original one,[5] because it made the point more clearly.

> Once upon a time two explorers came upon a clearing in the jungle. In the clearing were growing many flowers and many weeds. One explorer says, "Some gardener must tend this plot." The other disagrees, "There is no gardener." So they pitch their tents and set a watch. No gardener is ever seen. "But perhaps he is an invisible gardener." So they set up a barbed-wire fence. They electrify it. They patrol with bloodhounds. (For they remember how H. G. Wells's *The Invisible Man* could be both smelt and touched though he could not be seen.) But no shrieks ever suggest that some intruder has received a shock. No movements of the wire ever betray an invisible climber. The bloodhounds never give cry. Yet still the Believer is not convinced. "But there is a gardener, invisible, intangible, insensible to electric shocks, a gardener who has no scent and makes no sound, a gardener who comes secretly to look after the garden which he loves." At last the Sceptic despairs, "But what remains of your original assertion? Just how does what you call an invisible, intangible, eternally elusive gardener differ from an imaginary gardener or even from no gardener at all?"

By the time he had finished, the Simple Believer was in a bad way; for its point was only too clear to him. You see, he had started off by thinking that he was making perfectly good assertions about the existence of a being called God, and had in his imagination some sort of idea about what this being was like. Then, when he met the Simple Unbeliever, he came to see that what he had been saying was literally false. At first, when he discovered that a being of the sort he had been imagining couldn't live in the sky, he was comforted by the Sophisticated Believer's telling him that of course he had the wrong ideas about God; God did indeed exist, but he was not quite the sort of being that he had been imagining, and his location was not spatial in the way that he had thought; that in a sense he was everywhere and yet nowhere; that his hand was visible where no

[5] John Wisdom, "Gods," *Proc. Ar. Soc.*, XIV (1944/45); reprinted in *Logic and Language*, I, ed. A. Flew (Oxford: Blackwell, 1952); and in Wisdom, *Philosophy and Psychoanalysis* (Oxford: Blackwell, 1953).

hand (no literal hand, that is to say) was visible; that God's love was manifested even in events which, in our normal use of words, we should not regard as manifestations of love, or even of hate, but just as things that happen in the world. But as the process went on, it had begun to be a bit beyond him. He did at least understand the old literal ideas about God, even if they were false; but these new ideas—well, even if they were true, it was so very hard to say what they meant, and they seemed so far removed from the God he used to worship. True, he still got the old warm feeling when he thought about religion; but even that was beginning to fade away a bit.

And then he thought of another thing. His father was a clergyman, and his grandfather had been a bishop; and so he had naturally sometimes had occasion to try to persuade people, whose faith was going or gone, to come back into the fold. He had heard his father doing this in the pulpit, and he had tried in his private conversation to reproduce, and indeed to improve on, his father's arguments. But it did not seem to work, somehow. The trouble was that the people he was trying to reconvert (quite ordinary people) did not seem to understand what it was they were being asked to believe in. They would say things like this: "You tell us to go to church; but why? We understand you when you say that a certain man at the beginning of the A.D.s, whom we can agree was a very good man if all that you say about him is true, was wrongfully and painfully executed; but we don't see what this has got to do with our enduring even much less discomfort and a great deal of boredom by going to church now. When you start talking about God our mind somehow shuts up—and all the bright new liturgical gimmicks that your father is so keen on don't open it up again. We don't know what it is you are saying. You say God answers prayer. But when somebody prays to God and the thing prayed for doesn't happen, you say, 'God has thought it better not to answer this one; and of course he knows best.' But in that case what do you *mean* when you say God answers prayer?"

They just did not seem to understand what it was they were supposed to believe; and he found it hard to explain to them. He could have explained to them the things he believed in before he met the Simple Unbeliever; but he didn't really believe in *them* himself any more. And these new things that the Sophisticated Believer told him he ought to believe were somehow so difficult to explain, or even to understand. And after he had heard about the invisible gardener, the frightening thought occurred to him that the reason why he found it so difficult to explain what he was saying was that he wasn't really saying anything.

The Simple Believer's grandfather, as I have said, was a bishop, and he wrote a book about fossils that was a best seller among the faithful. In it he proved conclusively, in his own opinion, that fossils were of very recent origin, and certainly more recent than 4004 B.C.; that they all dated from round about the biblical date for the Flood. And so he thought he had proved the literal truth of the Genesis account, and saved the faith from the attacks of the scientists who were trying to subvert it. The Simple Believer had read his grandfather's book, and very good hard-hitting stuff it was; but it did not seem to help him in his present difficulty. His grandfather had thought he was having a real battle: it said in the Bible that the world was made in 4004 B.C.; and here were all these geologists and paleontologists saying that it was much older, and it was his job as a bishop to refute them. But what was it the job of his grandson the Simple Believer to refute or prove? For the worrying thing was that he did not believe any longer the things his grandfather was trying to prove—good solid assertions like "The world was made in 4004 B.C." No; *he* believed the scientists that his grandfather was attacking; his grandfather had lost that battle, for all his hard hitting.

But that would not have mattered if there were something substantial left now to fight about; the trouble was that, as a result of the Sophisticated Believer's qualifications, the faith had become so insubstantial that it was hard to see what one was supposed to defend. That perhaps explained why Christians were, taken all in all, so very like other people; in all the things that mattered they seemed to think just like anybody else. In his grandfather's day, if you were a Christian you thought one thing, and if you were not you thought something very different. You disagreed, for example, about the date and manner of the beginning of the world. But now, what are the Christian and the non-Christian disagreeing about? For the Christians have, on the advice of sophisticated believers, conceded all the points to the scientists that the scientists required. And so it came about that, while in his grandfather's day those who attacked Christianity were saying that its affirmations were false, in the Simple Believer's day, which is our own, the most dangerous and up-to-date attack comes from those who say that they are meaningless, that they assert nothing. And a great deal of public opinion has come round to the attackers' point of view.

So you can understand why the Simple Believer was unhappy. What was he to do? He did not feel that he could go back to the simple assertions of his grandfather, which the scientists had overthrown; but yet he did not any longer see much substance in the consolations of the Sophisticated Believer. If he went back to views of his grandfather, he would be saying what he believed to be false; but if he said what the Sophisticated Believer wanted him to say, he would be uttering words without meaning. It was when the Simple Believer was in this dilemma that I first got to know him. I understood his predicament very well, for it was one I had been in myself, and to a great extent was in still. He came to me for philosophical advice; but I was at a loss to know what to say to him. Would it be best, perhaps, to seek out some simple slick way of comforting him? The philosopher always has in his armory plenty of snap refutations that will readily deceive the inexpert. He does not always like to use these devices; but in defending what you think really matters, all's fair. The trouble is that, even if I could outwit the Sophisticated Unbeliever by any logical trick, I should not think that I had thereby helped the Simple Believer much. It would be like proving that the evidence of fossils was no good; it might deceive the layman for a time, but sooner or later the truth would prevail. After all, the God the Simple Believer believed in was a God of Truth; and it would be odd to try to defend faith in him by spurious arguments.

Nevertheless, I did very much want to help the Simple Believer— I will call him from now on the Believer, for he is simple no longer. There seemed to me to be something about his faith that put me to shame—something whose loss would make the world a worse place. And in so far as I had a little (though perhaps only a little) of this something myself, I wanted to strengthen it rather than destroy it; and for this purpose the Believer, for all his philosophical difficulties and perplexities, was a great example and source of strength to me. He might get into a muddle in his thought when sophisticated people tied him into knots; but to know him was to know that these knots somehow did not matter. If any of you know any people of the type I am describing, you know what I mean.

So in the end I hit upon this method. Instead of trying to teach the Believer what he ought to believe, I sought instead to learn from

him what he really did believe. This is a thing that cannot be done
entirely by kindness. It entails preventing the victim getting away
with any evasions and confusions; and so sometimes I seemed to be
trying to undermine his faith. I kept on dinning into him the arguments of the Sophisticated Unbeliever, and had sometimes even to
appear a Sophisticated Unbeliever myself. But I felt that the bru-
tality was worth while—for what I was trying to do was no less than
to find out what it was about his faith that really made him different
—and believe me it did make him different—from other men. It was
this that I wanted to find out, and if possible imitate.

I soon came to the conclusion that what the Believer believed in
weren't *assertions* in the narrow sense, as the term was used by the
Sophisticated Unbeliever. At least, though he may have believed
some assertions in this narrow sense, they were not central to his
faith. By this I mean that they could be abandoned or modified without his losing that whose basis I was seeking to discover. This much
was shown by his readiness to abandon these assertions when Unbelievers cast serious doubt upon them in argument. Of course, in a
sense, what the Believer believed in were assertions. But I did not
want to perform the usual philosophical trick of saying, "It all depends what you mean by an assertion." This is often a useful thing
to say—but only as a prelude to taking each of the things that might
be meant in turn, and examining its consequences. So to start with
I saw no harm in accepting the Sophisticated Unbeliever's criterion
of what were and were not assertions—the criterion was, you remember, that if the utterance was to express an assertion, there
had to be something which, if it occurred, would constitute a disproof of the assertion. But I did not want to admit that all meaningful utterances expressed assertions in this sense; for after all there
are plenty of utterances which are quite meaningful and yet do not
in this sense express assertions—for example, imperatives, questions,
expressions of wishes, and so on. There are, moreover, beliefs which
are not beliefs in the truth of assertions, in this narrow sense, and
yet which are fundamental to our whole life in this world, and still
more to our doing anything like science.

Let me explain this last point. Suppose you believed that everything that happens, happens by pure chance, and that therefore the
regularities that we have observed so far in the phenomena around
us have all been quite fortuitous; that the world might start behaving

tomorrow in a quite different manner, or in no consistent manner at all. Then it is obvious that we should not be able to make any scientific predictions about what was going to happen, and our science would become quite useless. It is only because we believe that there are some causal laws to be discovered, that we think it worth while to set about discovering them. But what sort of belief is this? Is it a belief in the truth of an assertion, in the Sophisticated Unbeliever's sense? Let us apply the test to it. "Just what would have to happen, not merely (morally and wrongly) to *tempt,* but also (logically and rightly) to *entitle"* the scientist to stop believing in or looking for causal laws?[6] The answer to this seems to be, as in the case of the religious believer and his God, "Nothing that could happen could have this effect."

Suppose that a scientist has a hypothesis which he is testing by experiment, and the experiment shows him that his hypothesis was false. He then, after trying the experiment again once or twice to make sure there has been no silly mistake, says, "My hypothesis was wrong; I must try a new one." That is to say, he does not stop believing in, or looking for, regularities in the world which can be stated in the form of scientific "laws"; he abandons this particular candidate for the status of a law, but only in order to look for another candidate. Thus, *whatever* happens, he still goes on looking for laws; nothing can make him abandon the search, for to abandon the search would be to stop being a scientist. He is just like the religious believer in this; in fact, we may say that the belief of the scientist is one kind of religious belief—a kind, moreover, which is not incompatible with what is called Christian belief, for it is part of it.[7]

I want to emphasize this point, because it is the most important that I have to make. When the scientist refuses to give up his search for causal explanations of things, even when any number of proposed explanations fail, he is acting in an essentially religious manner. Therefore, if you want to know what religion is, this is one of the very best illustrations to take. When the scientist says, "There must *be* an explanation of this, although none of the explanations that we have thought of so far work," he is manifesting just that refusal to doubt, which in religious contexts we call *faith.* And indeed it *is* faith; for the scientist does not *know* that there is an explanation.

[6] A. Flew, "Theology and Falsification," p. 99.
[7] See, e.g., P. E. Hodgson, in *The Tablet,* June 21, 1969.

For all he knows there may be no explanation. Indeed, even when he thinks he has found the explanation, how does he know that it is an explanation? For what is and what is not an explanation of something is not a question that can be settled by any sort of proof or appeal to the facts. To say that something is an explanation of something else is to hold just the kind of belief that the Sophisticated Unbeliever said was not belief in the truth of an assertion.

So then, to be a scientist is to be a kind of believer. And the Sophisticated Believer was quite right—perhaps it was the only thing he was right about—when he said that religion did not contradict science. But this is not, as he thought, because religion and science are different kinds of thing; it is because, though different in many respects, in this one crucial respect they are the same kind of thing. And, as I said, scientific belief is not incompatible with Christian belief. It is rather a *part* of Christian belief. It is a part of Christian belief to believe in the possibility of explaining things by means of scientific laws.

But scientific belief is not the whole of Christian belief. There are whole fields of human conduct outside the laboratory where scientific belief does not give us the answers to the questions we are (or ought to be) asking. It does not give us these answers, not because it is wrong, but because it does not apply in those fields. I will mention only one of those fields, that of morality. We cannot decide by experimental methods or by observation what we ought to do. That I ought to do this or that is another of those beliefs which I have to accept or reject (for what I do depends on this decision) but which are excluded by the Sophisticated Unbeliever's test from the realm of assertions. It is only if he ignores such questions that the scientist is able to make do with so limited a faith.

II

In my first lecture, near the end, I made a brief comparison between religious beliefs and moral judgments. It has been an extremely common move in these controversies to say that religious belief is a kind of moral belief or attitude. This is the suggestion which I am now going to explore. I shall not accept it as it stands; but I think that a great deal is to be learnt from it.

In order to avoid misunderstandings it is necessary to make it clear that I am not going myself to advance any thesis about the qualifications for being called a Christian. That is a terminological question which I am prepared to leave to others. I am going, rather, to explore a possible system of beliefs, which I think it reasonable to hold, and which I am myself inclined to hold. Whether these are to be called Christian or even religious beliefs is of less importance; for what serious students of this question ought to be troubled about is what they can believe, and not what they can call it. And whether the Christian imagery is an appropriate expression of such beliefs is a highly subjective matter which is to be settled by whoever has something to express and does or does not find the Christian language an adequate and fitting vehicle for what he is trying to say. I do not think that very many Christian churchgoers would like to be held to the letter of all that they say in church; they go because there is enough that they can sincerely (though not always literally) say, and that cannot be said at all succinctly in any other way, to make it more appropriate for them to be inside than outside. If, when I have published my views, it still seems unscandalous for me to go on going to church, I shall do so.

The best-known recent statement of the proposal to reduce religion to morality is that of Professor Braithwaite. Braithwaite's Eddington Lecture, called "An Empiricist's View of the Nature of Religious Belief," and reprinted in Professor John Hick's collection *The Existence of God*, struck me, at the time I heard it delivered in 1955, as by far the best thing on this subject that I had ever heard or read; and I have since then seen no reason to revise this opinion. His sincerity, and his refusal to take refuge in the evasions and the obscurities that are the occupational disease of those who write in this field, compel admiration. It is therefore distressing that, since the lecture was published, it has received almost no support, either from Christians or from non-Christians, and has come to be regarded as a rather ridiculous attempt to do what cannot be done. It may be that, if Braithwaite had wrapped up his views in the almost impenetrable darkness that is fashionable in this sort of writing, he would have got away with it. Perhaps he and not Tillich would have been the hero of the Bishop of Woolwich's book *Honest to God*. For in many ways the views of Braithwaite and the bishop are highly congenial to one another. It is the same lumps of orthodoxy that stick in the throats of both of them; and the motives of both go back to the diffi-

culties which I discussed in my first lecture—in particular the difficulty of assigning to statements of religious belief a logical status
which will leave them saying something that is, first of all, meaningful, and, secondly, not obviously false.

Braithwaite sums up his position as follows:

> A man is not, I think, a professing Christian unless he both
> proposes to live according to Christian moral principles, and
> associates his intention with thinking of Christian stories; but
> he need not believe that the empirical propositions presented
> by the stories correspond to empirical fact.[8]

Thus, to adopt a slogan, religion could be described, on Braithwaite's view, as morals helped out by mythology.

This crude description is, however, unfair to Braithwaite. For he
includes under the summary term "moral principles" a great deal
which, I am sure, he would distinguish from them if he were expounding his view more fully. Perhaps the term "way of life" would
represent more fairly what he means; but even so we shall have ourselves to go into more detail before we can do justice to his position.

I think that the clearest way of doing this will be to take what we
may call the minimum Braithwaitian position (corresponding to an
over-narrow interpretation of the passage that I have just quoted)
and to ask how Braithwaite might meet the objections to it that
would be made by an old-fashioned Christian believer, whether simple or sophisticated. There is, however, one style of criticism to which
I shall offer no reply, since an entirely devastating rebuttal of it has
already been given by Mr. J. C. Thornton in his article "Religious
Belief and 'Reductionism.'"[9] This is the style of those who by a palpably circular argument assume that the traditional interpretation of
Christian belief is the only admissible one, and then think that they
have refuted Braithwaite by showing that he does not conform to it.
Such a maneuver will not strengthen the faith of anybody who is in
serious doubt about the acceptability of the traditional interpretation.

Of the objections which I shall consider, I will start with
the smaller ones. First, it may be objected that merely to have certain ideas about what our duties are, even if we then go on to act

---

[8] R. B. Braithwaite, "An Empiricist's View of the Nature of Religious Belief,"
The Existence of God, ed. John Hick (New York: Macmillan, 1964), p. 246.
[9] J. C. Thornton, "Religious Belief and 'Reductionism,'" *Sophia* (1966),
pp. 3–16.

accordingly, is hardly to practice even the Christian virtue of charity —let alone faith and hope. Christian charity or love (*agape*) is not, it may be said, a kind of behavior, but a state or attitude of mind (loving my neighbor as myself). This Braithwaite can easily concede, and does concede:

> The superiority of religious conviction over the mere adoption of a moral code . . . arises from a religious conviction changing what the religious man wants. It may be hard enough to love your enemy, but once you have succeeded in doing so it is easy to behave lovingly towards him.[10]

So evidently the *agape* to which Braithwaite is referring is, unlike Kant's "practical love,"[11] a state of mind or attitude, and not merely the obedience to a moral code.

Nor need Braithwaite confine himself, as in his lecture he largely does, to the morality which consists in loving our neighbor as ourself. If he did, it might be objected that there is also the love of God to be considered. Before we can understand what could be meant, by one of Braithwaite's views, by "loving God," we shall first have to explain in what sense, for Braithwaite, God can exist to be the object of love. Here I want only to point out that, even for a humanist, and *a fortiori* for a Braithwaitian Christian, there can be more to morality than the love of neighbors; there is the whole sector of morality to be considered which is concerned with moral ideals, and which may have nothing to do with our neighbors. Since I said a lot about this in my book *Freedom and Reason*, I will not repeat it here.

Nor need Braithwaite confine himself to morality in the narrow sense. It may be that not only our moral attitudes, but all our wants, aspirations, and ideals should be included in that total attitude to life which Braithwaite wants to call religious belief. To be a Christian, then, is not merely to acknowledge certain duties, or even to aspire to certain virtues; it is also to have an entirely different idea of what is prudent or sensible. For if our desires become different, what is prudent—i.e., what is likely in the long run to conduce to the fulfillment of our desires—will radically change. Thus we are

[10] Braithwaite, "An Empiricist's View of the Nature of Religious Belief," p. 243.
[11] Immanuel Kant, *Groundwork*, 2d ed., p. 13; trans. in H. J. Paton, *The Moral Law* (New York: Barnes & Noble, 1950), p. 67.

bidden not to take thought for what we shall put on, but to seek first the Kingdom of God.

There is no reason why Braithwaite should not incorporate these modifications into his theory. For what he is trying to do is to get the better of the Sophisticated Unbeliever of my first lecture, who said that statements of religious belief are not falsifiable, and therefore say nothing. Braithwaite's maneuver consists in assimilating statements of religious belief to a class of utterances which can be unfalsifiable without lacking content. This class includes moral judgments, on Braithwaite's and my view of them; but it includes much else besides. The important thing for Braithwaite is, not to admit that religious statements are any kind of factual assertion. For if he admits that, it is open to the Sophisticated Unbeliever to place him in the dilemma of my first lecture: he has either to open his statements to factual refutation, in which case they get refuted; or else he has to acknowledge that in uttering them he is not really doing what, in a factual assertion, one is supposed to do.

It is time now to consider another objection which an old-fashioned Christian might make against Braithwaite's view. He might say, "Surely religious assertions *are* factual. For the Christian does not merely follow a way of life; he has the *hope* that this way of life is not vain or pointless. And this hope would be futile if the world were not ordered in a certain way." Here we get very close to one of the traditional moral arguments for the existence of God. The old-fashioned Christian would, indeed, surely put his objection in terms of the existence of God; he would say, "To be a Christian is not merely to be disposed to follow a way of life; it is to believe that God is there to *sustain* one in this way of life. Otherwise it would be pointless and stupid to follow, or try to follow, the way of life."

What can Braithwaite make of this objection? I think that he can go a long way to meet it. To begin with, he might say that the Christian may, indeed, be committed to certain factual assertions about the world, but that these are all empirical ones, and so are not at the mercy of the Sophisticated Unbeliever. Suppose that the Christian has certain wants, aspirations, ideals, moral principles, etc., which, on this view, constitute his religion. And suppose that, as he must, he believes that it is not futile to act in pursuit of these aspirations, etc. He need not believe that the aspirations are certain to be fulfilled, but only that there is a reasonable hope that they will be. Since the aspirations themselves are not very determinate—but sufficiently determinate to be meaningful—the empirical propositions to which he thus commits himself are not very determinate either. But they are far from being contentless.

The easiest example to take is that of the effects of our actions on people. How often do we not hear it said that if only we behave towards people in a Christian way—if we have the faith and trust to do this—they will respond in ways that would surprise an unbeliever. This is often expressed in terms of the working of the Holy Spirit in men's hearts. Now, it may be that if I have certain Christian aspirations which cannot be realized without the co-operation of other people, the proposition that it is not pointless to pursue these aspirations is one that can be called, in a sense, a factual one.

But we need not confine ourselves to the responses of other people. A Christian may believe that the inanimate world also is so ordered as not to make his endeavors pointless. In my first lecture I said that the attitude of the scientists was like this, and I said that this scientific attitude was a part, though only a part, of Christian belief. Now we are in a position to understand this better. Both the scientist and the religious believer can claim that among their beliefs are two classes of affirmations, both of which escape the Sophisticated Unbeliever's dilemma, but in different ways. The first, and philosophically less interesting, class is the one I have just mentioned. Both the scientist and the religious believer will find themselves making some assertions which, though they are assertions in the narrow sense, are sufficiently indeterminate to escape refutation by single or even by quite numerous counter-instances—they contain enough *ceteris paribus* clauses to look after the counter-instances, in all of which it will be claimed that other things were not, after all, equal. The scientist does not give up his claim to be able in principle to predict natural phenomena just because of the notorious failure of the Meteorological Office to predict the weather accurately. And the religious believer does not give up his belief that, on the whole, if you behave Christianly towards other people they will respond accordingly, just because he has had one or two disappointments.

The more interesting class of beliefs consists in those which are not in assertions, in the Sophisticated Unbeliever's narrow sense, at all, though they may be in assertions in some less restricted sense.

These are the beliefs I was referring to at the end of my first lecture. The scientist believes that there is scientific truth to be discovered, in the form of natural laws to which the processes of the world conform. This belief is not itself testable in the ordinary way (though the hypotheses which the scientist frames as candidates for the status of natural laws *are* testable). If a scientist has thought up some hypothesis, and when he tries it out by experiment it turns out to be false, he gives up the particular hypothesis, but does not give up the belief that there are laws to be discovered. This belief, therefore, is not a belief in the truth of an assertion in the narrow sense. Yet in another sense the belief is surely factual; it is "about the world." If the scientist, after repeated failures, did lose faith, not merely in his own abilities as a researcher, but in the possibility of anybody ever discovering laws which governed a certain range of phenomena, we should say that his beliefs about the character of those phenomena had changed, and not merely that he had adopted a different way of life.

If this is true of the scientist's belief that his researches are not pointless, may it not also be true of the Christian moralist's belief that his morality is not pointless? The scientist does not know that even the most long-established hypothesis may not be refuted by new evidence tomorrow. All that has been written about the problem of induction has not altered the fact that belief in the future regularity of the universe is an act of faith; and yet we base all our actions on this faith. The faith might be represented as faith in a prescription: "Don't give up hope." But this would be misleading if we did not at the same time emphasize that the hope which the scientist is not to give up is a hope that he or some other scientist will find answers to questions which are not prescriptive, but in any ordinary sense of the word, factual.

Similarly the moralist has to have the faith, not that he has found, but at least that it is possible to find, moral "policies" (as I am sure Braithwaite would call them) which are not pointless. It is not enough to be convinced that some kind of act is a duty. Without going now into the tangled and, I think, unnecessary controversy between the teleologists and the deontologists, I will merely record my conviction that what it is our duty to do must depend on what we should be doing if we initiated a certain train of events; and this depends on the consequences of alternative courses of action. But in this world consequences must always be to a large extent a matter of conjecture and of faith. We have to have faith and hope that our actions will turn out for the best; they are hostages to the world, and no practical morality could do without an ample faith that events will not frustrate its ends. It is extremely natural to express this faith in religious terms.

Here again we might be tempted to say that the faith is not factual but prescriptive. The prescription is, not to give up hope of finding a moral policy that is not futile. But here again we must reply that, though the faith is not faith in an assertion in the narrow sense, abandonment of it would entail a radical change in our view about what the world is like. We should not merely be ceasing to look for non-futile moral policies, but be doing so because we thought that the world was such that we would never find any.

When I speak of "non-futile moral policies," I shall certainly be misunderstood unless I add an explanation. I am not talking about the presence or absence of rewards for virtue. Sometimes a "moral argument" for God's existence is put in the following terms: there must be a sanction for morality; it must be shown that, in the end, the virtuous are rewarded and the wicked punished, or at least that for some other reason honesty is the best policy. That is not what I am talking about at all. I do as a matter of fact believe that as the world is ordered, honesty *is* the best policy—in the sense that if one were asking how to form the character of a child (or of oneself), considering solely his own selfish interests, one would be wisest to seek to implant in him the traditional virtues. In the actual world, there are no reliable rings of Gyges[12]—and that there are none, might also count as part of our religion. But that is not what I am talking about. Although virtue is the surest recipe for happiness, occasions undoubtedly arise on which the path of virtue leads to great suffering. On these occasions the virtuous man will, like Hermeias in Aristotle's poem,[13] accept the suffering as the price of virtue; just because his character has been formed in virtue, he will want the ends of morality to be achieved more than he wants to avoid the suffering. But even if this is what he above all wants—

[12] Plato, *Republic II*, 359–60.
[13] Aristotle, *Select Fragments*, ed. W. D. Ross (Oxford: Clarendon Press, 1952); cf. *Ethica Nicomachea*, ed. and trans. W. D. Ross (London: Oxford Univ. Press, 1931), 1169 a25.

even if he totally disregards his own selfish interests—he still needs
to have the kind of faith that I am speaking of. I am not advocating
the view that the virtuous man will do the virtuous thing and disregard the consequences; for what is the virtuous thing depends in
part on the consequences, if not for himself, for others. A man might
stoically cultivate his own perfection by doing an act which he
thought virtuous, even though it led to disaster for everybody; but
I would not call virtuous a man who could deliberately do such a
thing.

What I am trying to say is that, granted that the good man wishes
above all to realize the ends of morality—moral ideals—he can hardly
pursue this object unless he has faith in the possibility, as things are,
of realizing them. That is why faith and hope are virtues as well as
charity. And I must confess that faith in the divine providence has
always seemed to me to be one of the central features of the Christian religion, and one to which it is possible to cling even when
much else is in doubt. This faith that all shall be well is matched by
a feeling of thankfulness that all is well.

So, then, I want to say that religion cannot be reduced to morality,
even in an extended sense, unless we include also the faith that
saves moral endeavor from futility. But it is obvious that in saying
this I shall not have done very much to appease our old-fashioned
Christian objector. It is, indeed, evident that for a long time he has
been wanting to say that I have left out God from my account (or
rather from my tentative expansion of Braithwaite's account) of
religion. However, this objection cannot be made clear until we have
discovered what it would be to bring God in. I think that matters
may become clearer if we discuss something which I certainly have
left out, and that is what is called "the supernatural." Recently the
idea has been put forward more than once that religion can do without the supernatural; and so in leaving it out I do not feel so isolated
as in some other things that I have said. But first we must ask what
the supernatural is.

One absolutely crucial distinction that needs making here is
between two different senses of "supernatural." I shall use, to stand
for these two senses, the words "contranatural" and "transcendental."
An event may be said to be *contranatural* if it is contrary to the
ordinary natural laws. Miracles, for example, are, on the usual interpretation, contranatural. It has been said, of course, that if a

miracle were established to have happened, then we should revise our ideas about the natural law in question, and so there would be no breach of natural law. But there is an understandable sense in which a miracle is contrary to natural law—i.e., to those natural laws in which, after much experiment and observation of phenomena, we have considerable confidence.

It is a distinguishing feature of the contranatural that propositions stating that a contranatural event has occurred are perfectly meaningful empirical propositions. The controversy is about their truth, not about their significance. Thus it is an empirical proposition that the sun stood still for Joshua; what we quarrel about is whether it actually did stand still, or whether the story in the Bible is the result of credulity.

The *transcendental* is quite different. Let us suppose that someone alleges that there is a god in the fire who makes it burn; it would not burn without him, it is said, and to get him to make it burn you have to perform the right ritual, lay the sticks correctly, not put too much big stuff on top, etc. It so happens that my wife can always perform this ritual correctly, and I cannot; my fires always go out. But, it may be asked, what is the difference between the statement that there is a god who, if we perform the right ritual, makes the fire burn, and the statement that the fire will burn if we do the specified series of operations? I call this fire-god "transcendental" because his existence or non-existence makes no difference to observable phenomena. He is, as Wittgenstein might have said, idling —doing no work.

The Sophisticated Unbeliever's point in my first lecture could be put in terms of these two words. What the Simple Believer had been doing was that, when he came to think that his contranatural beliefs were false, he substituted for them beliefs in transcendental entities and events, with the results that we saw. Now, I do not believe myself that religion can last much longer, among educated people, unless it rejects both the contranatural and the transcendental. This is going to be very repugnant to old-fashioned believers; but I think that it is inescapable.

It is escapable, indeed, by the uneducated—and I must explain what I mean by that. I am going to call that kind of religion which relies on the supernatural, in either of its senses, *superstition*. If anybody does not like the implications of this word, or thinks it offensive, he need not disturb himself, because I shall not use these implications in my argument. Now, there are three things, I want to say, which cannot, all three, co-exist together in the present state of knowledge. They are superstition, science, and philosophy. By science I mean not merely the practice of science, but the acceptance of its results by non-scientists. By philosophy, I mean the ability to reason logically about these and other subjects with enough familiarity with the verbal traps that lie in one's path not to fall into them —the ability, that is to say, to see the issues clearly and not to be deceived by sophistries, whether intentional or inadvertent.

Now, there is no difficulty in science co-existing with superstition. There are many scientists who achieve it. All that is necessary is to be philosophically naïve; it will then be possible to construct systems of belief which are essentially superstitious, but not to notice that they involve elements which are either contranatural, and therefore incompatible with scientific beliefs, or transcendental, and therefore idle. It is likewise not difficult to be a superstitious philosopher, if one is not concerned about science. If one is willing boldly to deny facts which nearly all scientists would accept, one can easily suppose, for example, that the nether regions are just as Dante describes them, and one's system of the world need not fall into any *logical* errors. But when we try to put together all these three things, science, philosophy, and superstition, one of them is bound to succumb. That is what I meant when I said that an educated man has to abandon superstition, i.e., the belief in the supernatural. It is wrong of me, I know, to say all this without arguing for it; but this ground has been gone over so often by abler expositors than I am (Russell, for example), that I do not feel like entering upon it now, even if there were time. If any Christians do not, when they have understood the issues clearly, feel the overwhelming force of these arguments, I envy them, but address myself rather to those who do feel their force, and to whom, therefore, I may be able to say something helpful.

The problem for me, therefore, as apparently for some more august people, is, Can religion do without the supernatural? In facing this question we ought not to be put off by a move which is often made. It is sometimes said that, if we banish the supernatural from religion, we leave no difference between Christianity and humanism. This notion that Christianity has got to be *different* is a very difficult one to overcome. But, I ask, suppose that someone produced an interpretation of Christianity that could be accepted by the best humanists, would this necessarily be a bad thing? We have, at present, in our civilization, a very absurd state of affairs. I constantly meet people who evidently share my outlook on life quite as much as my fellow-Christians do, and who yet call themselves humanists. It is a source of scandal to me that I am supposed to have to make myself different from these people, some of whom I very much admire. Of course there *are* differences between us; but so there are between me and a great many Christians. And it is no use saying that the reason why I can say this about the humanists is that I am not a very solid Christian; I am quite sure that the same could be said by a great many extremely solid Christians. If any of you think that you are solid Christians, you can verify this for yourselves. So I should not be at all sorry if it could be shown that there is a type of Christianity which is compatible with humanism.

I know that I said in my first lecture that the Believer's faith made him different from other men. But the point is, was it faith in the supernatural that made him different, or was it a faith that could be had by somebody who did not believe in the supernatural? That really is the crux of our whole problem.

We must, however, face the fact that in abandoning the supernatural we shall have to abandon some things which have been thought to be very central to traditional Christianity. This is, of course, why left-wing theologians, when they get on to these topics, are apt to become impenetrably obscure.

> So well-bred spaniels civilly delight
> In mumbling of the game they dare not bite.[14]

I will take two of these topics which I think are among the most difficult, namely prayer, and the after life. The problem of prayer arises mainly from the rejection of the transcendental; that of the after life from the rejection of the contranatural. But, as we shall see, there is an overlap.

In thinking about prayer, it will be as well to have particular examples in mind. In preparing this lecture, I had especially two. The first is from Arthur Bryant's *The Turn of the Tide*. This book is a history of the Second World War based on Lord Alanbrooke's diaries

[14] Alexander Pope, *An Epistle from Mr. Pope to Dr. Arbuthnot* (London: J. Wright for L. Gilbert, 1734), 313.

and recollections. Lord Alanbrooke is writing, in retrospect, about the day in November 1941 when Churchill asked him to become Chief of the Imperial General Staff.

> I am not [he says] an exceptionally religious person, but I am not ashamed to confess that as soon as he was out of the room my first impulse was to kneel down and pray to God for guidance and support in the task I had undertaken. As I look back at the years that followed I can now see clearly how well this prayer was answered.[15]

The second example is more extended; in a recent book called *Fire in Coventry*,[16] Canon Stephen Verney describes the prayers of clergy and people in preparation for the consecration of the cathedral and diocese of Coventry, and the remarkable way in which these were answered. He is convinced that something powerful, which he calls the Holy Spirit, took hold of the diocese and that observable effects happened which would not have happened unless there had been prayer and it had been answered. Both these books are well worth reading by anybody who wishes to study this question. Another is *Miracle on the River Kwai*, by Ernest Gordon.[17]

When a prayer is answered, what to the naked eye, as it were, happens is this. A person conceives of or imagines a being more powerful than himself, to whom he makes certain requests, or whose guidance he simply awaits. Afterwards, certain ideas for action come into his head, and certain external events take place which are conducive to the success of the actions, and which are interpreted as the answer to the prayer. We have to ask what part the transcendental has to play in this. My answer would be, None at all. For what is the difference between there being a transcendental God who listens to the prayer and directs events accordingly, and it just being the case that the events take place? Braithwaite would no doubt speak of what the person praying imagines or conceives as a "story," and would say that it makes no difference to his being a Christian or not whether it is thought of as a true story or a myth. But this really misses the point. The point is that, where the transcendental is con-

---

[15] Arthur Bryant, *The Turn of the Tide* (Garden City, N.Y.: Doubleday, 1959), p. 266.
[16] Canon Stephen Verney, *Fire in Coventry* (Westwood, N.J.: Revell, 1964).
[17] Ernest Gordon, *Miracle on the River Kwai* (London: Collins, 1963).

cerned, there is no difference between a true story and a myth; it is therefore wrong to speak of the person who prays having an *illusion* that there is somebody that he is praying to. If prayer is important in religion—and I am convinced that it is—it cannot be that its importance rests upon the existence of a transcendental being whose existence could not, in principle, make itself felt in the world as we see it.

Since Canon Verney's book is called *Fire in Coventry*, may I recur to what I said earlier about fire. I said that, in making an ordinary fire, we might think of what we did as a ritual to propitiate a fire-god, who then, if propitiated, caused the fire to burn; but that there is really no empirical difference between this story and the chemist's account of the matter, viz., that if certain prior conditions are carefully created, a certain chemical reaction will take place. The transcendental "god" is really idling. And I venture to suggest that the same is true of the larger-scale spiritual conflagration which took place, according to Canon Verney, in Coventry, and that this does not in the least diminish its importance for good or its significance for religion. Surely we do not want to relegate God to a position of logically guaranteed ineffectiveness.

The question of the after life is an even more difficult one. I was struck, in reading *The Turn of the Tide*, by the fact that Lord Alanbrooke (in spite of his protestations, a devout man, who was often in situations of extreme danger), says almost nothing about the after life. Nor, in my conversations with most clergymen, have I been able to obtain from them any clear idea of what they believe on this question. My impression is that belief in the after life does not now have the importance for Christians that it once had—perhaps because they have become convinced by scientists and philosophers that it is not very plausible to believe in personal survival in a literal sense. I am not myself a follower of those philosophers who allege that no sense can be given to the statement that we shall survive the death (the literal death) of our bodies. I believe that this statement is meaningful, but unbelievable. This is so, whether what we are required to believe is that the soul can exist without any body, or (more orthodoxly) that the body will rise again at the last day, and that we shall then again have experiences, including memories of what passed before our deaths. I think that symbolic significance can be given to either of these doctrines, on the lines advocated by sophis-

ticated believers. But I think it would be better if this stumbling
block in the way of belief were removed by some entirely plain speaking on the part of Christians, making clear what is the substance
which this shadow veils.

If this necessitated a revision or reinterpretation of the Creeds,
this should be accepted. The Creeds are not scriptural, and were
written a very long time ago in the light of philosophical and cosmological ideas which nobody would now accept. Even if they were
scriptural, this would not be so important; for in the same way as
we are not bound to believe, just because St. Paul says that the seed
has to die in the earth before the corn can come up,[18] that this is
in fact what happens, so we are not bound to believe, just because
Jesus spoke in terms of theological and philosophical ideas and terminology different from any to which we can attach truth or significance, that this is the way in which the Christian religion has
now to be expressed. A lot has changed about the Christian religion
in the course of the centuries; and, just as change in other matters
is now faster than it has ever been, we must expect religion to change
faster too. Either that, or it will cease to be practiced altogether; but
I am confident that Christians will prove at least as adaptable in the
future as they have in the past.

Since I know that the orthodox, who are still numerous, will disagree with nearly everything that I have said in this lecture, I must
end with a warning. Changes in the intellectual climate can be divided into two classes. First, there are the quick and superficial ones
—fashions in thinking. The ebb and flow of these signifies nothing
for the future. We have religious revivals; Oxford Movements; Moral
Rearmaments; and so on. And on the other side we have equally
transitory humanist movements. This has been going on at least since
the sixteenth century; and very similar things happened in ancient
times before the rise of Christianity. There are those who fix their
eyes on these relatively superficial movements, and, because they
ebb and flow, think that underneath nothing has changed.

But there is a second kind of intellectual movement, which goes
on all the time, and mostly in the same direction. It is a function of
the increasing education (if you like, sophistication) of the bulk
of mankind, and of our increasing knowledge of, and control over,

[18] I Corinthians 15:36.

nature. Though the movement goes on almost continuously, there are certain steps or stages in it which can be marked. And at certain times it does move faster than at others. Those who have the required intellectual penetration ought to discern the signs of the times, and be guided by them. At the present time, we can see clearly that the movement is accelerating—just because education has fairly suddenly become more widespread. And we can see also that a clearly marked stage in the process has been reached.

Let me now try to explain these rather prophetic remarks. At most times in past history the orthodox have been able to rely on a vast reservoir of uneducated people. Whatever the ebb and flow of intellectual fashions among the sophisticated, they have been only on the surface, because, even where there is an educated class, its little enlightenments can never compete on equal terms with the superstitions of the masses. But when people start to be educated—or even half-educated—in really large numbers, a quite different stage is reached; and that is where we have got to now.

Another very important factor in our present situation is a new attitude to morality. Ever since Kant (indeed, ever since Hume, and perhaps ever since Protagoras) it has been *possible* for people to insist on the autonomy of morals—its independence of human or divine authority. Indeed, it has been *necessary*, if they were to think morally, in the sense in which that word is now generally understood. But for all that, few people up to the present time have entirely cut themselves free from the kind of pre-moral, heteronomous thinking which previously sufficed. But now their numbers are increasing dramatically. You are seeing a symptom of this every time you find a teenager asking, "But why *should* I behave in the way you—or anybody else—calls morally right?"

This situation would be extremely dangerous, were it not that the remedy has arisen at the same time. This too we owe to Kant. To replace the more or less socially effective, though basically irrational disciplines of heteronomy, we now have available a way of moral thinking which can do the same job within an autonomous, rational framework of thought. This means that the God of the orthodox, who was never competent to provide us with the basis of our morality, can now be seen to be unnecessary for this purpose. And the realization of this fact by an increasing number of people can only present the gravest threat to the orthodox position. I was therefore not surprised to see Professor Flew hailing my book *Freedom and Reason*[19] (which is in spirit Kantian) as a step on the road to a viable humanist morality.[20] That would make it a nail in the coffin of much orthodox Christianity.

Once people realize that they can have a rational morality without the orthodox God, and cannot have one with him, one of his chief props (indeed, perhaps, his only surviving prop with any strength) will have disappeared. And it is this situation for which Christians ought to be preparing. I will now discuss various strategies which they might adopt.

The first is to ignore what educated people are saying, and concentrate on ministering to the wholly uneducated, to whom the old stories can still seem true. In some parts of the world it is possible to do even better, and actually prevent the spread of education, or confine its content to topics thought to be harmless. But the result of such a strategy would be to make the Church into the Church of that diminishing minority of mankind which education had not reached.

The second possible strategy (which is not incompatible with the first) is to fight, at the intellectual level, what is bound to be nevertheless a losing battle. I think that it is as impossible that a fully educated population should believe in the God of the orthodox as it is that the present-day population of England, or New England, should believe in witchcraft. Still, at this high intellectual level there is scope for unlimited spoiling maneuvers. For to be clear about these matters is exceedingly difficult; whereas anybody whose intentions are mainly polemical has an easy task. These discussions have reached a degree of subtlety which is beyond the attainment of most people; therefore, when a new argument is produced—or often an old and discarded one revived in a form that is more intricate and whose invalidity is therefore harder to detect—the only possible courses are, either to ignore it (and this can be dangerous) or else to spend a great deal of time taking it to pieces. Those who are trying to make things clearer are thus at the mercy of those who are not; either they leave themselves defenseless, or they abandon hope of advancing the subject and devote themselves to polemics. This, I

[19] R. M. Hare, *Freedom and Reason* (Oxford: Clarendon Press, 1963).
[20] Anthony Flew in the *Rationalist Annual* (1964).

think, is one of the reasons why the philosophy of religion has in recent times attracted relatively few first-rate philosophers.

However, I do not think that these intellectual delaying actions are going to do the orthodox much good in the long run; because I believe that *magna est veritas, et*—in the long run—*praevalebit.* Therefore I think that Christians—and by this I mean not just the orthodox, but all those who are ready to profess and call themselves Christians—are bound to consider what they should do in the situation, which must come in the end, in which the orthodox have plainly lost the intellectual battle. But I am inclined to think that the question of what they are to do turns into one which has more terminology than substance about it. What it comes down to is really this: if the position for which I have been arguing is acceptable, are we to *call* it a Christian or a humanist position? Now this, as I said earlier, is a less important question than whether it *is* acceptable; but nevertheless, since I am sure that a great deal of breath is going to be spent in the next few decades on this terminological question, it is worth giving a few minutes to it.

While orthodoxy held the field among those who call themselves Christians, there seemed to be no two ways about it. The position which I have been defending could be said to be obviously a humanist one, and incompatible with Christianity. But I wonder whether this is still the case. We must reflect that there was a time when it was thought—and that there are people who still think— that you cannot be a Christian (at least not a non-heretical one) unless you believe in transubstantiation, or in the immaculate conception, or in the Genesis story of the creation, taken literally. We have to allow that ideas about what is requisite for being said to be a Christian can change, and may change radically and, in the present circumstances, rapidly.

Therefore, I would say that at present, though it is certainly possible for a person who holds views like mine to be called a humanist, it is not necessary. And perhaps it might be misleading. For "humanist" is an even vaguer term than "Christian" (it often means "non-Christian, non-Muslim, non-Jew, non-Hindu, etc.," and has no positive content of its own); and on the other hand it is sometimes used to describe positions from which I should strongly dissent (for example, the view that humanity is the only proper object of worship). My differences from even orthodox Christianity are, however, less important than they might seem. For, first of all, I agree on all prescriptive matters—that is to say, on everything that concerns what we should do, whether it is morals or prudence or science or whatever it is—I agree with Christians, or at any rate with a highly representative group of them, about everything that could determine our conduct.

Secondly, I agree with Christians, or at any rate with a fairly typical group of them, about all ordinary empirical matters of fact. In a sense, for example, I expect prayers to be answered—in the rather weak sense, that is to say, in which most Christians expect them to be answered, which is compatible with them not being answered in the way that we were thinking of when we prayed. And I do believe in divine providence (that, incidentally, is the main reason why I have such a firm conviction that the truth will prevail in philosophy, despite all the maneuvers that are available to falsehood). I believe, that is to say, that matters are so ordered in the world that there is a point in trying to live by the precepts to which Christians subscribe.

My differences with those who can perhaps still be called typical Christians concern, of course, the supernatural. And I am obviously not alone in this; for it is becoming quite fashionable among Christians to reject the supernatural. Now, the supernatural, as I said, is divided into the contranatural and the transcendental. As regards the transcendental, I cannot believe that the differences between those who accept it and those who reject it have the slightest substance. For really they are both believing the same thing, but saying it in different words—even if the words *are* different, which they are not always. I have, I hope, argued convincingly that the transcendent God is bound always to be an idle element in our religious life. His existence or non-existence cannot possibly make any difference, either to what we ought to do, or to what is going to be the case. His transcendence logically rules this out.

On the other hand, the differences between those who accept and those who reject the contranatural are of substance. But I think that it is legitimate to ask Christians who say that they differ from me about this to cross their hearts and declare whether they themselves really do believe in the contranatural (when it has been freed from transcendentalist "interpretations"). I am certain that a great many Christians—Modern Churchmen, for example—do not; and

I am convinced that still more would not, if they had become sufficiently clear about the distinction between the contranatural and the transcendental, and were therefore more aware of what is happening when we say, "You are not bound to take this doctrine literally." They are able to cling to the contranatural only because, when the belief seems to be threatened, they at once take refuge in the transcendental, without realizing that they have entirely altered, and indeed trivialized, their position. The danger once past, they emerge from their hiding places and think that they can go on as before believing in the contranatural. But these maneuvers cannot long survive the serious study of philosophy.

I conclude, therefore, that not very much separates me even from what would now be called typical Christians; and I think that in a fairly short time my views will not seem so unusual as perhaps they do now. Not that *my* views are important; I have only spent so long discussing them because I am convinced that the dilemma in which I now find myself is one which, in the near future, very large numbers of thoughtful Christians are going to have to face. The dilemma is really this. If we call ourselves Christians, we run the risk of being thought dishonest, because to call oneself a Christian is, at present, to create in the minds of many people the impression that one believes in the supernatural. But perhaps since *Honest to God* this danger has become more remote. On the other hand, if we call ourselves humanists, we run, I am convinced, much greater risks. For we shall be thought to be abandoning, possibly the prescriptive principles which I said were essential to Christianity, and most certainly the other beliefs which I said were also part of it—beliefs in the ordering of the world so as to give morality a point. I think that there is still some danger that if one says that one is a humanist, one will be thought to be supporting, if not some kind of moral nihilism, at any rate a morality without visible means of support. And this I do not want to do.

How this dilemma will work itself out is a matter for uncertain speculation. It may be that the orthodox will succeed in capturing for good and all the name "Christian." This may not make very much difference to what anybody actually believes; for, as I said, the dispute that I am now discussing is a terminological one. But it will have the result that the name "Christian" is reserved for a diminishing body of people, composed in varying proportions of the ingenu-

ous and the disingenuous. Then most of us will be (suitably
qualified) humanists, and we shall reserve the names "religion" and
"Christianity" for positions that we have left behind, in much the
same way as we now reserve the name "superstition."

I cannot believe that this is the best outcome. What I should like
to see happen, and what I think shows some signs of happening,
is that the name "Christian" is extended to cover positions like that
which I have been defending; and that people who think as I do,
or in more or less similar ways, will still think—as is indeed the case
—that they have enough in common with typical Christians to make
it less misleading to call them Christians than to call them anything
else.

It has been maliciously said of Professor Braithwaite that he may
have given a true account of the faith of King's Senior Combination
Room, but not of that of the saints and martyrs. But it needs to be
asked (given that we obviously do not believe, and do not, in order
to be called Christians, have to believe, everything that was believed
by every saint and martyr) what it was in their beliefs that made
them into saints and into martyrs, and whether mankind in the future can be got to go on believing in this. I should regard the opinions of any fellow of King's who was prepared to call himself a
Christian as of great relevance in answering both these questions.

Some years ago, Braithwaite came to talk to a college society in
Oxford, and told us the story of his religious life, and how he came
to be baptized, and about his religious beliefs. At the end of the
meeting, he bravely asked if he might take a vote on the question
whether he was a Christian or not. Unfortunately I cannot remember the exact figures; but they were distributed fairly evenly between
"Yes," "No," and "Don't know." But what was more significant was
this. I had a strong impression (which could not have been made
any more than an impression without lengthy and possibly embar-
rassing researches) that, on the whole, the people who said he was a
Christian were the Christians, and the people who said he was not
were the non-Christians. The reason is obvious. If one is a Christian,
and is trying to hang on to one's Christianity, one does not want
to set up for oneself unnecessary hurdles; therefore it is in one's interest to admit that a man of Braithwaite's left-wing views is, after
all, a Christian. These people, I am sure, showed a very sound feeling for what is essential to Christianity and what is not, and were

not merely displaying Christian charity. The non-Christians, on the other hand, were in the opposite position. What they were trying to do was to justify their rejection of Christianity; and therefore it suited their book to make it difficult to be a Christian, in order that, in arguments with Christians, they could saddle the Christians with as absurd views as possible. Therefore it was in their interest to insist that Braithwaite was not a Christian; for, if he *is* a Christian, a lot of very promising arguments against Christianity go by the board.

I hope that by telling you this story I have succeeded in my object of showing how trivial, really, is the terminological question, once the matter behind it is made clear. The important thing is what one believes, and not what one calls it; and therefore, not being so brave as Braithwaite, I am not going to take any vote on what you call what *I* believe, but shall content myself with thanking you for being so patient with me.

INDEX